D0103727

A Kodansha Comics Trade Paperback Original.

In/Spectre volume 1 copyright © 2015 Kyo Shirodaira/Chashiba Katase
English translation copyright © 2016 Kyo Shirodaira/Chashiba Katase

All rights reserved.

Published in the United States by Kodansha Comics,
an imprint of Kodansha USA Publishing, LLC, New York.

Publication rights for this English edition arranged through Kodansha Ltd.,
Tokyo.

First published in Japan in 2015 by Kodansha Ltd., Tokyo, as *Kyokou Suiri*
volume 1.

ISBN 978-1-63236-379-4

Printed in the United States of America.

www.kodanshacomics.com

9 8 7 6 5 4 3 2 1

Translation: Alethea Nibley & Athena Nibley
Lettering: Lys Blakeslee
Editing: Ajani Oloye
Kodansha Comics edition cover design: Phil Balsman

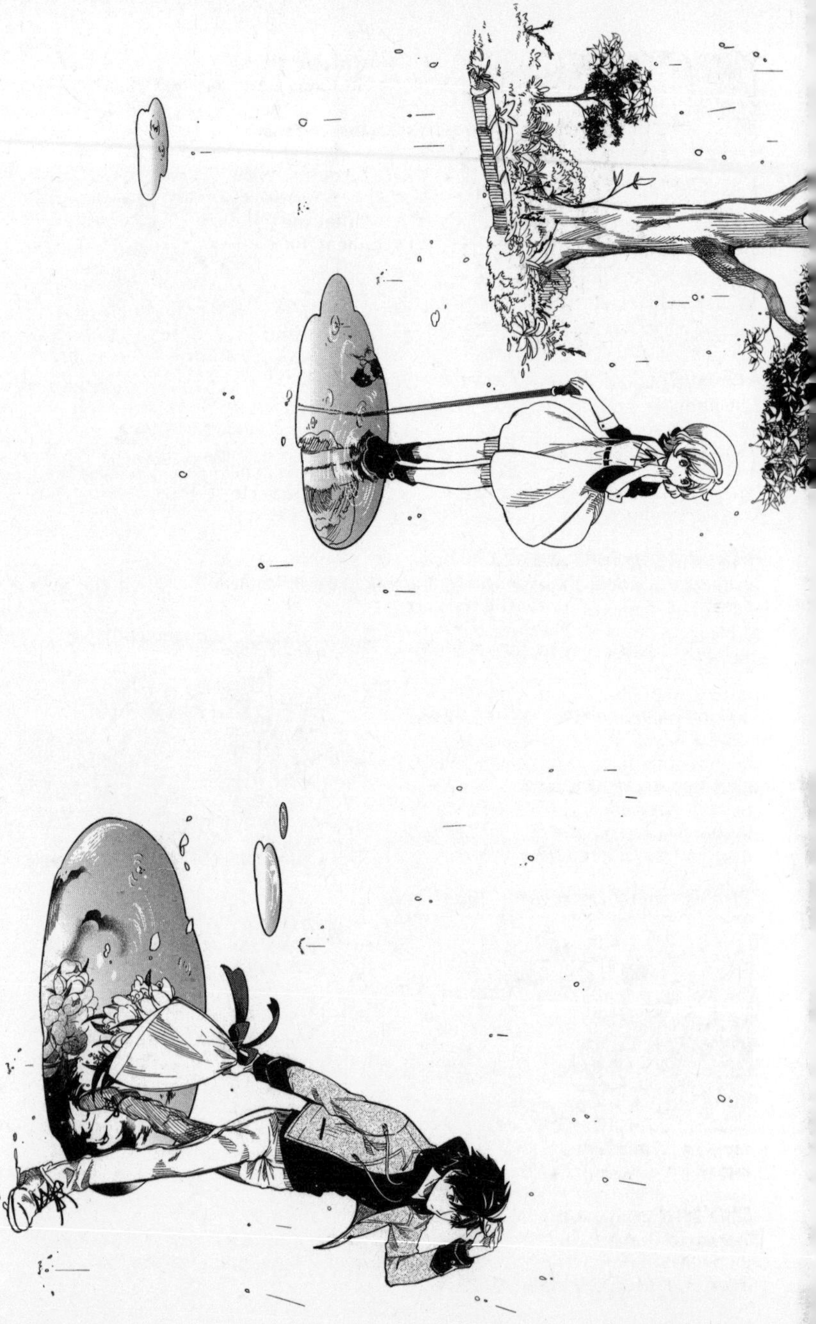

STORY: KYO SHIRODAIRA
MANGA: CHASHIBA KATASE

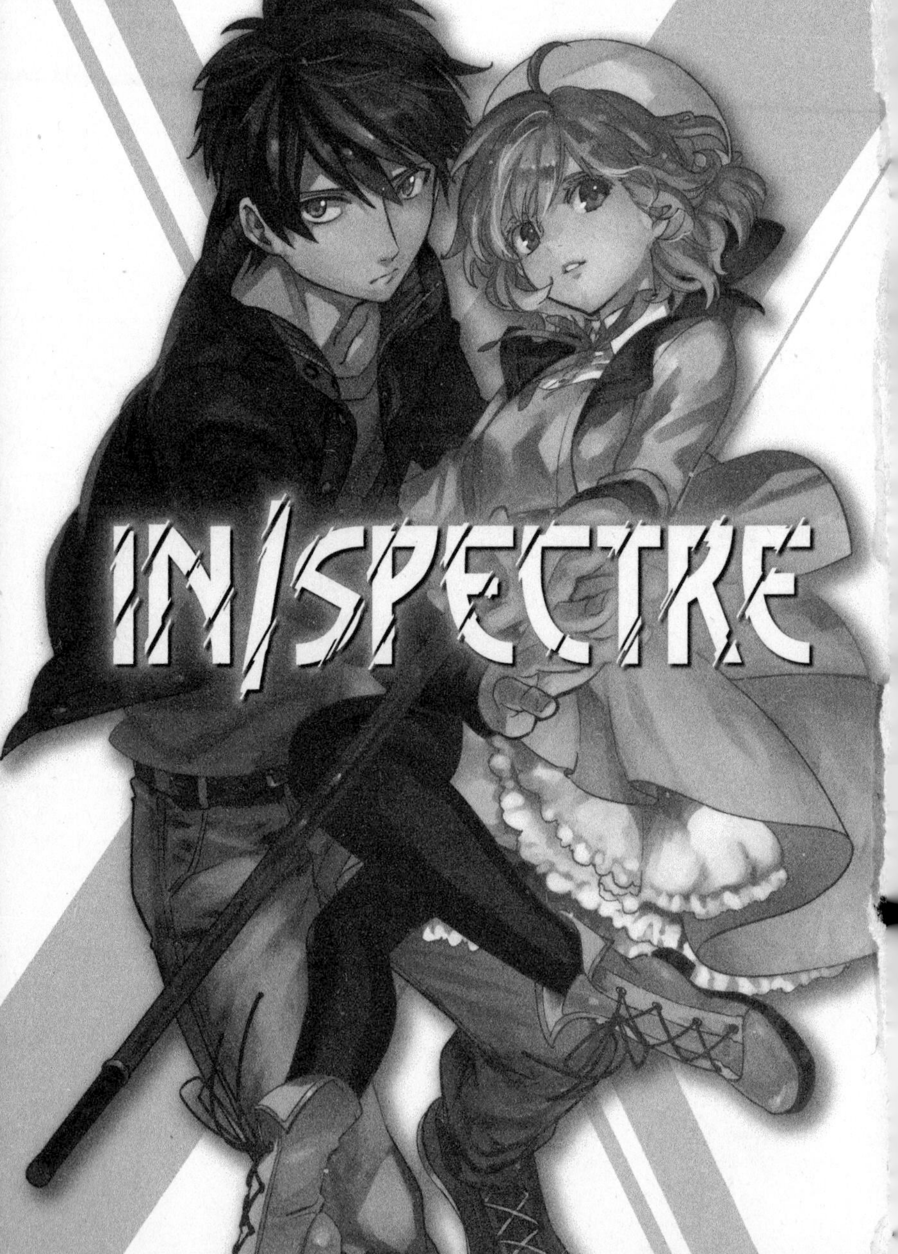
IN/SPECTRE

NOVEL VERSION CHARACTER DESIGNS
HIRO KIYOHARA

CONTENTS

CHAPTER 1: "ONE EYE, ONE LEG"   3

CHAPTER 2: "RUMORS OF THE STEEL MAN"   87

BONUS MANGA   166

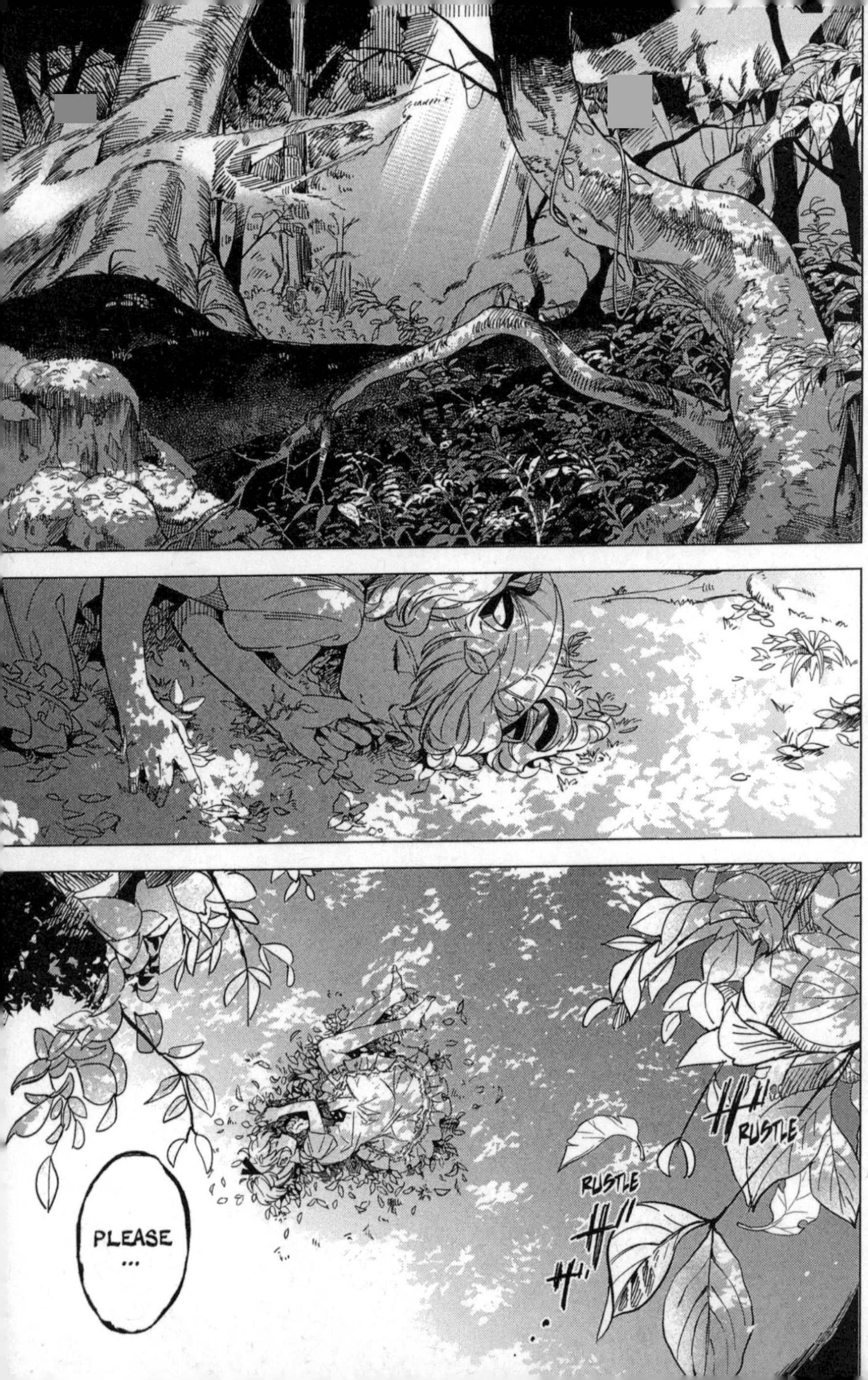
RUSTLE
RUSTLE
PLEASE ...

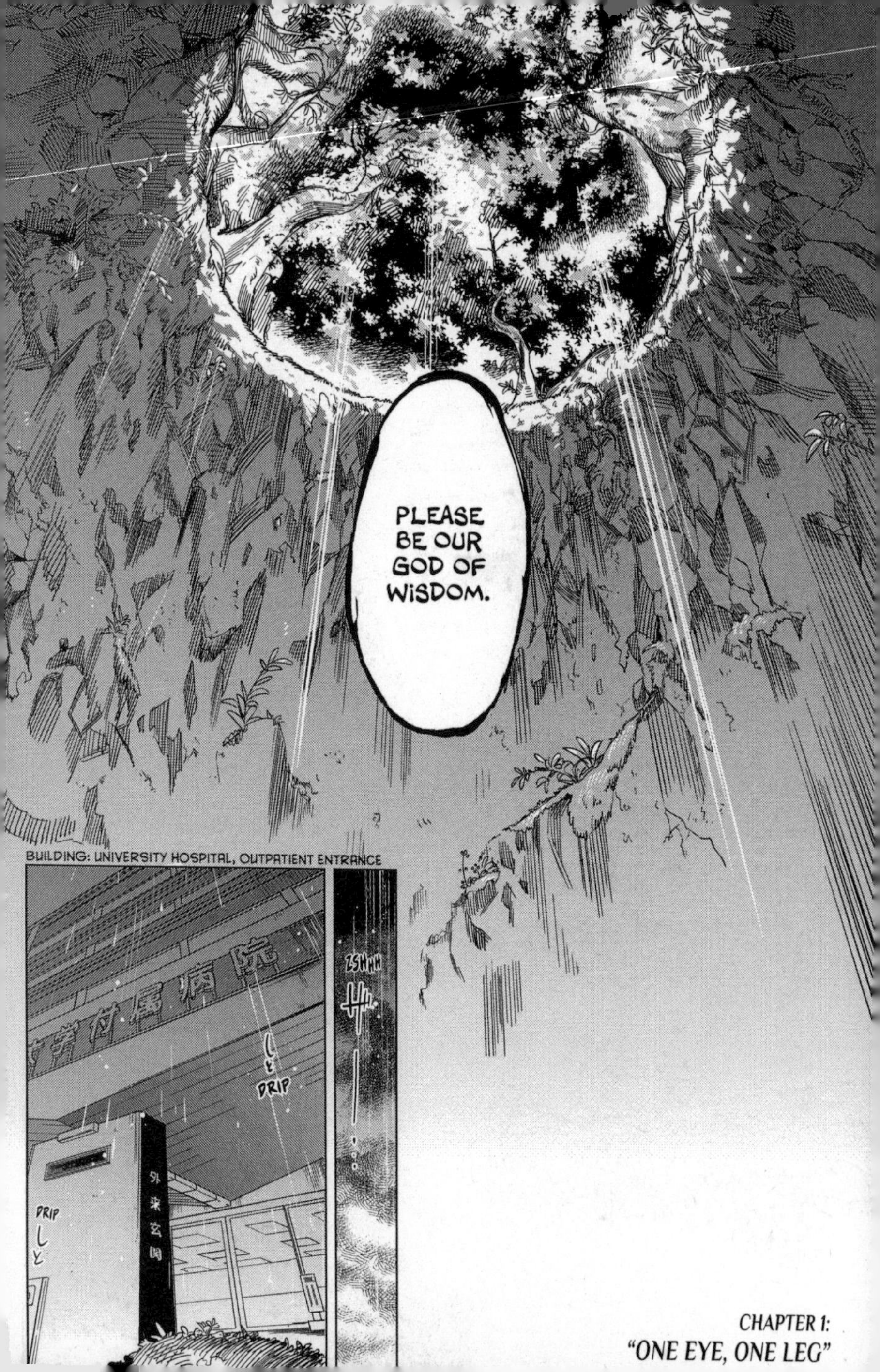
PLEASE BE OUR GOD OF WISDOM.
ZSHHH
BUILDING: UNIVERSITY HOSPITAL, OUTPATIENT ENTRANCE
しと
DRIP
外来玄関
DRIP
しと

CHAPTER 1:
"ONE EYE, ONE LEG"

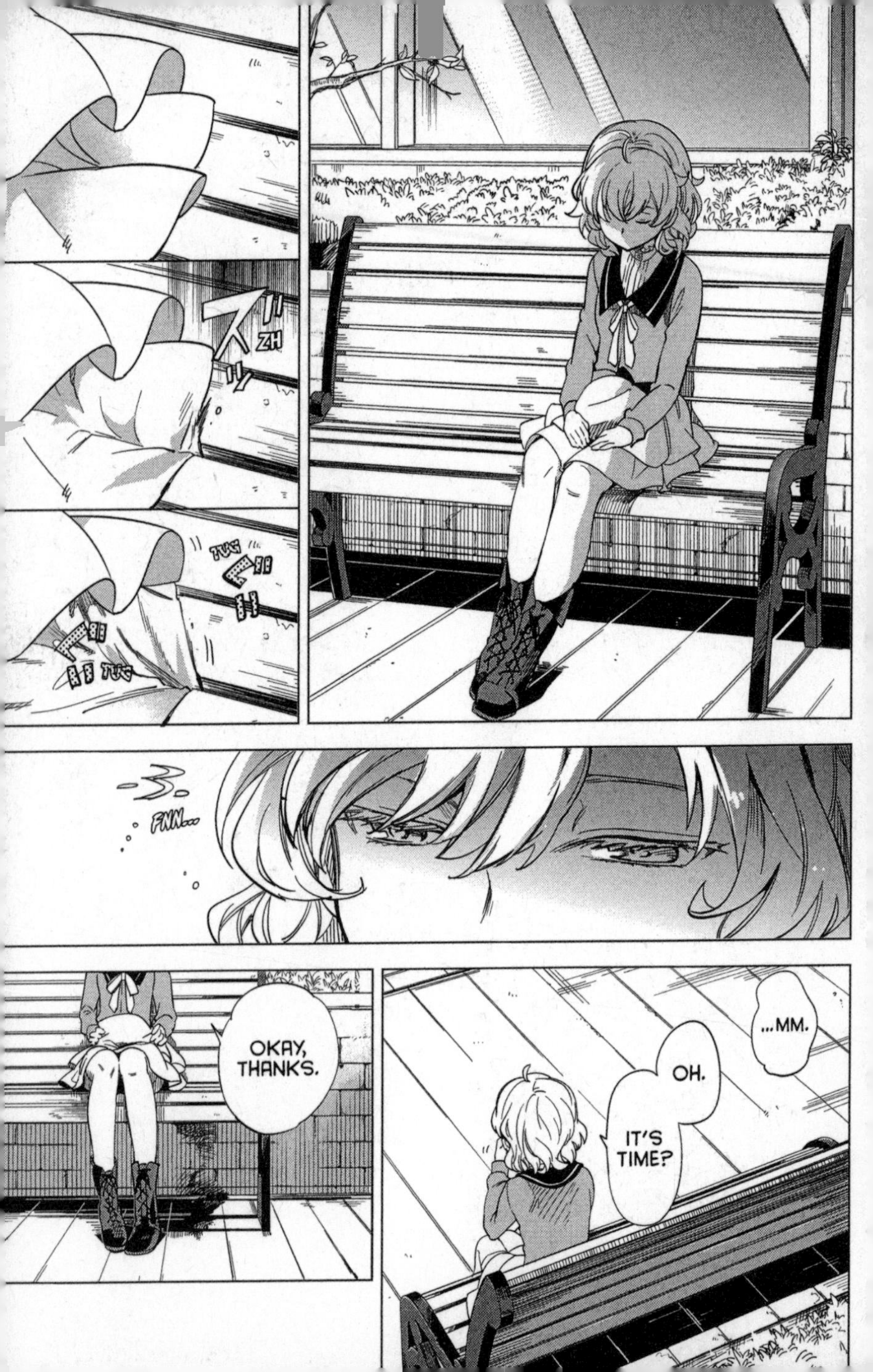
ZH
TUG
TUG
FNN...
...MM.
OH.
IT'S TIME?
OKAY, THANKS.

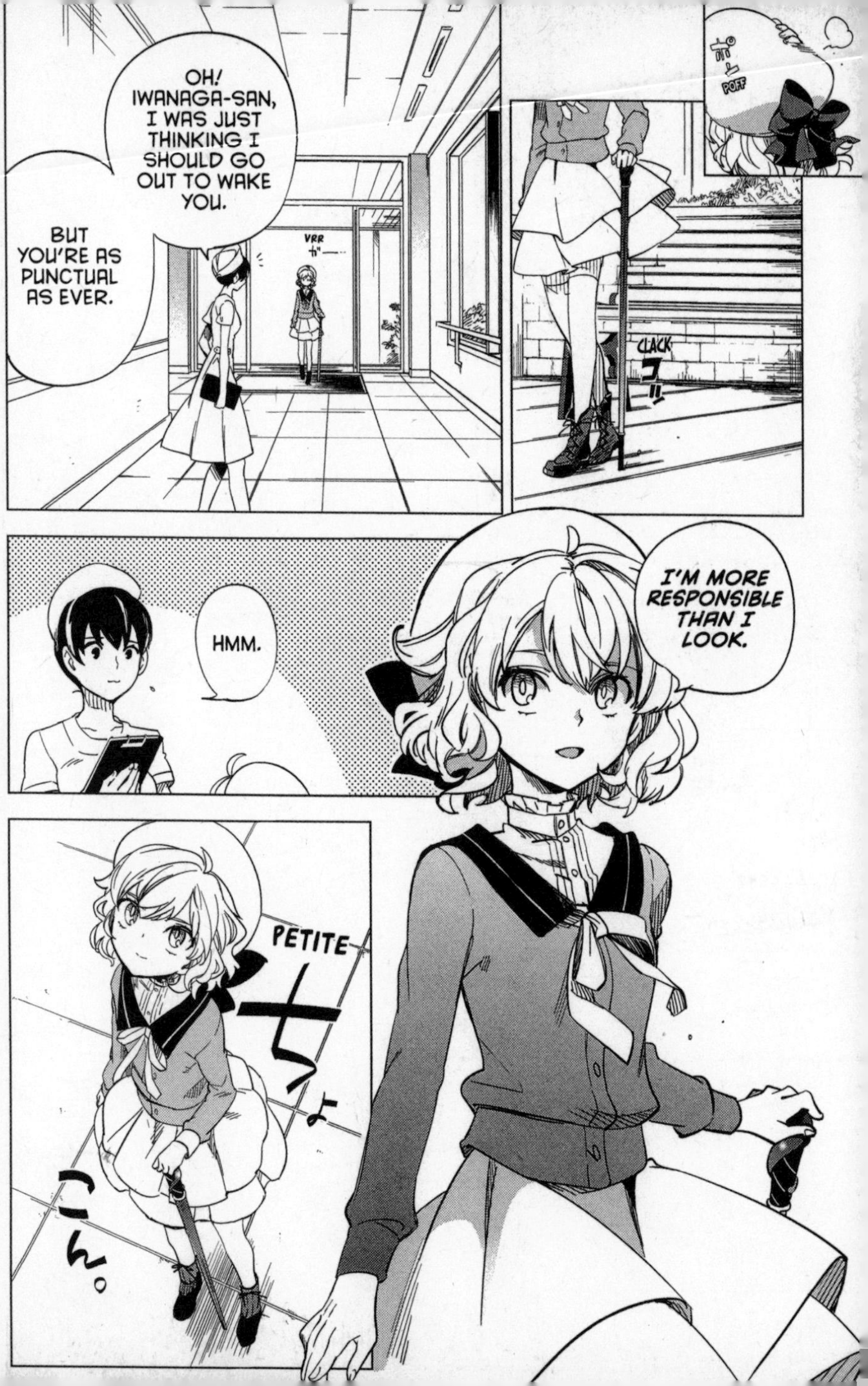
POFF
CLACK
OH! IWANAGA-SAN, I WAS JUST THINKING I SHOULD GO OUT TO WAKE YOU.
VRR
BUT YOU'RE AS PUNCTUAL AS EVER.
I'M MORE RESPONSIBLE THAN I LOOK.
HMM.
PETITE

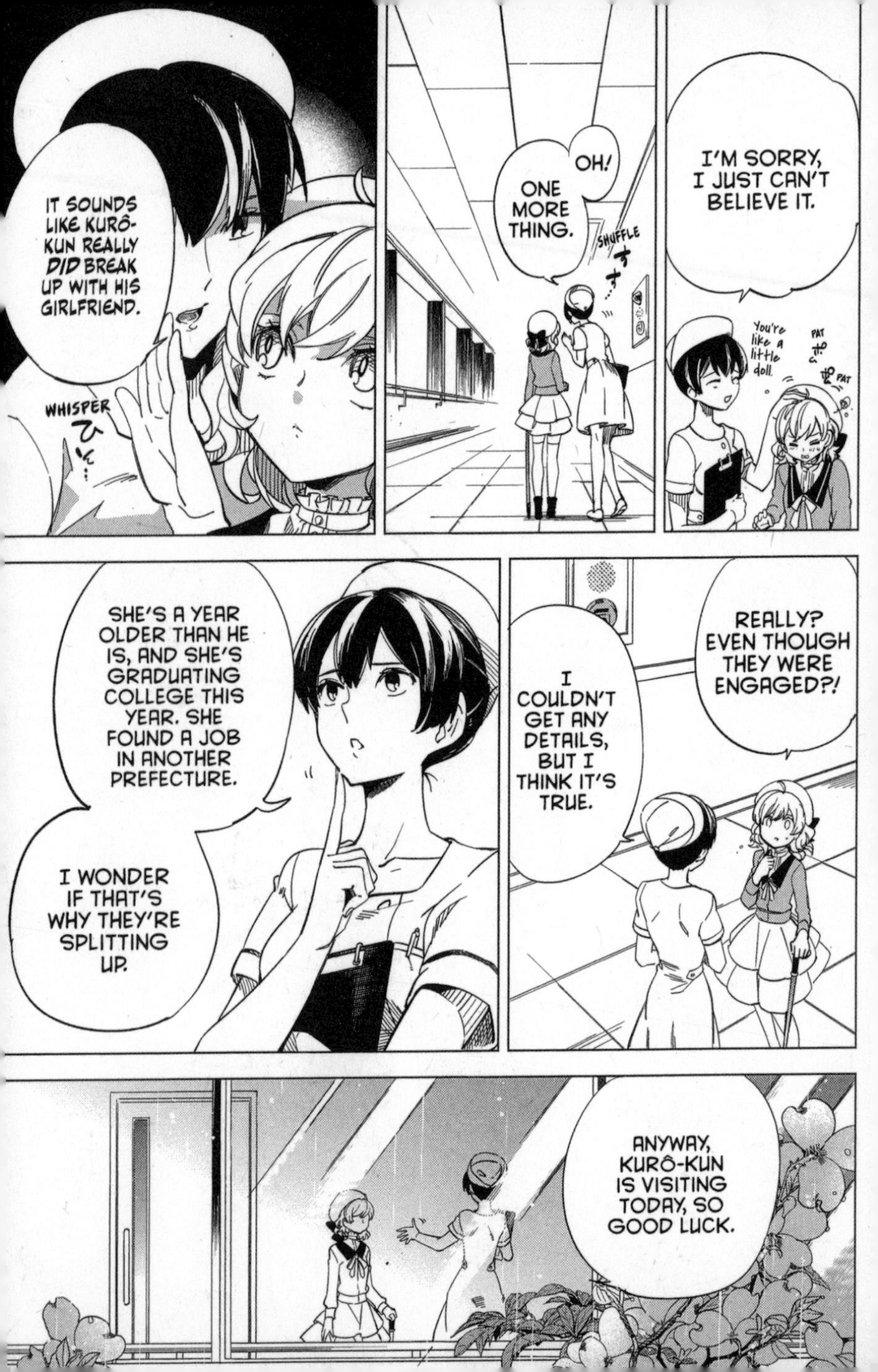
I'M SORRY, I JUST CAN'T BELIEVE IT.
You're like a little doll.
PAT
PAT
OH!
ONE MORE THING.
SHUFFLE
IT SOUNDS LIKE KURÔ-KUN REALLY DID BREAK UP WITH HIS GIRLFRIEND.
WHISPER
REALLY? EVEN THOUGH THEY WERE ENGAGED?!
I COULDN'T GET ANY DETAILS, BUT I THINK IT'S TRUE.
SHE'S A YEAR OLDER THAN HE IS, AND SHE'S GRADUATING COLLEGE THIS YEAR. SHE FOUND A JOB IN ANOTHER PREFECTURE.
I WONDER IF THAT'S WHY THEY'RE SPLITTING UP.
ANYWAY, KURÔ-KUN IS VISITING TODAY, SO GOOD LUCK.

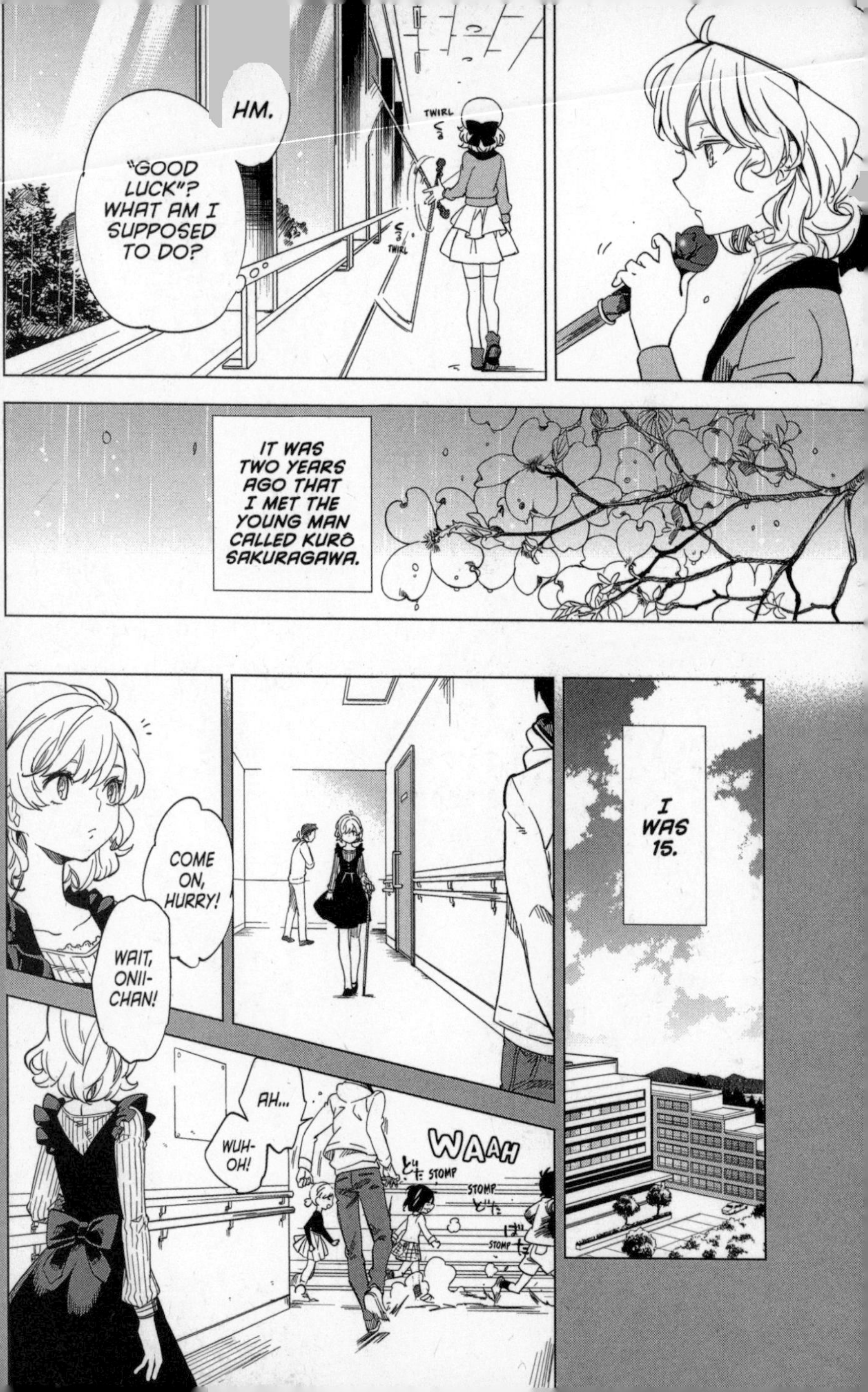
TWIRL
HM.
"GOOD LUCK"? WHAT AM I SUPPOSED TO DO?
TWIRL
IT WAS TWO YEARS AGO THAT I MET THE YOUNG MAN CALLED KURÔ SAKURAGAWA.
I WAS 15.
COME ON, HURRY!
WAIT, ONII-CHAN!
WAAH
STOMP
STOMP
STOMP
AH...
WUH-OH!

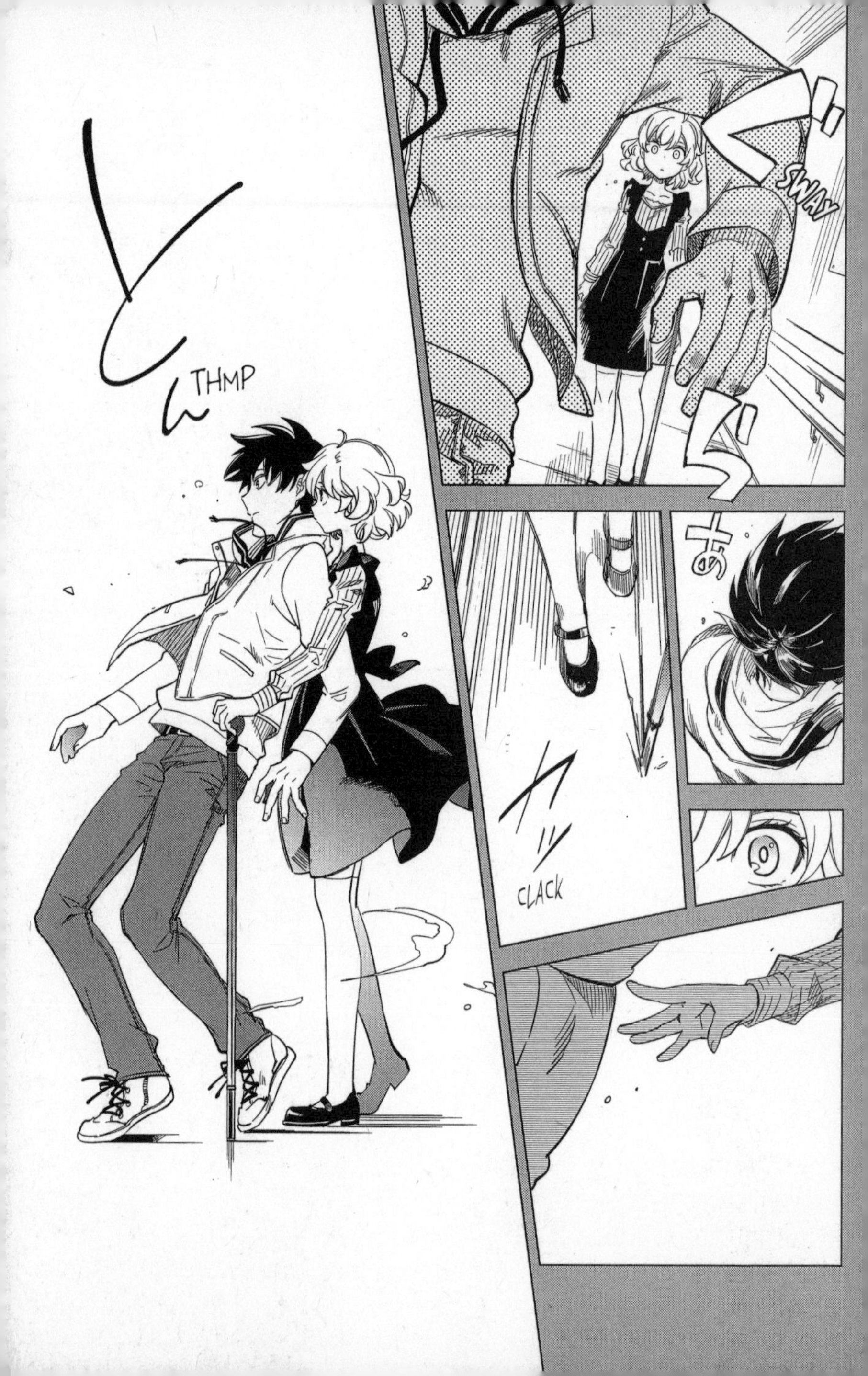
SWAY
あ
カッ
CLACK
とん
THMP

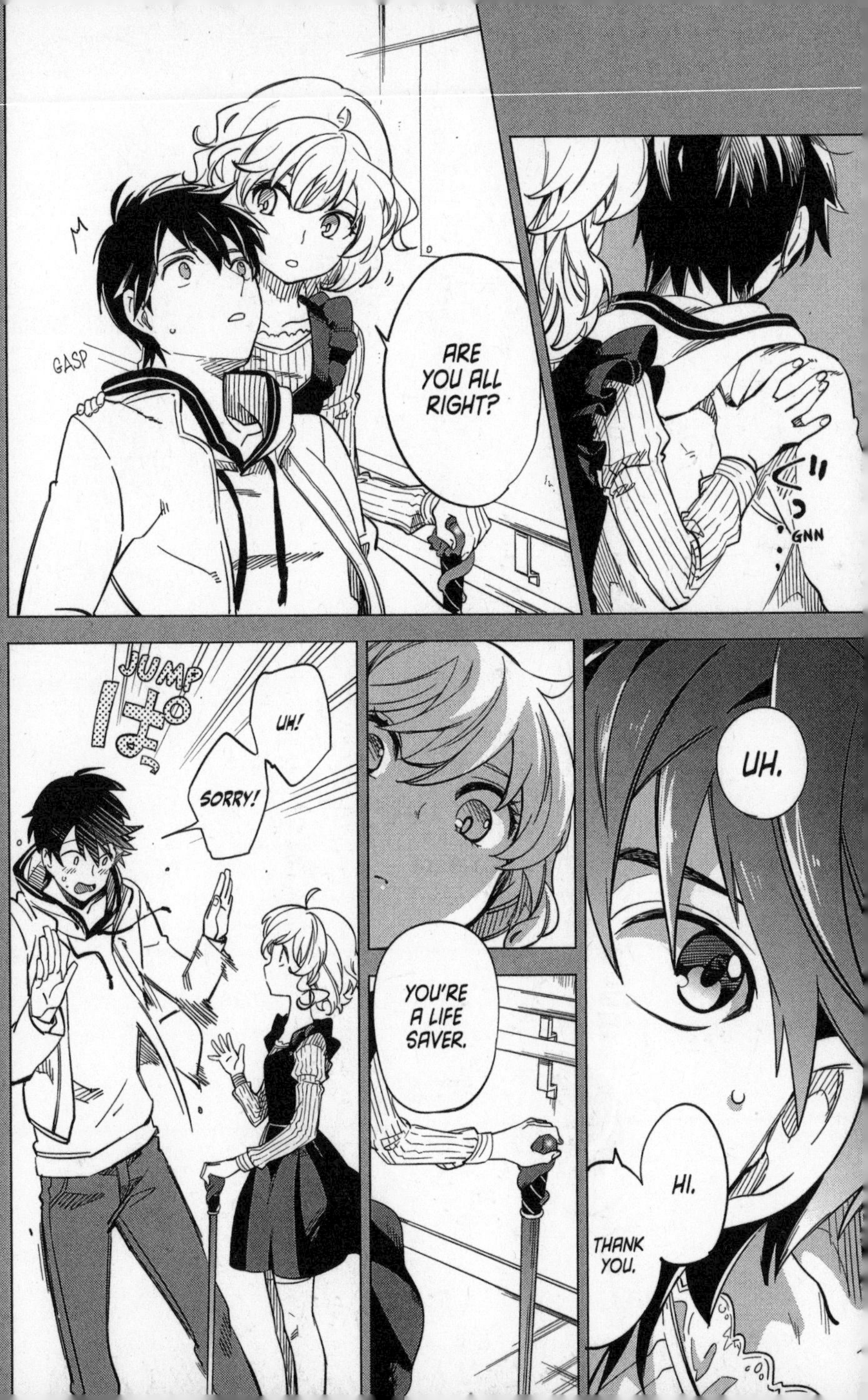
ぐっ
GNN
ARE YOU ALL RIGHT?
GASP
UH.
HI.
THANK YOU.
YOU'RE A LIFE SAVER.
JUMP
ぱっ
UH!
SORRY!

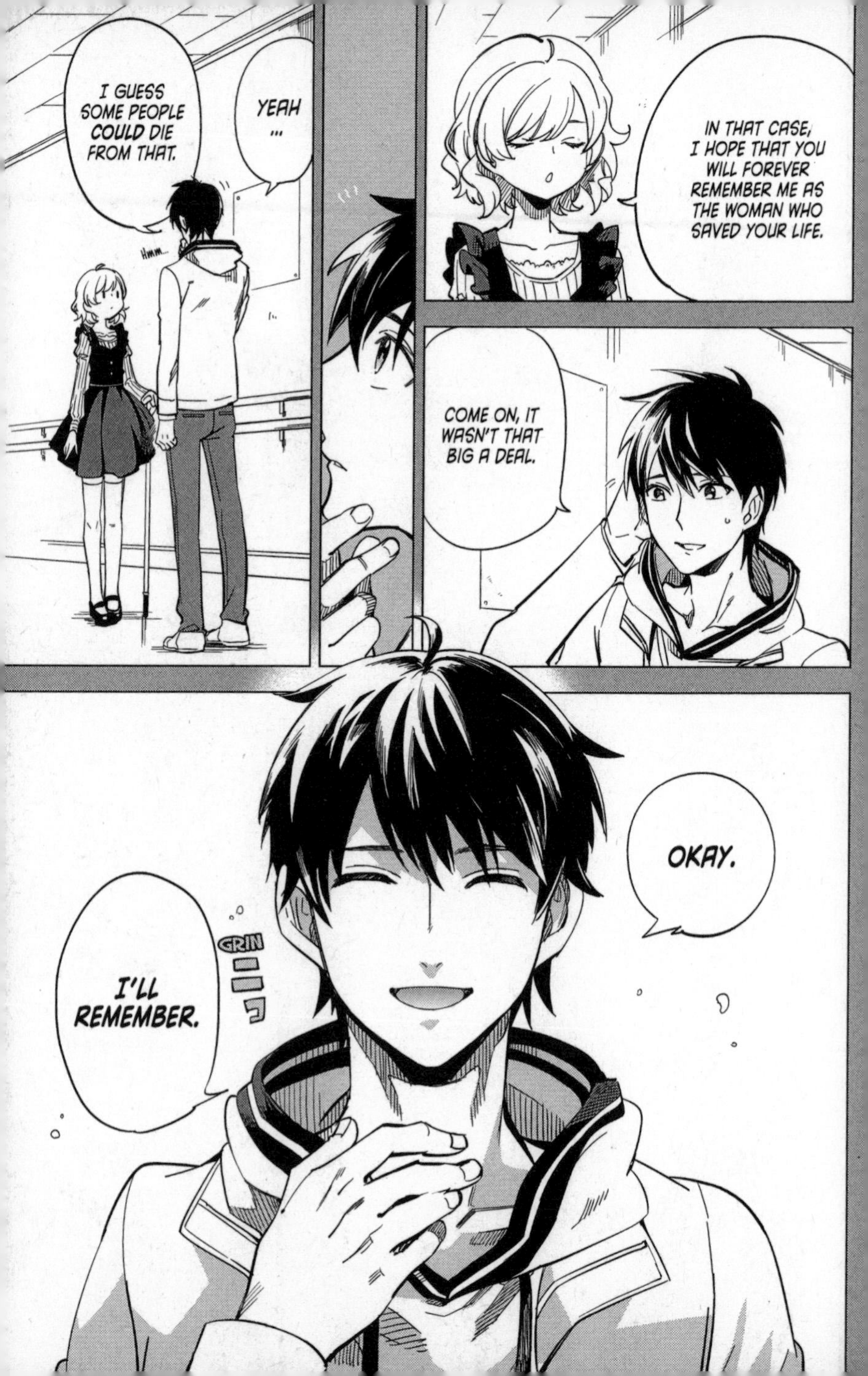
I GUESS SOME PEOPLE COULD DIE FROM THAT.
YEAH ...
Hmm...
IN THAT CASE, I HOPE THAT YOU WILL FOREVER REMEMBER ME AS THE WOMAN WHO SAVED YOUR LIFE.
COME ON, IT WASN'T THAT BIG A DEAL.
OKAY.
GRIN
I'LL REMEMBER.

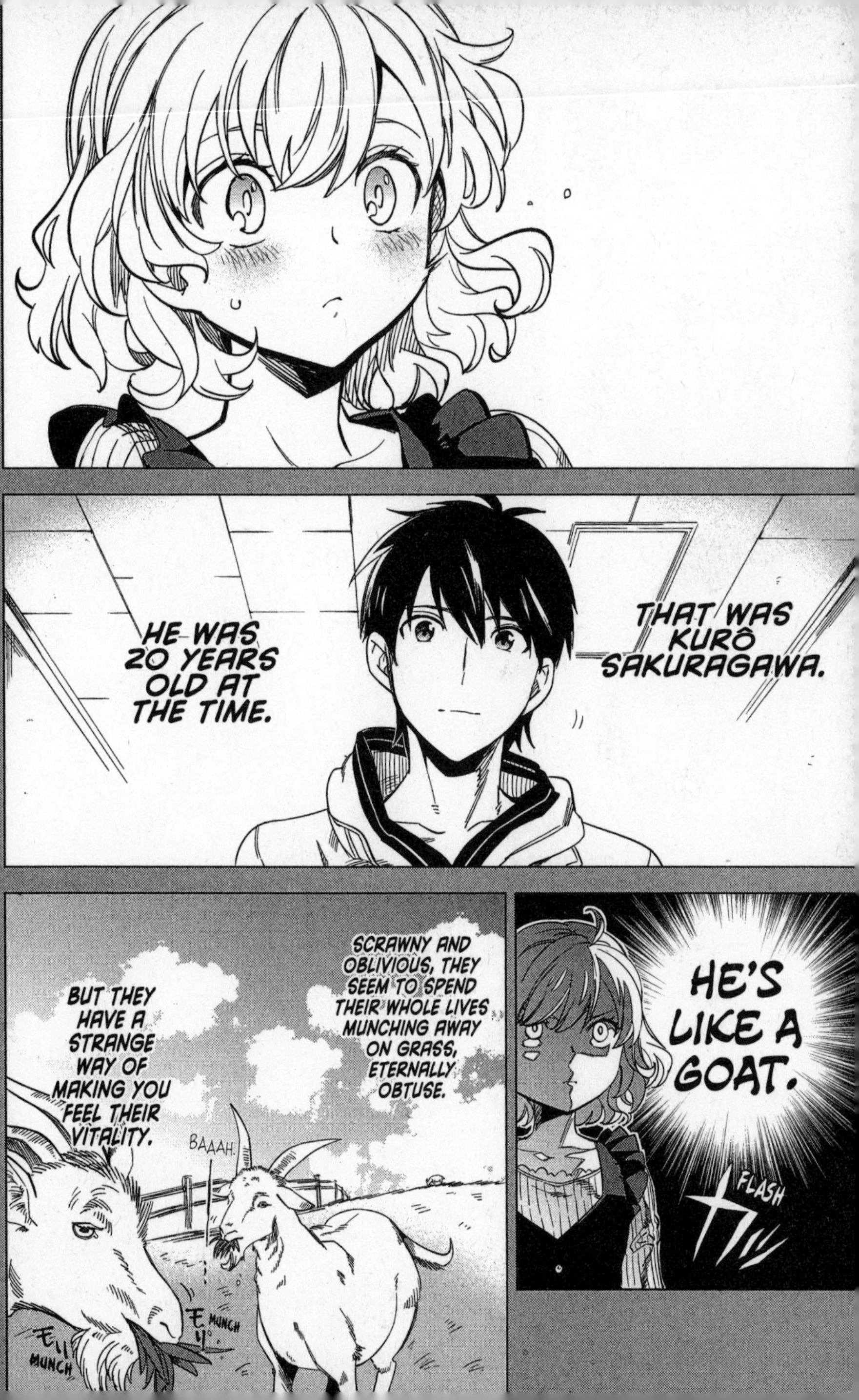
THAT WAS KURÔ SAKURAGAWA.
HE WAS 20 YEARS OLD AT THE TIME.
HE'S LIKE A GOAT.
FLASH
SCRAWNY AND OBLIVIOUS, THEY SEEM TO SPEND THEIR WHOLE LIVES MUNCHING AWAY ON GRASS, ETERNALLY OBTUSE.
BUT THEY HAVE A STRANGE WAY OF MAKING YOU FEEL THEIR VITALITY.
BAAAH.
MUNCH
MUNCH

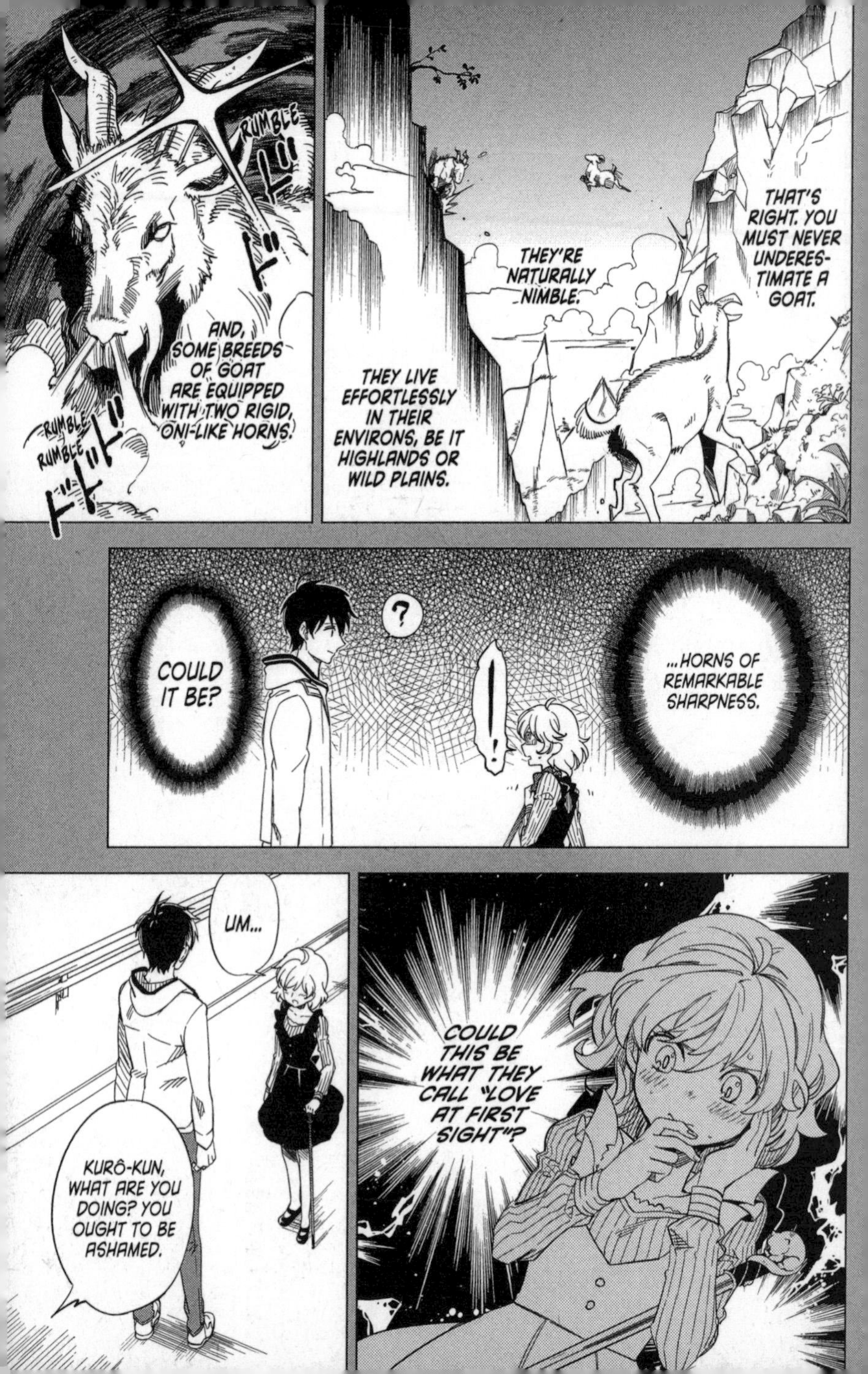
THAT'S RIGHT. YOU MUST NEVER UNDERES-TIMATE A GOAT.
THEY'RE NATURALLY NIMBLE.
THEY LIVE EFFORTLESSLY IN THEIR ENVIRONS, BE IT HIGHLANDS OR WILD PLAINS.
RUMBLE
AND, SOME BREEDS OF GOAT ARE EQUIPPED WITH TWO RIGID, ONI-LIKE HORNS.
RUMBLE RUMBLE
...HORNS OF REMARKABLE SHARPNESS.
?
!
COULD IT BE?
COULD THIS BE WHAT THEY CALL "LOVE AT FIRST SIGHT"?
UM...
KURÔ-KUN, WHAT ARE YOU DOING? YOU OUGHT TO BE ASHAMED.

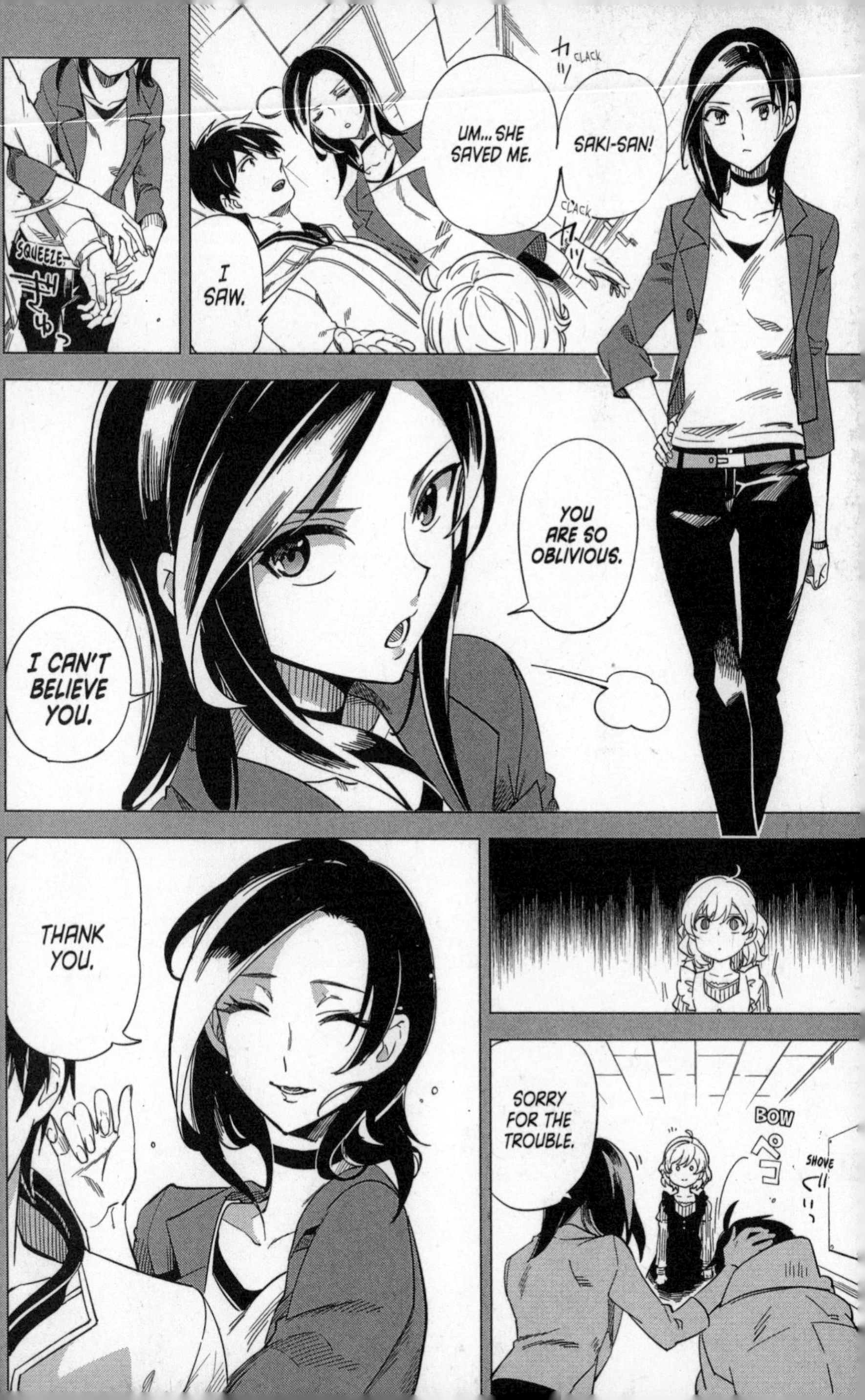

CLACK
SAKI-SAN!
UM... SHE SAVED ME.
CLACK
I SAW.
SQUEEZE
YOU ARE SO OBLIVIOUS.
I CAN'T BELIEVE YOU.
SORRY FOR THE TROUBLE.
BOW
SHOVE
THANK YOU.

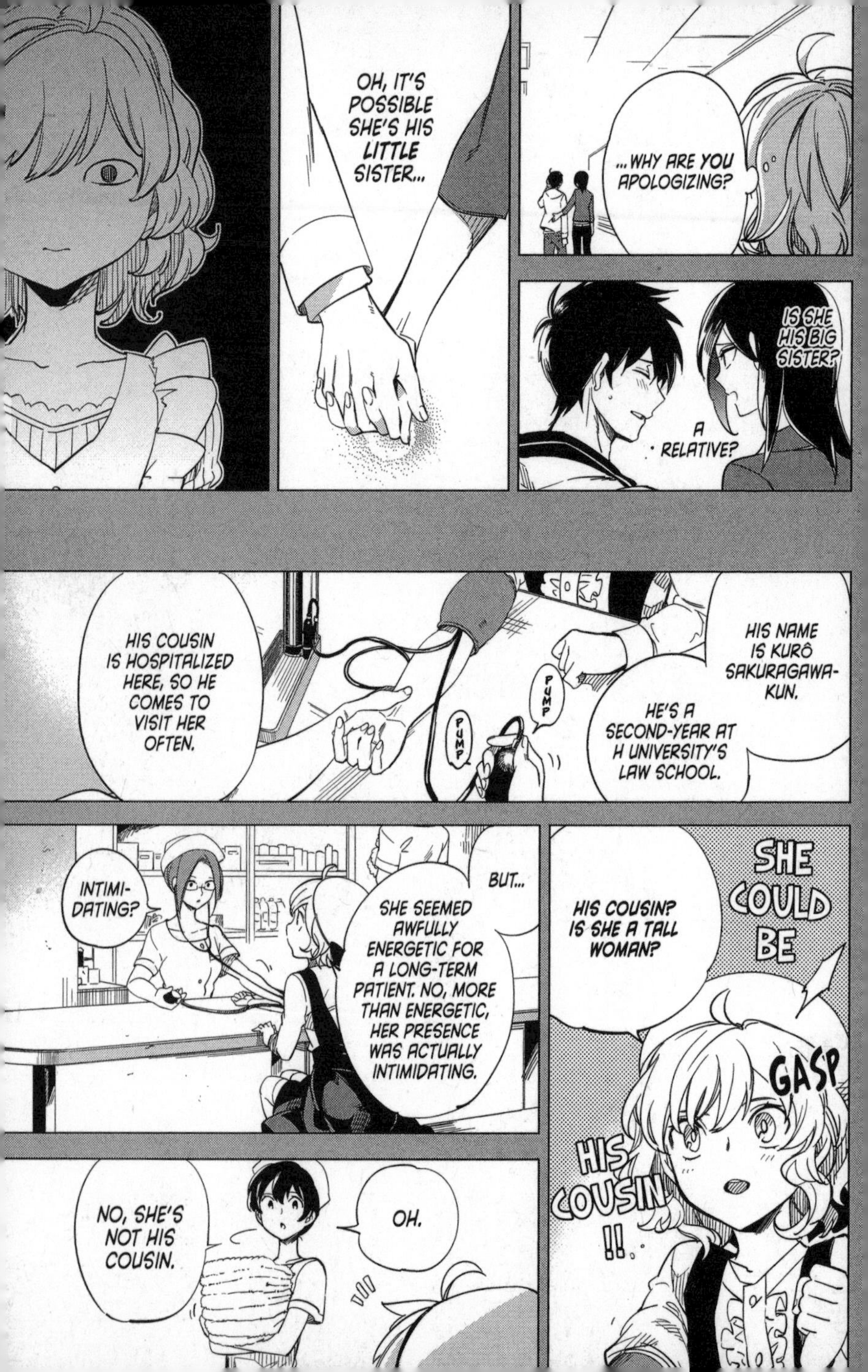
...WHY ARE YOU APOLOGIZING?
IS SHE HIS BIG SISTER?
A RELATIVE?
OH, IT'S POSSIBLE SHE'S HIS LITTLE SISTER...
HIS NAME IS KURÔ SAKURAGAWA-KUN.
HE'S A SECOND-YEAR AT H UNIVERSITY'S LAW SCHOOL.
PUMP
PUMP
HIS COUSIN IS HOSPITALIZED HERE, SO HE COMES TO VISIT HER OFTEN.
SHE COULD BE
HIS COUSIN? IS SHE A TALL WOMAN?
GASP
HIS COUSIN!!
BUT...
SHE SEEMED AWFULLY ENERGETIC FOR A LONG-TERM PATIENT. NO, MORE THAN ENERGETIC, HER PRESENCE WAS ACTUALLY INTIMIDATING.
INTIMI-DATING?
OH.
NO, SHE'S NOT HIS COUSIN.

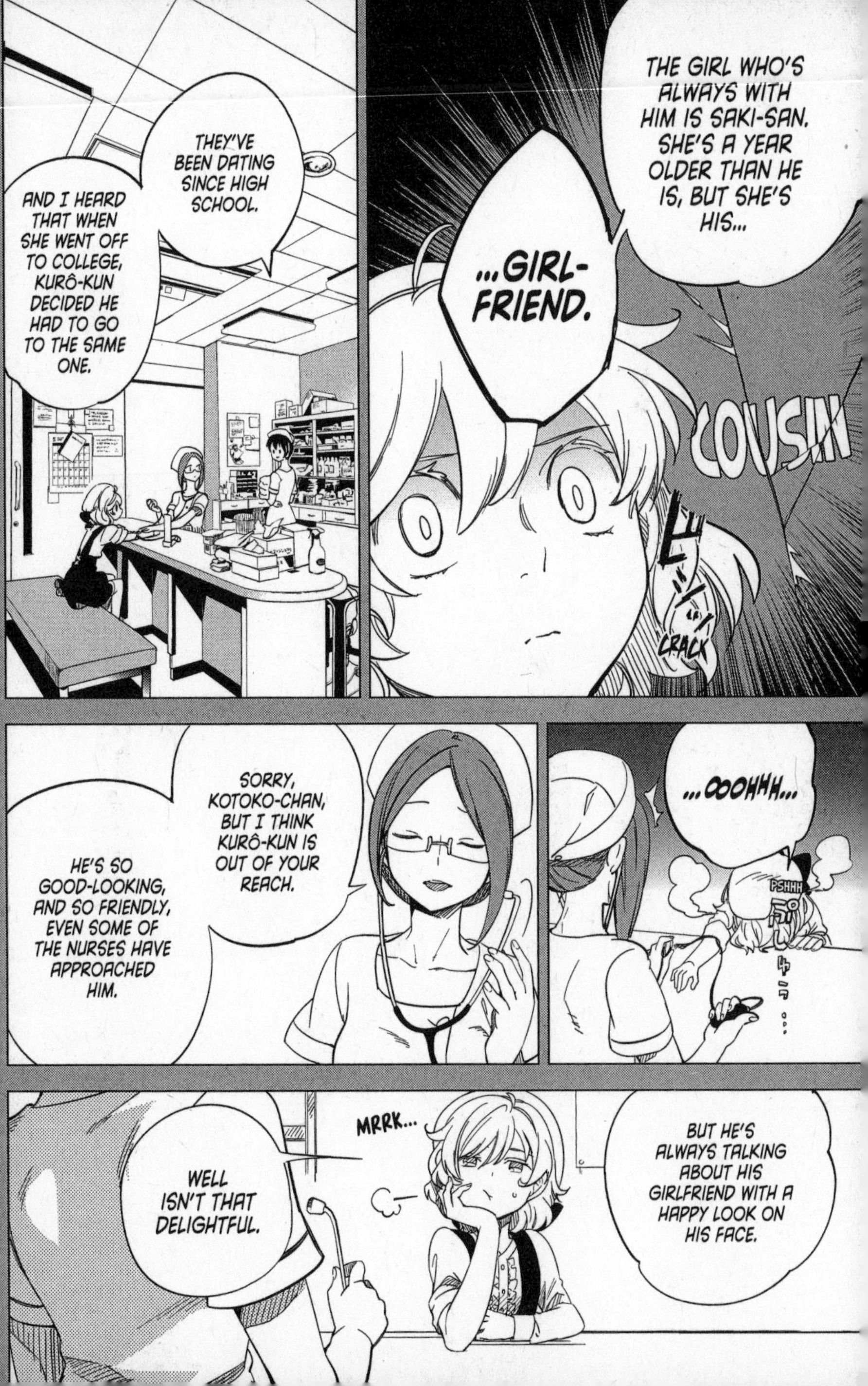
THE GIRL WHO'S ALWAYS WITH HIM IS SAKI-SAN. SHE'S A YEAR OLDER THAN HE IS, BUT SHE'S HIS...
...GIRL-FRIEND.
COUSIN
CRACK
THEY'VE BEEN DATING SINCE HIGH SCHOOL.
AND I HEARD THAT WHEN SHE WENT OFF TO COLLEGE, KURÔ-KUN DECIDED HE HAD TO GO TO THE SAME ONE.
...OOOHHH...
PSHHH
SORRY, KOTOKO-CHAN, BUT I THINK KURÔ-KUN IS OUT OF YOUR REACH.
HE'S SO GOOD-LOOKING, AND SO FRIENDLY, EVEN SOME OF THE NURSES HAVE APPROACHED HIM.
BUT HE'S ALWAYS TALKING ABOUT HIS GIRLFRIEND WITH A HAPPY LOOK ON HIS FACE.
MRRK...
WELL ISN'T THAT DELIGHTFUL.

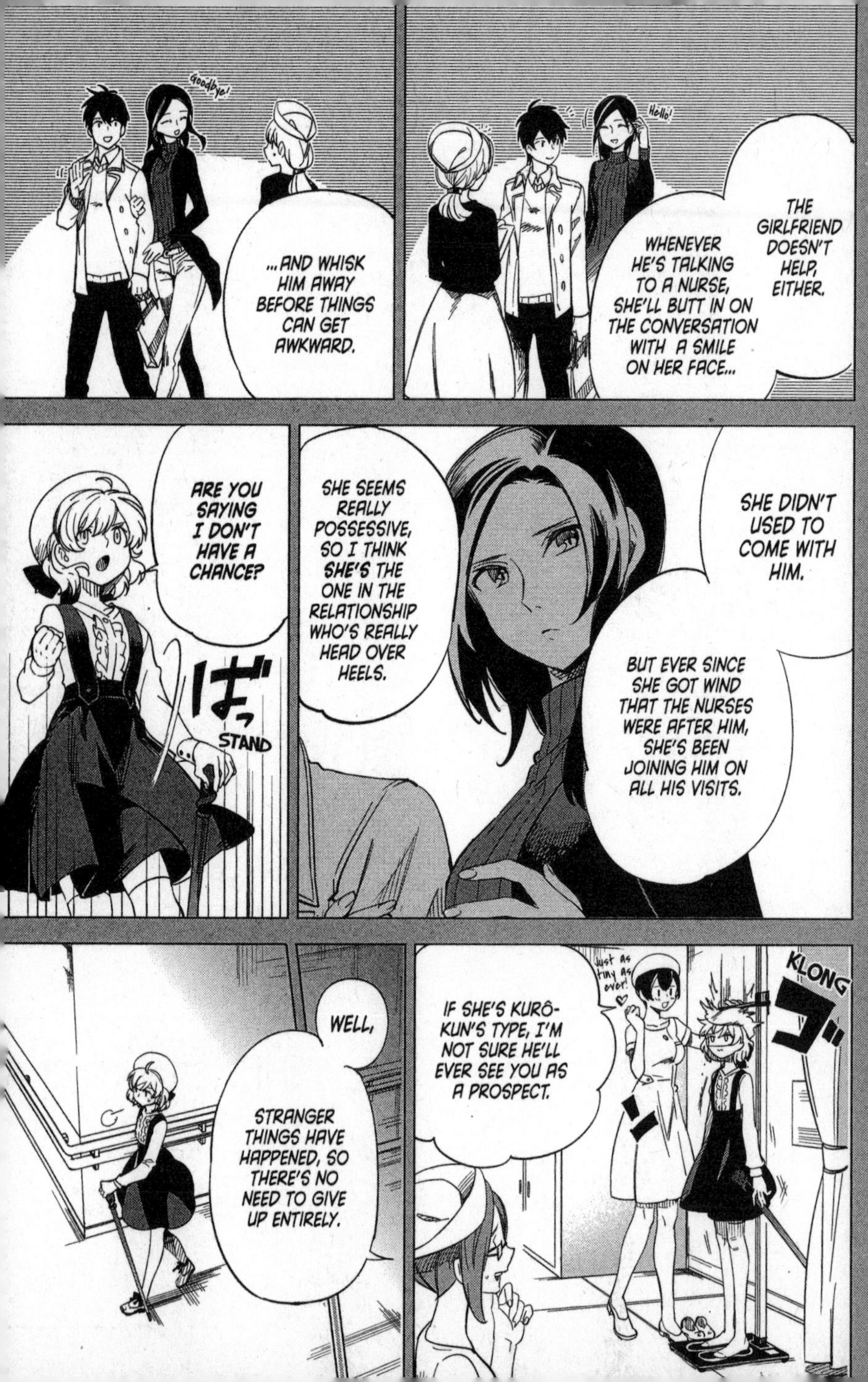
THE GIRLFRIEND DOESN'T HELP, EITHER.
Hello!
WHENEVER HE'S TALKING TO A NURSE, SHE'LL BUTT IN ON THE CONVERSATION WITH A SMILE ON HER FACE...
Goodbye!
...AND WHISK HIM AWAY BEFORE THINGS CAN GET AWKWARD.
SHE DIDN'T USED TO COME WITH HIM.
BUT EVER SINCE SHE GOT WIND THAT THE NURSES WERE AFTER HIM, SHE'S BEEN JOINING HIM ON ALL HIS VISITS.
SHE SEEMS REALLY POSSESSIVE, SO I THINK SHE'S THE ONE IN THE RELATIONSHIP WHO'S REALLY HEAD OVER HEELS.
ARE YOU SAYING I DON'T HAVE A CHANCE?
ばっ
STAND
KLONG
ゴッ
Just as tiny as ever!
IF SHE'S KURÔ-KUN'S TYPE, I'M NOT SURE HE'LL EVER SEE YOU AS A PROSPECT.
WELL,
STRANGER THINGS HAVE HAPPENED, SO THERE'S NO NEED TO GIVE UP ENTIRELY.

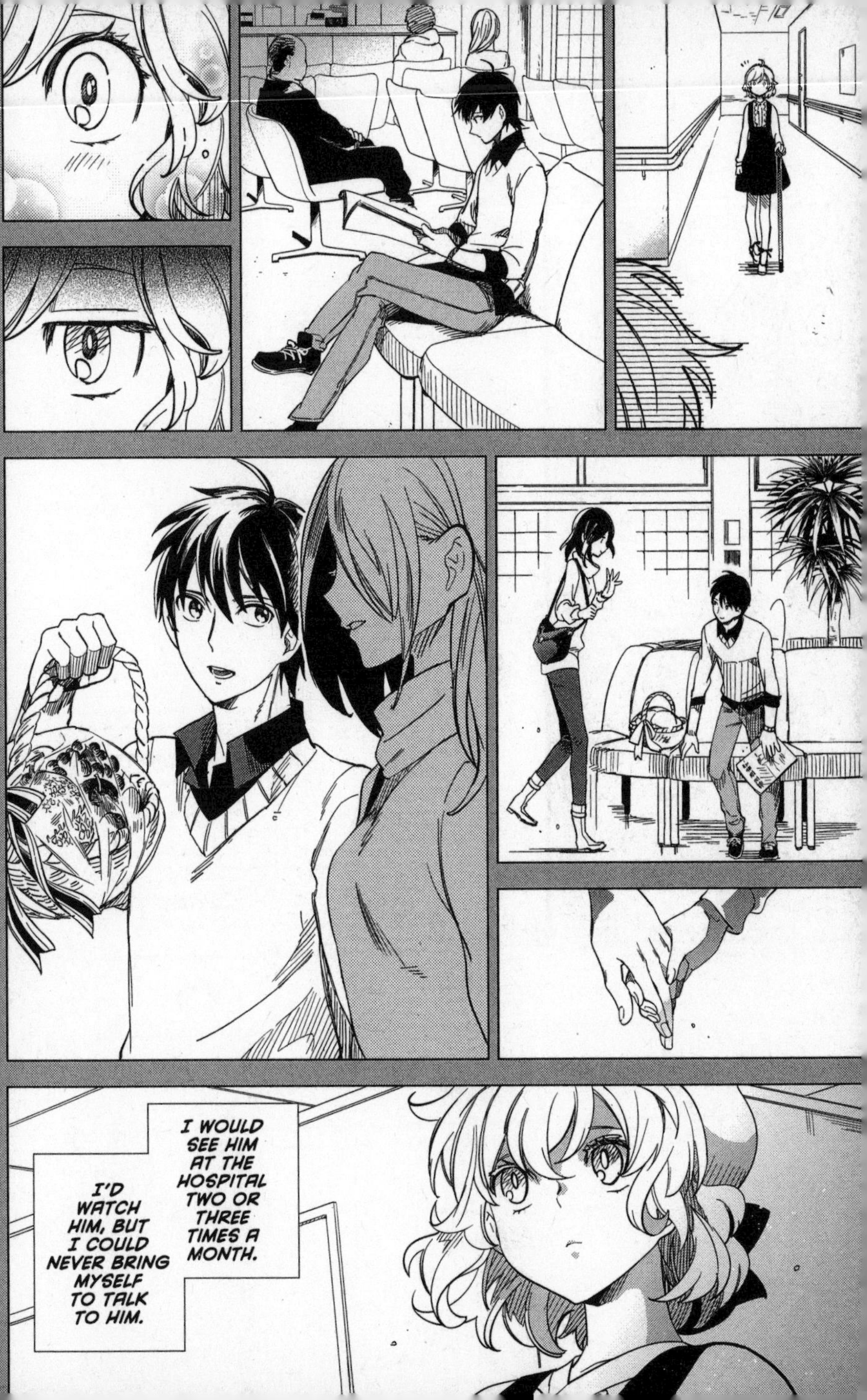
I WOULD SEE HIM AT THE HOSPITAL TWO OR THREE TIMES A MONTH.
I'D WATCH HIM, BUT I COULD NEVER BRING MYSELF TO TALK TO HIM.

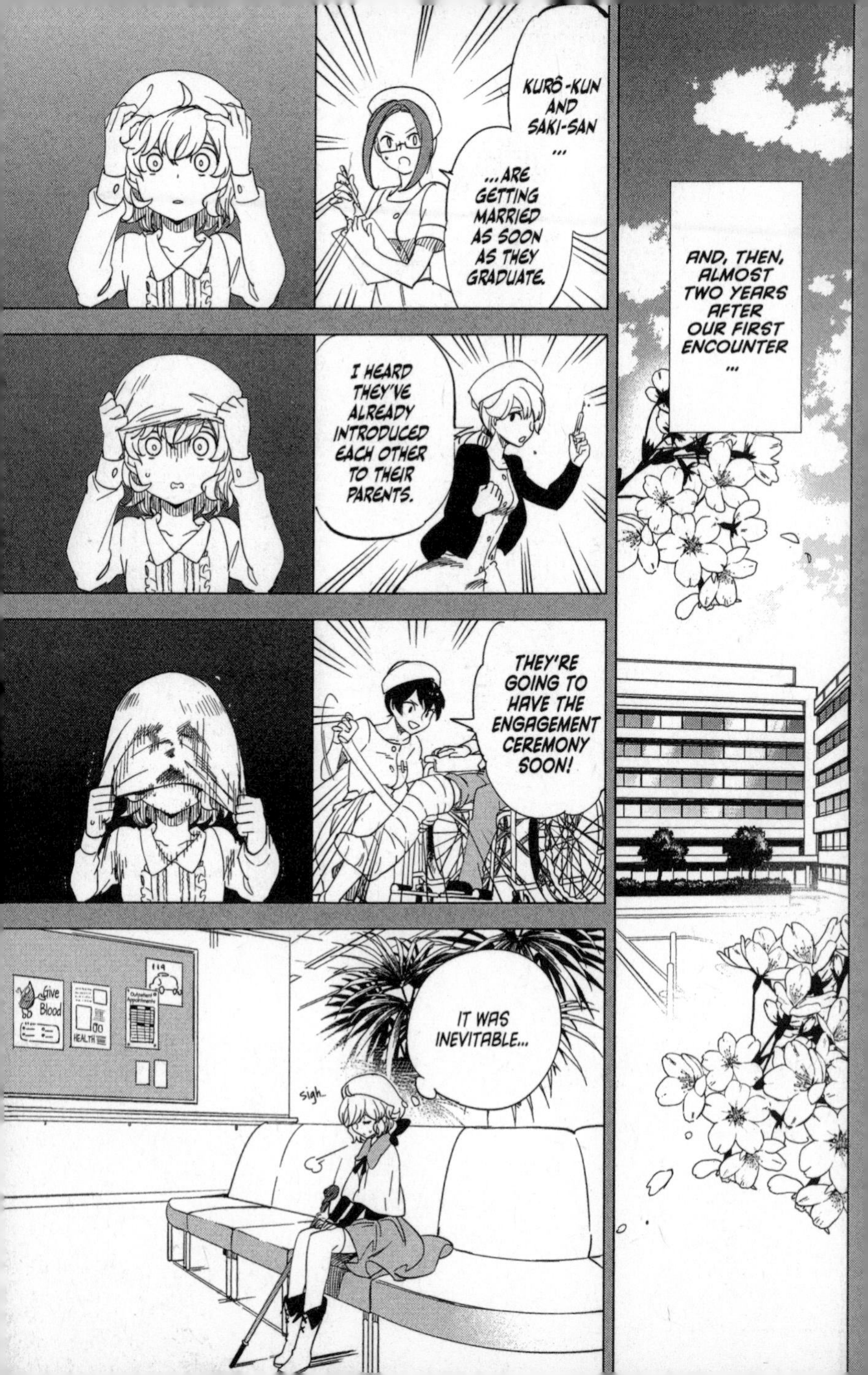
AND, THEN, ALMOST TWO YEARS AFTER OUR FIRST ENCOUNTER ...
KURÔ-KUN AND SAKI-SAN ...
...ARE GETTING MARRIED AS SOON AS THEY GRADUATE.
I HEARD THEY'VE ALREADY INTRODUCED EACH OTHER TO THEIR PARENTS.
THEY'RE GOING TO HAVE THE ENGAGEMENT CEREMONY SOON!
IT WAS INEVITABLE...
Give Blood
HEALTH
sigh

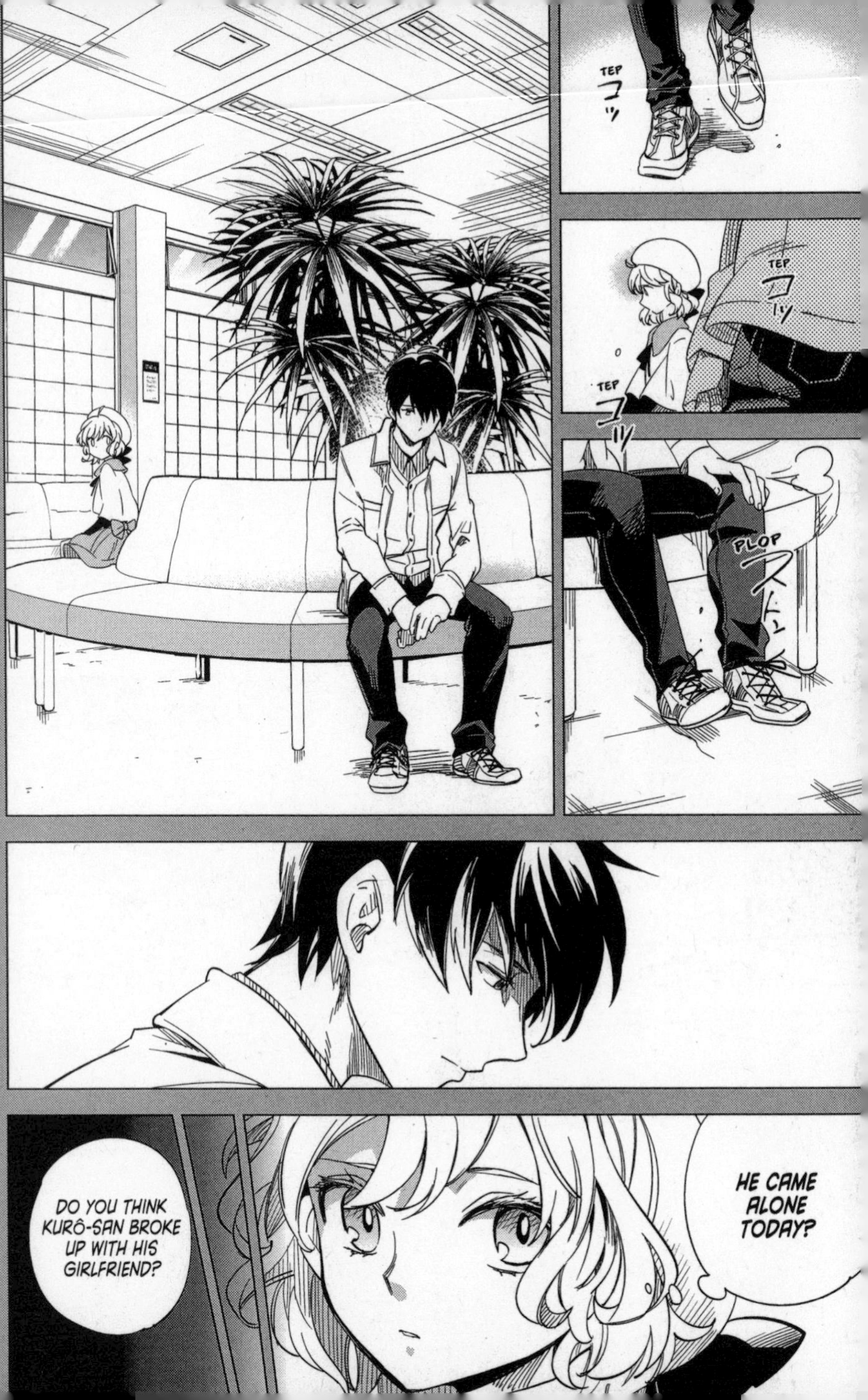
TEP
コッ
TEP
コッ
TEP
コッ
PLOP
ストン
HE CAME ALONE TODAY?
DO YOU THINK KURÔ-SAN BROKE UP WITH HIS GIRLFRIEND?

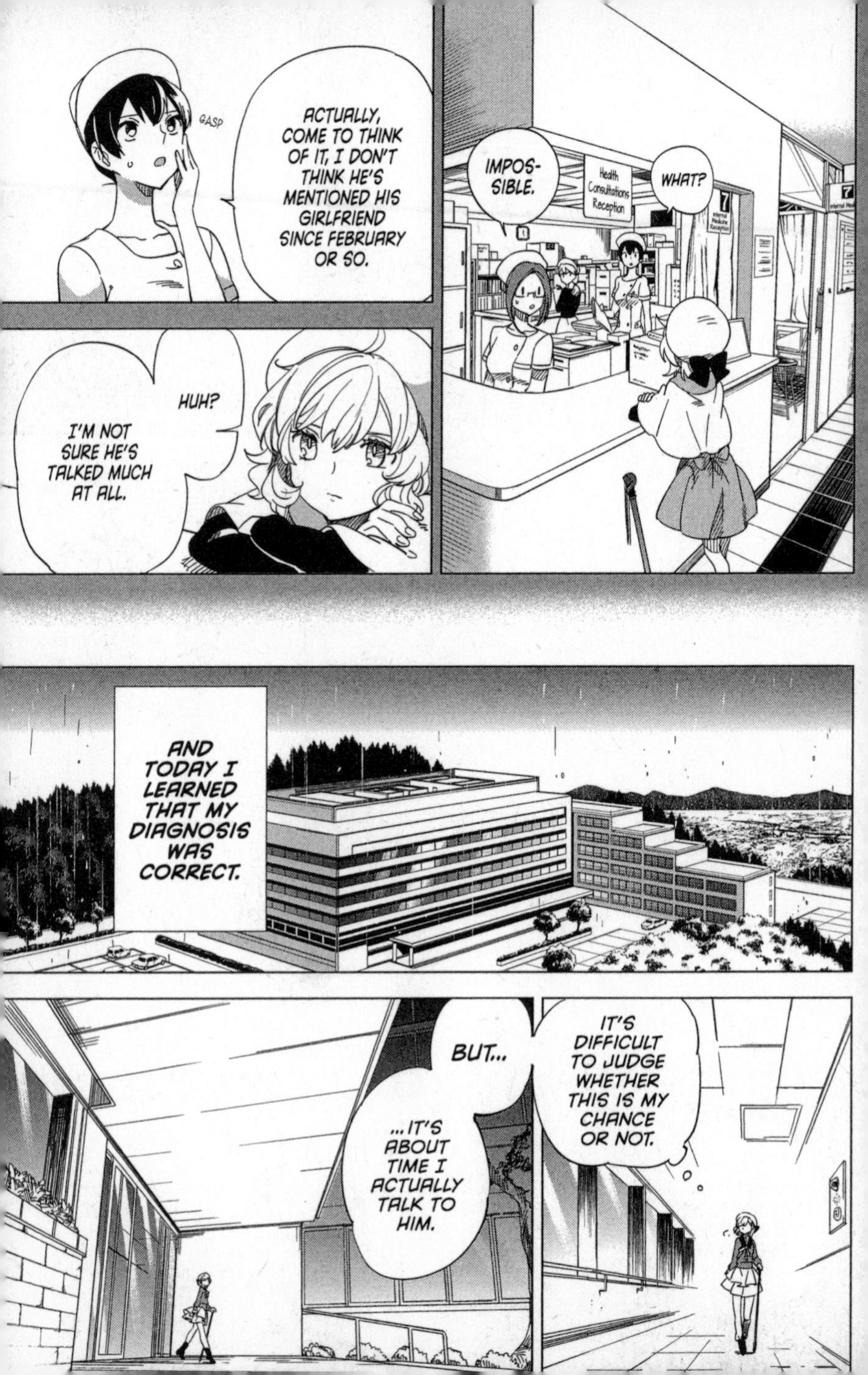
WHAT?
IMPOS-SIBLE.
Health Consultations Reception
GASP
ACTUALLY, COME TO THINK OF IT, I DON'T THINK HE'S MENTIONED HIS GIRLFRIEND SINCE FEBRUARY OR SO.
HUH?
I'M NOT SURE HE'S TALKED MUCH AT ALL.
AND TODAY I LEARNED THAT MY DIAGNOSIS WAS CORRECT.
IT'S DIFFICULT TO JUDGE WHETHER THIS IS MY CHANCE OR NOT.
BUT...
...IT'S ABOUT TIME I ACTUALLY TALK TO HIM.

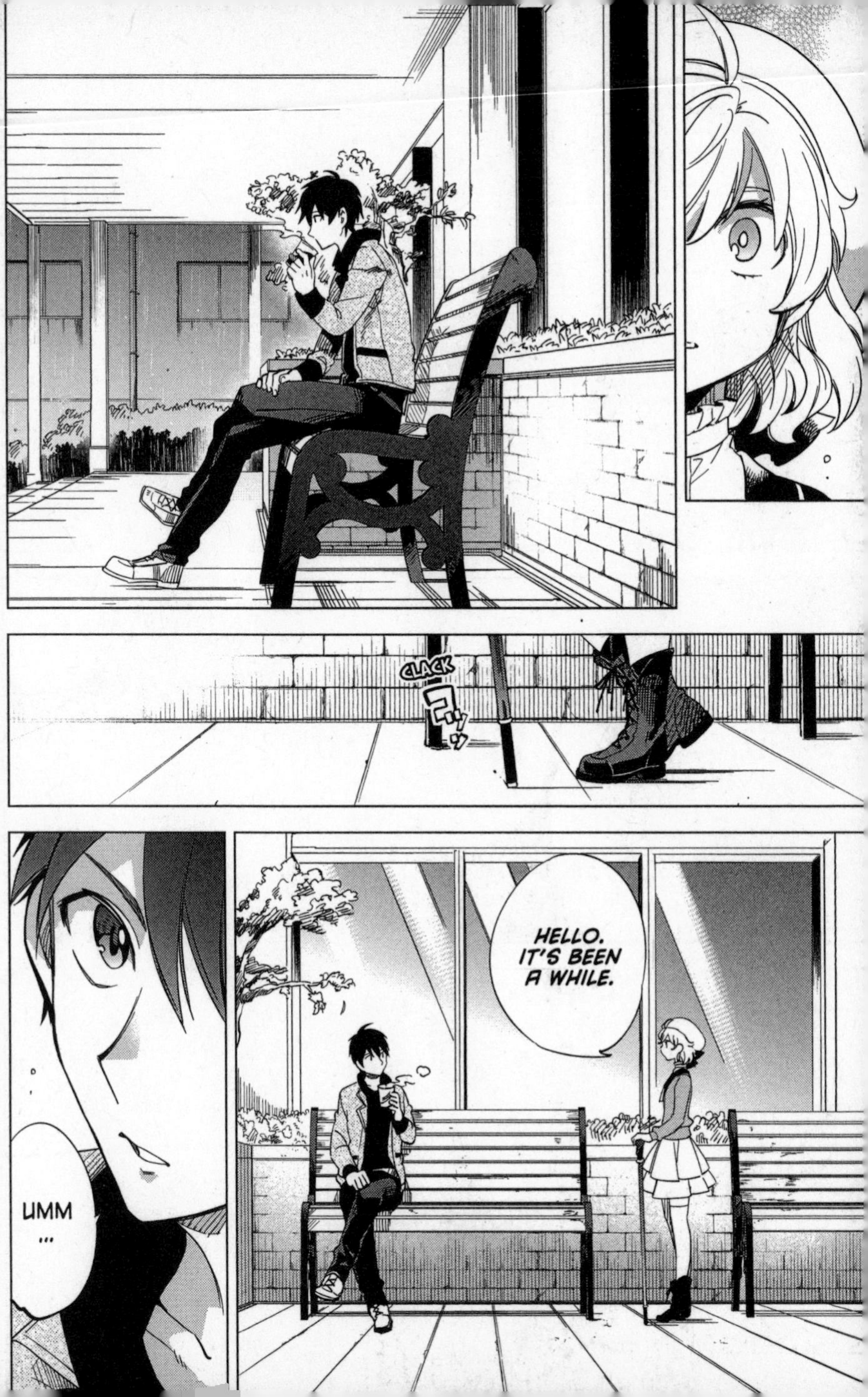
CLACK
HELLO. IT'S BEEN A WHILE.
UMM ...

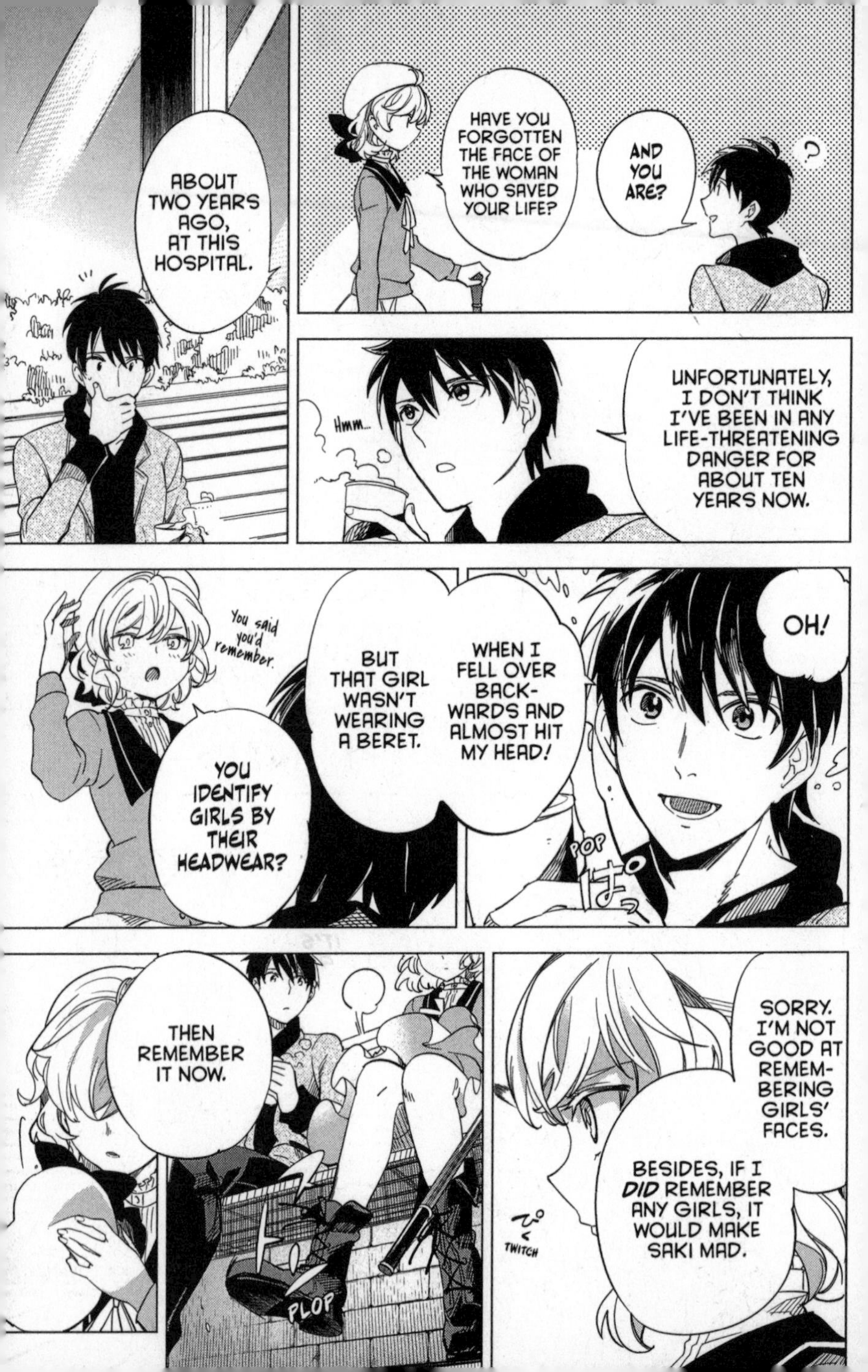
AND YOU ARE?
HAVE YOU FORGOTTEN THE FACE OF THE WOMAN WHO SAVED YOUR LIFE?
UNFORTUNATELY, I DON'T THINK I'VE BEEN IN ANY LIFE-THREATENING DANGER FOR ABOUT TEN YEARS NOW.
Hmm...
ABOUT TWO YEARS AGO, AT THIS HOSPITAL.
OH!
WHEN I FELL OVER BACK-WARDS AND ALMOST HIT MY HEAD!
POP
BUT THAT GIRL WASN'T WEARING A BERET.
You said you'd remember.
YOU IDENTIFY GIRLS BY THEIR HEADWEAR?
SORRY. I'M NOT GOOD AT REMEM-BERING GIRLS' FACES.
BESIDES, IF I DID REMEMBER ANY GIRLS, IT WOULD MAKE SAKI MAD.
TWITCH
THEN REMEMBER IT NOW.
PLOP

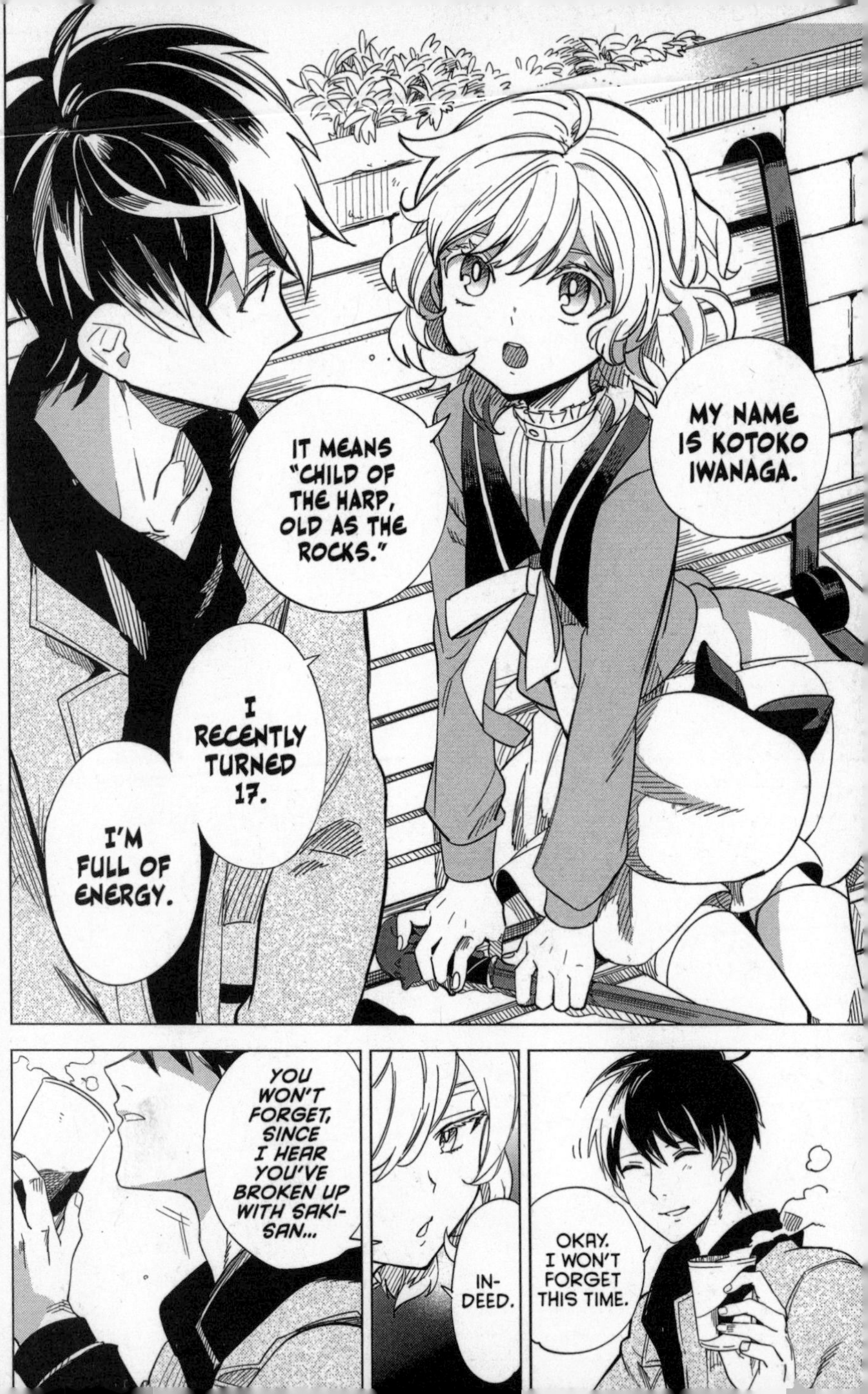
MY NAME IS KOTOKO IWANAGA.
IT MEANS "CHILD OF THE HARP, OLD AS THE ROCKS."
I RECENTLY TURNED 17.
I'M FULL OF ENERGY.
OKAY. I WON'T FORGET THIS TIME.
IN-DEED.
YOU WON'T FORGET, SINCE I HEAR YOU'VE BROKEN UP WITH SAKI-SAN...

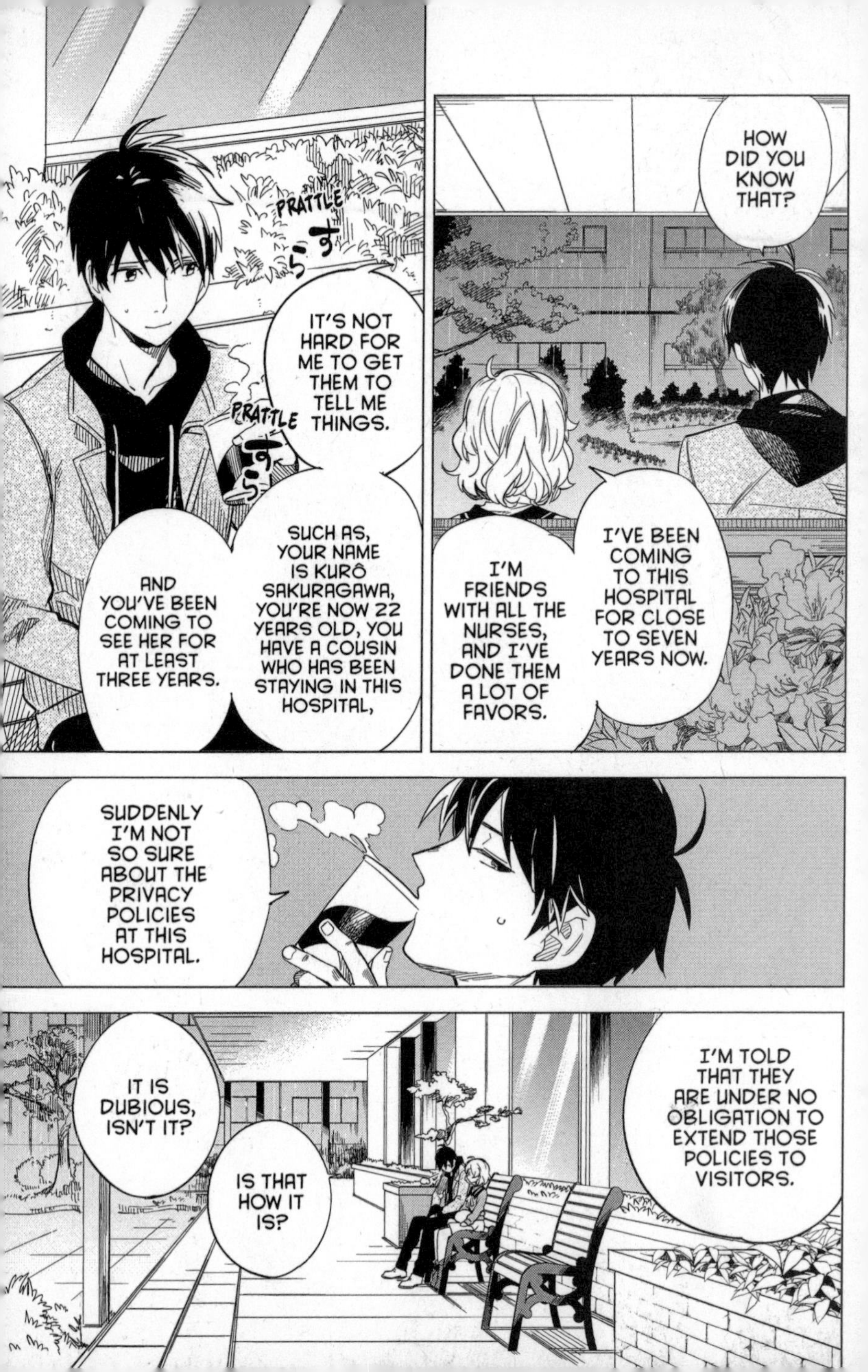
HOW DID YOU KNOW THAT?
I'VE BEEN COMING TO THIS HOSPITAL FOR CLOSE TO SEVEN YEARS NOW.
I'M FRIENDS WITH ALL THE NURSES, AND I'VE DONE THEM A LOT OF FAVORS.
PRATTLE
すら
IT'S NOT HARD FOR ME TO GET THEM TO TELL ME THINGS.
PRATTLE
すら
SUCH AS, YOUR NAME IS KURÔ SAKURAGAWA, YOU'RE NOW 22 YEARS OLD, YOU HAVE A COUSIN WHO HAS BEEN STAYING IN THIS HOSPITAL,
AND YOU'VE BEEN COMING TO SEE HER FOR AT LEAST THREE YEARS.
SUDDENLY I'M NOT SO SURE ABOUT THE PRIVACY POLICIES AT THIS HOSPITAL.
I'M TOLD THAT THEY ARE UNDER NO OBLIGATION TO EXTEND THOSE POLICIES TO VISITORS.
IT IS DUBIOUS, ISN'T IT?
IS THAT HOW IT IS?

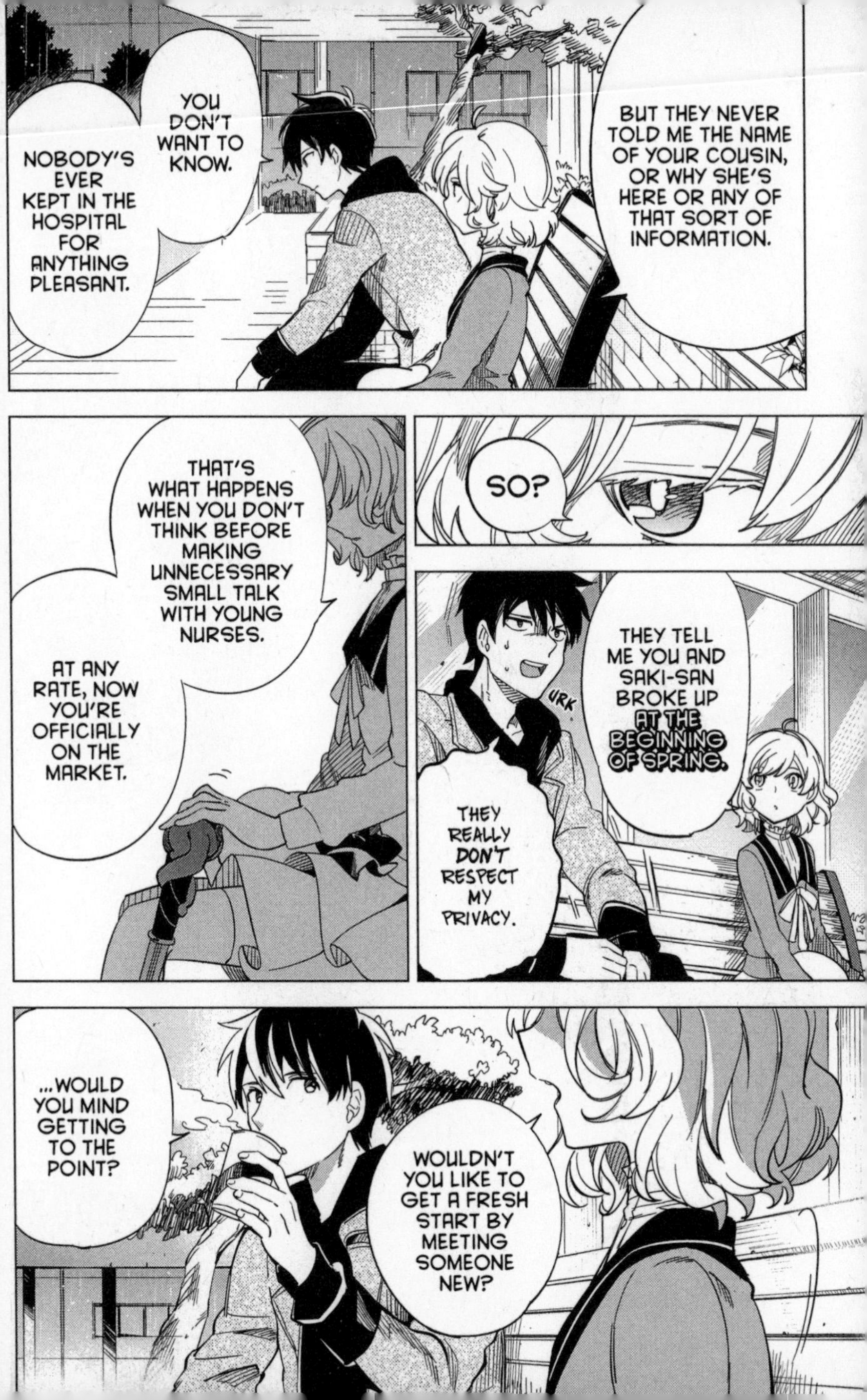
BUT THEY NEVER TOLD ME THE NAME OF YOUR COUSIN, OR WHY SHE'S HERE OR ANY OF THAT SORT OF INFORMATION.
YOU DON'T WANT TO KNOW.
NOBODY'S EVER KEPT IN THE HOSPITAL FOR ANYTHING PLEASANT.
SO?
THEY TELL ME YOU AND SAKI-SAN BROKE UP AT THE BEGINNING OF SPRING.
URK
THEY REALLY DON'T RESPECT MY PRIVACY.
THAT'S WHAT HAPPENS WHEN YOU DON'T THINK BEFORE MAKING UNNECESSARY SMALL TALK WITH YOUNG NURSES.
AT ANY RATE, NOW YOU'RE OFFICIALLY ON THE MARKET.
WOULDN'T YOU LIKE TO GET A FRESH START BY MEETING SOMEONE NEW?
...WOULD YOU MIND GETTING TO THE POINT?

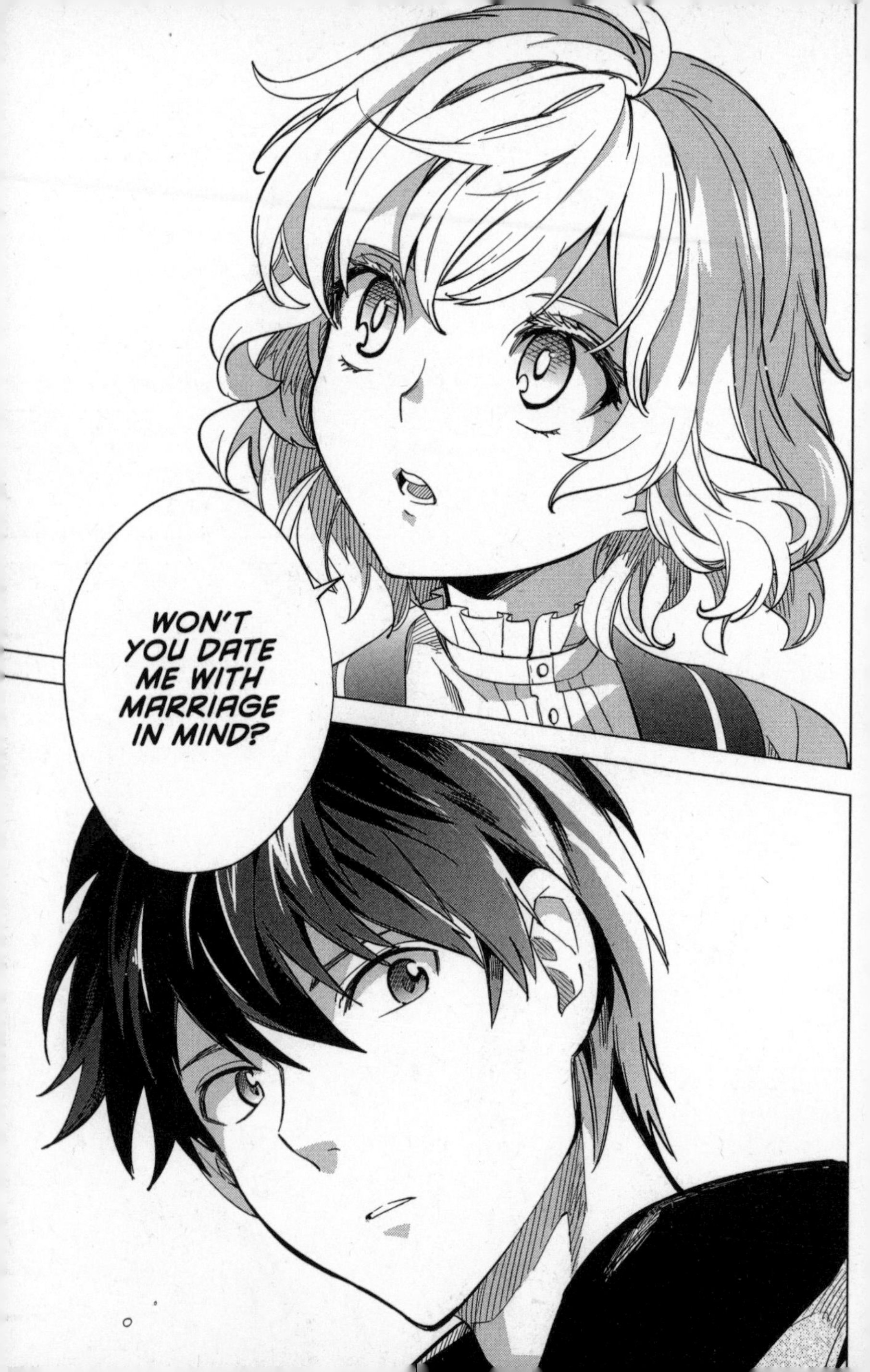
WON'T YOU DATE ME WITH MARRIAGE IN MIND?

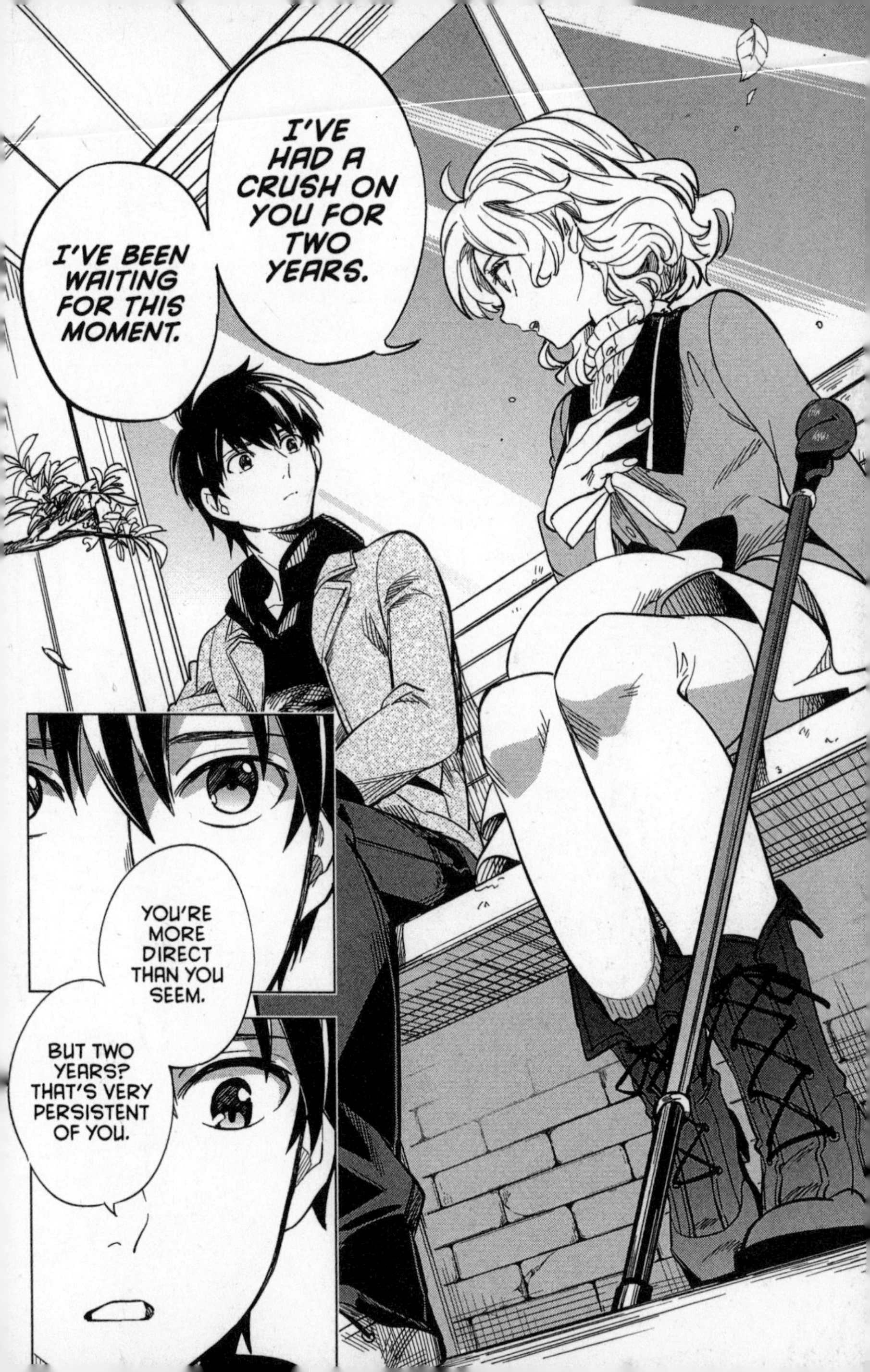
I'VE HAD A CRUSH ON YOU FOR TWO YEARS.
I'VE BEEN WAITING FOR THIS MOMENT.
YOU'RE MORE DIRECT THAN YOU SEEM.
BUT TWO YEARS? THAT'S VERY PERSISTENT OF YOU.

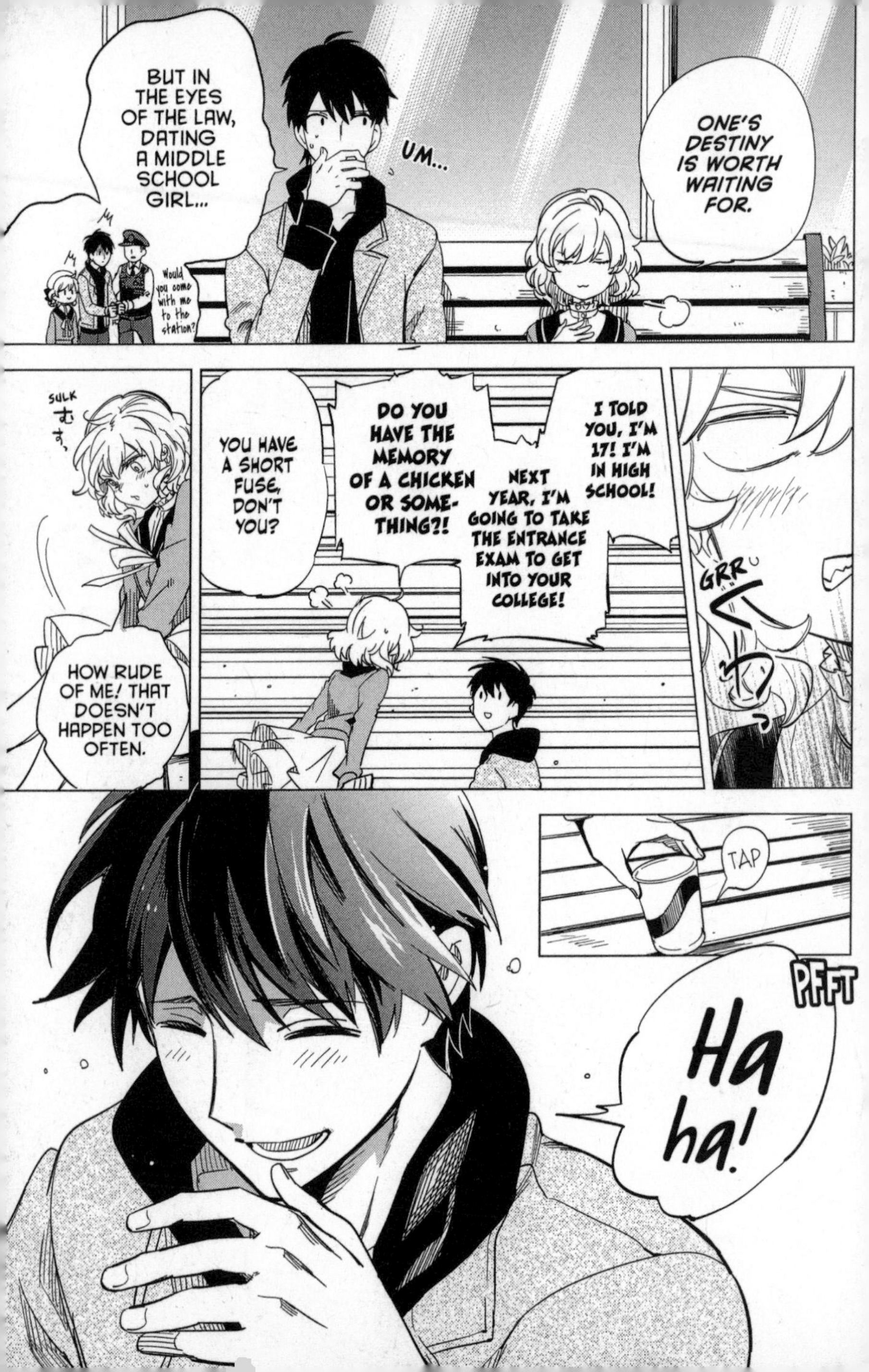
ONE'S DESTINY IS WORTH WAITING FOR.
UM...
BUT IN THE EYES OF THE LAW, DATING A MIDDLE SCHOOL GIRL...
Would you come with me to the station?
GRR
I TOLD YOU, I'M 17! I'M IN HIGH SCHOOL!
NEXT YEAR, I'M GOING TO TAKE THE ENTRANCE EXAM TO GET INTO YOUR COLLEGE!
DO YOU HAVE THE MEMORY OF A CHICKEN OR SOME-THING?!
YOU HAVE A SHORT FUSE, DON'T YOU?
SULK
むす
HOW RUDE OF ME! THAT DOESN'T HAPPEN TOO OFTEN.
TAP
PFFT
Ha ha!

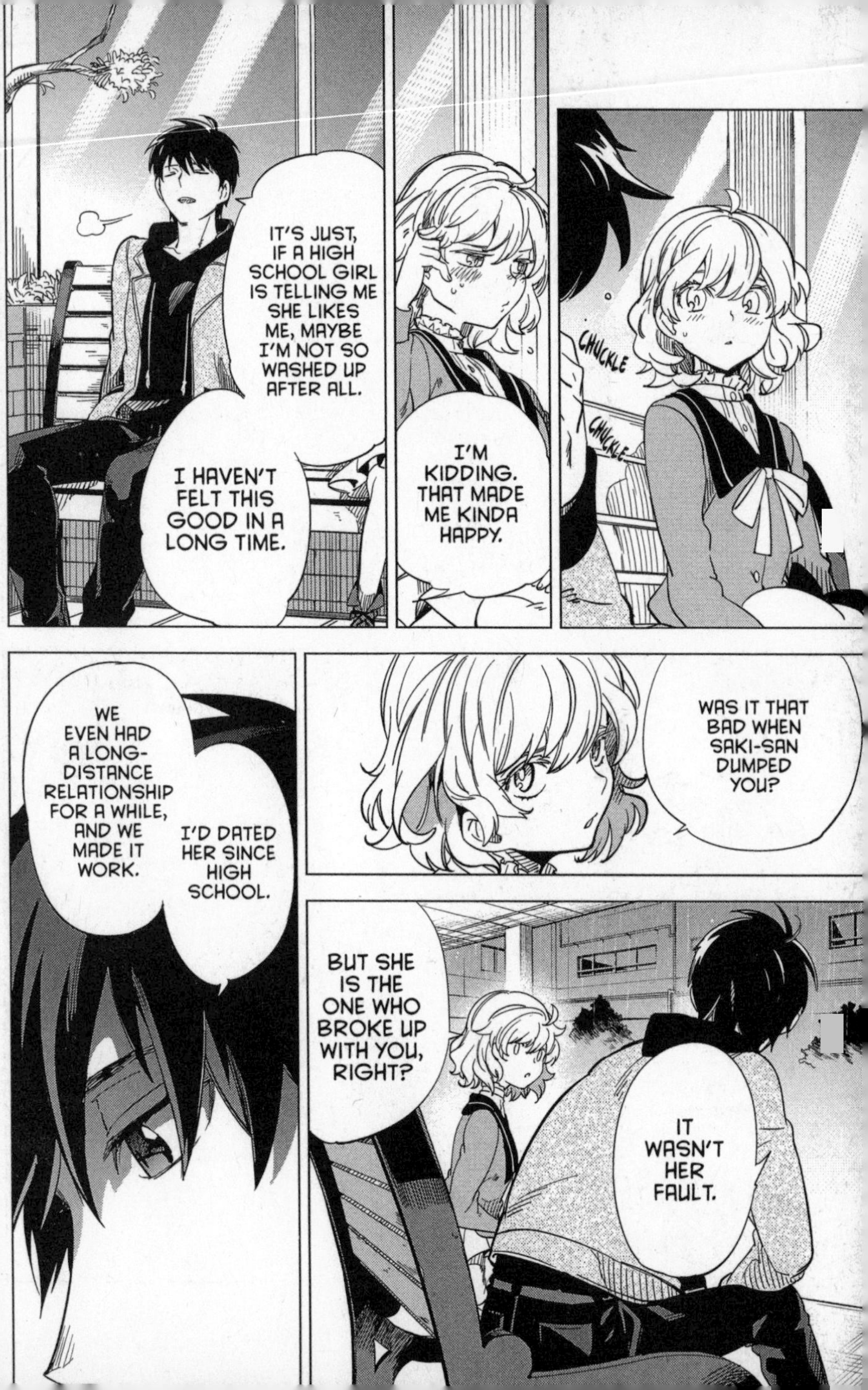
CHUCKLE
CHUCKLE
I'M KIDDING. THAT MADE ME KINDA HAPPY.
IT'S JUST, IF A HIGH SCHOOL GIRL IS TELLING ME SHE LIKES ME, MAYBE I'M NOT SO WASHED UP AFTER ALL.
I HAVEN'T FELT THIS GOOD IN A LONG TIME.
WAS IT THAT BAD WHEN SAKI-SAN DUMPED YOU?
BUT SHE IS THE ONE WHO BROKE UP WITH YOU, RIGHT?
IT WASN'T HER FAULT.
I'D DATED HER SINCE HIGH SCHOOL.
WE EVEN HAD A LONG-DISTANCE RELATIONSHIP FOR A WHILE, AND WE MADE IT WORK.

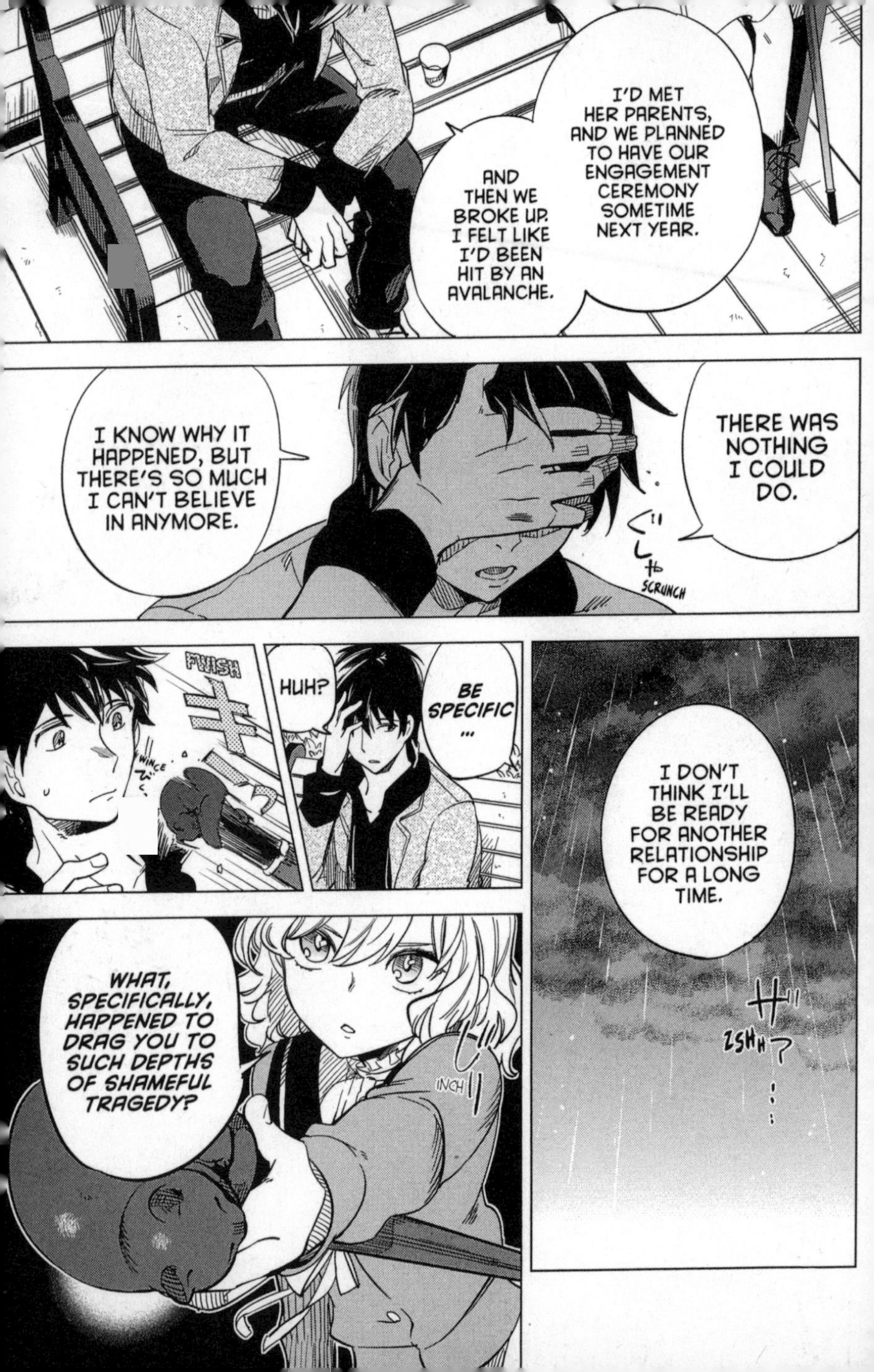
I'D MET HER PARENTS, AND WE PLANNED TO HAVE OUR ENGAGEMENT CEREMONY SOMETIME NEXT YEAR.
AND THEN WE BROKE UP. I FELT LIKE I'D BEEN HIT BY AN AVALANCHE.
THERE WAS NOTHING I COULD DO.
SCRUNCH
I KNOW WHY IT HAPPENED, BUT THERE'S SO MUCH I CAN'T BELIEVE IN ANYMORE.
I DON'T THINK I'LL BE READY FOR ANOTHER RELATIONSHIP FOR A LONG TIME.
ZSHHH
BE SPECIFIC ...
HUH?
FWISH
WINCE
WHAT, SPECIFICALLY, HAPPENED TO DRAG YOU TO SUCH DEPTHS OF SHAMEFUL TRAGEDY?
INCH

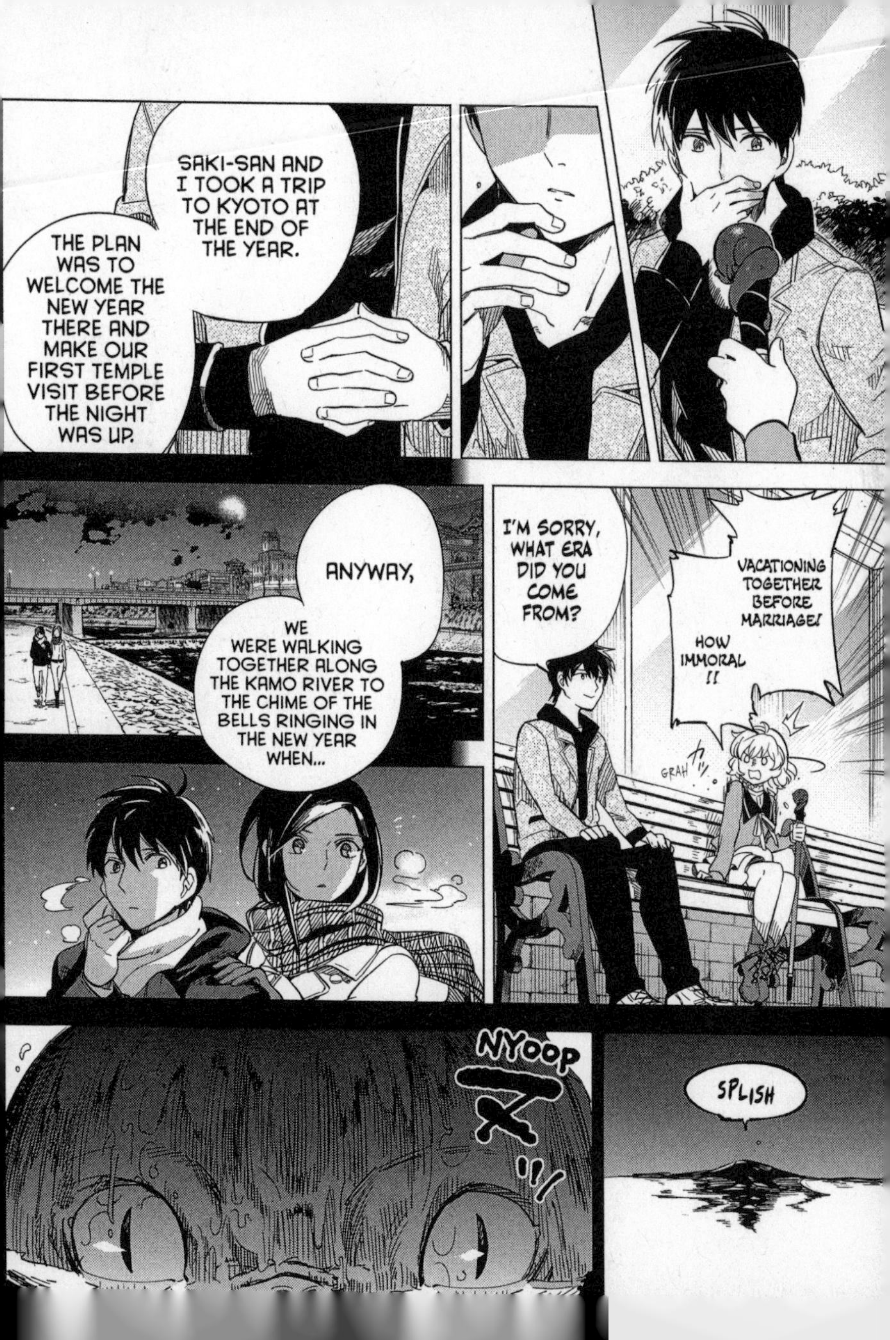
SAKI-SAN AND I TOOK A TRIP TO KYOTO AT THE END OF THE YEAR.
THE PLAN WAS TO WELCOME THE NEW YEAR THERE AND MAKE OUR FIRST TEMPLE VISIT BEFORE THE NIGHT WAS UP.
VACATIONING TOGETHER BEFORE MARRIAGE!
HOW IMMORAL !!
GRAH
I'M SORRY, WHAT ERA DID YOU COME FROM?
ANYWAY,
WE WERE WALKING TOGETHER ALONG THE KAMO RIVER TO THE CHIME OF THE BELLS RINGING IN THE NEW YEAR WHEN...
SPLISH
NYOOP

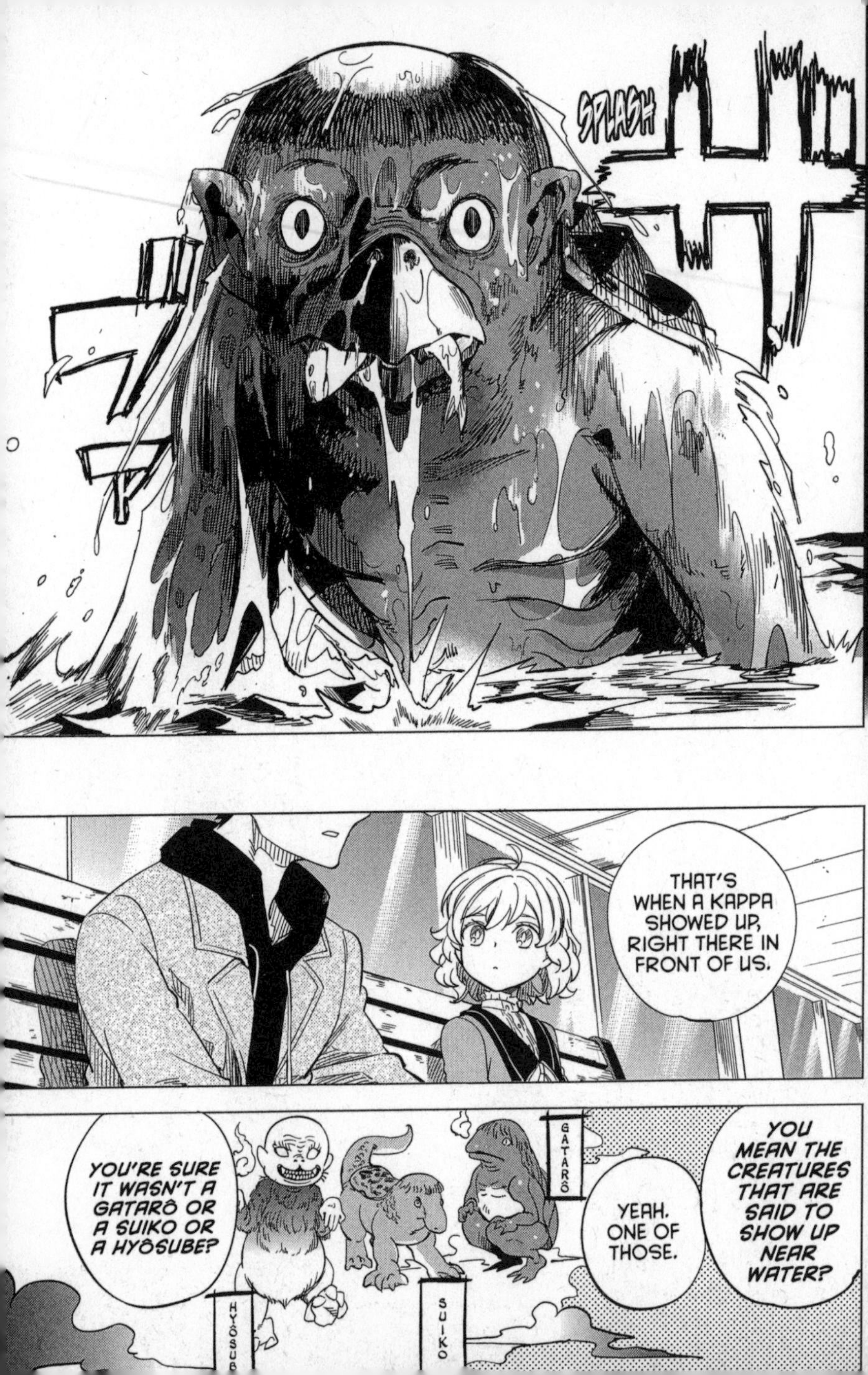
SPLASH
THAT'S WHEN A KAPPA SHOWED UP, RIGHT THERE IN FRONT OF US.
YOU MEAN THE CREATURES THAT ARE SAID TO SHOW UP NEAR WATER?
GATARÔ
YEAH. ONE OF THOSE.
YOU'RE SURE IT WASN'T A GATARÔ OR A SUIKO OR A HYÔSUBE?
SUIKO

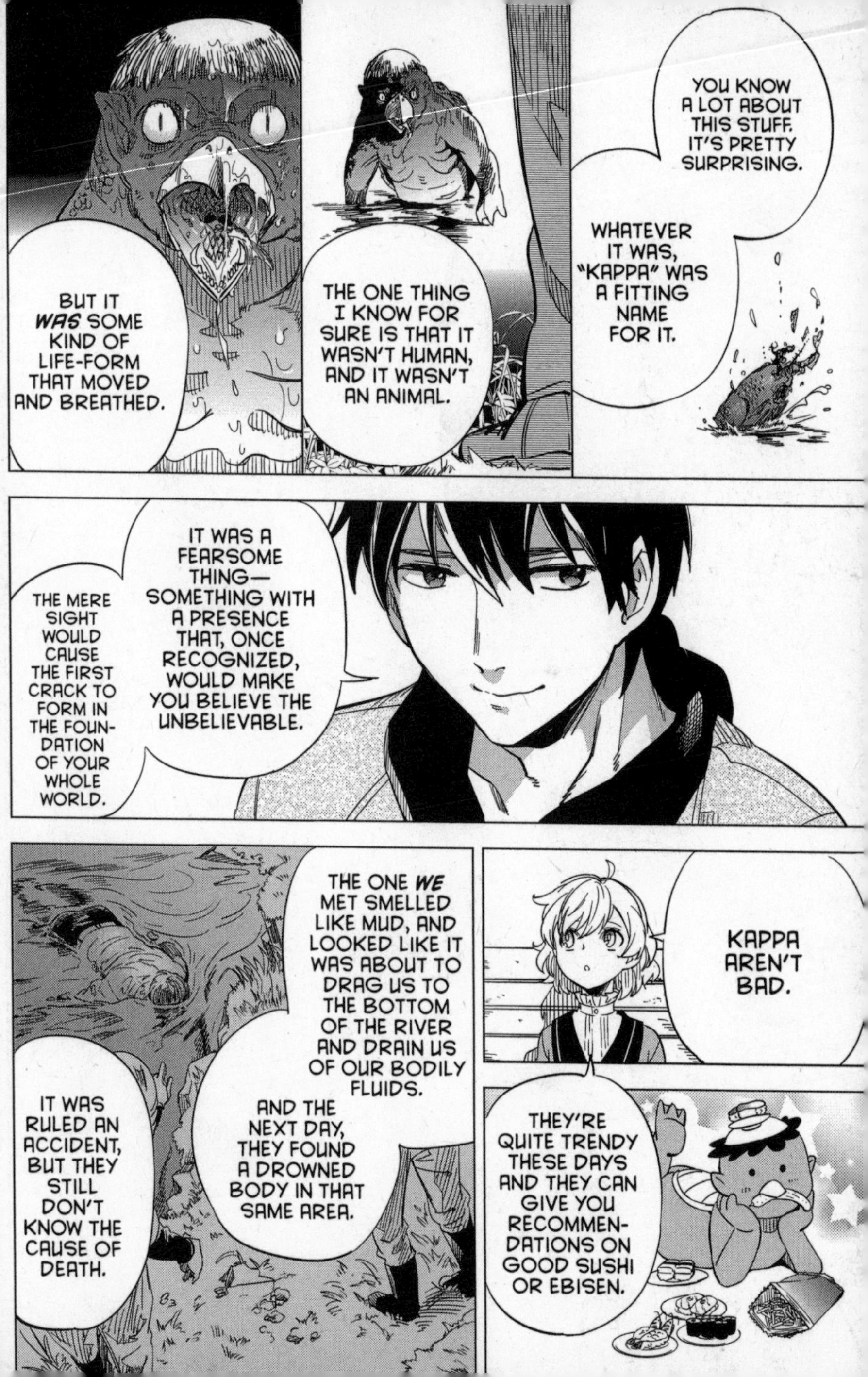
YOU KNOW A LOT ABOUT THIS STUFF. IT'S PRETTY SURPRISING.
WHATEVER IT WAS, "KAPPA" WAS A FITTING NAME FOR IT.
THE ONE THING I KNOW FOR SURE IS THAT IT WASN'T HUMAN, AND IT WASN'T AN ANIMAL.
BUT IT *WAS* SOME KIND OF LIFE-FORM THAT MOVED AND BREATHED.
IT WAS A FEARSOME THING—SOMETHING WITH A PRESENCE THAT, ONCE RECOGNIZED, WOULD MAKE YOU BELIEVE THE UNBELIEVABLE.
THE MERE SIGHT WOULD CAUSE THE FIRST CRACK TO FORM IN THE FOUN-DATION OF YOUR WHOLE WORLD.
KAPPA AREN'T BAD.
THEY'RE QUITE TRENDY THESE DAYS AND THEY CAN GIVE YOU RECOMMEN-DATIONS ON GOOD SUSHI OR EBISEN.
THE ONE *WE* MET SMELLED LIKE MUD, AND LOOKED LIKE IT WAS ABOUT TO DRAG US TO THE BOTTOM OF THE RIVER AND DRAIN US OF OUR BODILY FLUIDS.
AND THE NEXT DAY, THEY FOUND A DROWNED BODY IN THAT SAME AREA.
IT WAS RULED AN ACCIDENT, BUT THEY STILL DON'T KNOW THE CAUSE OF DEATH.

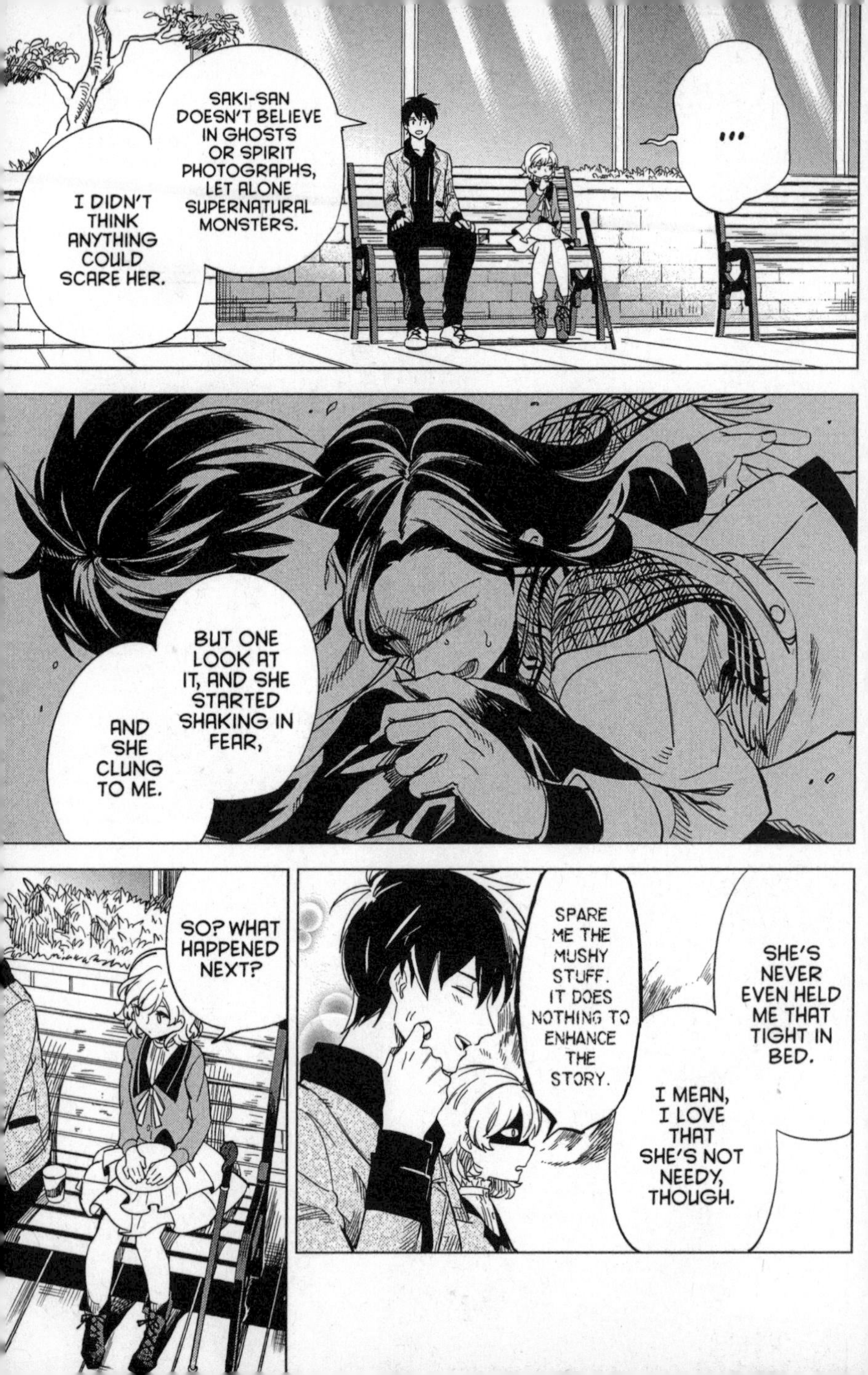
...
SAKI-SAN DOESN'T BELIEVE IN GHOSTS OR SPIRIT PHOTOGRAPHS, LET ALONE SUPERNATURAL MONSTERS.
I DIDN'T THINK ANYTHING COULD SCARE HER.
BUT ONE LOOK AT IT, AND SHE STARTED SHAKING IN FEAR,
AND SHE CLUNG TO ME.
SHE'S NEVER EVEN HELD ME THAT TIGHT IN BED.
SPARE ME THE MUSHY STUFF. IT DOES NOTHING TO ENHANCE THE STORY.
I MEAN, I LOVE THAT SHE'S NOT NEEDY, THOUGH.
SO? WHAT HAPPENED NEXT?

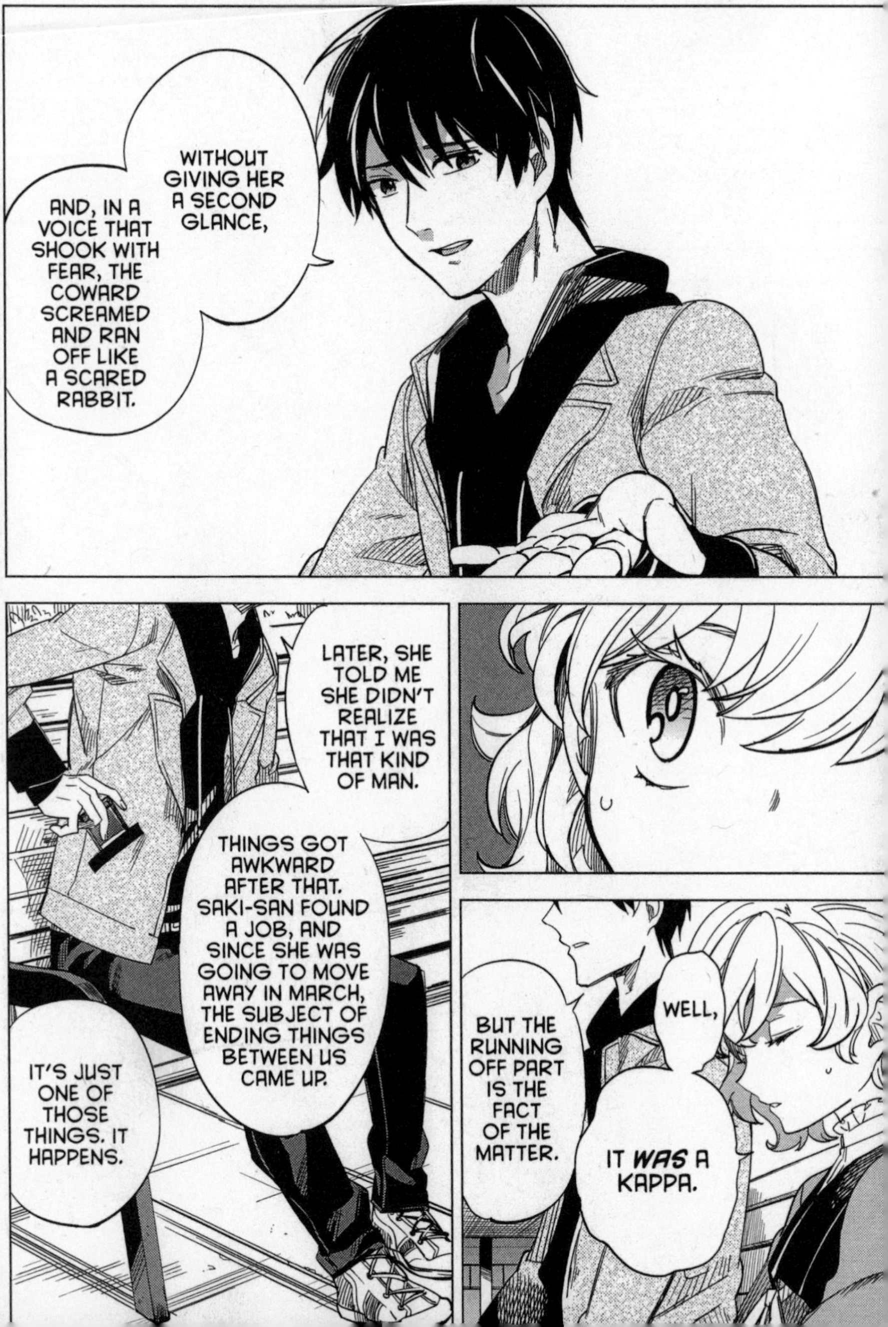
WITHOUT GIVING HER A SECOND GLANCE,
AND, IN A VOICE THAT SHOOK WITH FEAR, THE COWARD SCREAMED AND RAN OFF LIKE A SCARED RABBIT.
WELL,
IT *WAS* A KAPPA.
BUT THE RUNNING OFF PART IS THE FACT OF THE MATTER.
LATER, SHE TOLD ME SHE DIDN'T REALIZE THAT I WAS THAT KIND OF MAN.
THINGS GOT AWKWARD AFTER THAT. SAKI-SAN FOUND A JOB, AND SINCE SHE WAS GOING TO MOVE AWAY IN MARCH, THE SUBJECT OF ENDING THINGS BETWEEN US CAME UP.
IT'S JUST ONE OF THOSE THINGS. IT HAPPENS.

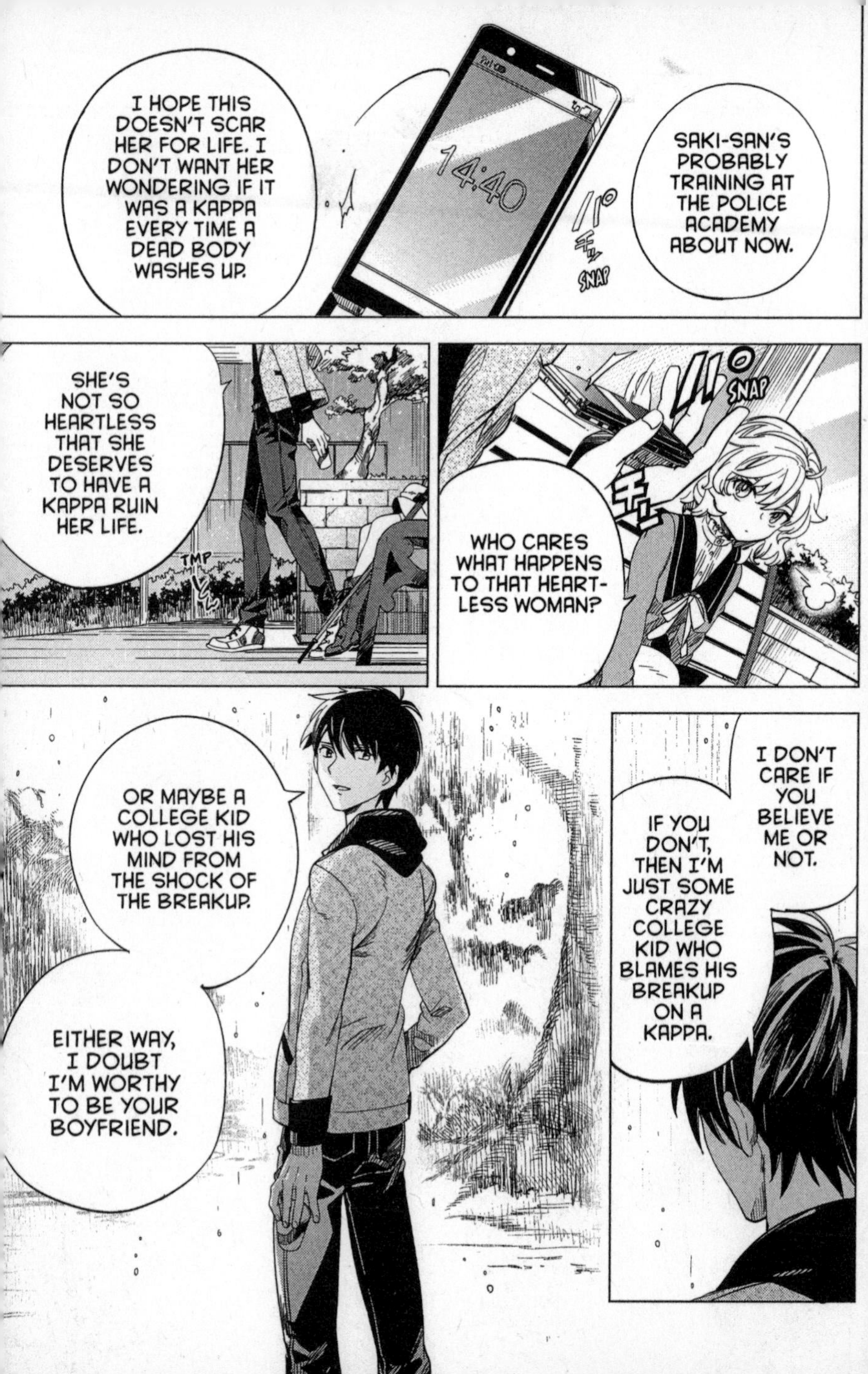
SAKI-SAN'S PROBABLY TRAINING AT THE POLICE ACADEMY ABOUT NOW.
SNAP
I HOPE THIS DOESN'T SCAR HER FOR LIFE. I DON'T WANT HER WONDERING IF IT WAS A KAPPA EVERY TIME A DEAD BODY WASHES UP.
SNAP
WHO CARES WHAT HAPPENS TO THAT HEART-LESS WOMAN?
SHE'S NOT SO HEARTLESS THAT SHE DESERVES TO HAVE A KAPPA RUIN HER LIFE.
TMP
I DON'T CARE IF YOU BELIEVE ME OR NOT.
IF YOU DON'T, THEN I'M JUST SOME CRAZY COLLEGE KID WHO BLAMES HIS BREAKUP ON A KAPPA.
OR MAYBE A COLLEGE KID WHO LOST HIS MIND FROM THE SHOCK OF THE BREAKUP.
EITHER WAY, I DOUBT I'M WORTHY TO BE YOUR BOYFRIEND.

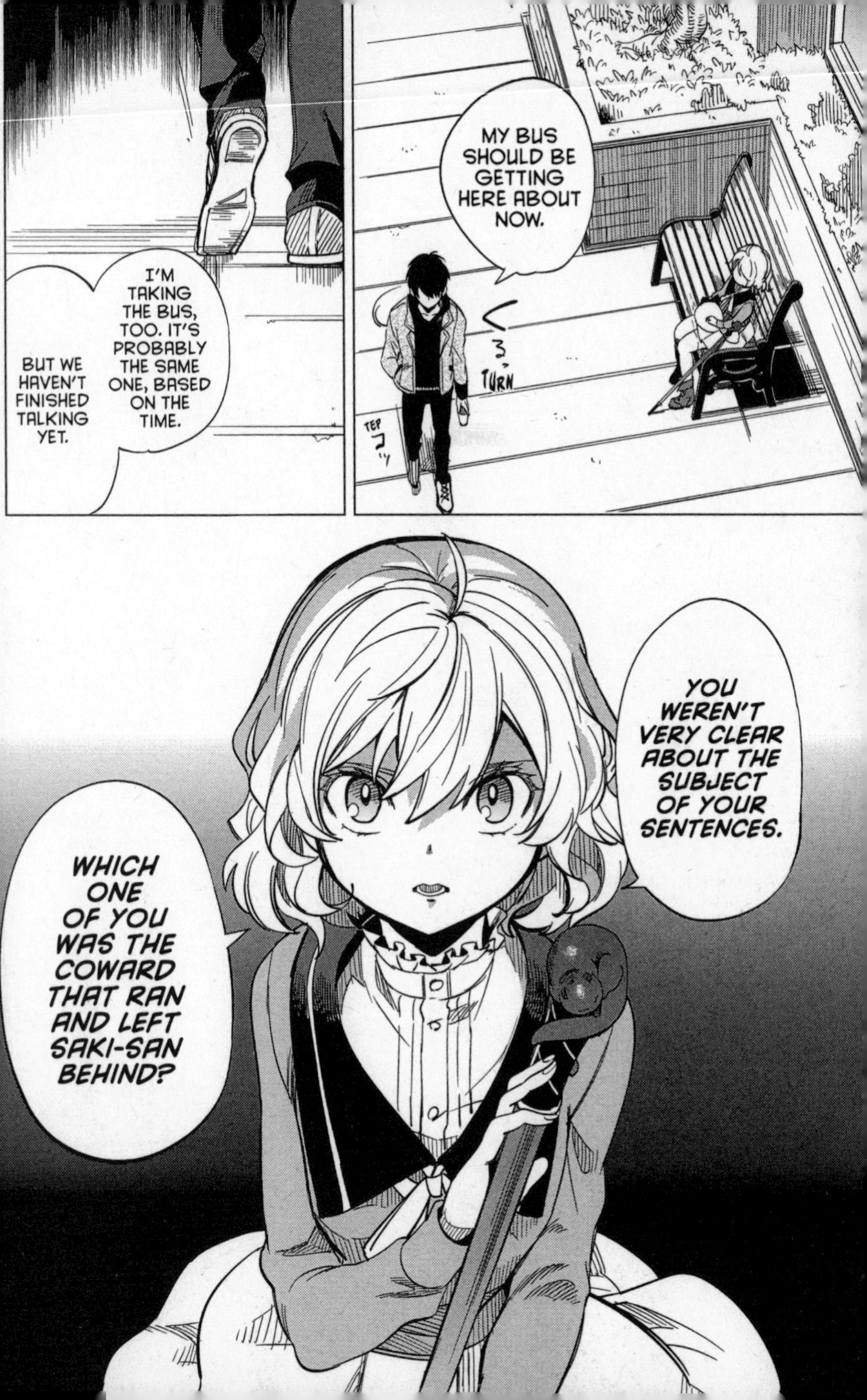
MY BUS SHOULD BE GETTING HERE ABOUT NOW.
TURN
TEP
I'M TAKING THE BUS, TOO. IT'S PROBABLY THE SAME ONE, BASED ON THE TIME.
BUT WE HAVEN'T FINISHED TALKING YET.
YOU WEREN'T VERY CLEAR ABOUT THE SUBJECT OF YOUR SENTENCES.
WHICH ONE OF YOU WAS THE COWARD THAT RAN AND LEFT SAKI-SAN BEHIND?

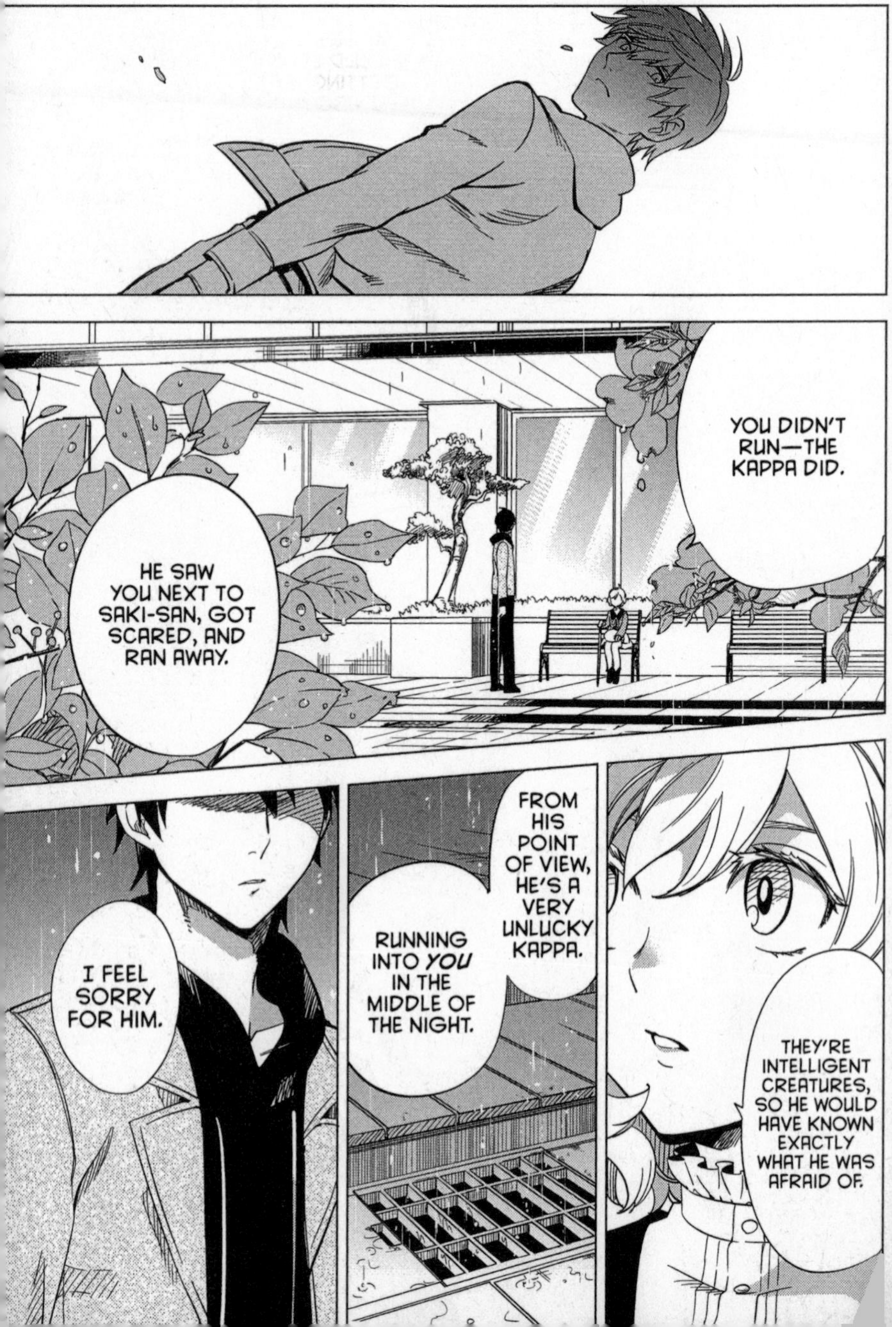
YOU DIDN'T RUN—THE KAPPA DID.
HE SAW YOU NEXT TO SAKI-SAN, GOT SCARED, AND RAN AWAY.
THEY'RE INTELLIGENT CREATURES, SO HE WOULD HAVE KNOWN EXACTLY WHAT HE WAS AFRAID OF.
FROM HIS POINT OF VIEW, HE'S A VERY UNLUCKY KAPPA.
RUNNING INTO *YOU* IN THE MIDDLE OF THE NIGHT.
I FEEL SORRY FOR HIM.

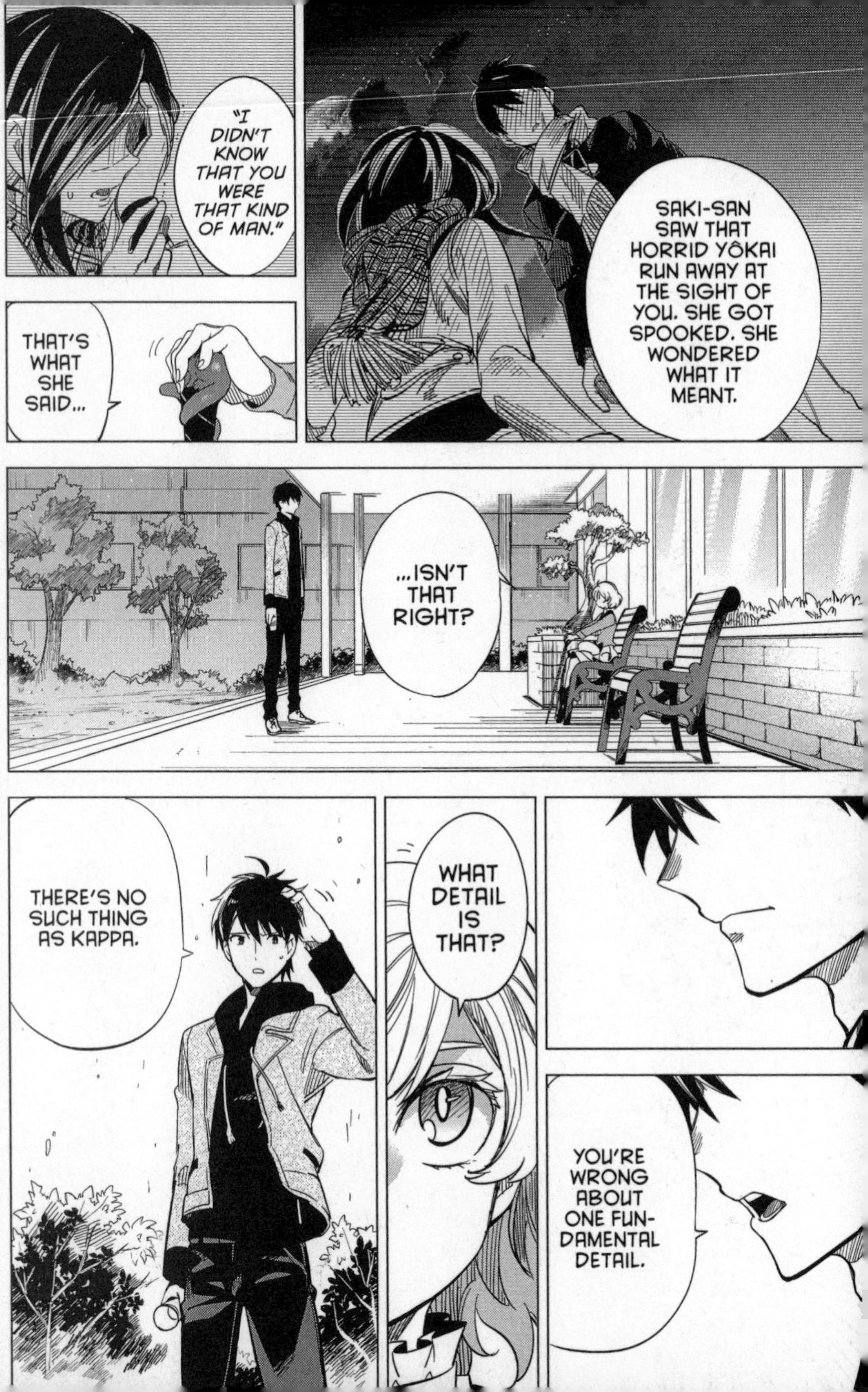
SAKI-SAN SAW THAT HORRID YÔKAI RUN AWAY AT THE SIGHT OF YOU. SHE GOT SPOOKED. SHE WONDERED WHAT IT MEANT.
"I DIDN'T KNOW THAT YOU WERE THAT KIND OF MAN."
THAT'S WHAT SHE SAID...
...ISN'T THAT RIGHT?
YOU'RE WRONG ABOUT ONE FUN-DAMENTAL DETAIL.
WHAT DETAIL IS THAT?
THERE'S NO SUCH THING AS KAPPA.

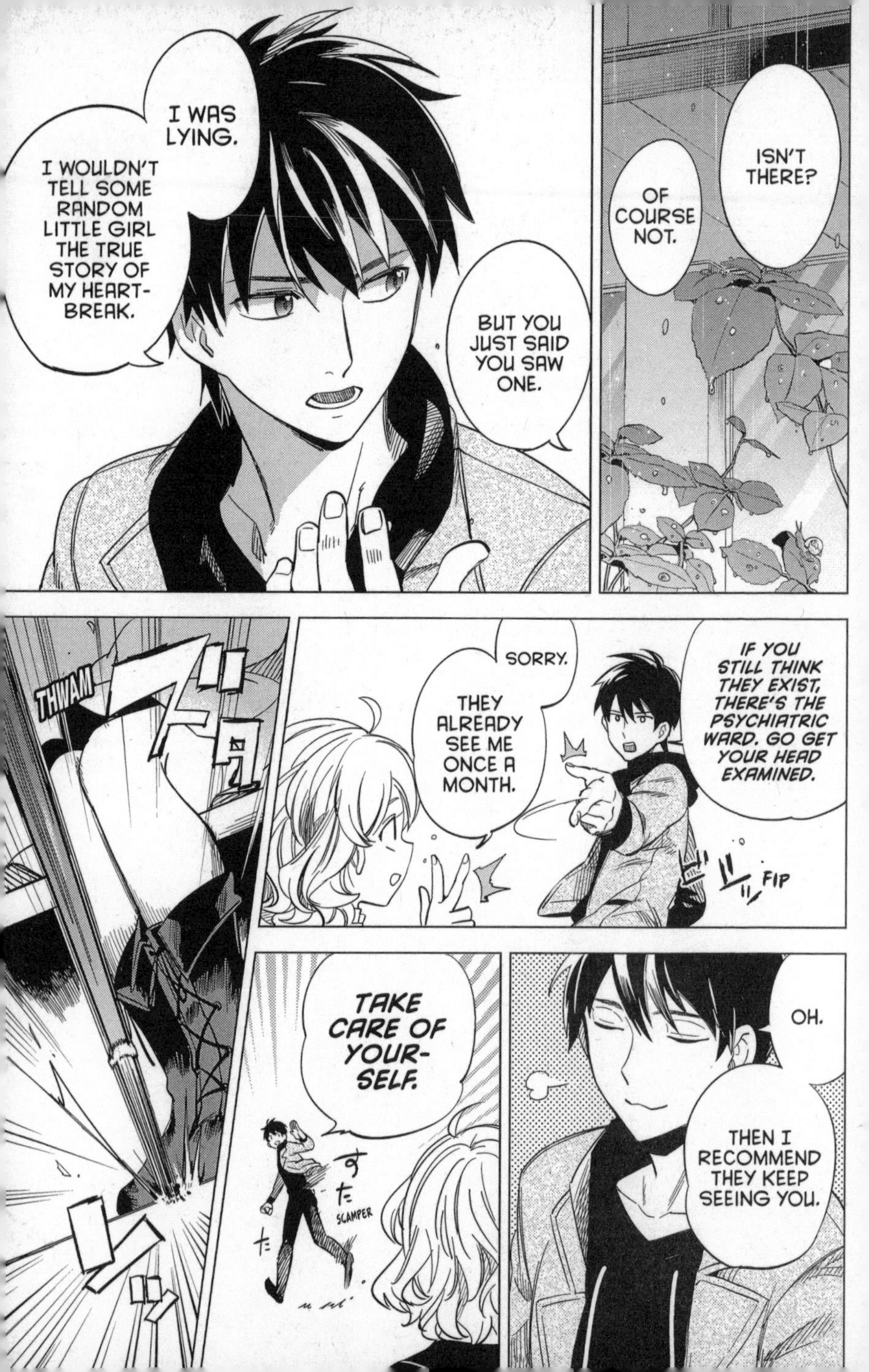

ISN'T THERE?
OF COURSE NOT.
BUT YOU JUST SAID YOU SAW ONE.
I WAS LYING.
I WOULDN'T TELL SOME RANDOM LITTLE GIRL THE TRUE STORY OF MY HEART-BREAK.
IF YOU STILL THINK THEY EXIST, THERE'S THE PSYCHIATRIC WARD. GO GET YOUR HEAD EXAMINED.
FIP
SORRY.
THEY ALREADY SEE ME ONCE A MONTH.
OH.
THEN I RECOMMEND THEY KEEP SEEING YOU.
TAKE CARE OF YOUR-SELF.
SCAMPER
THWAM

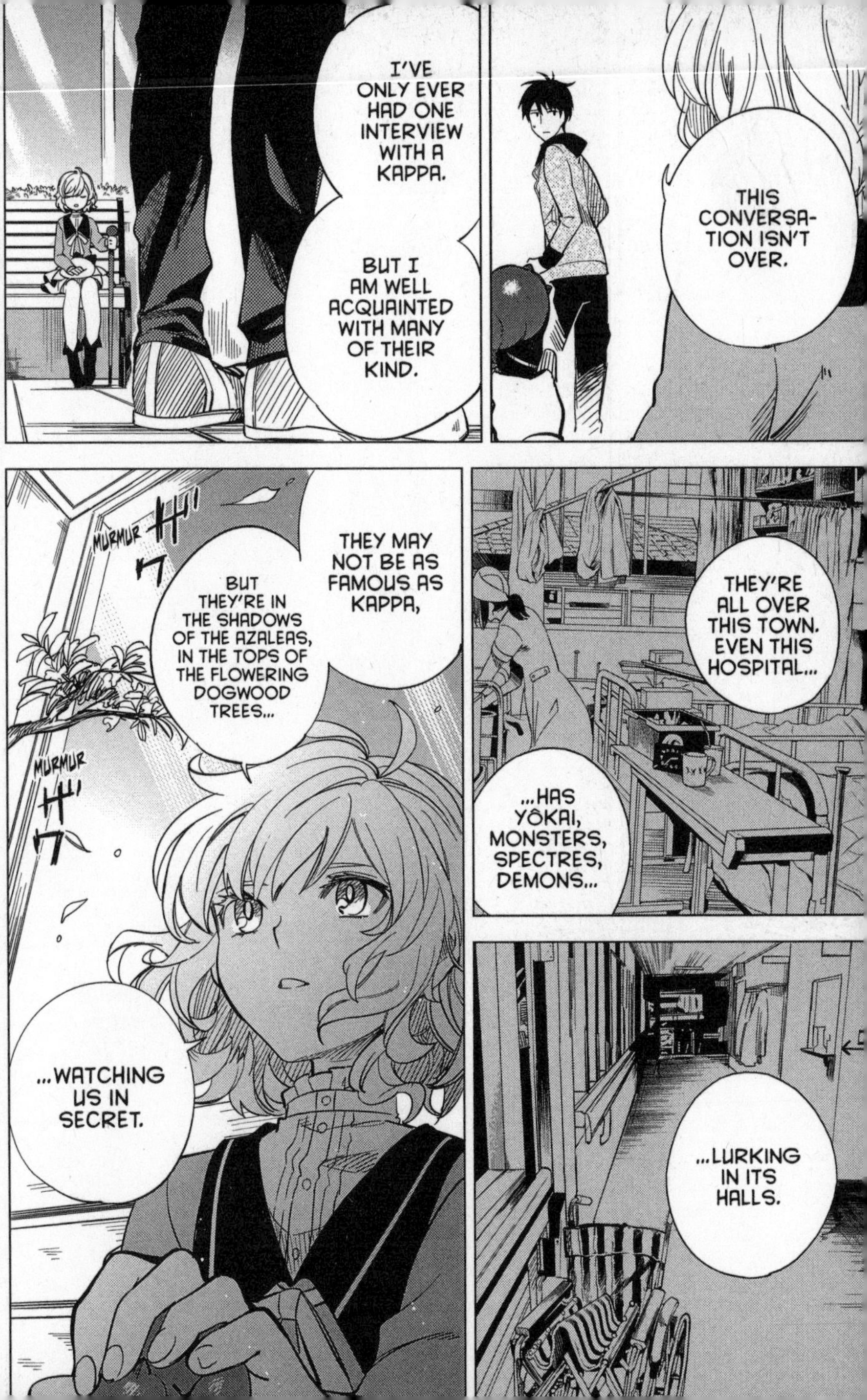
THIS CONVERSATION ISN'T OVER.
I'VE ONLY EVER HAD ONE INTERVIEW WITH A KAPPA.
BUT I AM WELL ACQUAINTED WITH MANY OF THEIR KIND.
THEY'RE ALL OVER THIS TOWN. EVEN THIS HOSPITAL...
...HAS YÔKAI, MONSTERS, SPECTRES, DEMONS...
...LURKING IN ITS HALLS.
THEY MAY NOT BE AS FAMOUS AS KAPPA,
BUT THEY'RE IN THE SHADOWS OF THE AZALEAS, IN THE TOPS OF THE FLOWERING DOGWOOD TREES...
MURMUR
MURMUR
...WATCHING US IN SECRET.

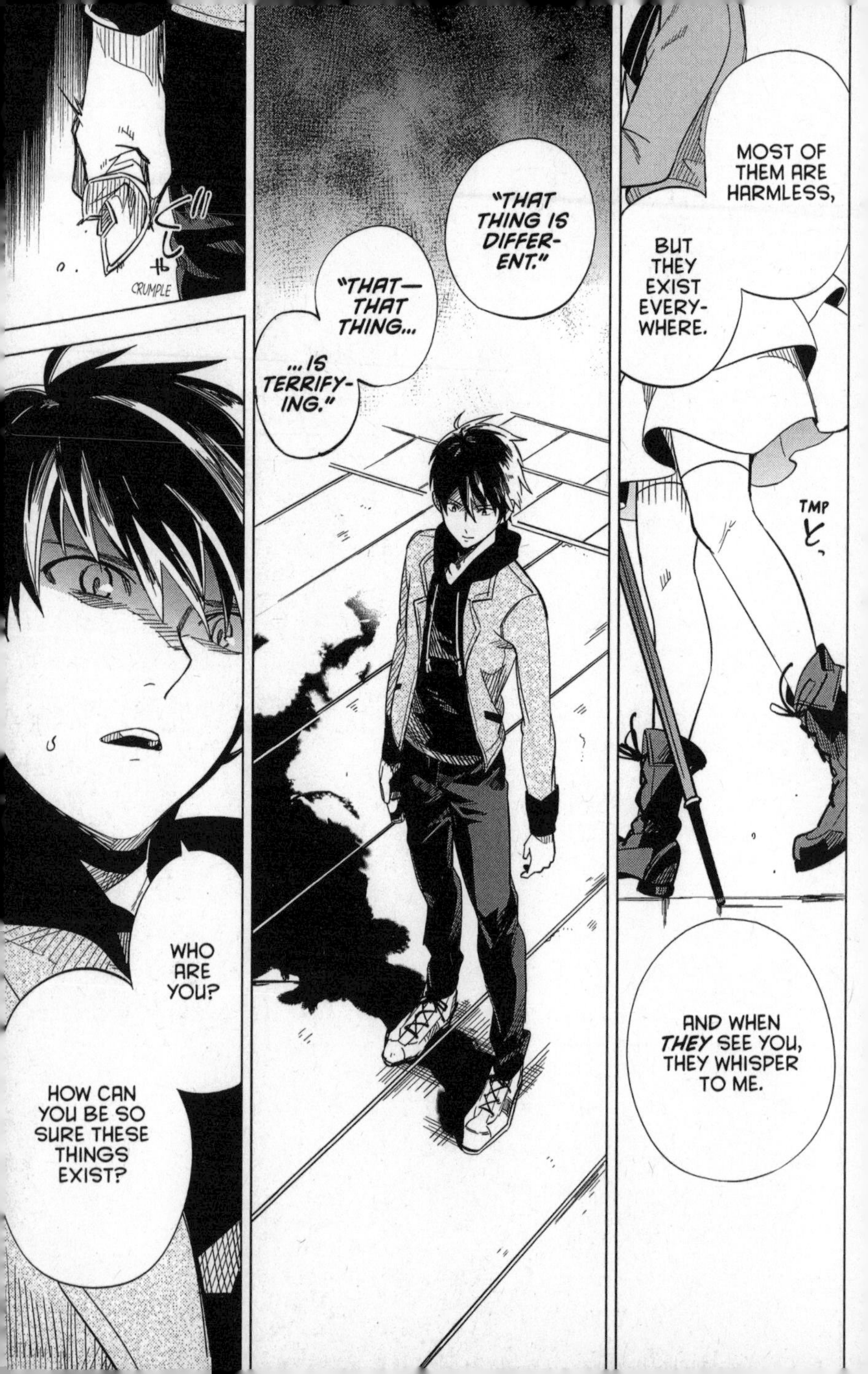
MOST OF THEM ARE HARMLESS,
BUT THEY EXIST EVERY-WHERE.
TMP
AND WHEN *THEY* SEE YOU, THEY WHISPER TO ME.
"THAT THING IS DIFFER-ENT."
"THAT— THAT THING...
...IS TERRIFY-ING."
CRUMPLE
WHO ARE YOU?
HOW CAN YOU BE SO SURE THESE THINGS EXIST?

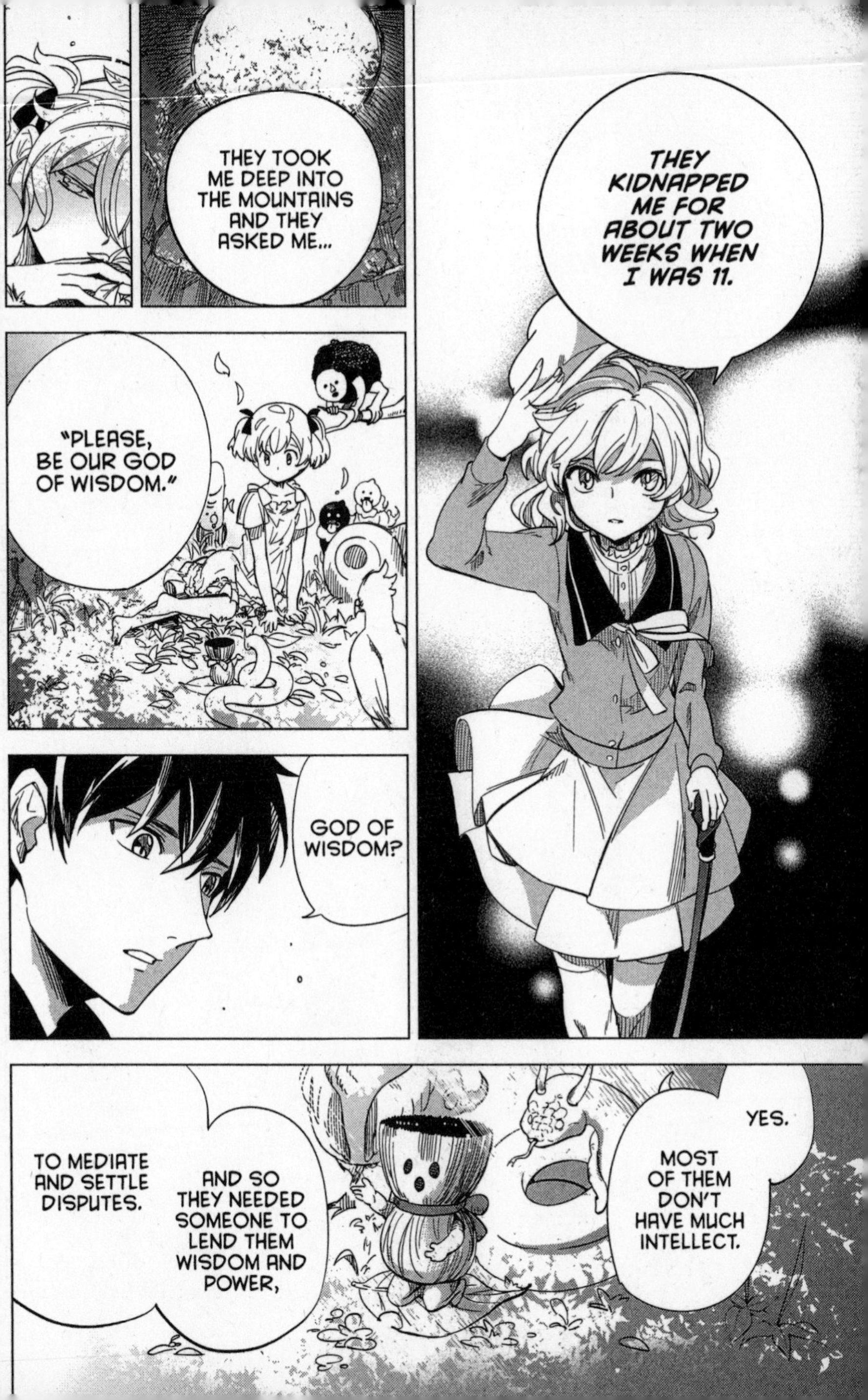
THEY KIDNAPPED ME FOR ABOUT TWO WEEKS WHEN I WAS 11.
THEY TOOK ME DEEP INTO THE MOUNTAINS AND THEY ASKED ME...
"PLEASE, BE OUR GOD OF WISDOM."
GOD OF WISDOM?
YES.
MOST OF THEM DON'T HAVE MUCH INTELLECT.
AND SO THEY NEEDED SOMEONE TO LEND THEM WISDOM AND POWER,
TO MEDIATE AND SETTLE DISPUTES.

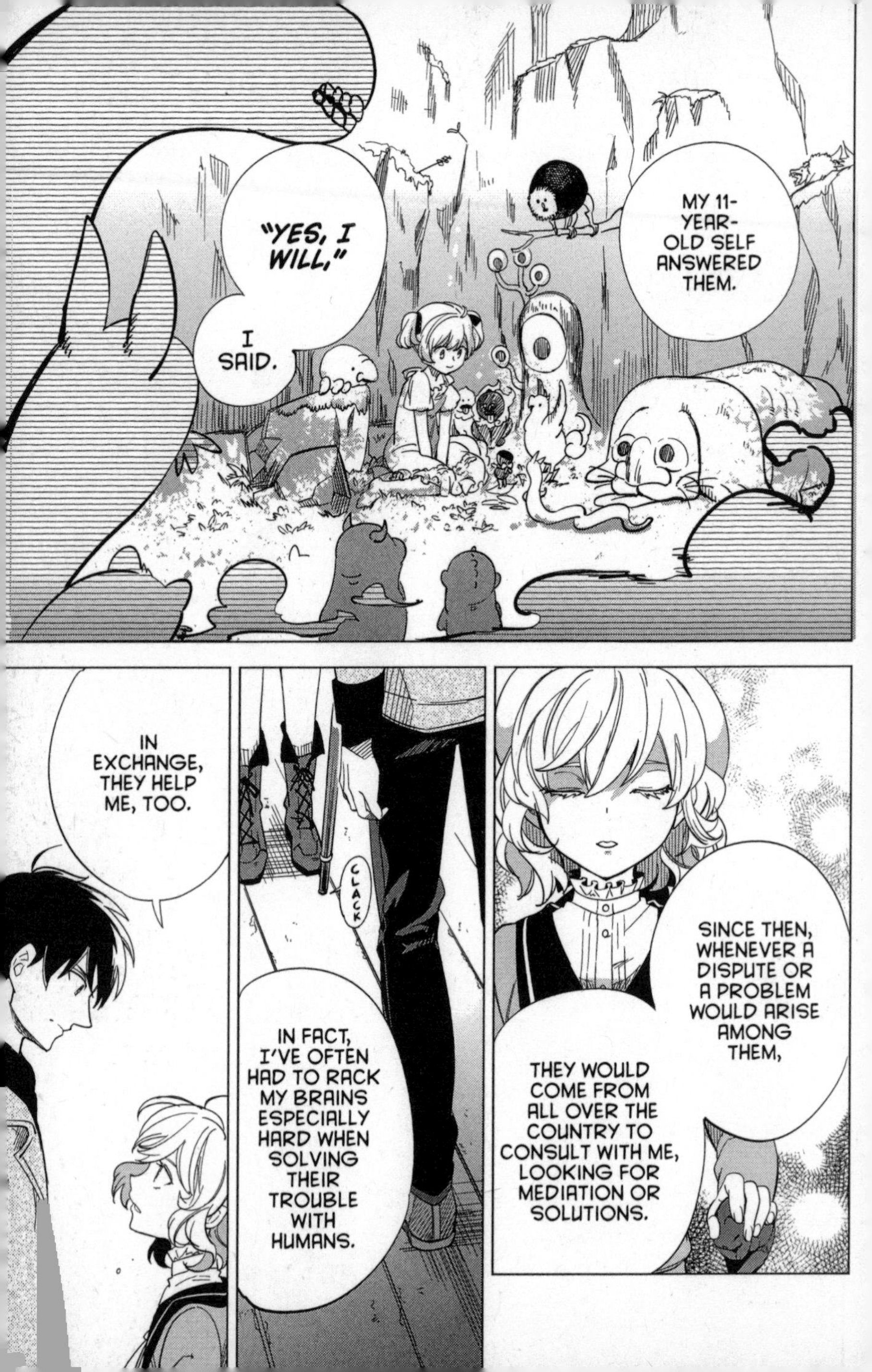
MY 11-YEAR-OLD SELF ANSWERED THEM.
"YES, I WILL,"
I SAID.
SINCE THEN, WHENEVER A DISPUTE OR A PROBLEM WOULD ARISE AMONG THEM,
THEY WOULD COME FROM ALL OVER THE COUNTRY TO CONSULT WITH ME, LOOKING FOR MEDIATION OR SOLUTIONS.
CLACK
IN FACT, I'VE OFTEN HAD TO RACK MY BRAINS ESPECIALLY HARD WHEN SOLVING THEIR TROUBLE WITH HUMANS.
IN EXCHANGE, THEY HELP ME, TOO.

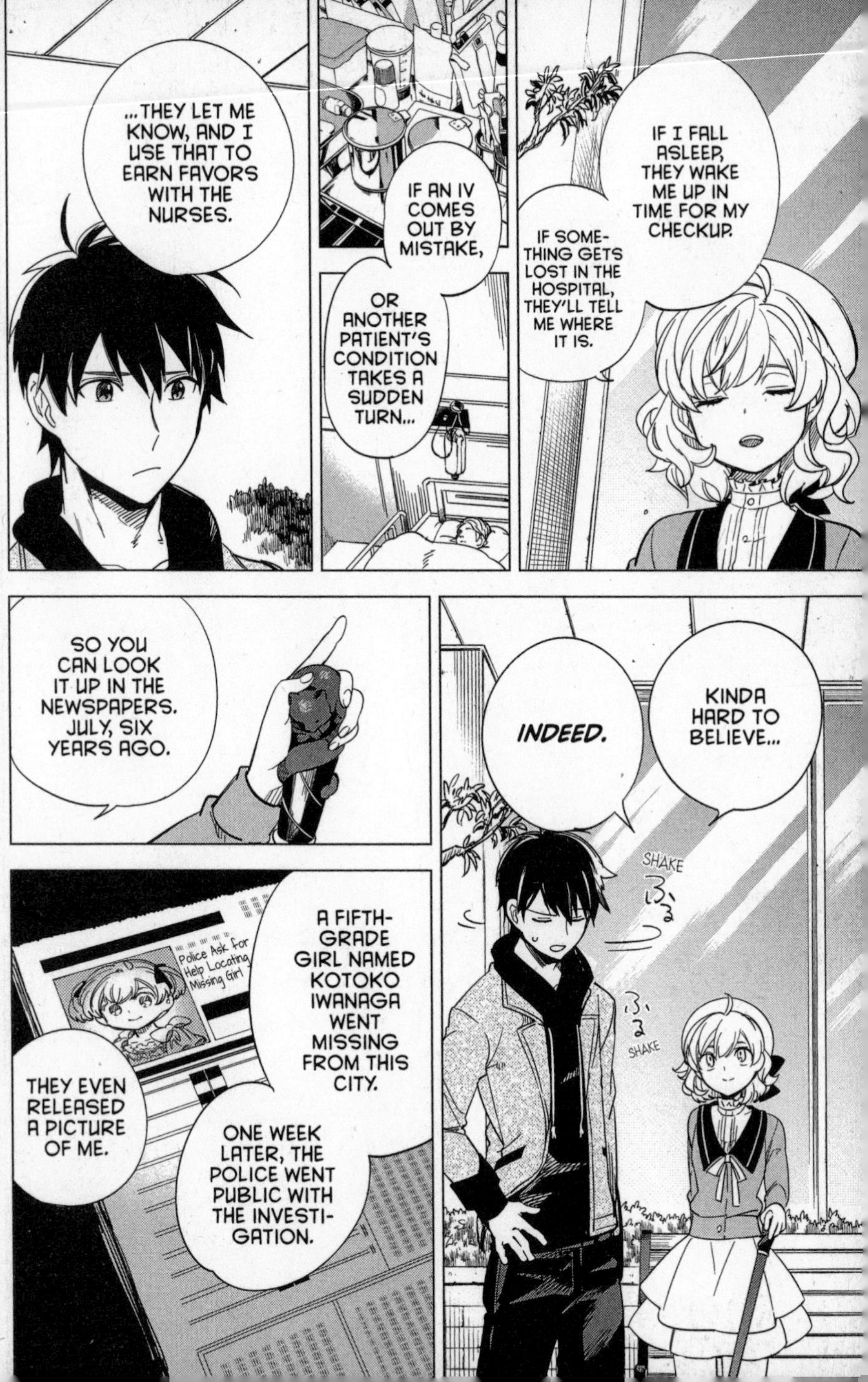
IF I FALL ASLEEP, THEY WAKE ME UP IN TIME FOR MY CHECKUP.
IF SOME-THING GETS LOST IN THE HOSPITAL, THEY'LL TELL ME WHERE IT IS.
IF AN IV COMES OUT BY MISTAKE,
OR ANOTHER PATIENT'S CONDITION TAKES A SUDDEN TURN...
...THEY LET ME KNOW, AND I USE THAT TO EARN FAVORS WITH THE NURSES.
KINDA HARD TO BELIEVE...
INDEED.
SHAKE
ふる
ふる
SHAKE
SO YOU CAN LOOK IT UP IN THE NEWSPAPERS. JULY, SIX YEARS AGO.
A FIFTH-GRADE GIRL NAMED KOTOKO IWANAGA WENT MISSING FROM THIS CITY.
Police Ask for Help Locating Missing Girl
ONE WEEK LATER, THE POLICE WENT PUBLIC WITH THE INVESTI-GATION.
THEY EVEN RELEASED A PICTURE OF ME.

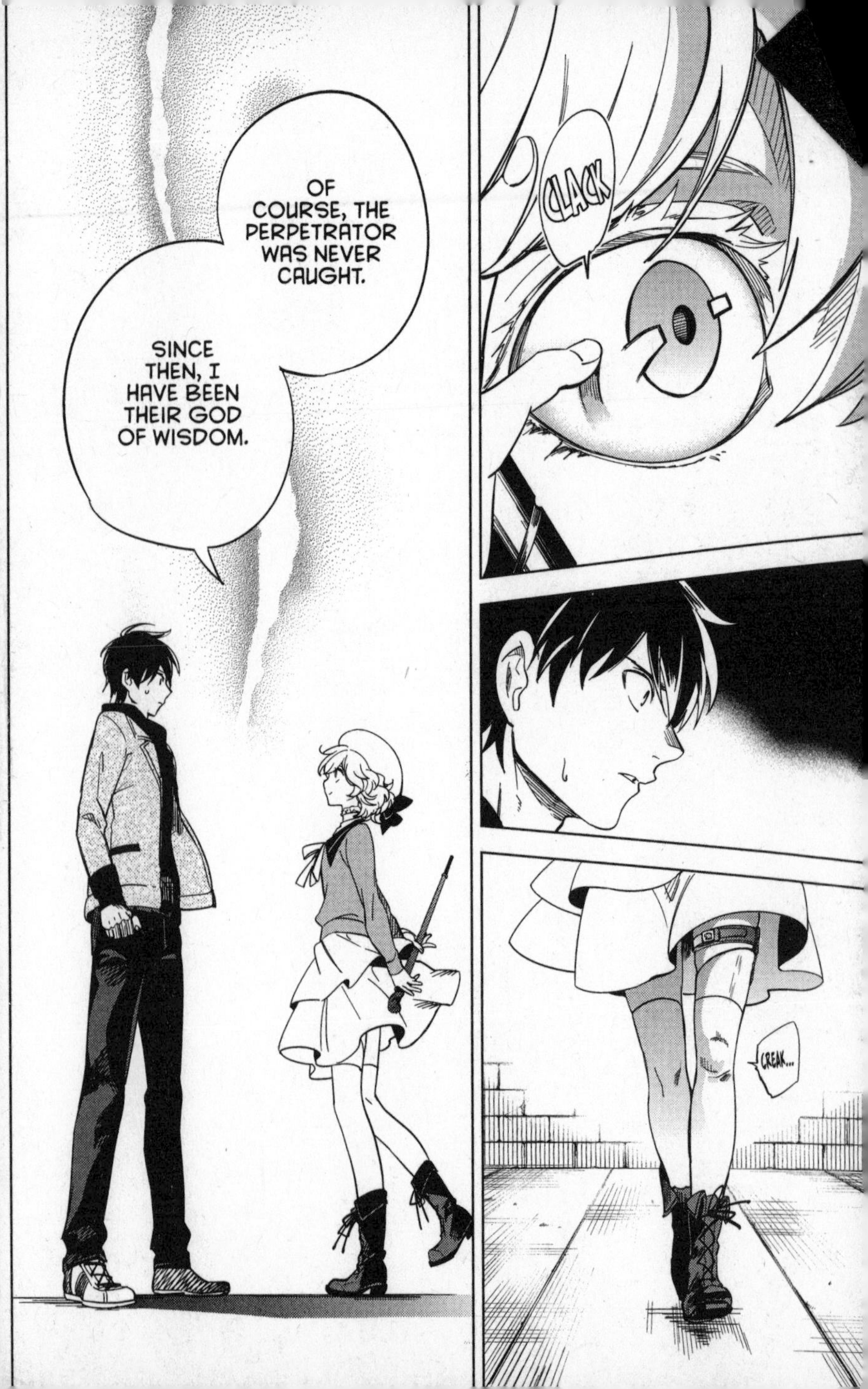
CLACK
CREAK...
OF COURSE, THE PERPETRATOR WAS NEVER CAUGHT.
SINCE THEN, I HAVE BEEN THEIR GOD OF WISDOM.

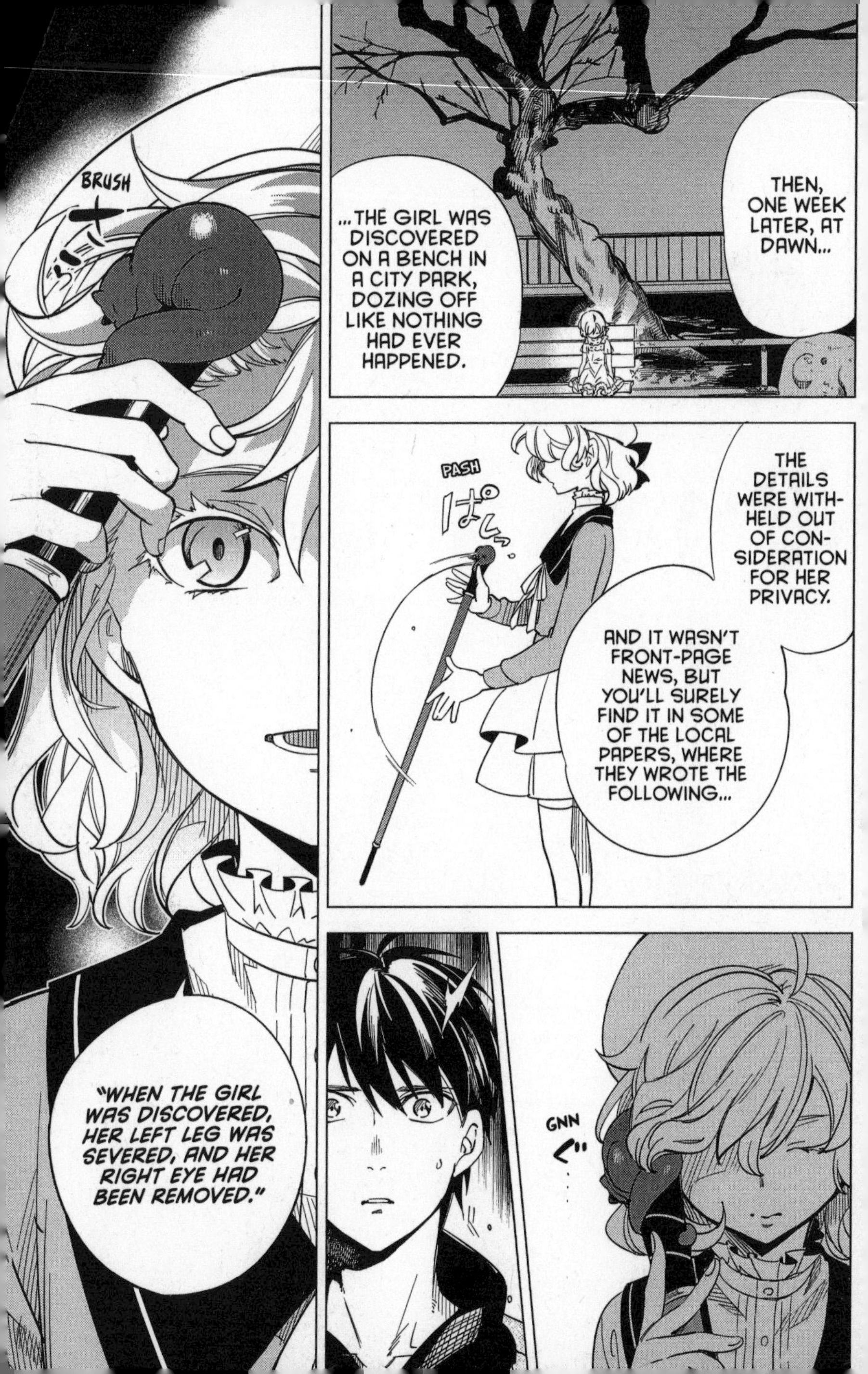
THEN, ONE WEEK LATER, AT DAWN...
...THE GIRL WAS DISCOVERED ON A BENCH IN A CITY PARK, DOZING OFF LIKE NOTHING HAD EVER HAPPENED.
THE DETAILS WERE WITH-HELD OUT OF CON-SIDERATION FOR HER PRIVACY.
PASH
ぱしっ
AND IT WASN'T FRONT-PAGE NEWS, BUT YOU'LL SURELY FIND IT IN SOME OF THE LOCAL PAPERS, WHERE THEY WROTE THE FOLLOWING...
GNN
BRUSH
"WHEN THE GIRL WAS DISCOVERED, HER LEFT LEG WAS SEVERED, AND HER RIGHT EYE HAD BEEN REMOVED."

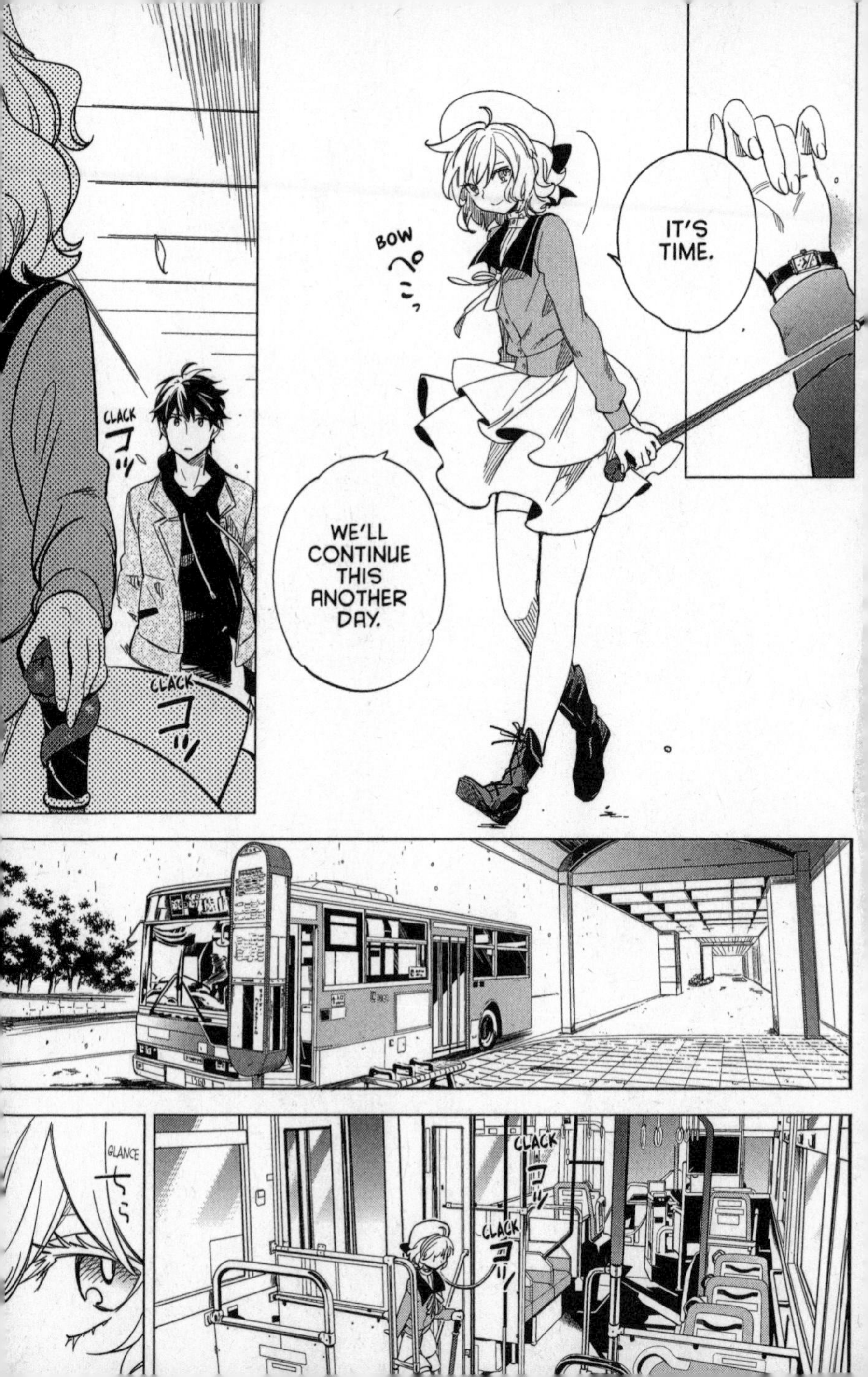
IT'S TIME.
BOW
ぺこっ
WE'LL CONTINUE THIS ANOTHER DAY.
CLACK
コッ
CLACK
コッ
CLACK
コッ
CLACK
コッ
GLANCE
ちら

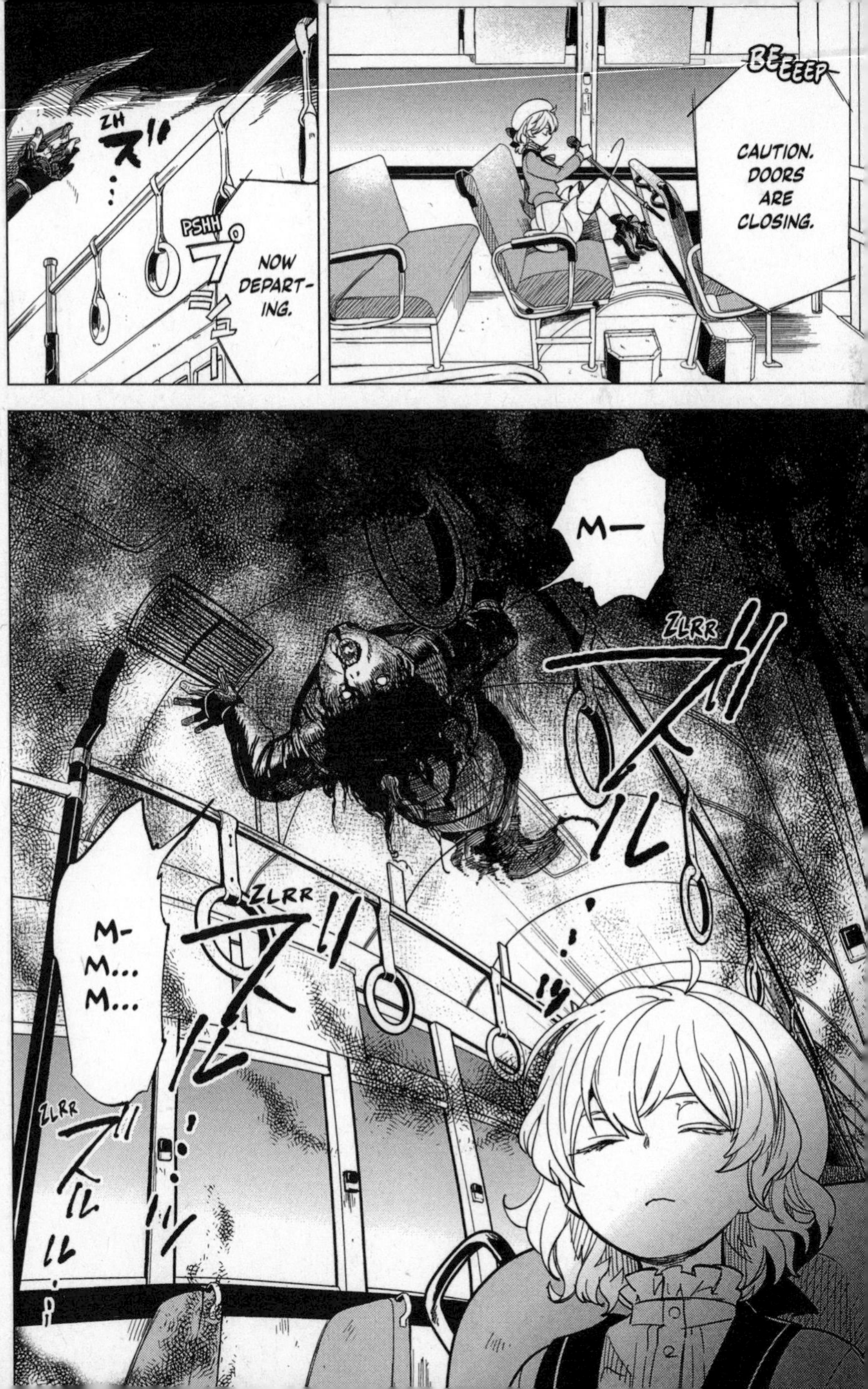
BEEEEP
CAUTION. DOORS ARE CLOSING.
ZH
PSHH
NOW DEPART-ING.
M—
ZLRR
M-M... M...
ZLRR
ZLRR

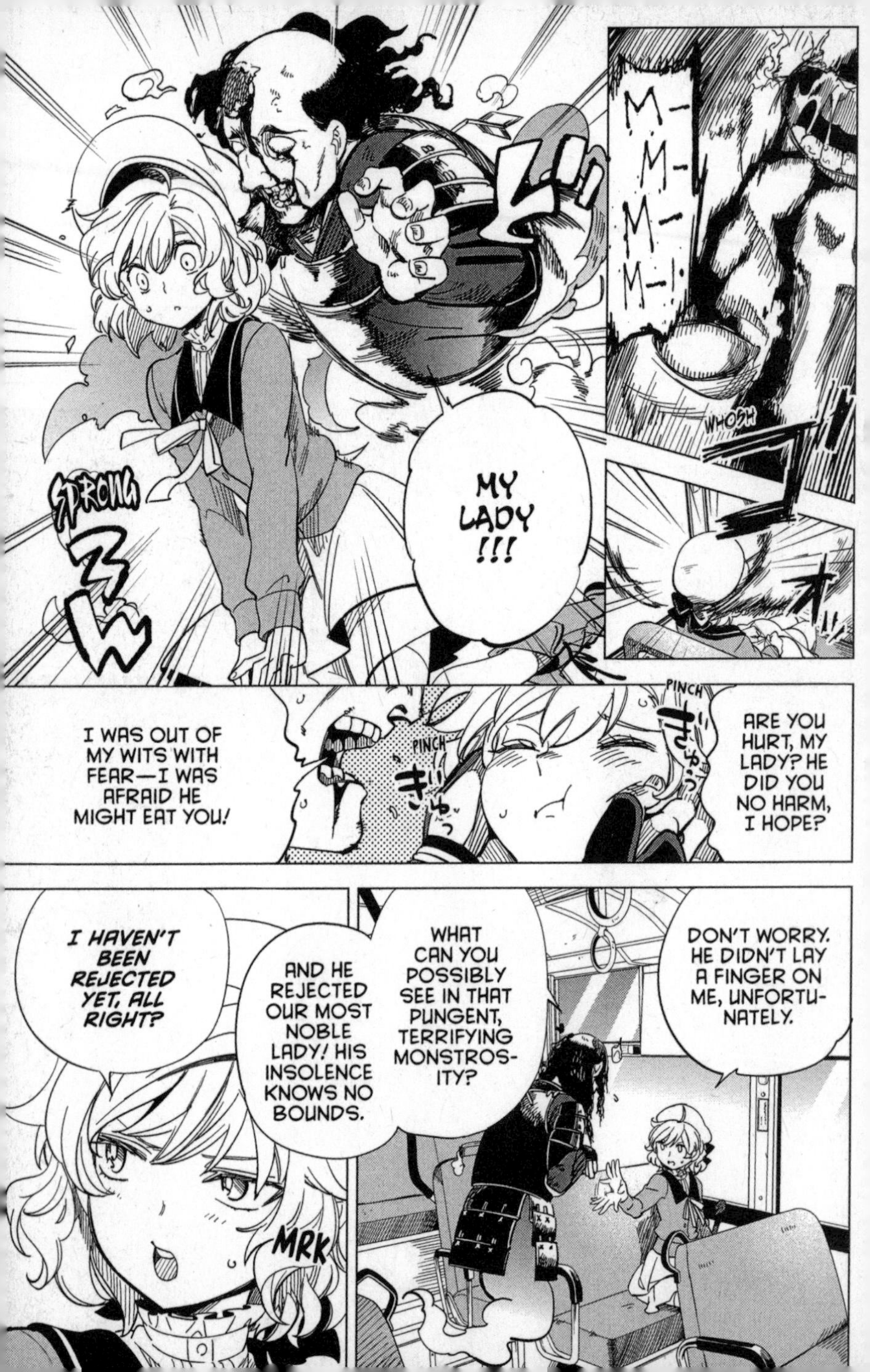
M-M-M-M-!
WHOSH
MY LADY!!!
SPRONG
ARE YOU HURT, MY LADY? HE DID YOU NO HARM, I HOPE?
PINCH
PINCH
I WAS OUT OF MY WITS WITH FEAR—I WAS AFRAID HE MIGHT EAT YOU!
DON'T WORRY. HE DIDN'T LAY A FINGER ON ME, UNFORTU-NATELY.
WHAT CAN YOU POSSIBLY SEE IN THAT PUNGENT, TERRIFYING MONSTROS-ITY?
AND HE REJECTED OUR MOST NOBLE LADY! HIS INSOLENCE KNOWS NO BOUNDS.
I HAVEN'T BEEN REJECTED YET, ALL RIGHT?
MRK

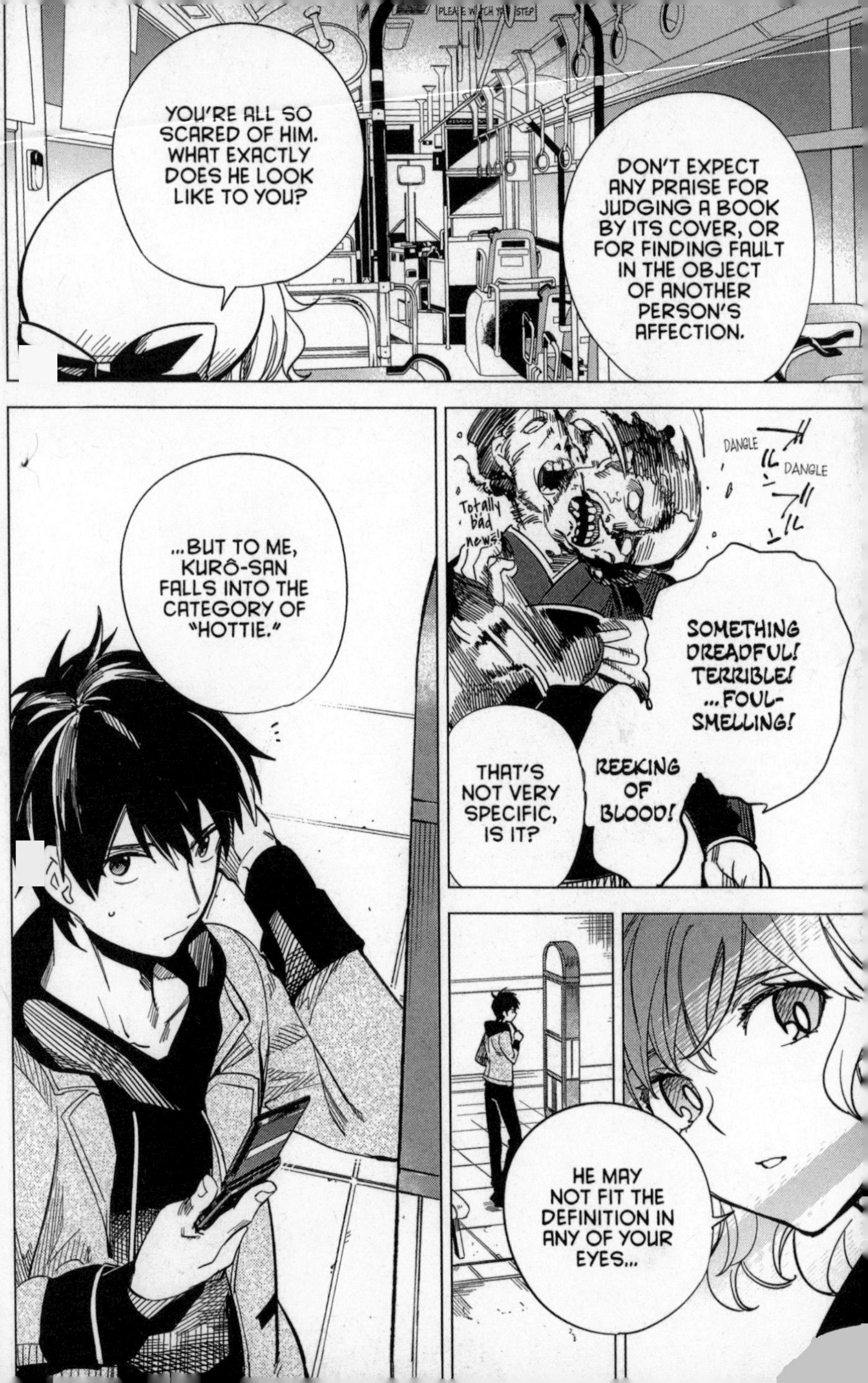
DON'T EXPECT ANY PRAISE FOR JUDGING A BOOK BY ITS COVER, OR FOR FINDING FAULT IN THE OBJECT OF ANOTHER PERSON'S AFFECTION.
YOU'RE ALL SO SCARED OF HIM. WHAT EXACTLY DOES HE LOOK LIKE TO YOU?
DANGLE
DANGLE
Totally bad news!
SOMETHING DREADFUL! TERRIBLE! ...FOUL-SMELLING!
REEKING OF BLOOD!
THAT'S NOT VERY SPECIFIC, IS IT?
HE MAY NOT FIT THE DEFINITION IN ANY OF YOUR EYES...
...BUT TO ME, KURÔ-SAN FALLS INTO THE CATEGORY OF "HOTTIE."

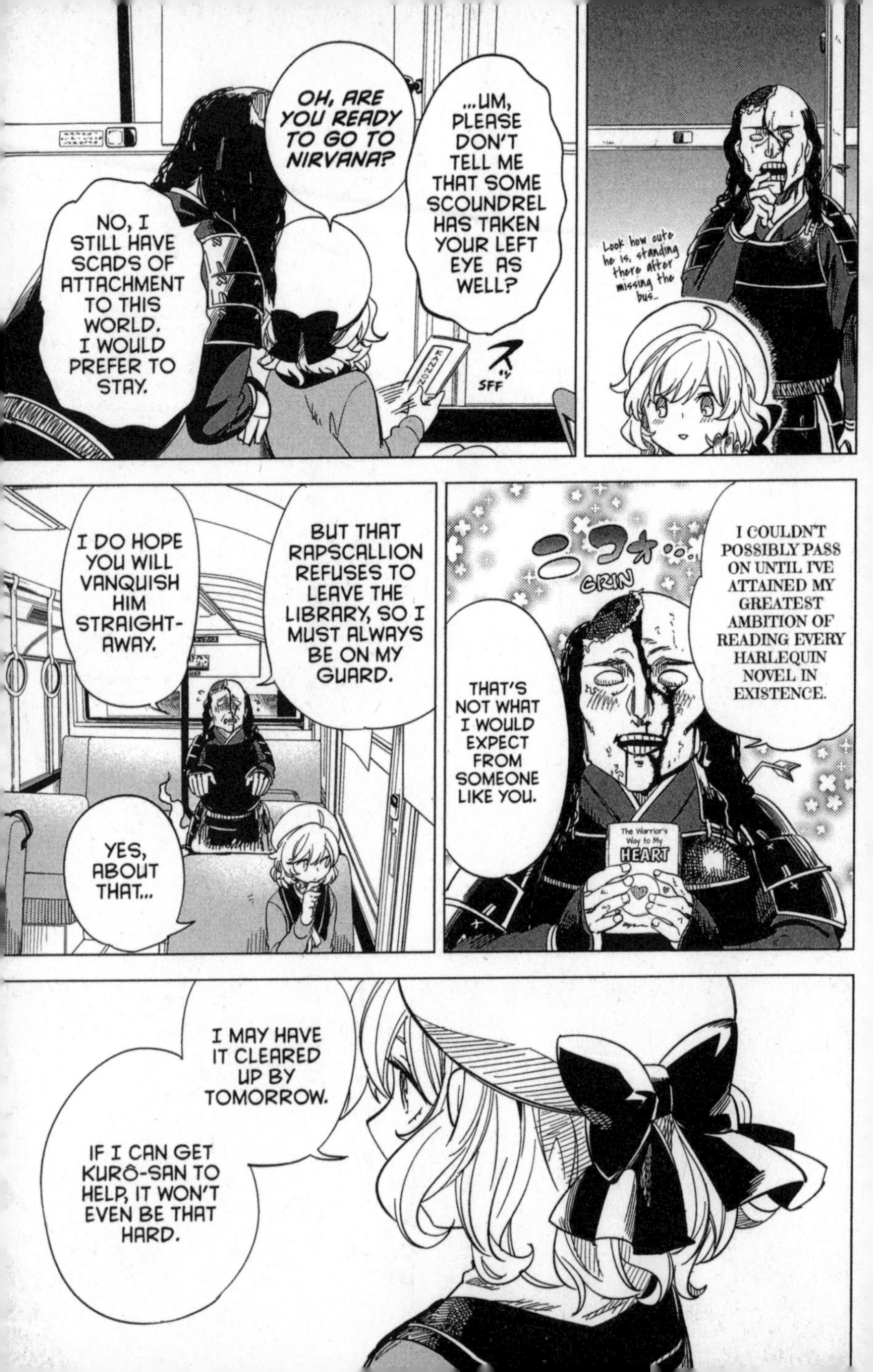
Look how cute he is, standing there after missing the bus...
...UM, PLEASE DON'T TELL ME THAT SOME SCOUNDREL HAS TAKEN YOUR LEFT EYE AS WELL?
OH, ARE YOU READY TO GO TO NIRVANA?
NO, I STILL HAVE SCADS OF ATTACHMENT TO THIS WORLD. I WOULD PREFER TO STAY.
SFF
I COULDN'T POSSIBLY PASS ON UNTIL I'VE ATTAINED MY GREATEST AMBITION OF READING EVERY HARLEQUIN NOVEL IN EXISTENCE.
GRIN
THAT'S NOT WHAT I WOULD EXPECT FROM SOMEONE LIKE YOU.
The Warrior's Way to My HEART
BUT THAT RAPSCALLION REFUSES TO LEAVE THE LIBRARY, SO I MUST ALWAYS BE ON MY GUARD.
I DO HOPE YOU WILL VANQUISH HIM STRAIGHT-AWAY.
YES, ABOUT THAT...
I MAY HAVE IT CLEARED UP BY TOMORROW.
IF I CAN GET KURÔ-SAN TO HELP, IT WON'T EVEN BE THAT HARD.

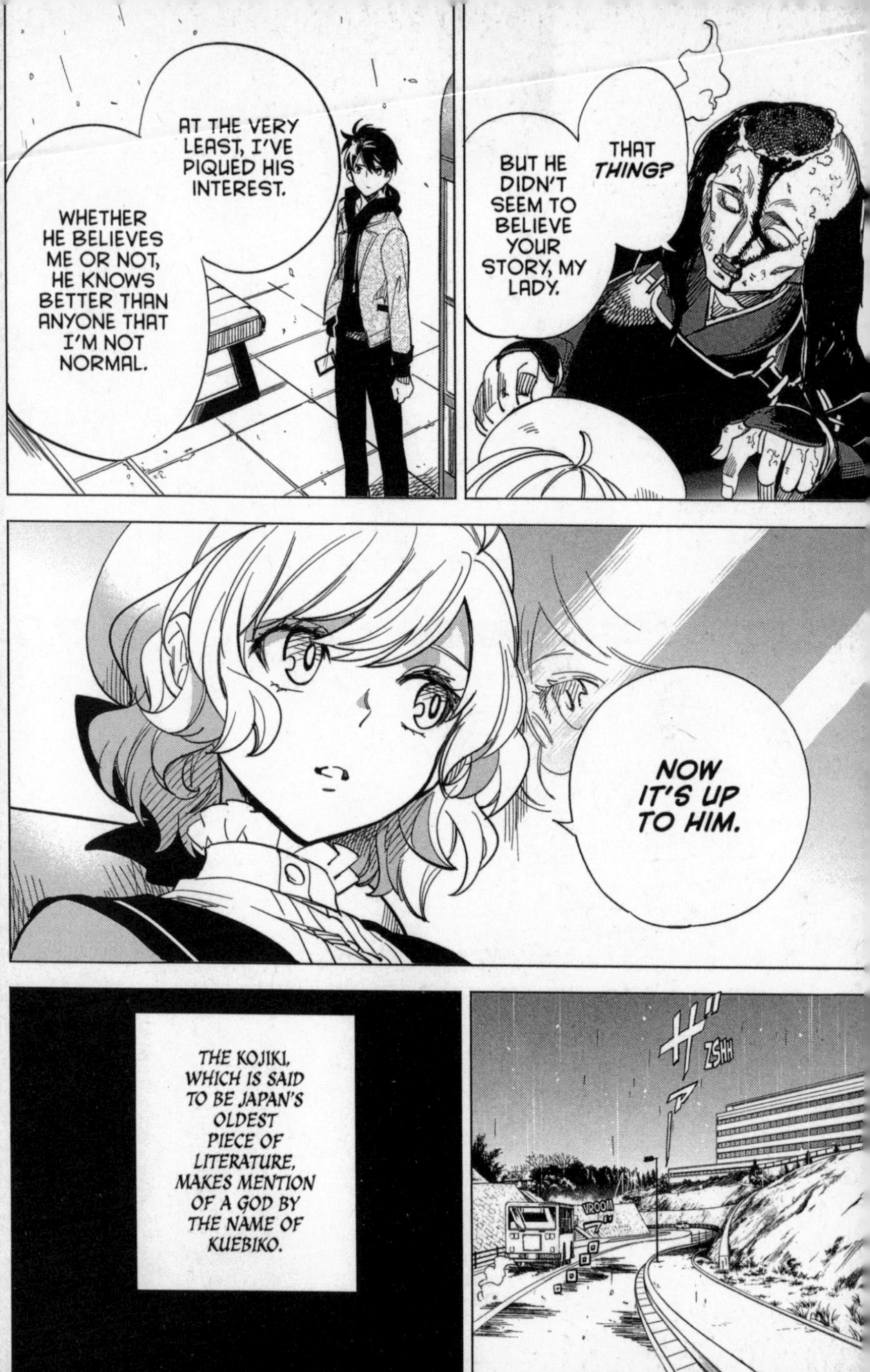
THAT THING?
BUT HE DIDN'T SEEM TO BELIEVE YOUR STORY, MY LADY.
AT THE VERY LEAST, I'VE PIQUED HIS INTEREST.
WHETHER HE BELIEVES ME OR NOT, HE KNOWS BETTER THAN ANYONE THAT I'M NOT NORMAL.
NOW IT'S UP TO HIM.
ZSHH
VROOM
THE KOJIKI, WHICH IS SAID TO BE JAPAN'S OLDEST PIECE OF LITERATURE, MAKES MENTION OF A GOD BY THE NAME OF KUEBIKO.

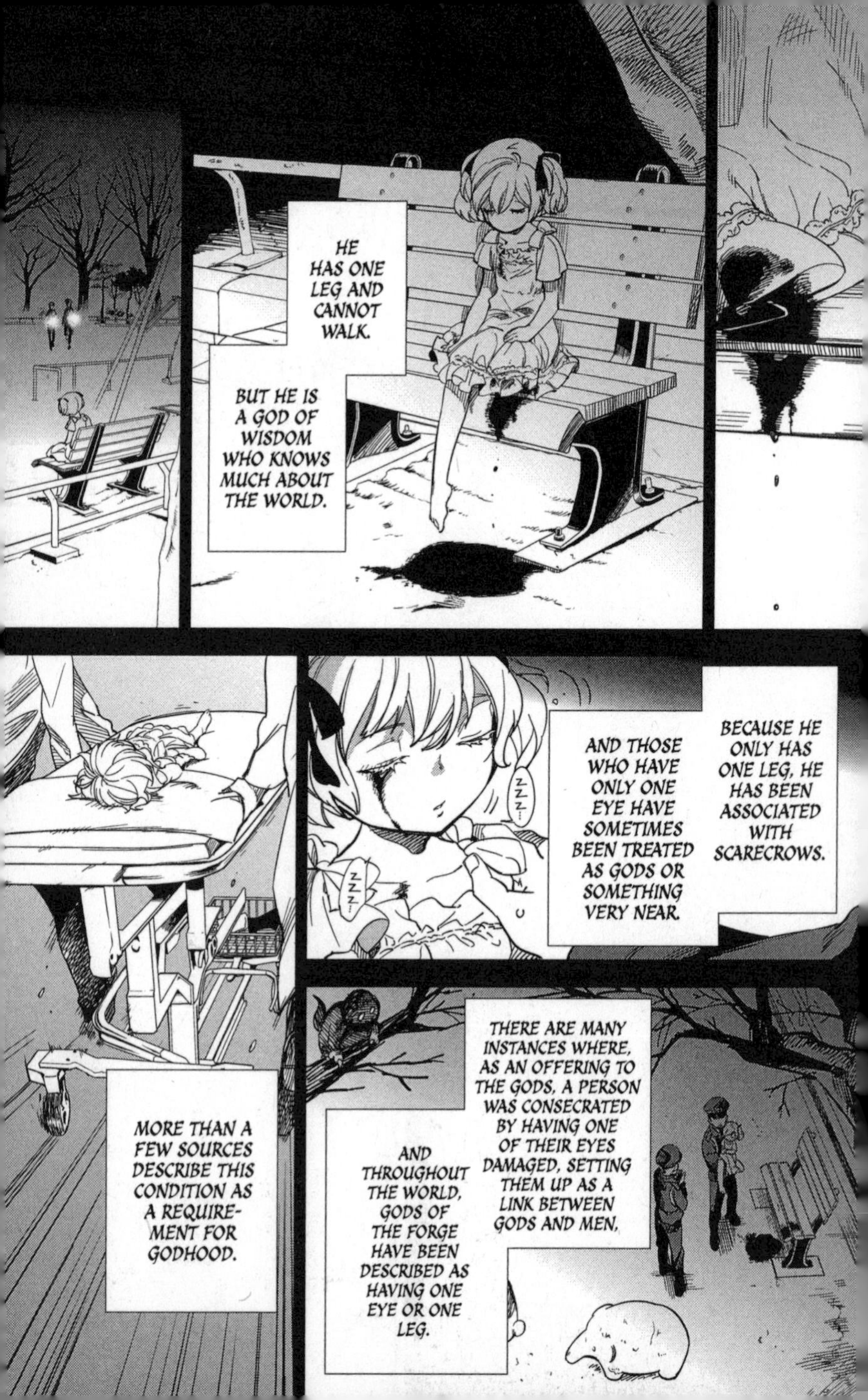
HE HAS ONE LEG AND CANNOT WALK.
BUT HE IS A GOD OF WISDOM WHO KNOWS MUCH ABOUT THE WORLD.
BECAUSE HE ONLY HAS ONE LEG, HE HAS BEEN ASSOCIATED WITH SCARECROWS.
AND THOSE WHO HAVE ONLY ONE EYE HAVE SOMETIMES BEEN TREATED AS GODS OR SOMETHING VERY NEAR.
ZZZ...
ZZZ...
THERE ARE MANY INSTANCES WHERE, AS AN OFFERING TO THE GODS, A PERSON WAS CONSECRATED BY HAVING ONE OF THEIR EYES DAMAGED, SETTING THEM UP AS A LINK BETWEEN GODS AND MEN,
AND THROUGHOUT THE WORLD, GODS OF THE FORGE HAVE BEEN DESCRIBED AS HAVING ONE EYE OR ONE LEG.
MORE THAN A FEW SOURCES DESCRIBE THIS CONDITION AS A REQUIREMENT FOR GODHOOD.

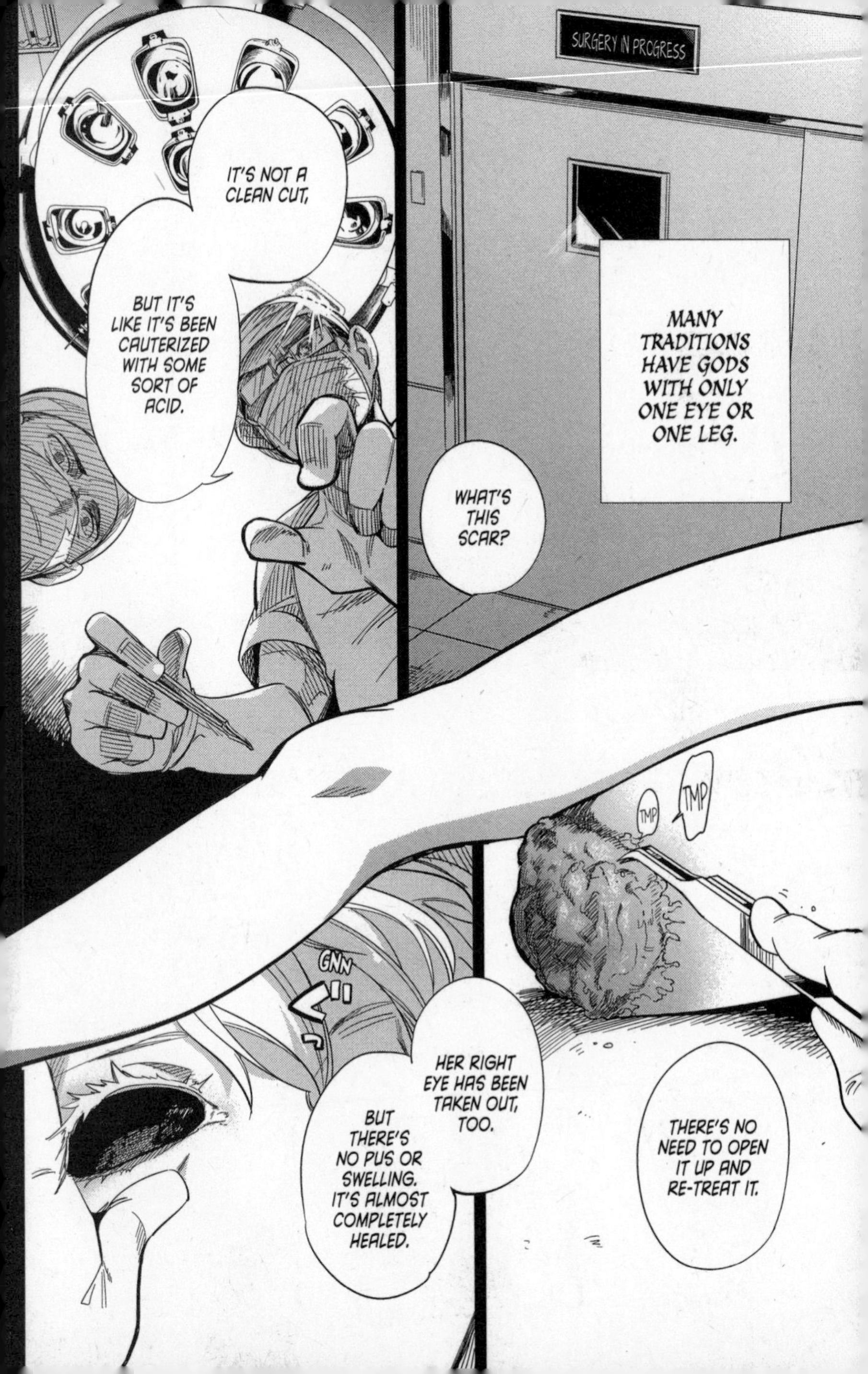
SURGERY IN PROGRESS
MANY TRADITIONS HAVE GODS WITH ONLY ONE EYE OR ONE LEG.
WHAT'S THIS SCAR?
IT'S NOT A CLEAN CUT,
BUT IT'S LIKE IT'S BEEN CAUTERIZED WITH SOME SORT OF ACID.
TMP
TMP
THERE'S NO NEED TO OPEN IT UP AND RE-TREAT IT.
GNN
HER RIGHT EYE HAS BEEN TAKEN OUT, TOO.
BUT THERE'S NO PUS OR SWELLING. IT'S ALMOST COMPLETELY HEALED.

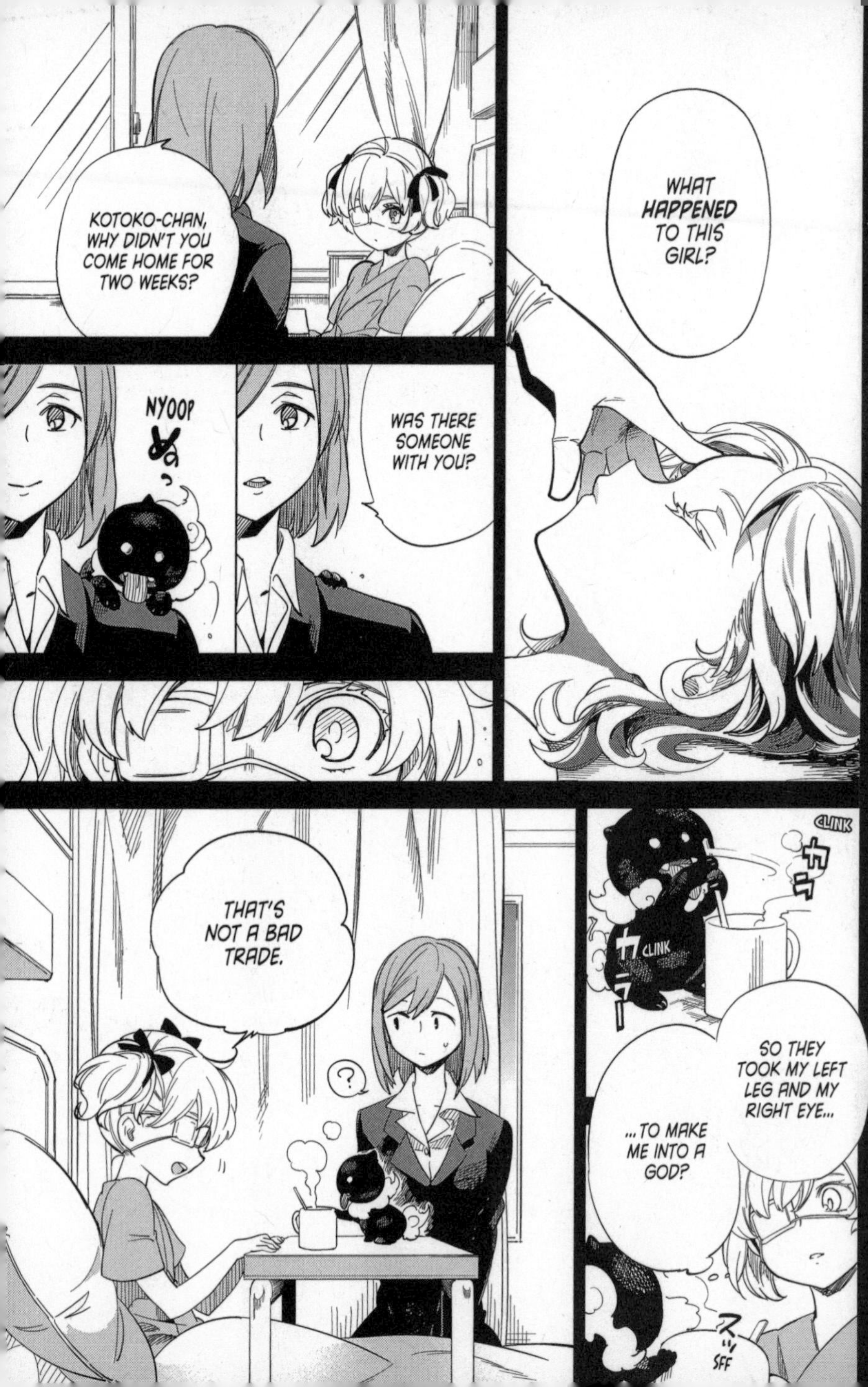
WHAT HAPPENED TO THIS GIRL?
KOTOKO-CHAN, WHY DIDN'T YOU COME HOME FOR TWO WEEKS?
WAS THERE SOMEONE WITH YOU?
NYOOP
ぬっ
CLINK
カラ
CLINK
カラー
SO THEY TOOK MY LEFT LEG AND MY RIGHT EYE...
...TO MAKE ME INTO A GOD?
スッ
SFF
THAT'S NOT A BAD TRADE.
?

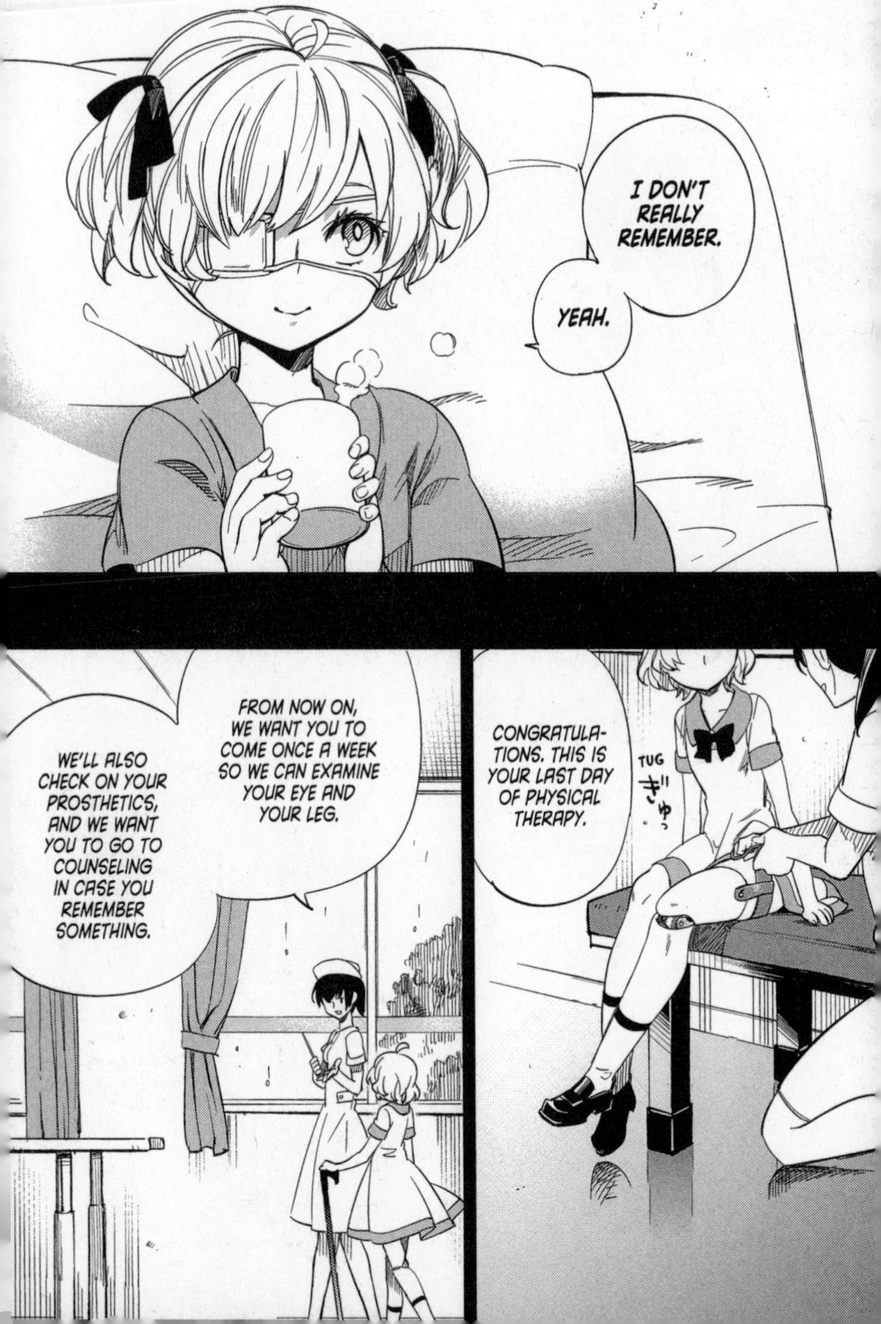
I DON'T REALLY REMEMBER.
YEAH.
CONGRATULA-TIONS. THIS IS YOUR LAST DAY OF PHYSICAL THERAPY.
TUG
ぎゅっ
FROM NOW ON, WE WANT YOU TO COME ONCE A WEEK SO WE CAN EXAMINE YOUR EYE AND YOUR LEG.
WE'LL ALSO CHECK ON YOUR PROSTHETICS, AND WE WANT YOU TO GO TO COUNSELING IN CASE YOU REMEMBER SOMETHING.

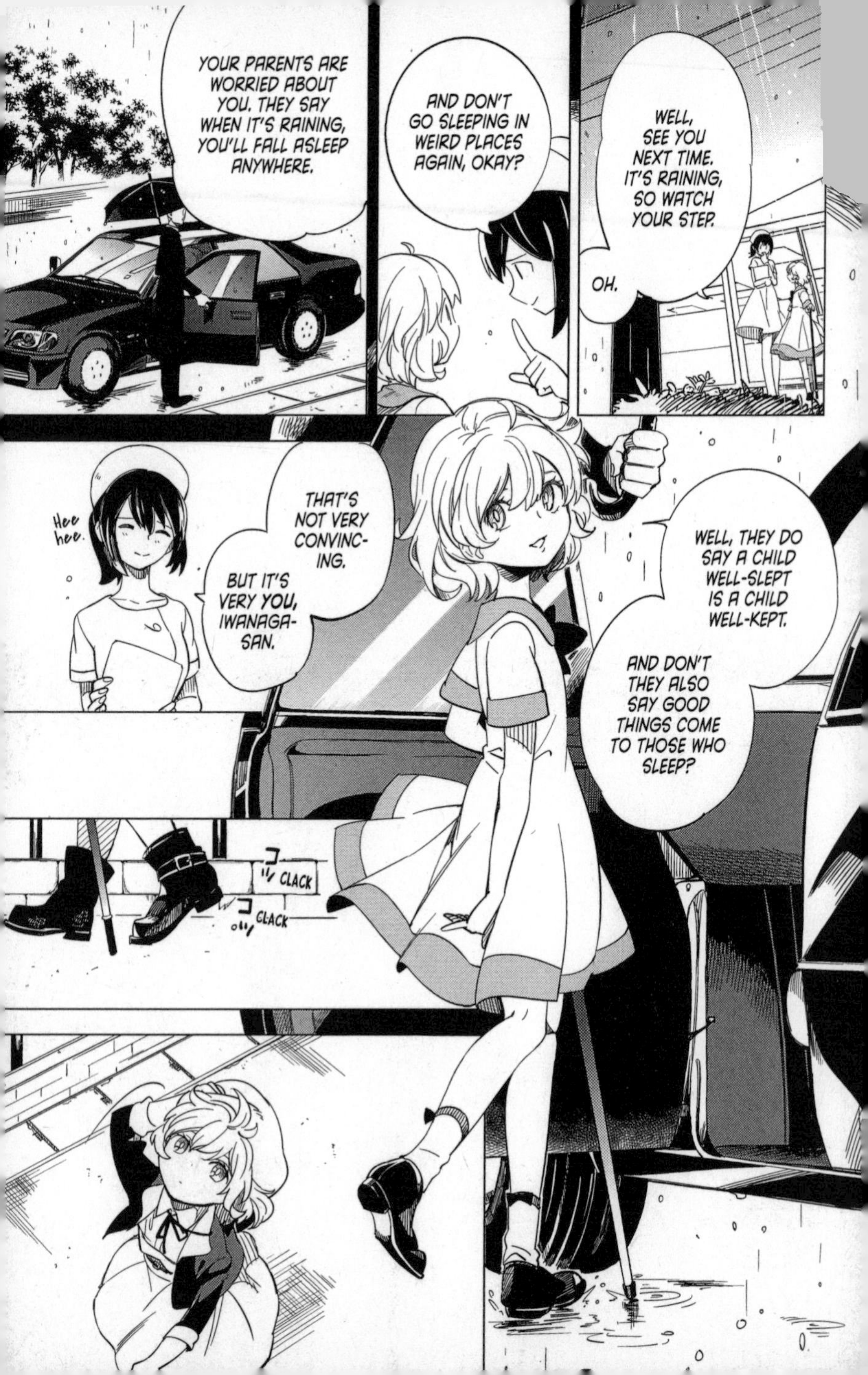
WELL, SEE YOU NEXT TIME. IT'S RAINING, SO WATCH YOUR STEP.
OH.
AND DON'T GO SLEEPING IN WEIRD PLACES AGAIN, OKAY?
YOUR PARENTS ARE WORRIED ABOUT YOU. THEY SAY WHEN IT'S RAINING, YOU'LL FALL ASLEEP ANYWHERE.
WELL, THEY DO SAY A CHILD WELL-SLEPT IS A CHILD WELL-KEPT.
AND DON'T THEY ALSO SAY GOOD THINGS COME TO THOSE WHO SLEEP?
THAT'S NOT VERY CONVINCING.
BUT IT'S VERY YOU, IWANAGA-SAN.
Hee hee.
CLACK
CLACK

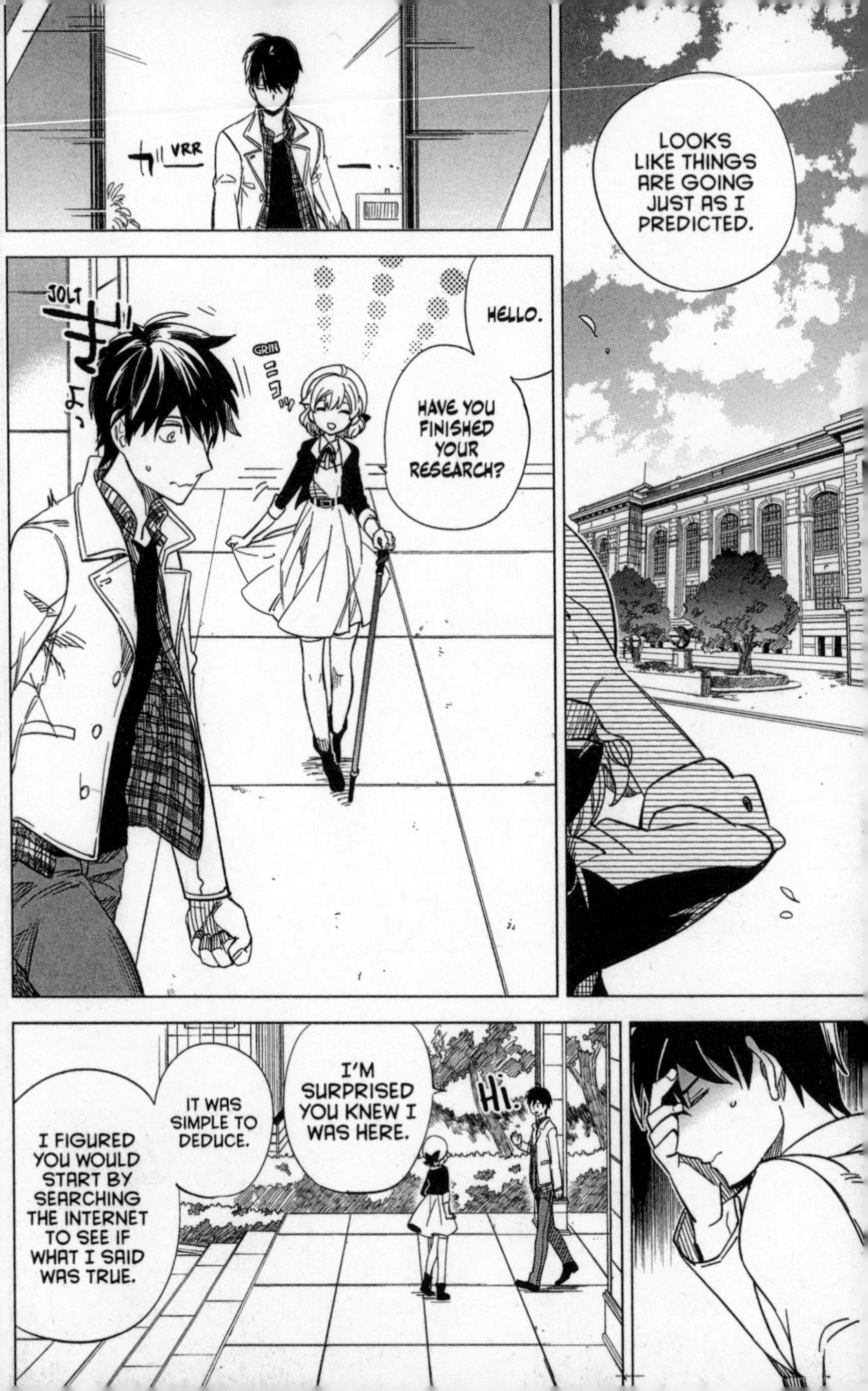
LOOKS LIKE THINGS ARE GOING JUST AS I PREDICTED.
VRR
JOLT
GRIN
HELLO.
HAVE YOU FINISHED YOUR RESEARCH?
HI.
I'M SURPRISED YOU KNEW I WAS HERE.
IT WAS SIMPLE TO DEDUCE.
I FIGURED YOU WOULD START BY SEARCHING THE INTERNET TO SEE IF WHAT I SAID WAS TRUE.

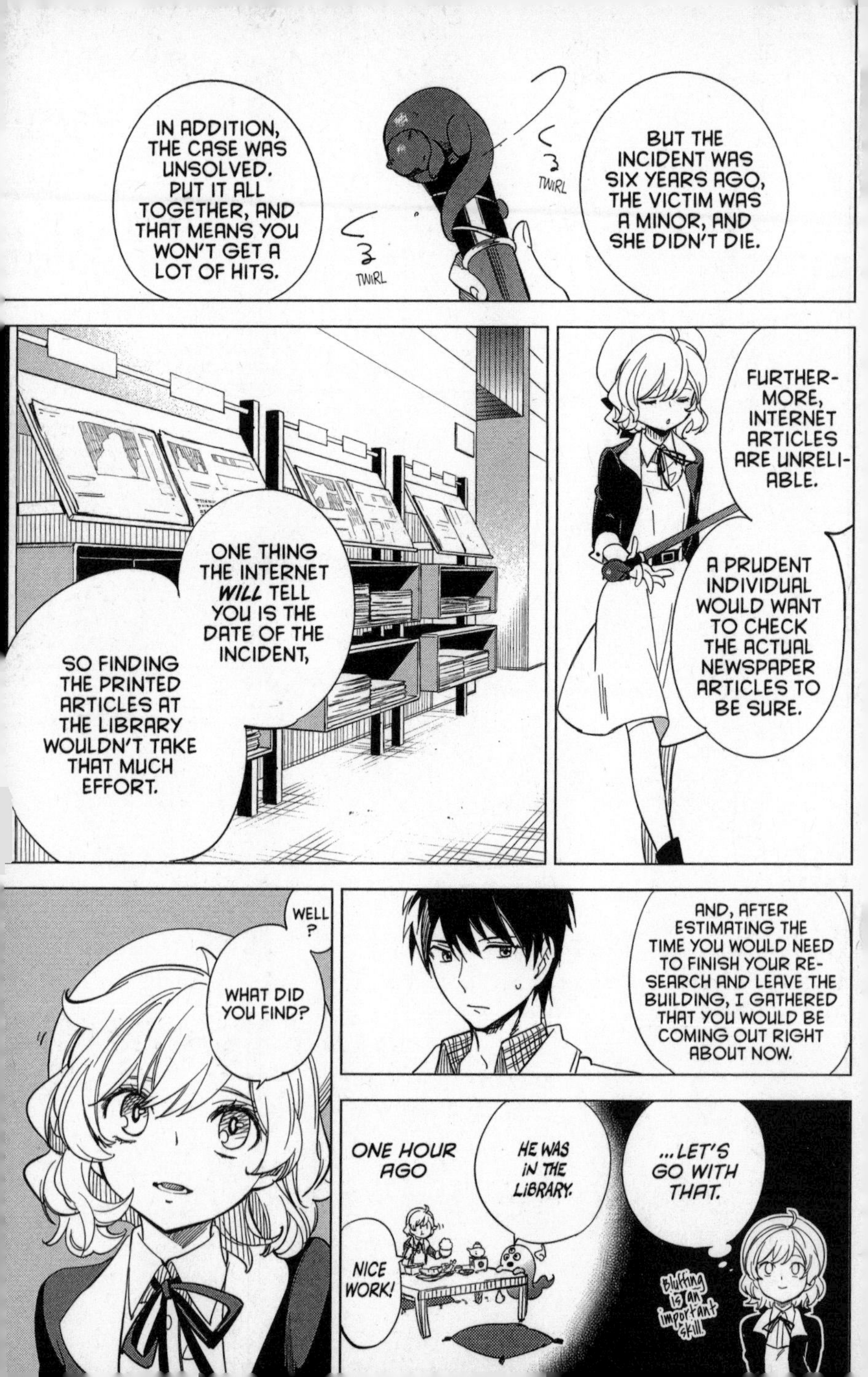
BUT THE INCIDENT WAS SIX YEARS AGO, THE VICTIM WAS A MINOR, AND SHE DIDN'T DIE.
TWIRL
TWIRL
IN ADDITION, THE CASE WAS UNSOLVED. PUT IT ALL TOGETHER, AND THAT MEANS YOU WON'T GET A LOT OF HITS.
FURTHER-MORE, INTERNET ARTICLES ARE UNRELI-ABLE.
A PRUDENT INDIVIDUAL WOULD WANT TO CHECK THE ACTUAL NEWSPAPER ARTICLES TO BE SURE.
ONE THING THE INTERNET *WILL* TELL YOU IS THE DATE OF THE INCIDENT,
SO FINDING THE PRINTED ARTICLES AT THE LIBRARY WOULDN'T TAKE THAT MUCH EFFORT.
AND, AFTER ESTIMATING THE TIME YOU WOULD NEED TO FINISH YOUR RE-SEARCH AND LEAVE THE BUILDING, I GATHERED THAT YOU WOULD BE COMING OUT RIGHT ABOUT NOW.
ONE HOUR AGO
HE WAS IN THE LIBRARY.
NICE WORK!
...LET'S GO WITH THAT.
Bluffing is an important skill.
WELL?
WHAT DID YOU FIND?

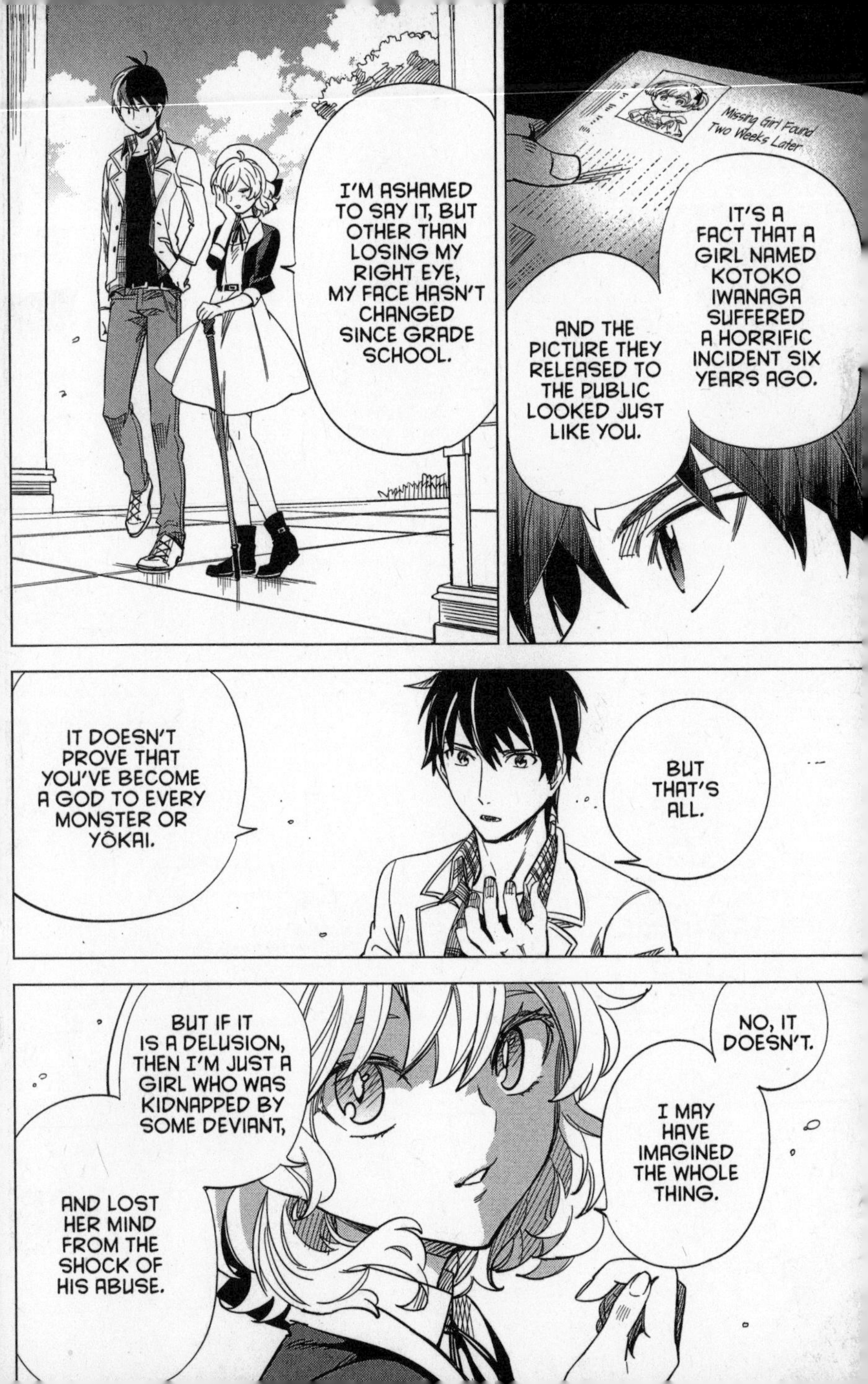
Missing Girl Found Two Weeks Later
IT'S A FACT THAT A GIRL NAMED KOTOKO IWANAGA SUFFERED A HORRIFIC INCIDENT SIX YEARS AGO.
AND THE PICTURE THEY RELEASED TO THE PUBLIC LOOKED JUST LIKE YOU.
I'M ASHAMED TO SAY IT, BUT OTHER THAN LOSING MY RIGHT EYE, MY FACE HASN'T CHANGED SINCE GRADE SCHOOL.
BUT THAT'S ALL.
IT DOESN'T PROVE THAT YOU'VE BECOME A GOD TO EVERY MONSTER OR YÔKAI.
NO, IT DOESN'T.
I MAY HAVE IMAGINED THE WHOLE THING.
BUT IF IT IS A DELUSION, THEN I'M JUST A GIRL WHO WAS KIDNAPPED BY SOME DEVIANT,
AND LOST HER MIND FROM THE SHOCK OF HIS ABUSE.

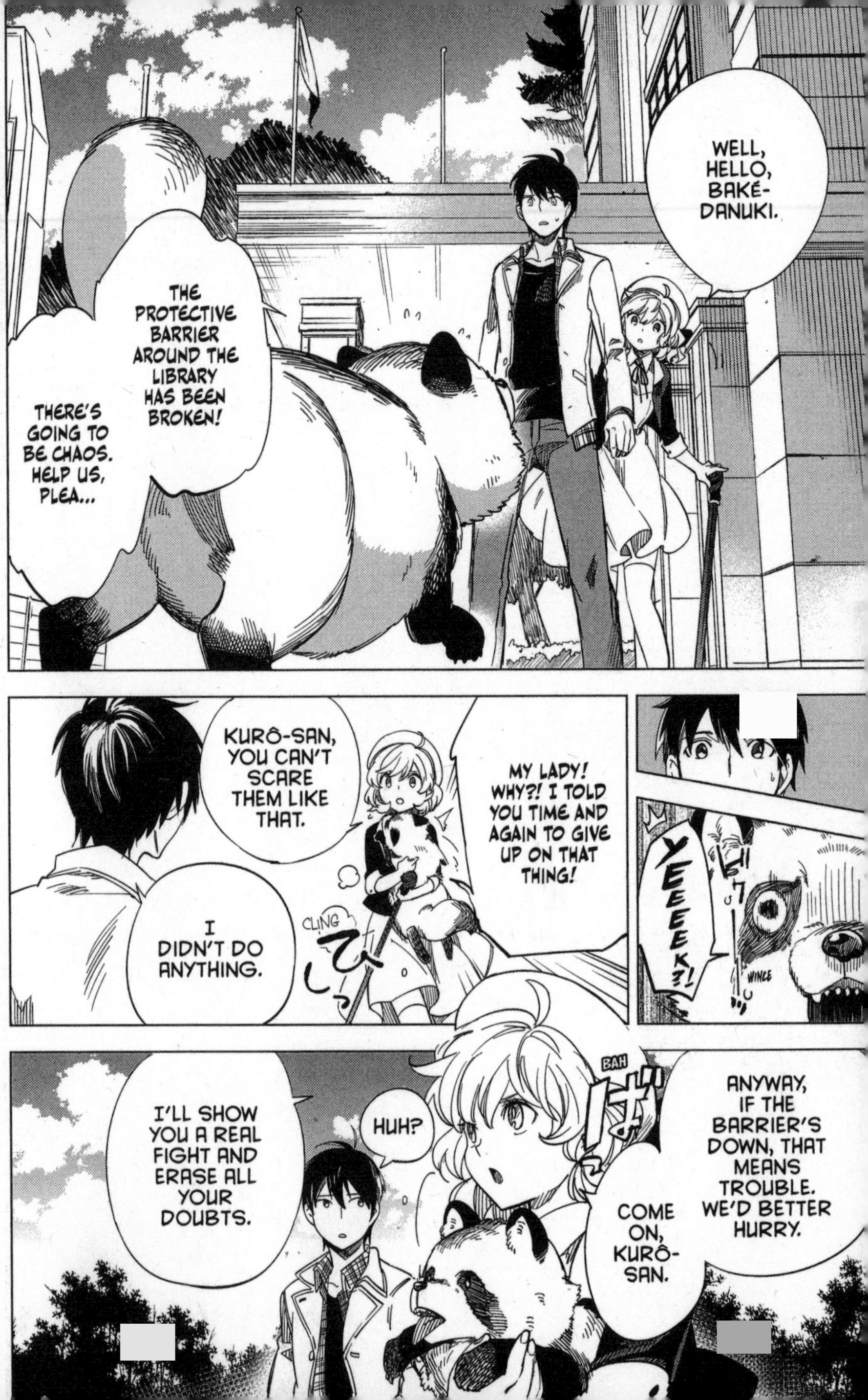
WELL, HELLO, BAKÉ-DANUKI.
THE PROTECTIVE BARRIER AROUND THE LIBRARY HAS BEEN BROKEN!
THERE'S GOING TO BE CHAOS. HELP US, PLEA...
YEEEEK?!
WINCE
MY LADY! WHY?! I TOLD YOU TIME AND AGAIN TO GIVE UP ON THAT THING!
KURÔ-SAN, YOU CAN'T SCARE THEM LIKE THAT.
CLING
I DIDN'T DO ANYTHING.
ANYWAY, IF THE BARRIER'S DOWN, THAT MEANS TROUBLE. WE'D BETTER HURRY.
BAH
COME ON, KURÔ-SAN.
HUH?
I'LL SHOW YOU A REAL FIGHT AND ERASE ALL YOUR DOUBTS.

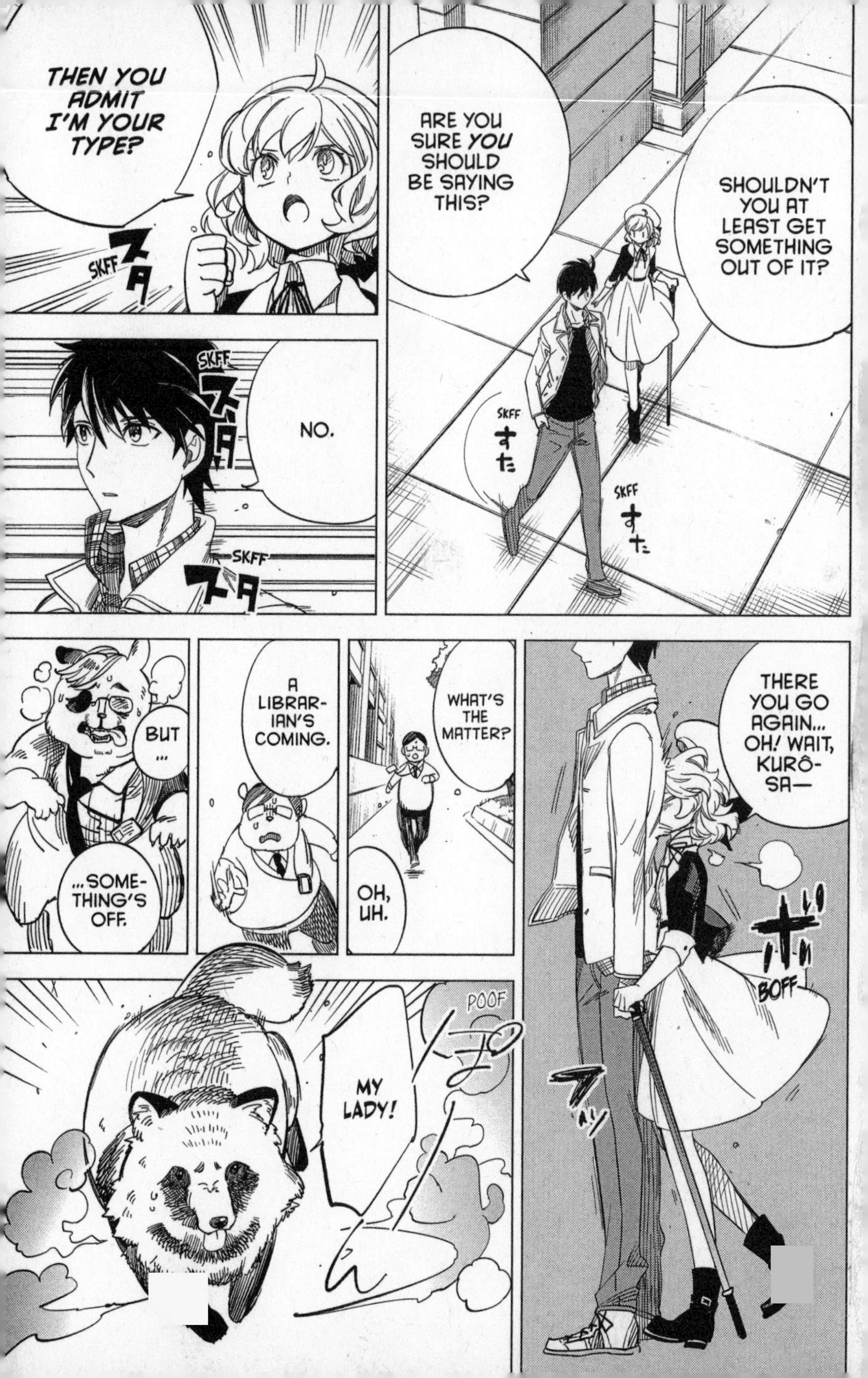

SHOULDN'T YOU AT LEAST GET SOMETHING OUT OF IT?
ARE YOU SURE *YOU* SHOULD BE SAYING THIS?
SKFF すた
SKFF すた
THEN YOU ADMIT I'M YOUR TYPE?
SKFF スタ
NO.
SKFF スタ
SKFF スタ
THERE YOU GO AGAIN... OH! WAIT, KURÔ-SA—
BOFF
WHAT'S THE MATTER?
OH, UH.
A LIBRAR-IAN'S COMING.
BUT ...
...SOME-THING'S OFF.
POOF
MY LADY!

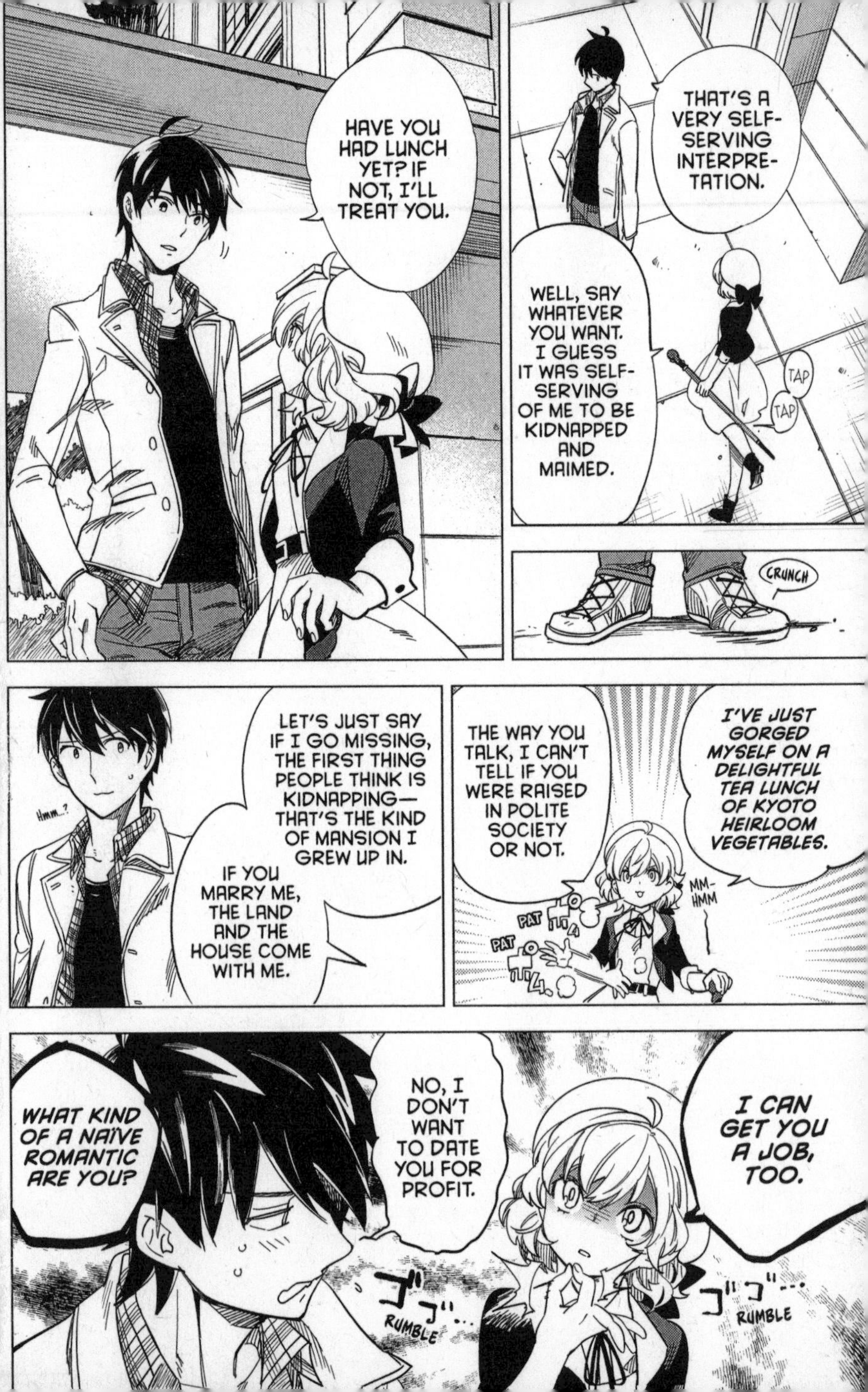

THAT'S A VERY SELF-SERVING INTERPRETATION.
WELL, SAY WHATEVER YOU WANT. I GUESS IT WAS SELF-SERVING OF ME TO BE KIDNAPPED AND MAIMED.
TAP
TAP
CRUNCH
HAVE YOU HAD LUNCH YET? IF NOT, I'LL TREAT YOU.
I'VE JUST GORGED MYSELF ON A DELIGHTFUL TEA LUNCH OF KYOTO HEIRLOOM VEGETABLES.
MM-HMM
PAT
PAT
THE WAY YOU TALK, I CAN'T TELL IF YOU WERE RAISED IN POLITE SOCIETY OR NOT.
LET'S JUST SAY IF I GO MISSING, THE FIRST THING PEOPLE THINK IS KIDNAPPING—THAT'S THE KIND OF MANSION I GREW UP IN.
IF YOU MARRY ME, THE LAND AND THE HOUSE COME WITH ME.
Hmm...?
I CAN GET YOU A JOB, TOO.
RUMBLE
NO, I DON'T WANT TO DATE YOU FOR PROFIT.
RUMBLE
WHAT KIND OF A NAÏVE ROMANTIC ARE YOU?

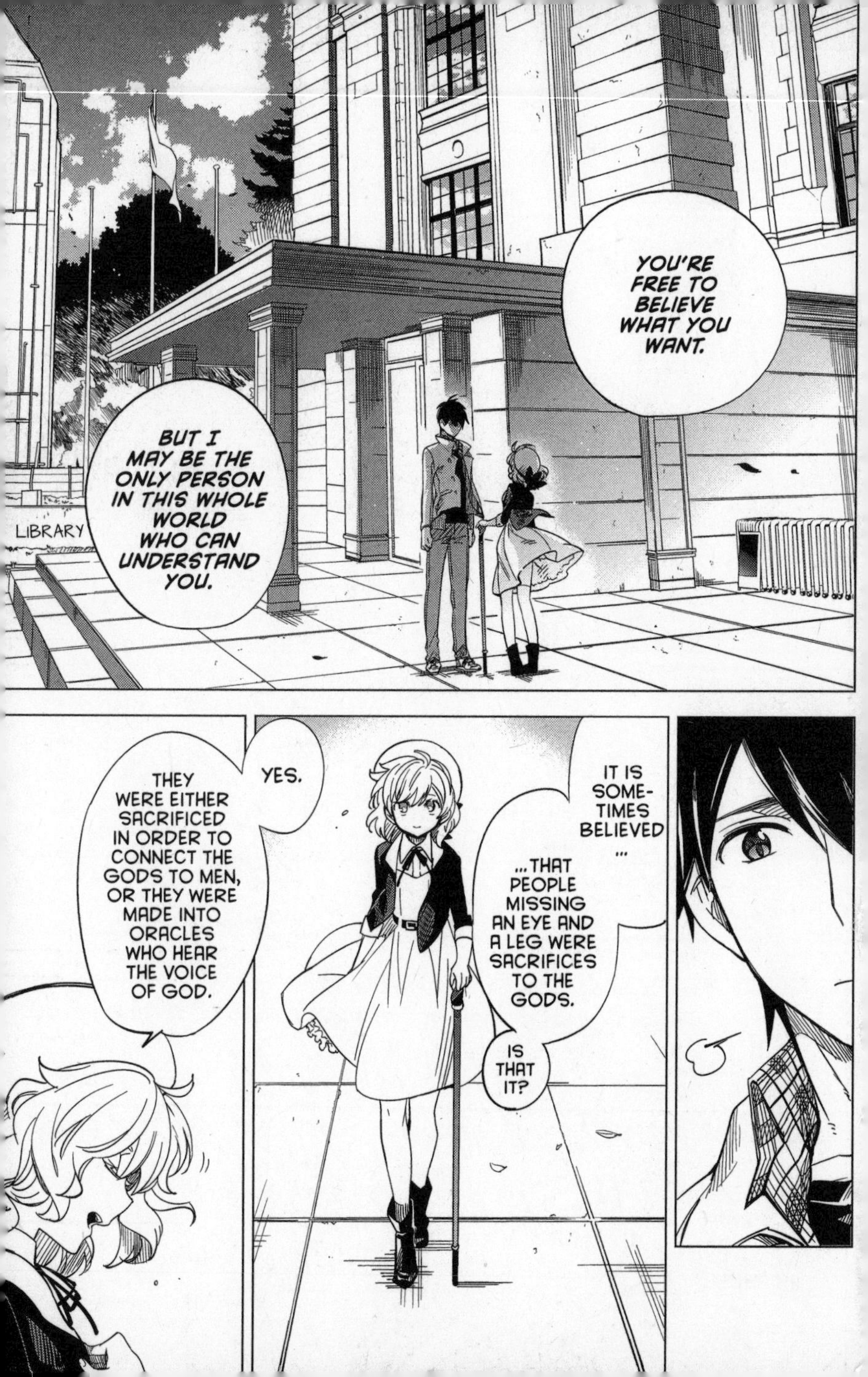
YOU'RE FREE TO BELIEVE WHAT YOU WANT.
BUT I MAY BE THE ONLY PERSON IN THIS WHOLE WORLD WHO CAN UNDERSTAND YOU.
LIBRARY
IT IS SOMETIMES BELIEVED...
...THAT PEOPLE MISSING AN EYE AND A LEG WERE SACRIFICES TO THE GODS.
IS THAT IT?
YES.
THEY WERE EITHER SACRIFICED IN ORDER TO CONNECT THE GODS TO MEN, OR THEY WERE MADE INTO ORACLES WHO HEAR THE VOICE OF GOD.

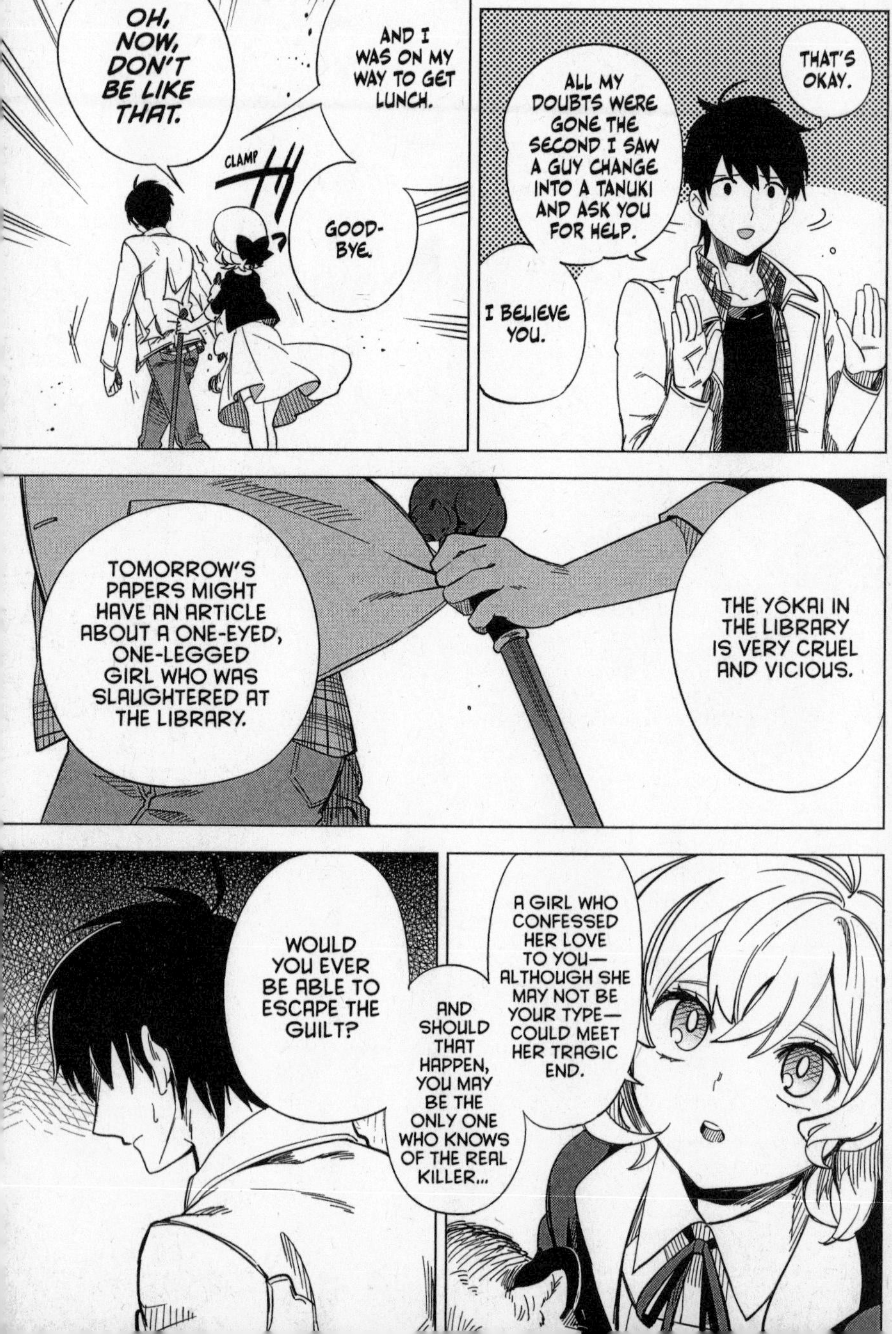
THAT'S OKAY.
ALL MY DOUBTS WERE GONE THE SECOND I SAW A GUY CHANGE INTO A TANUKI AND ASK YOU FOR HELP.
I BELIEVE YOU.
AND I WAS ON MY WAY TO GET LUNCH.
GOOD-BYE.
OH, NOW, DON'T BE LIKE THAT.
CLAMP
THE YÔKAI IN THE LIBRARY IS VERY CRUEL AND VICIOUS.
TOMORROW'S PAPERS MIGHT HAVE AN ARTICLE ABOUT A ONE-EYED, ONE-LEGGED GIRL WHO WAS SLAUGHTERED AT THE LIBRARY.
A GIRL WHO CONFESSED HER LOVE TO YOU—ALTHOUGH SHE MAY NOT BE YOUR TYPE—COULD MEET HER TRAGIC END.
AND SHOULD THAT HAPPEN, YOU MAY BE THE ONLY ONE WHO KNOWS OF THE REAL KILLER...
WOULD YOU EVER BE ABLE TO ESCAPE THE GUILT?

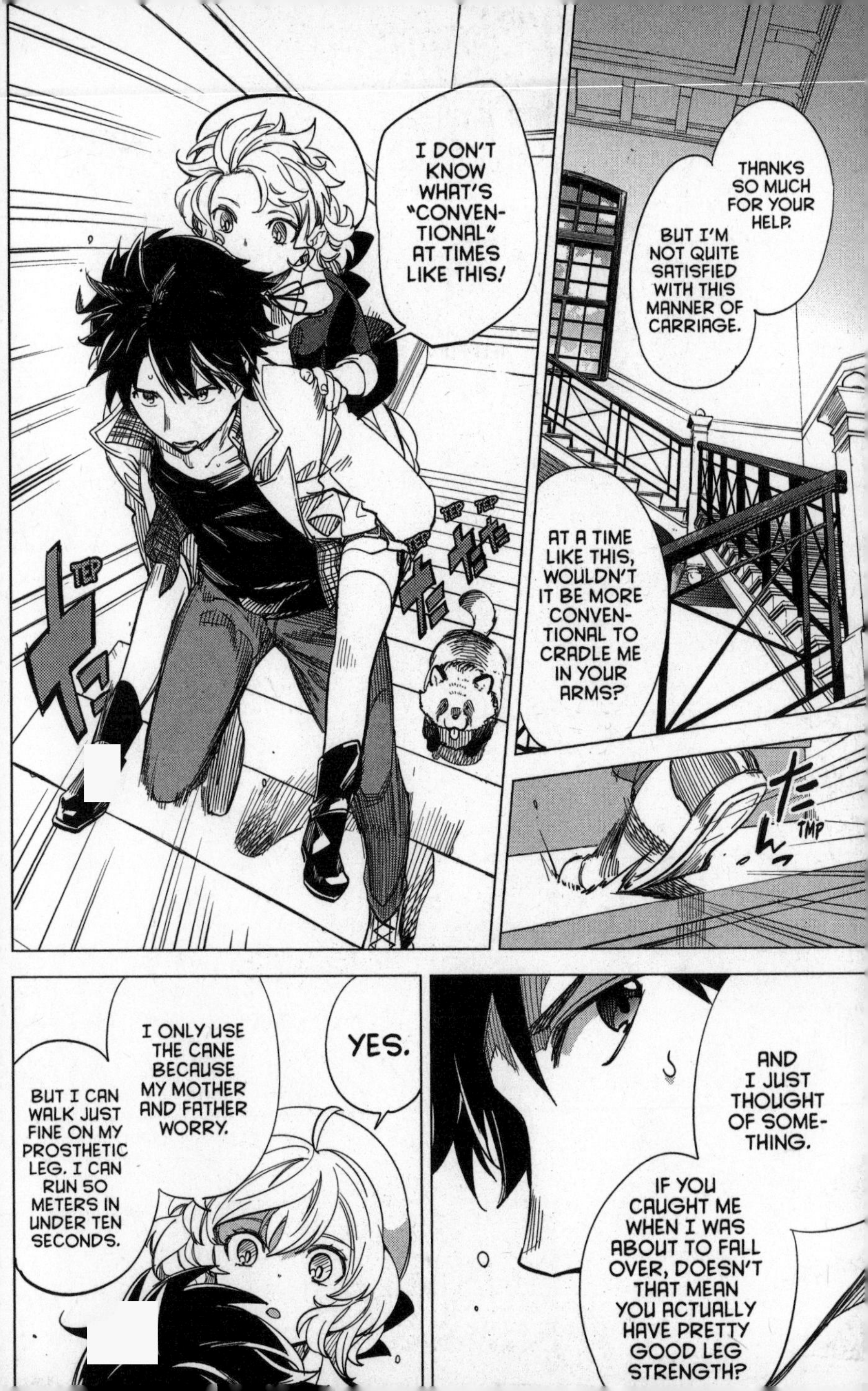
THANKS SO MUCH FOR YOUR HELP.
BUT I'M NOT QUITE SATISFIED WITH THIS MANNER OF CARRIAGE.
AT A TIME LIKE THIS, WOULDN'T IT BE MORE CONVEN-TIONAL TO CRADLE ME IN YOUR ARMS?
TMP
I DON'T KNOW WHAT'S "CONVEN-TIONAL" AT TIMES LIKE THIS!
TEP TEP TEP
TEP
AND I JUST THOUGHT OF SOME-THING.
IF YOU CAUGHT ME WHEN I WAS ABOUT TO FALL OVER, DOESN'T THAT MEAN YOU ACTUALLY HAVE PRETTY GOOD LEG STRENGTH?
YES.
I ONLY USE THE CANE BECAUSE MY MOTHER AND FATHER WORRY.
BUT I CAN WALK JUST FINE ON MY PROSTHETIC LEG. I CAN RUN 50 METERS IN UNDER TEN SECONDS.

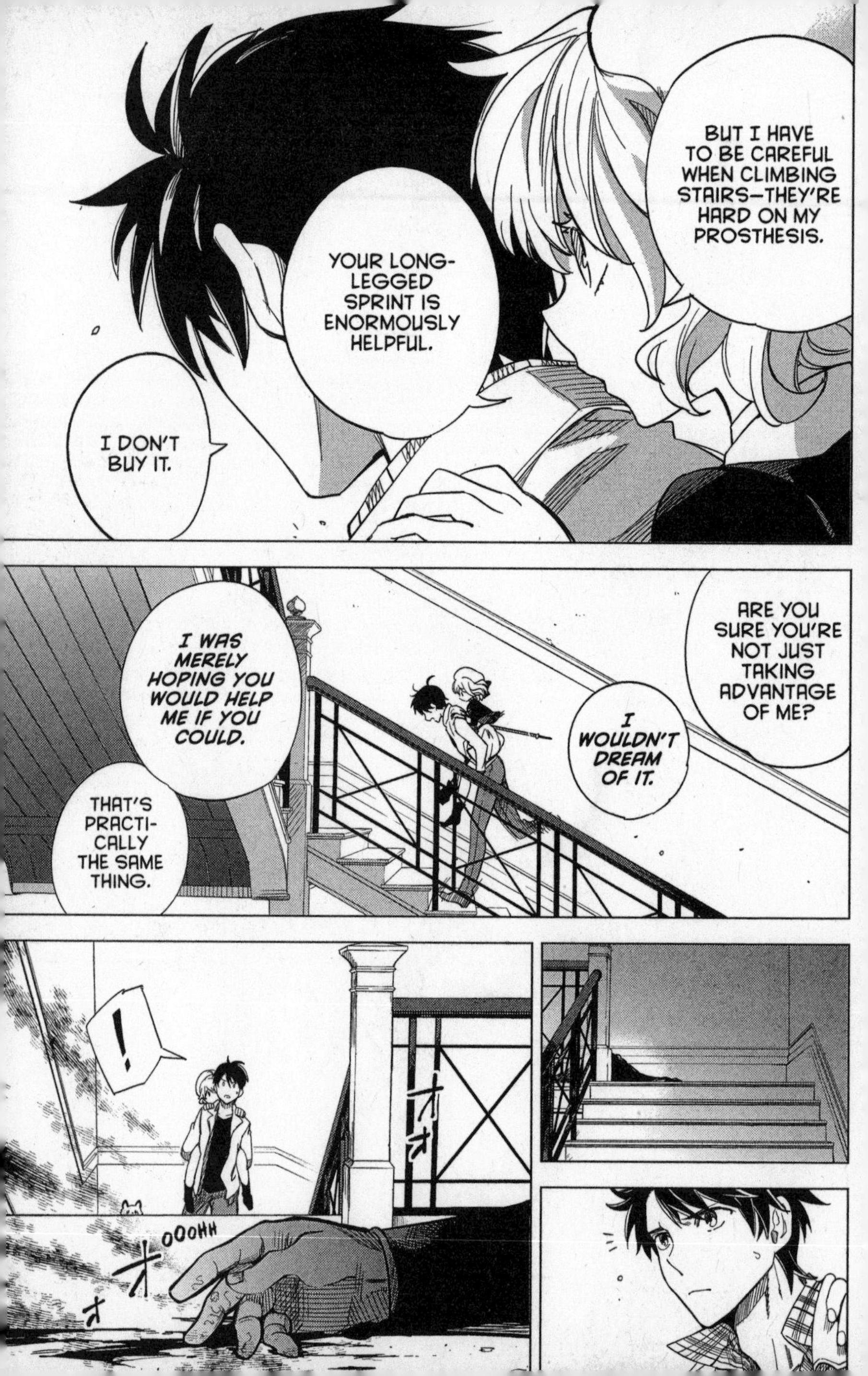
BUT I HAVE TO BE CAREFUL WHEN CLIMBING STAIRS—THEY'RE HARD ON MY PROSTHESIS.
YOUR LONG-LEGGED SPRINT IS ENORMOUSLY HELPFUL.
I DON'T BUY IT.
ARE YOU SURE YOU'RE NOT JUST TAKING ADVANTAGE OF ME?
I WOULDN'T DREAM OF IT.
I WAS MERELY HOPING YOU WOULD HELP ME IF YOU COULD.
THAT'S PRACTI-CALLY THE SAME THING.
!
OOOHH

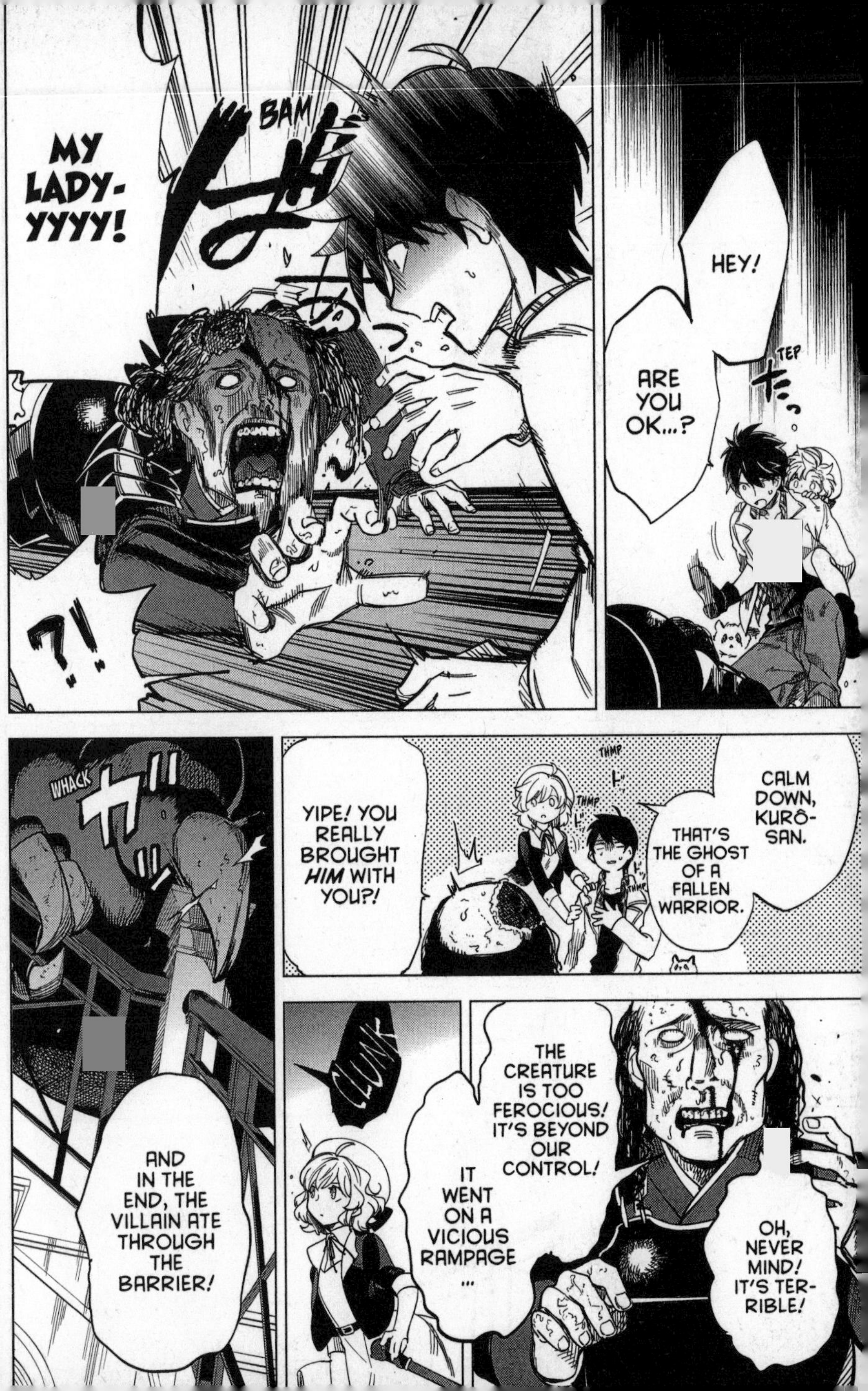
HEY!
ARE YOU OK...?
TEP
BAM
MY LADY-YYYY!
?!
CALM DOWN, KURÔ-SAN.
THAT'S THE GHOST OF A FALLEN WARRIOR.
THMP
THMP
THMP
YIPE! YOU REALLY BROUGHT *HIM* WITH YOU?!
OH, NEVER MIND! IT'S TER-RIBLE!
THE CREATURE IS TOO FEROCIOUS! IT'S BEYOND OUR CONTROL!
IT WENT ON A VICIOUS RAMPAGE ...
CLUNK
WHACK
AND IN THE END, THE VILLAIN ATE THROUGH THE BARRIER!

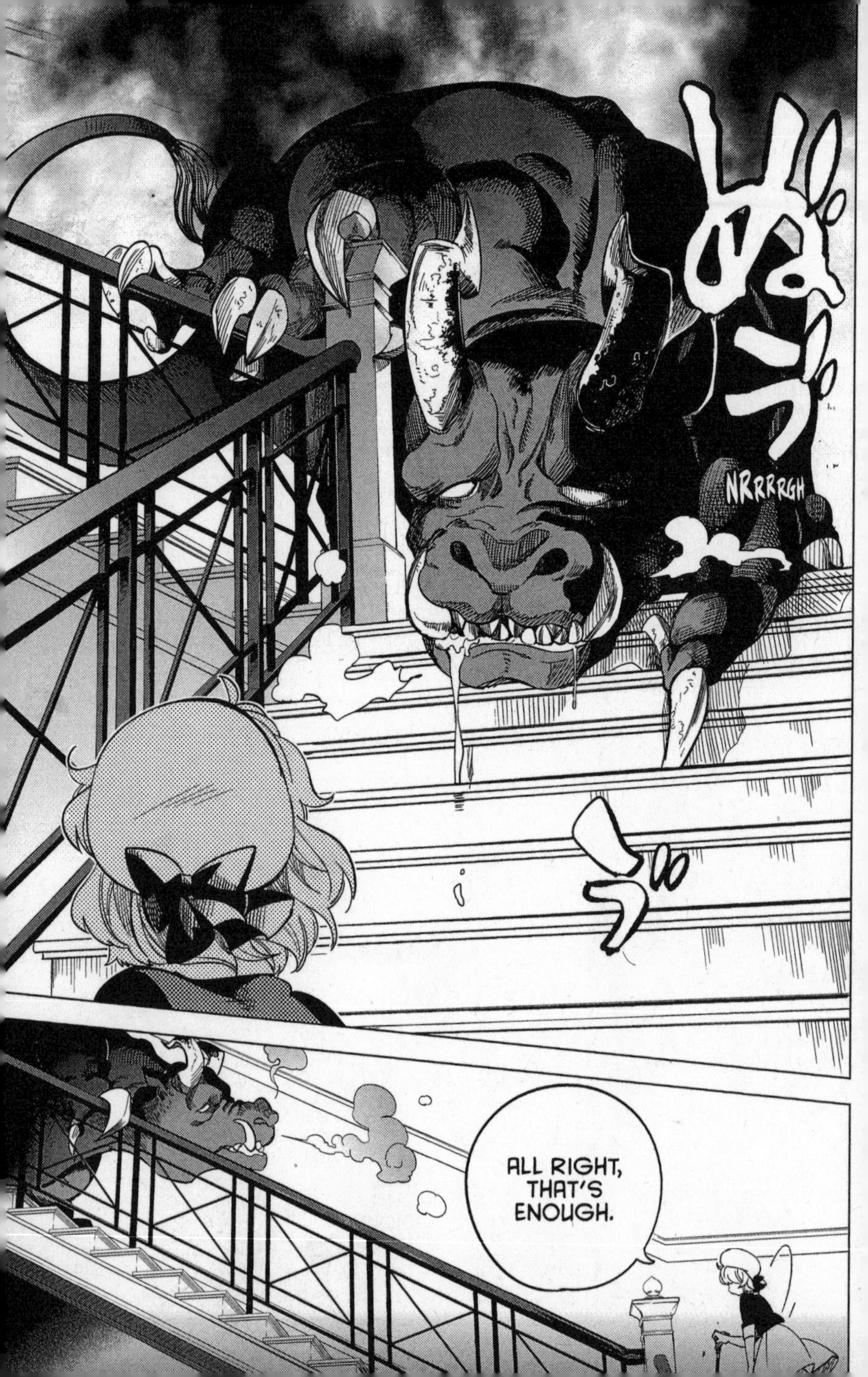
NRRRRGH
ALL RIGHT, THAT'S ENOUGH.

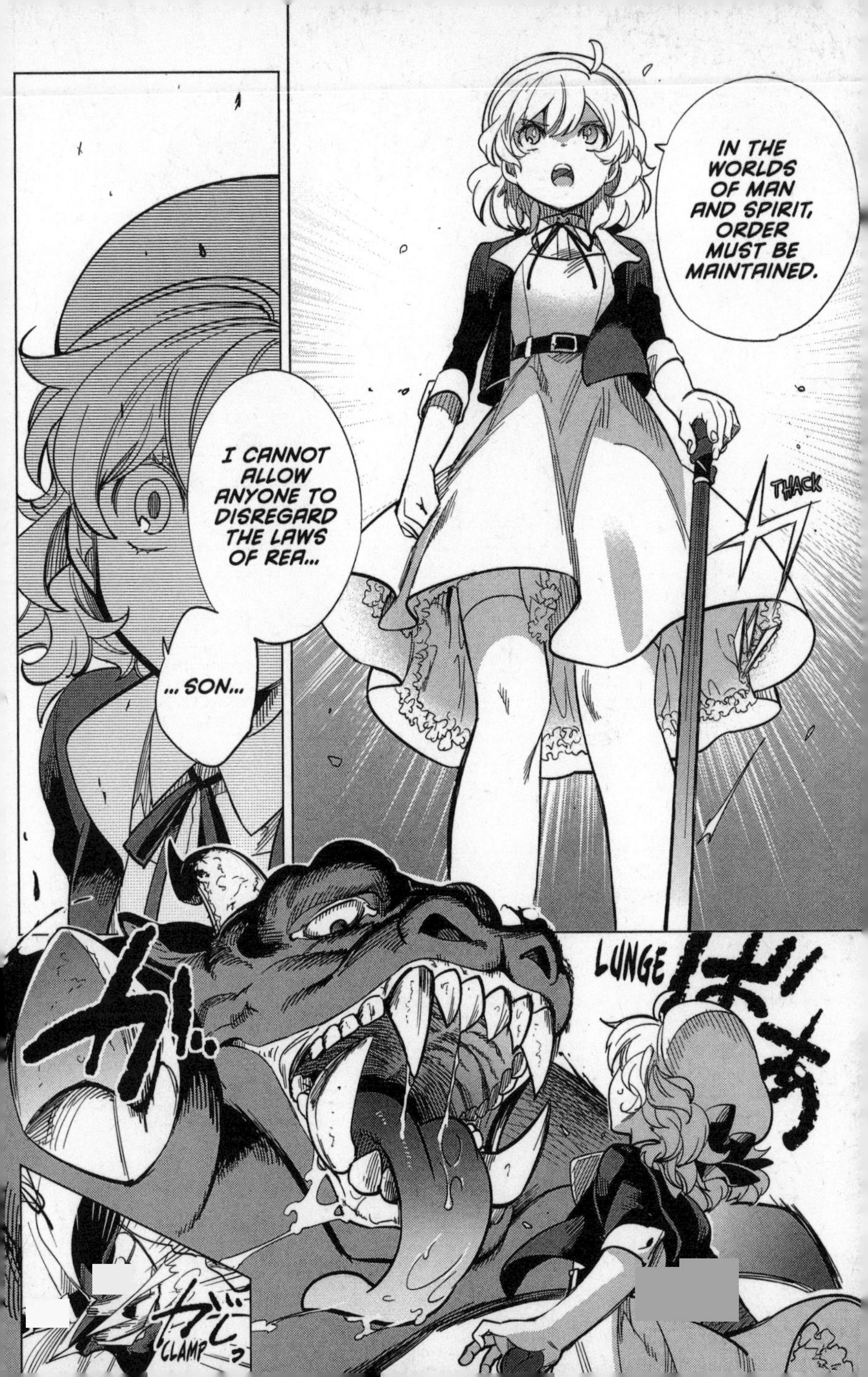
IN THE WORLDS OF MAN AND SPIRIT, ORDER MUST BE MAINTAINED.
I CANNOT ALLOW ANYONE TO DISREGARD THE LAWS OF REA...
THACK
...SON...
LUNGE
CLAMP

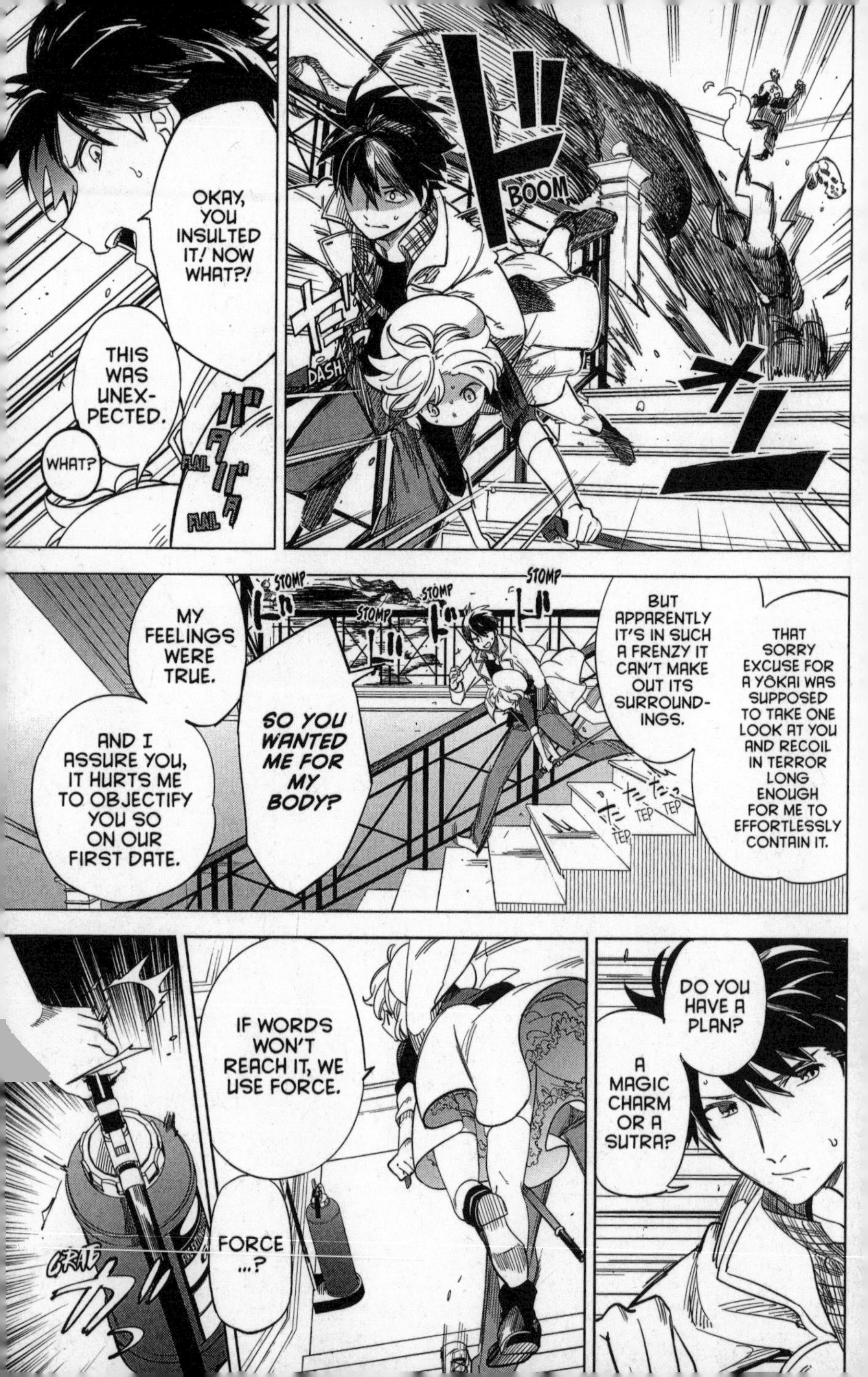
BOOM
DASH
OKAY, YOU INSULTED IT! NOW WHAT?!
THIS WAS UNEXPECTED.
WHAT?
FLAIL
FLAIL
THAT SORRY EXCUSE FOR A YÔKAI WAS SUPPOSED TO TAKE ONE LOOK AT YOU AND RECOIL IN TERROR LONG ENOUGH FOR ME TO EFFORTLESSLY CONTAIN IT.
BUT APPARENTLY IT'S IN SUCH A FRENZY IT CAN'T MAKE OUT ITS SURROUNDINGS.
STOMP
STOMP
STOMP
STOMP
TEP
TEP
TEP
SO YOU WANTED ME FOR MY BODY?
MY FEELINGS WERE TRUE.
AND I ASSURE YOU, IT HURTS ME TO OBJECTIFY YOU SO ON OUR FIRST DATE.
DO YOU HAVE A PLAN?
A MAGIC CHARM OR A SUTRA?
IF WORDS WON'T REACH IT, WE USE FORCE.
FORCE ...?
GRAB

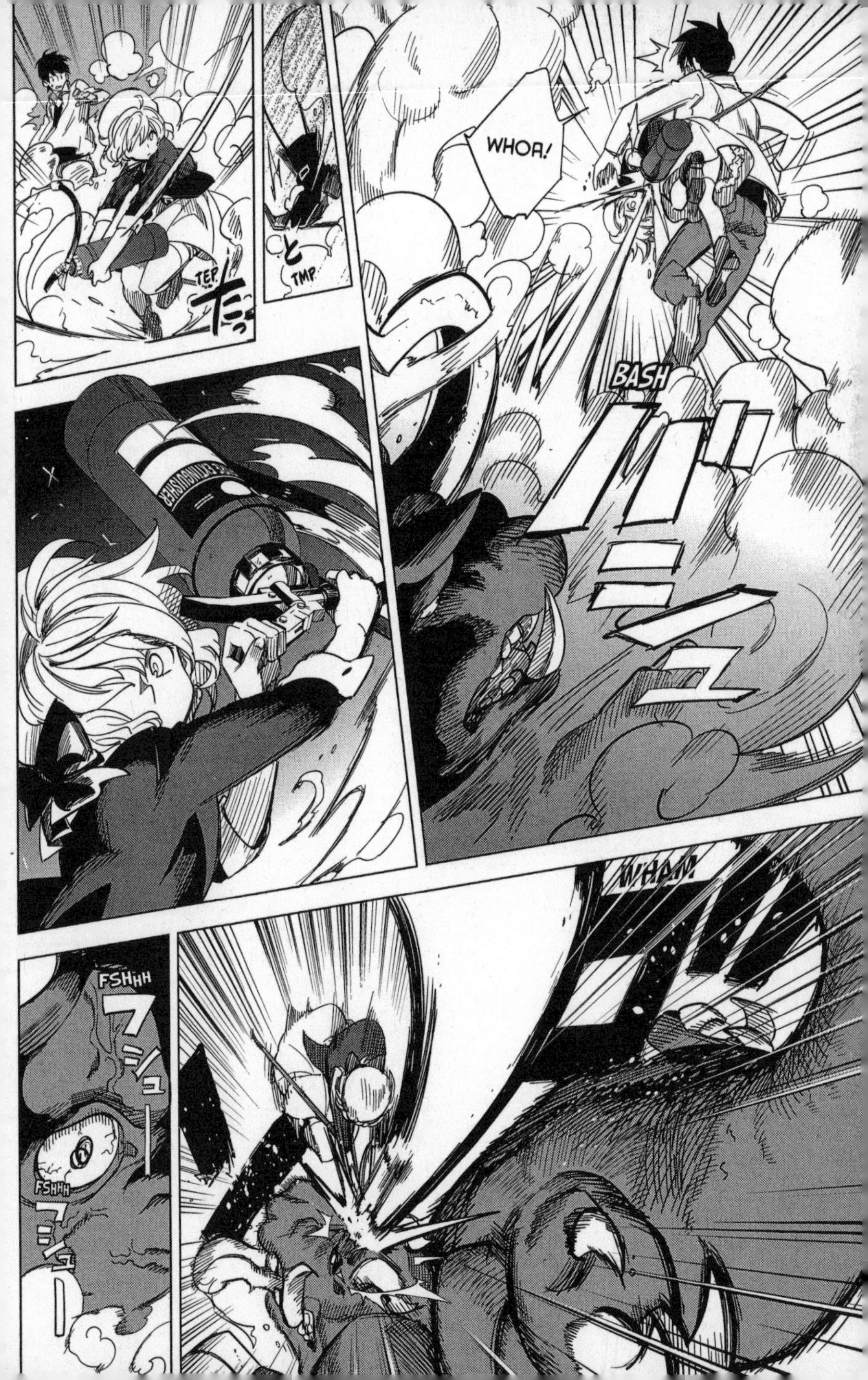
WHOA!
BASH
バシュ
TMP
と
TEP
たっ
WHAM!
FSHHH
フシュー
FSHHH
フシュー

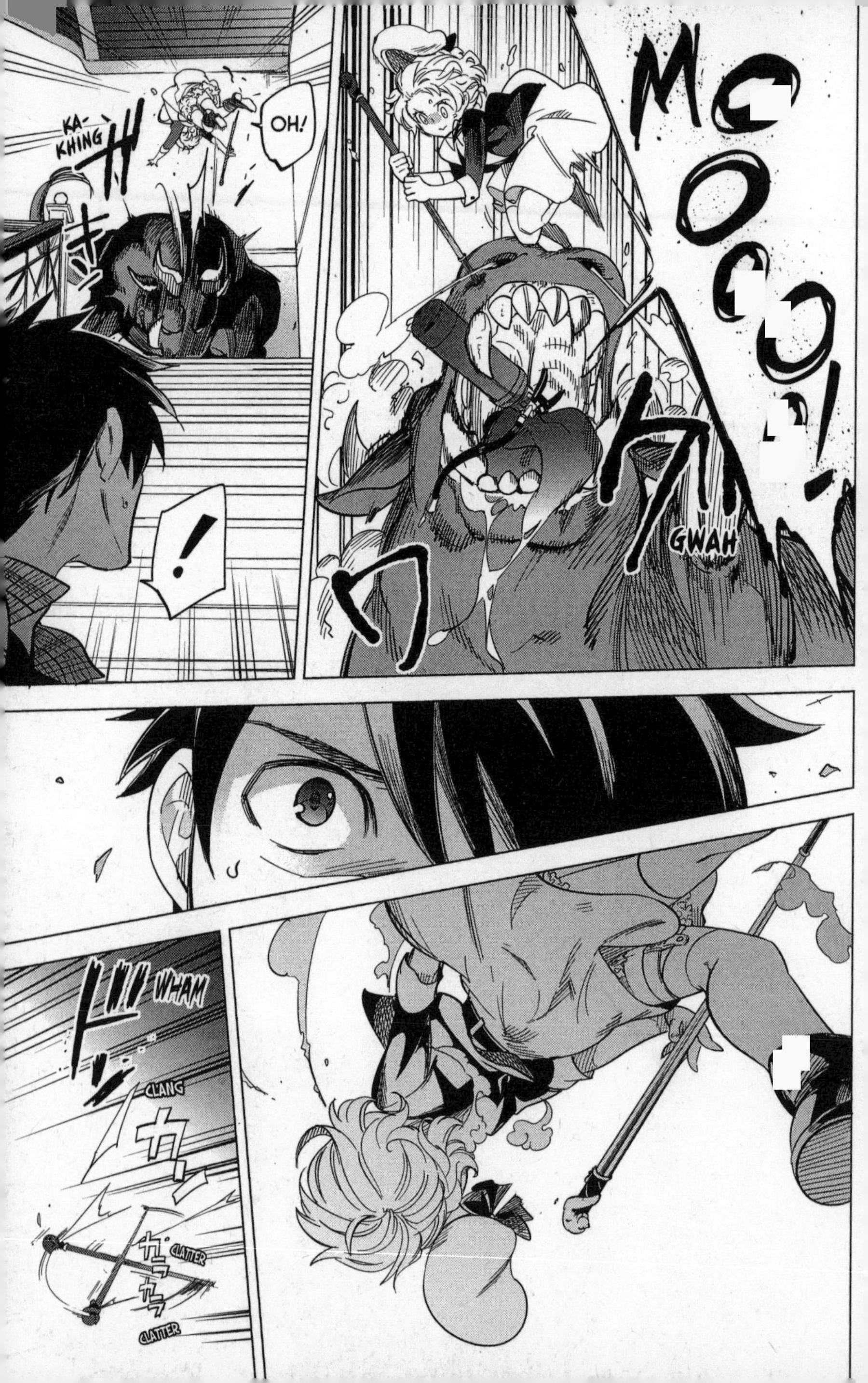
MOOOO!
GWAH
KA-KHING
OH!
!
WHAM
CLANG
CLATTER
CLATTER

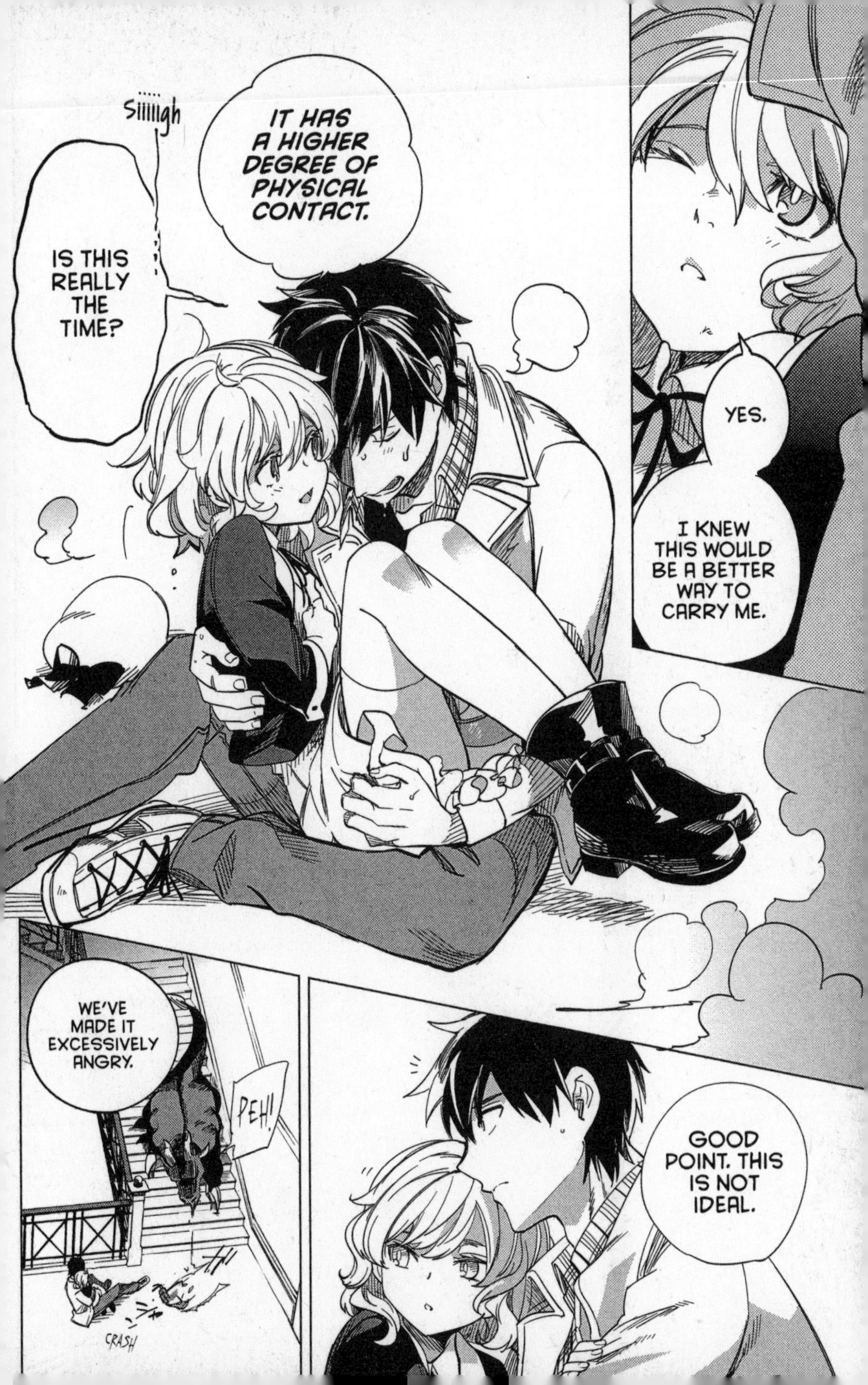
YES.
I KNEW THIS WOULD BE A BETTER WAY TO CARRY ME.
IT HAS A HIGHER DEGREE OF PHYSICAL CONTACT.
Siiiiigh
IS THIS REALLY THE TIME?
GOOD POINT. THIS IS NOT IDEAL.
WE'VE MADE IT EXCESSIVELY ANGRY.
PEH!
CRASH

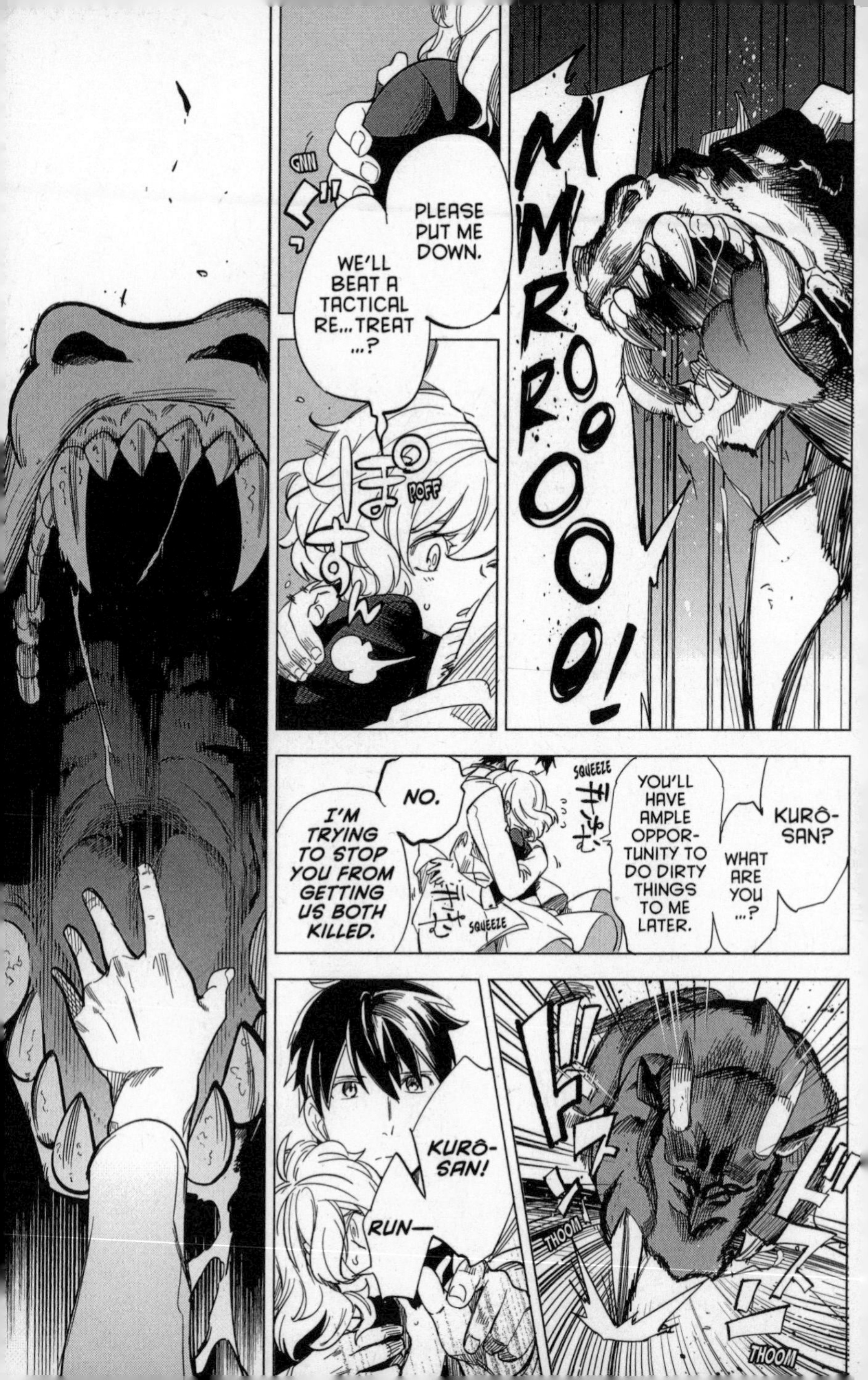
MMROOOOOO!
GNN
PLEASE PUT ME DOWN.
WE'LL BEAT A TACTICAL RE...TREAT ...?
POFF
KURÔ-SAN?
WHAT ARE YOU ...?
YOU'LL HAVE AMPLE OPPORTUNITY TO DO DIRTY THINGS TO ME LATER.
SQUEEZE
SQUEEZE
NO.
I'M TRYING TO STOP YOU FROM GETTING US BOTH KILLED.
THOOM
THOOM
KURÔ-SAN!
RUN—

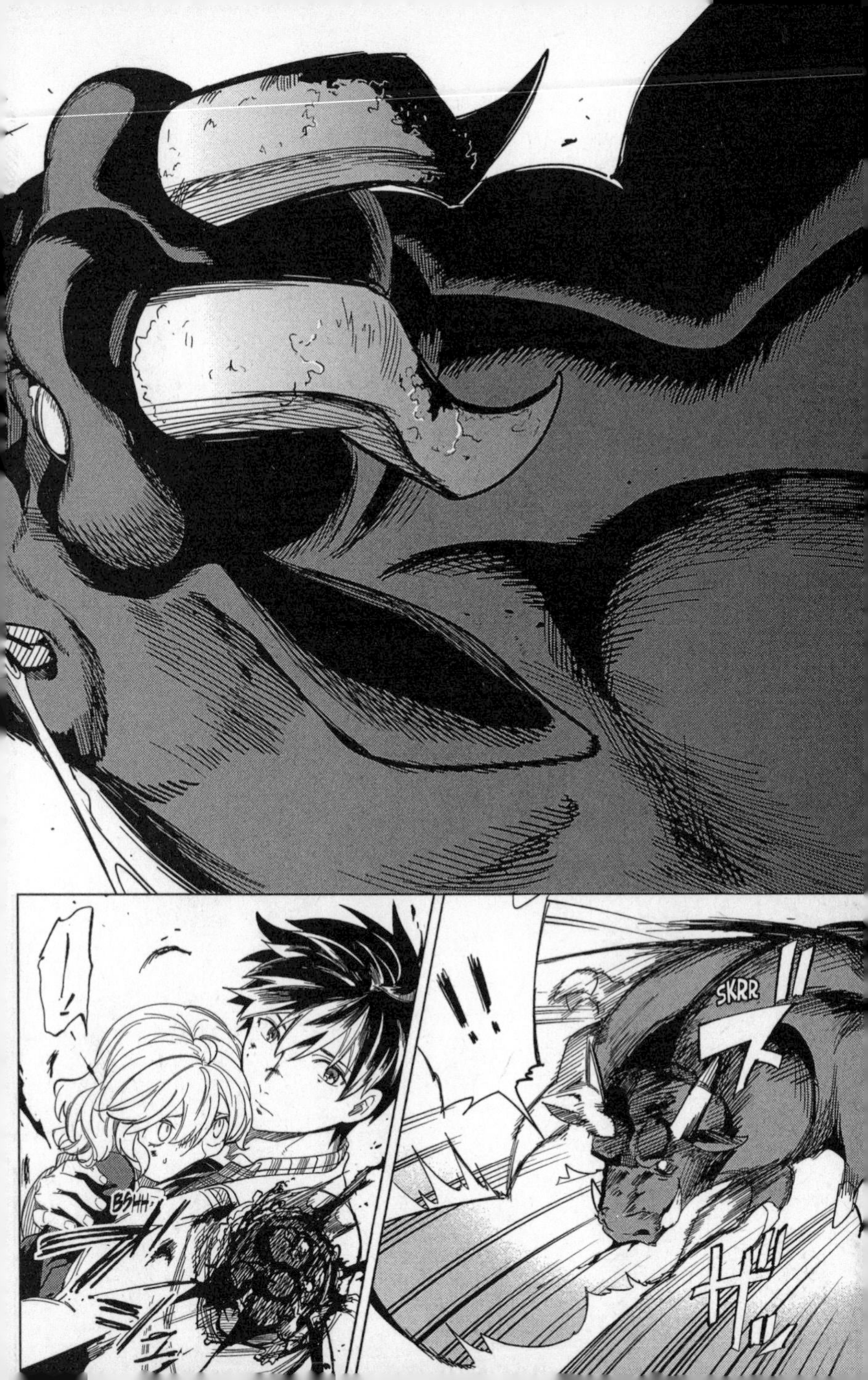
SKRR
!!
!
BSHH

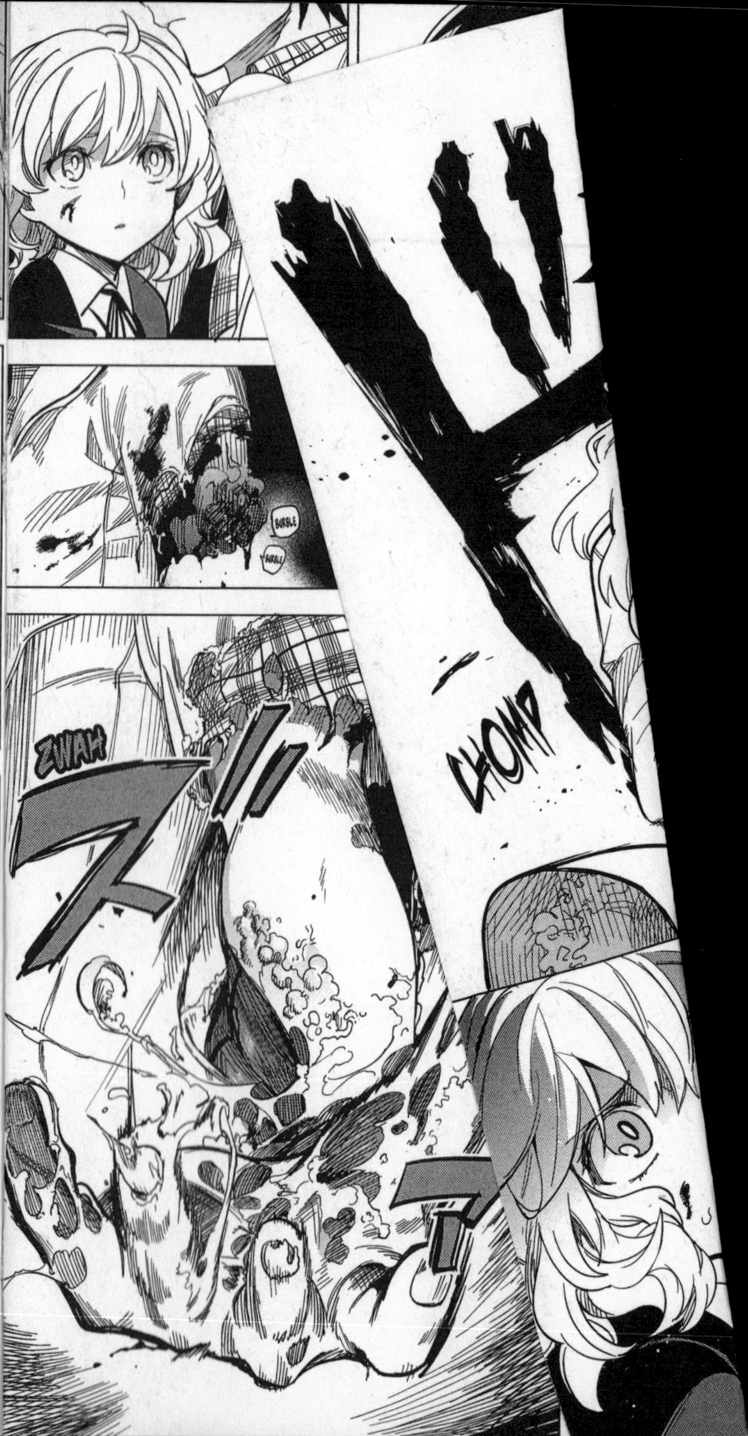
CHOMP
BURBLE
BURBLE
ZWAH

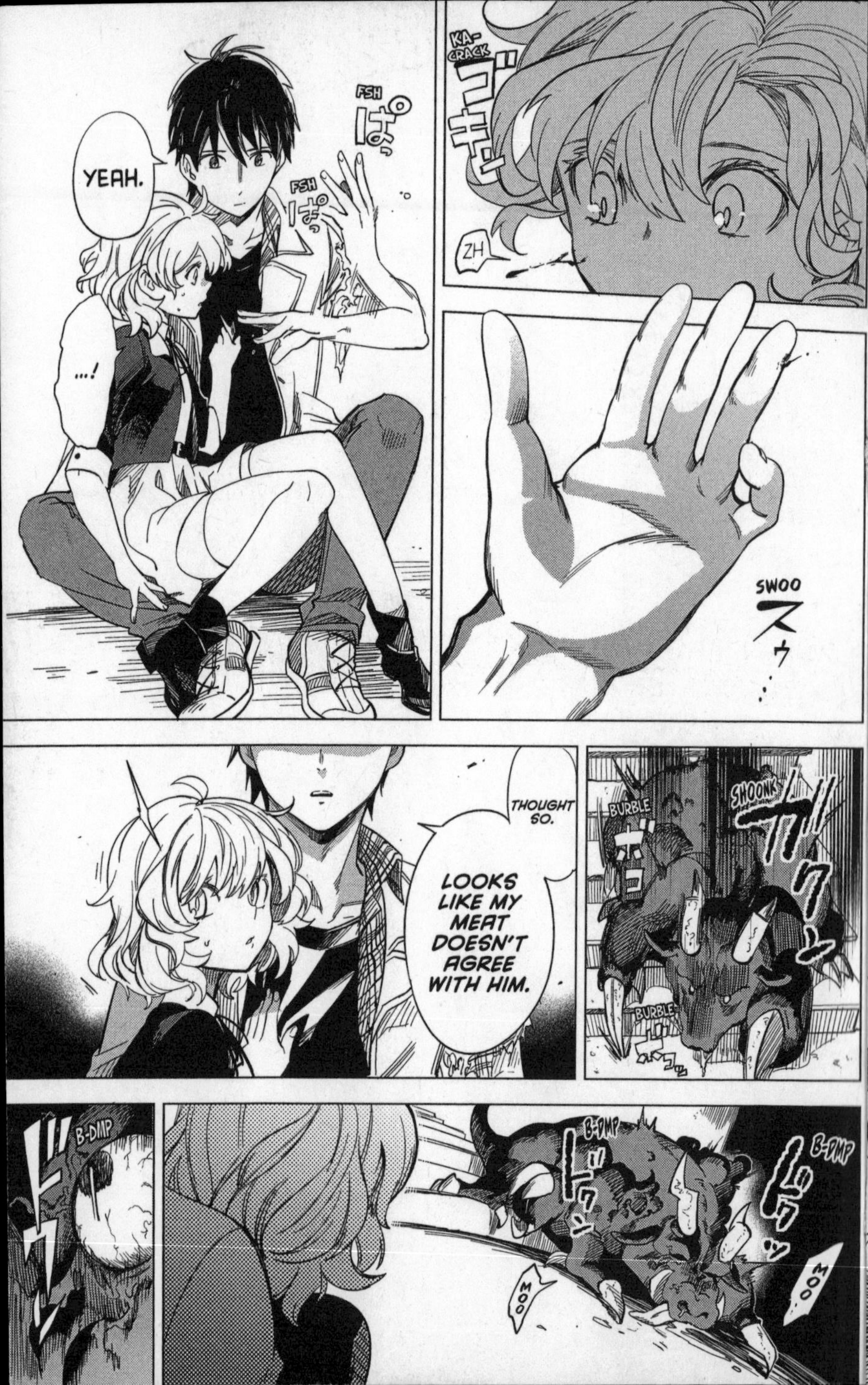
KA-CRACK
ZH
SWOO
スゥ…
FSH
ぱっ
FSH
ぱっ
YEAH.
...!
SHOONK
BURBLE
BURBLE
THOUGHT SO.
LOOKS LIKE MY MEAT DOESN'T AGREE WITH HIM.
B-DMP
B-DMP
MOO
MOO
B-DMP

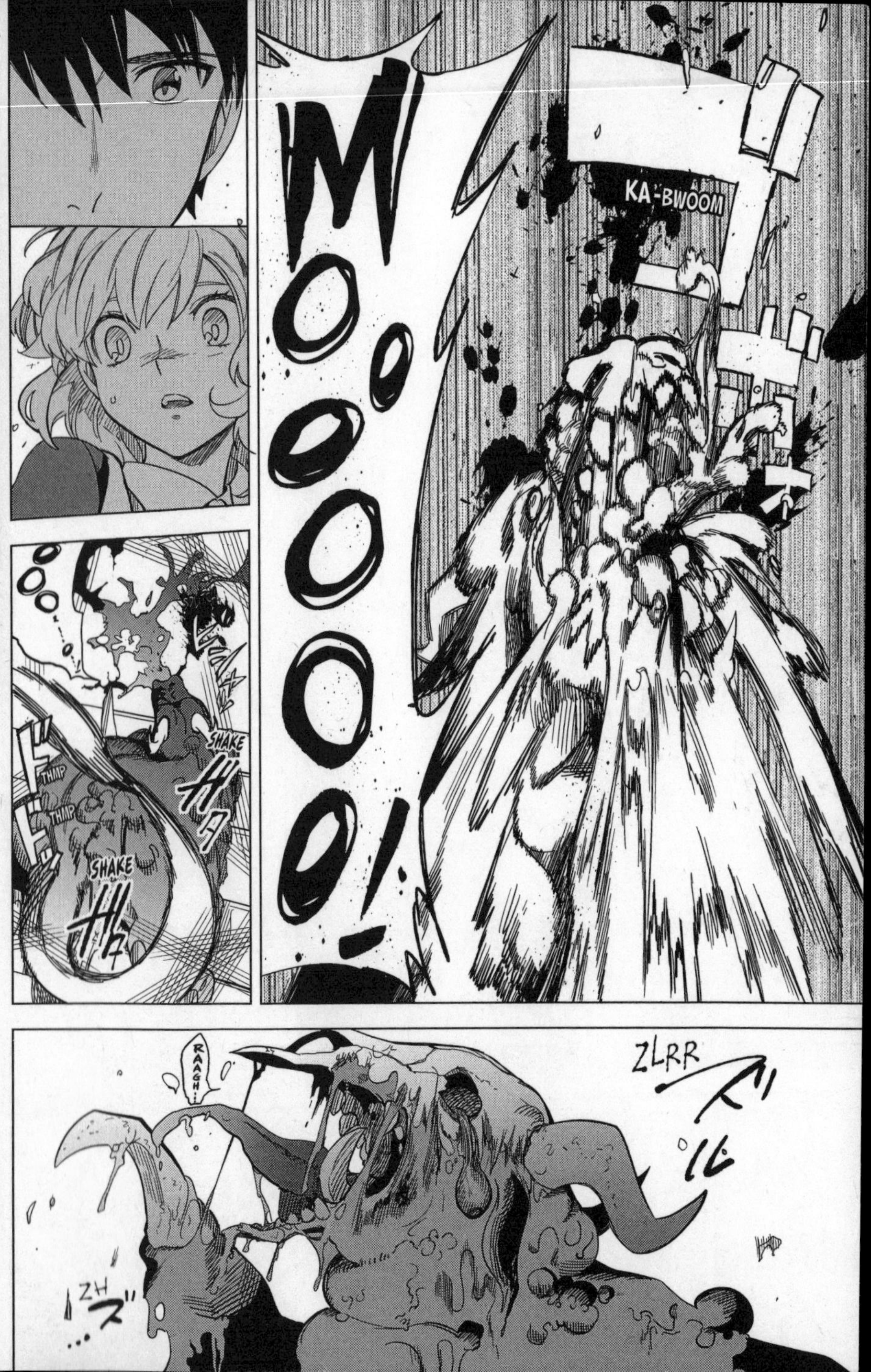
MOOOOOOO!
KA-BWOOM
OOO...O!
SHAKE
THMP
THMP
SHAKE
RAAGH!
ZLRR
ZH
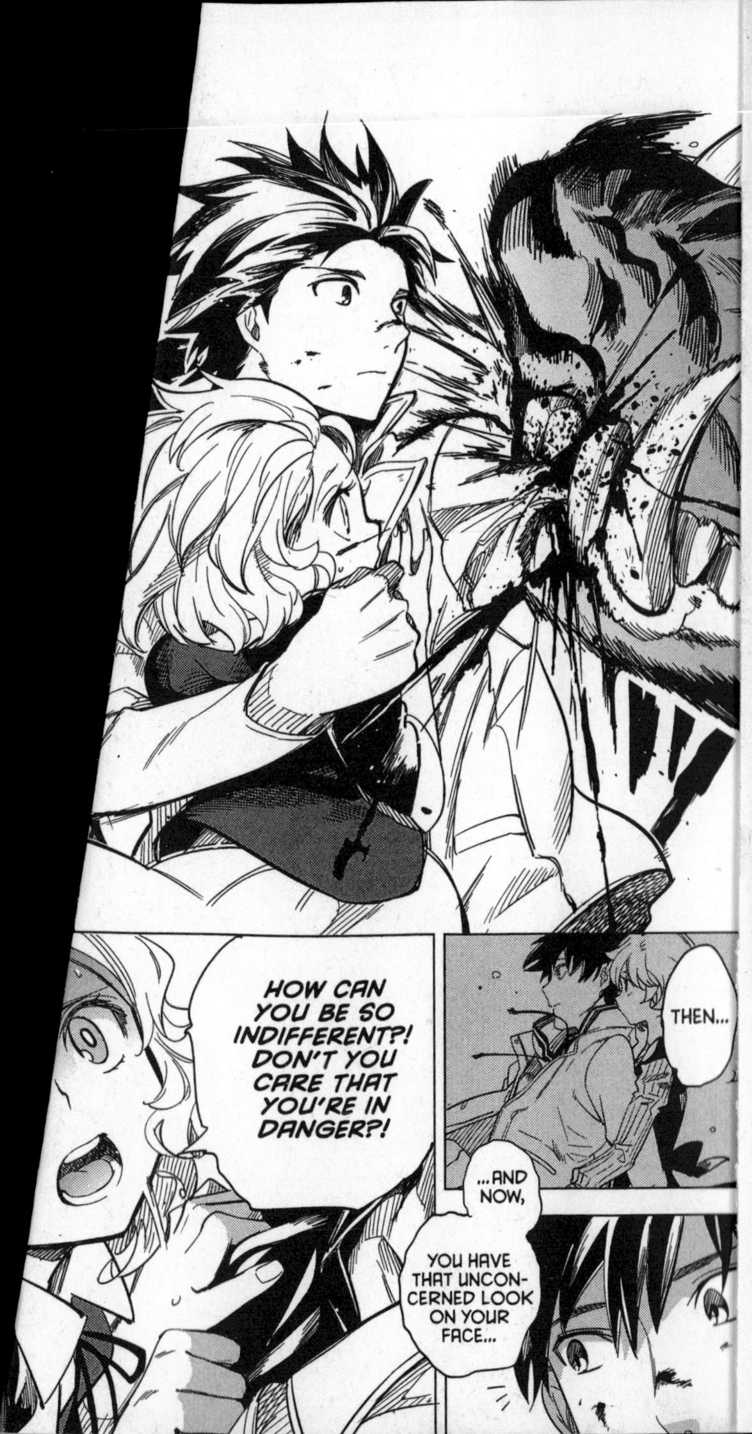
THEN...
...AND NOW,
YOU HAVE THAT UNCON-CERNED LOOK ON YOUR FACE...
HOW CAN YOU BE SO INDIFFERENT?! DON'T YOU CARE THAT YOU'RE IN DANGER?!

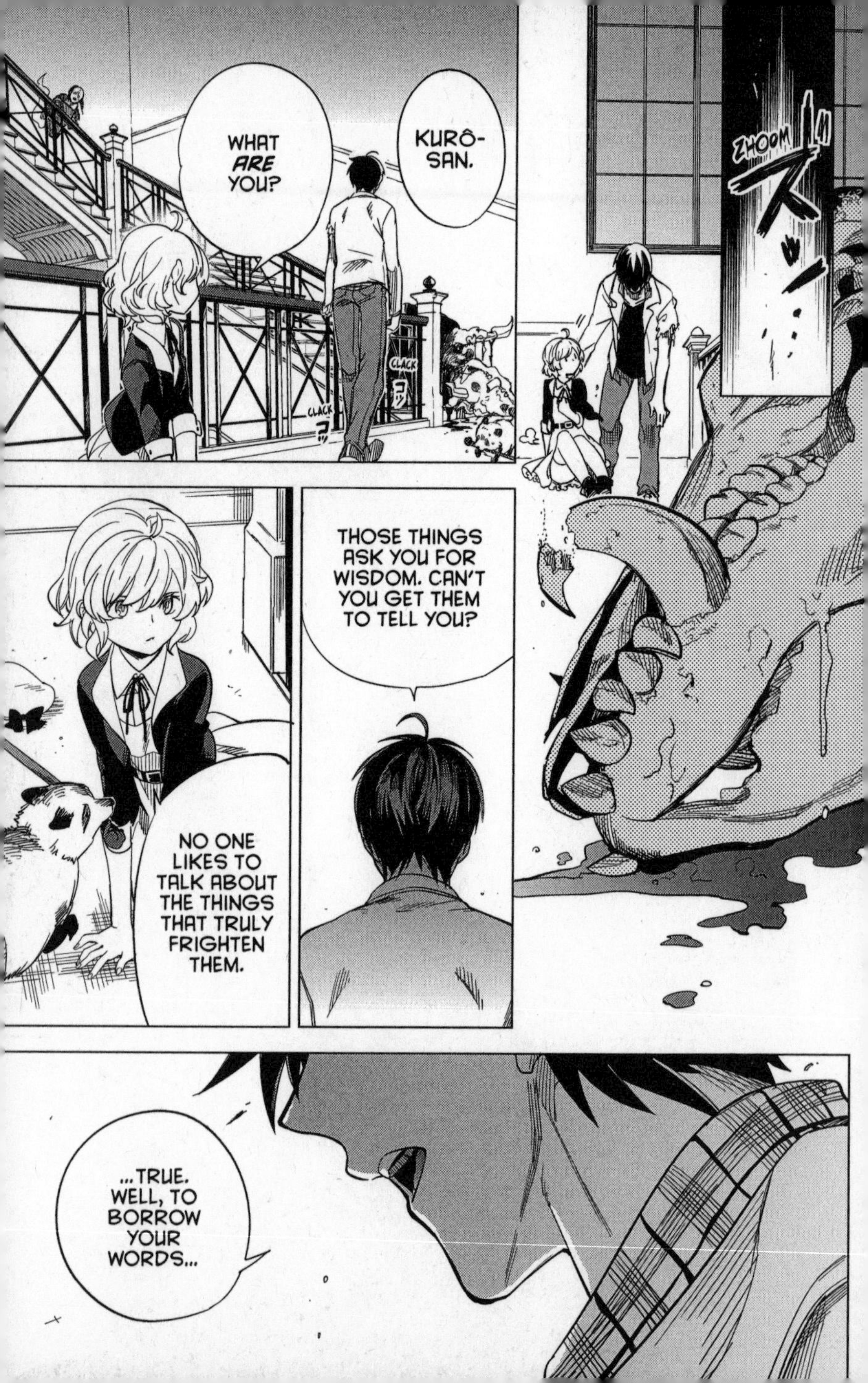
ZHOOM
CLACK
CLACK
KURÔ-SAN.
WHAT *ARE* YOU?
THOSE THINGS ASK YOU FOR WISDOM. CAN'T YOU GET THEM TO TELL YOU?
NO ONE LIKES TO TALK ABOUT THE THINGS THAT TRULY FRIGHTEN THEM.
...TRUE. WELL, TO BORROW YOUR WORDS...

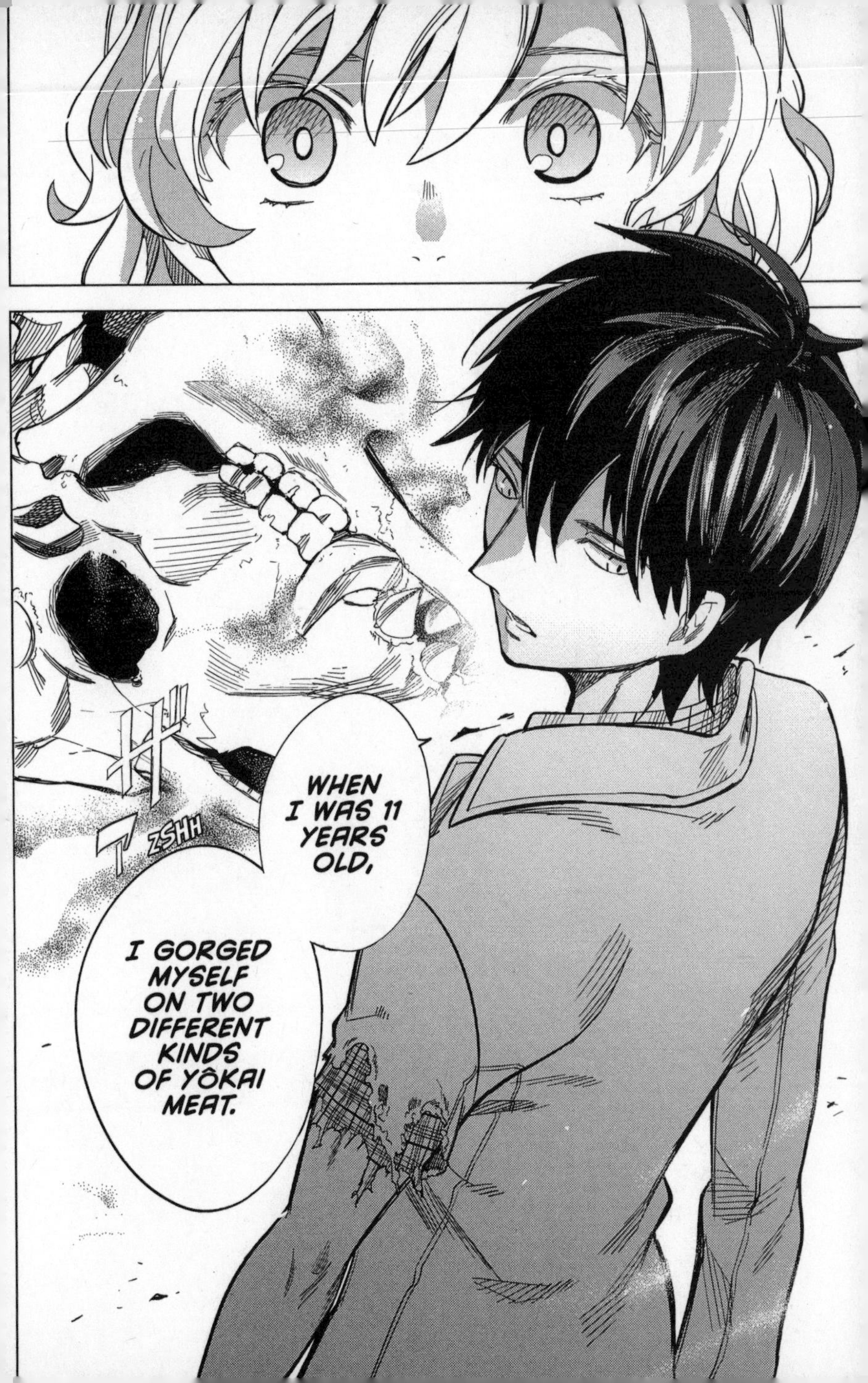
ZSHH
WHEN I WAS 11 YEARS OLD,
I GORGED MYSELF ON TWO DIFFERENT KINDS OF YÔKAI MEAT.

IN/SPECTRE

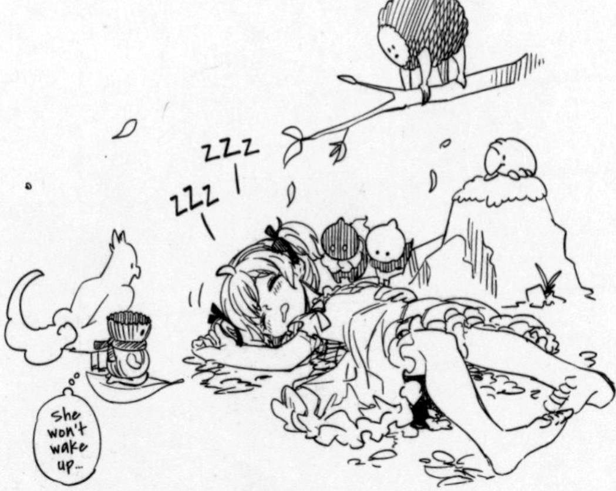
ZZZ
ZZZ
She won't wake up...

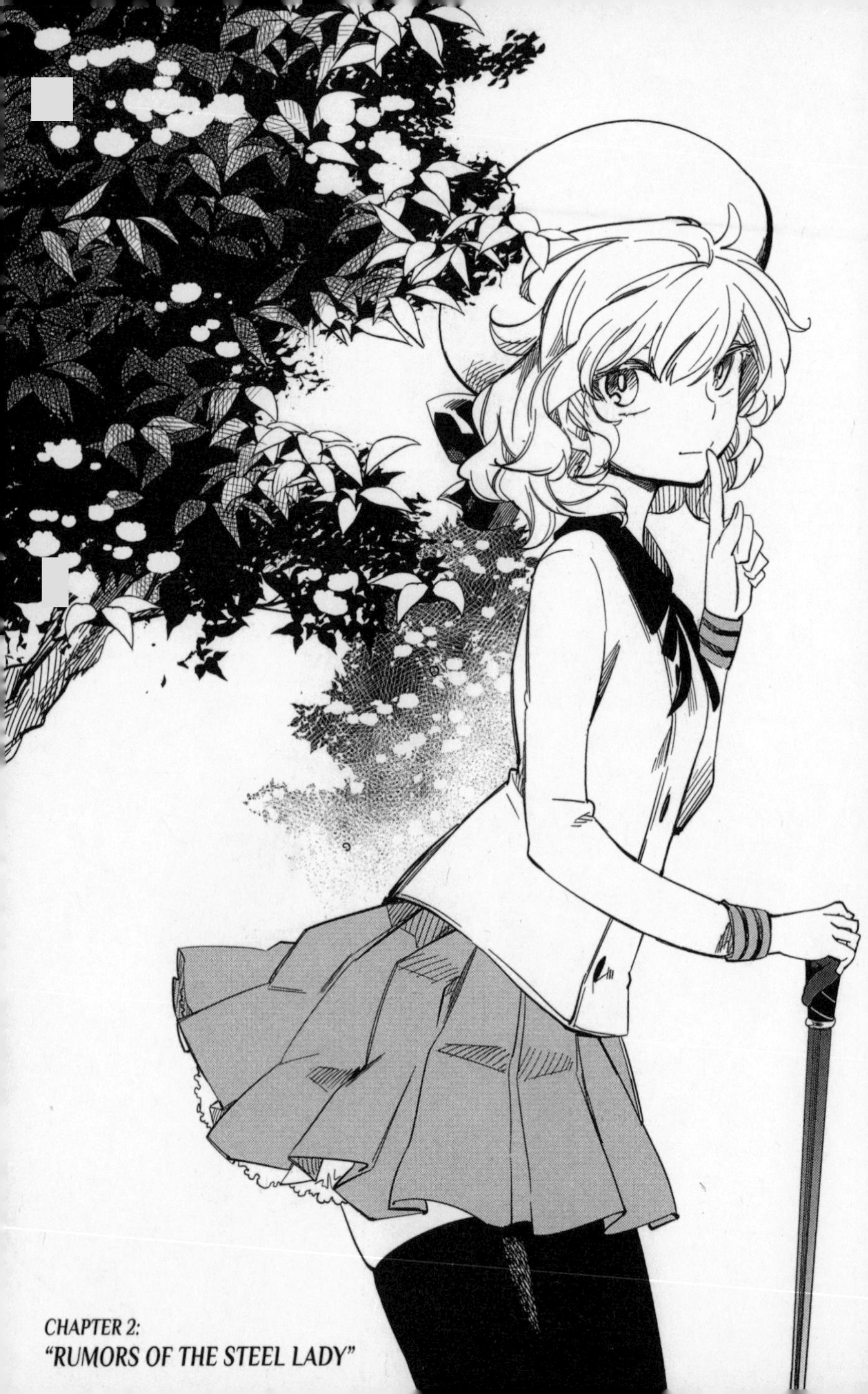

CHAPTER 2:
“RUMORS OF THE STEEL LADY”

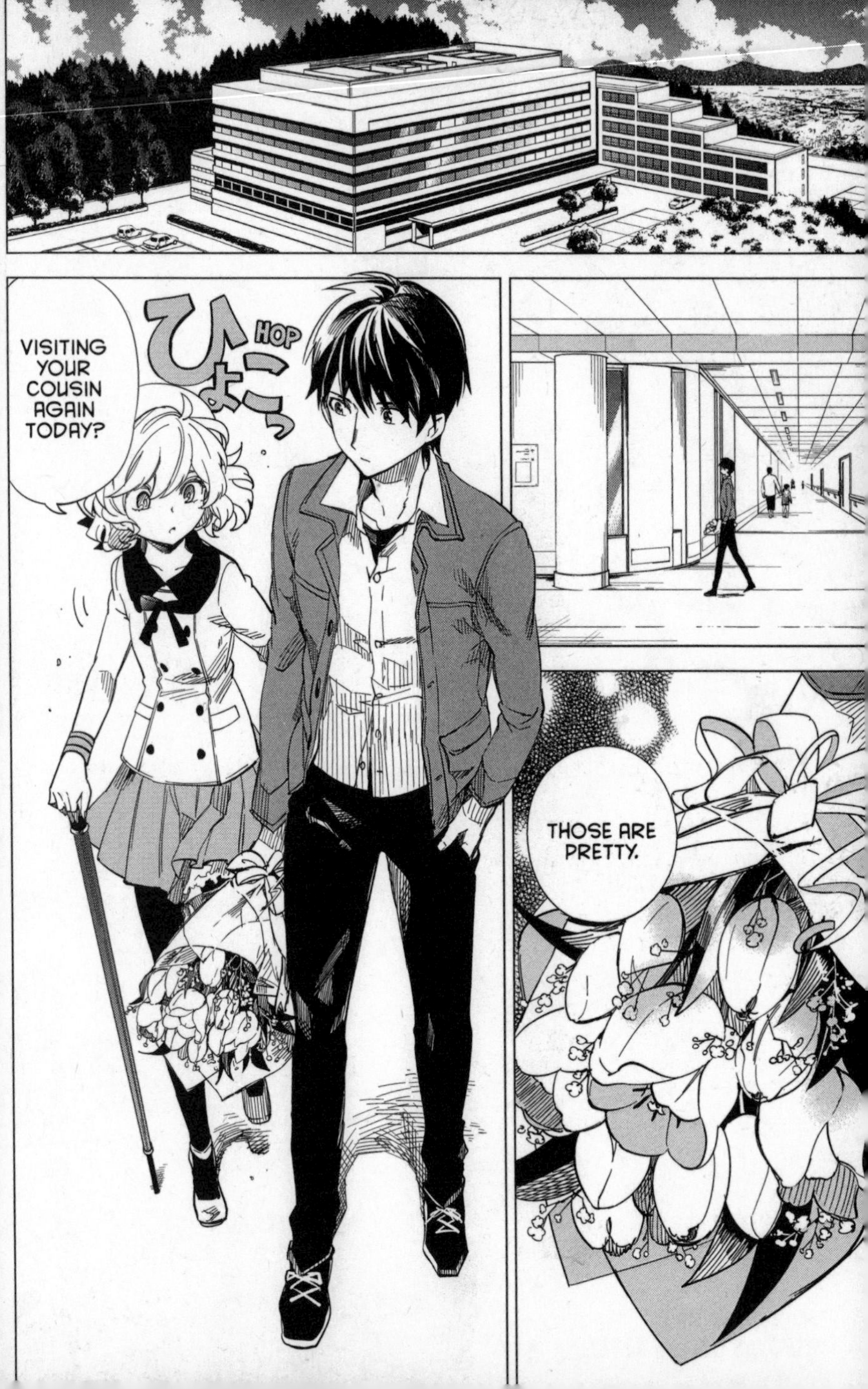
THOSE ARE PRETTY.
ひょこっ HOP
VISITING YOUR COUSIN AGAIN TODAY?

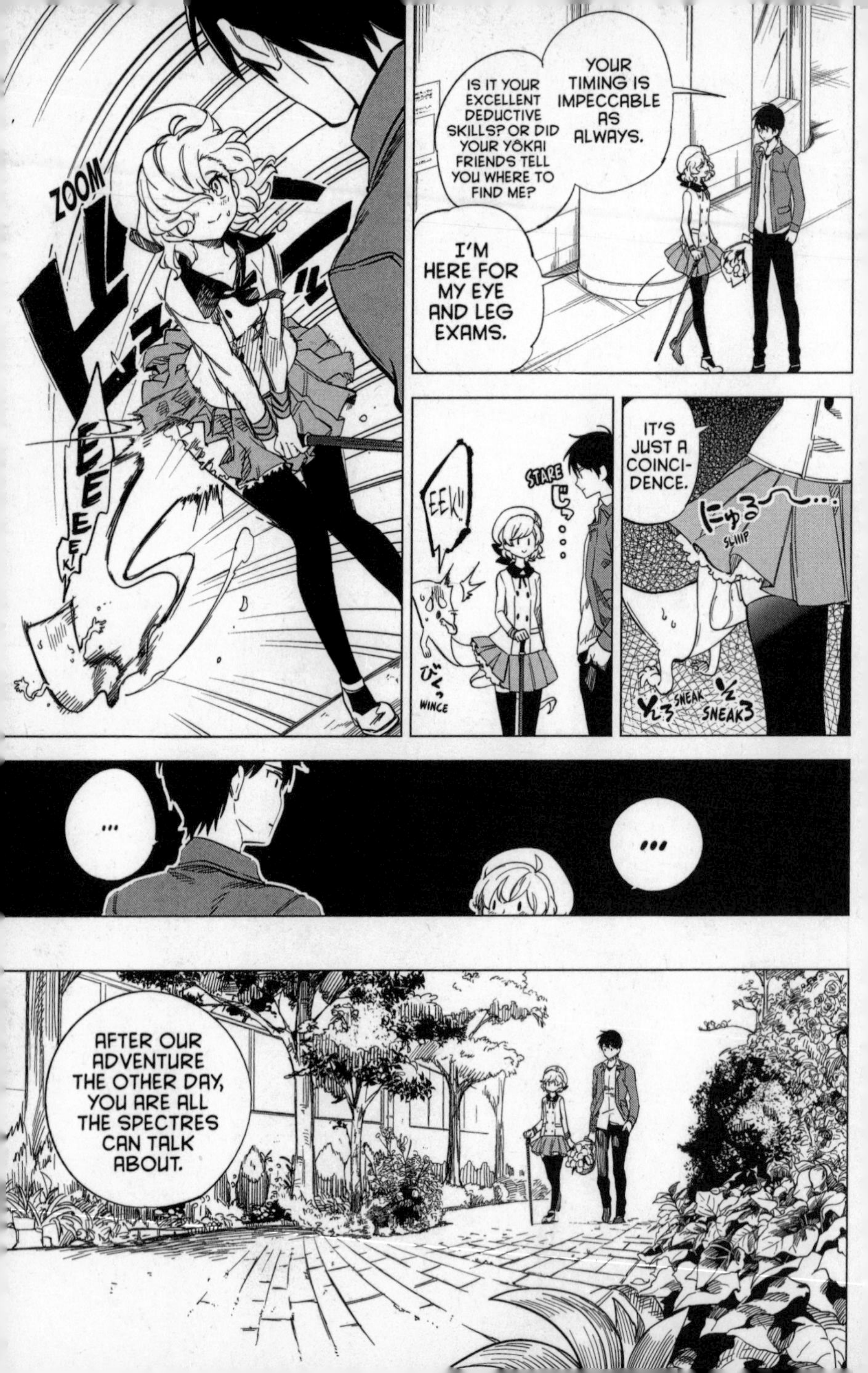
YOUR TIMING IS IMPECCABLE AS ALWAYS.
IS IT YOUR EXCELLENT DEDUCTIVE SKILLS? OR DID YOUR YŌKAI FRIENDS TELL YOU WHERE TO FIND ME?
I'M HERE FOR MY EYE AND LEG EXAMS.
IT'S JUST A COINCIDENCE.
にゅる〜〜…
SLIIIP
SNEAK
SNEAK
STARE
EEK!!
びくっ
WINCE
ZOOM
EEEEEEK!
...
...
AFTER OUR ADVENTURE THE OTHER DAY, YOU ARE ALL THE SPECTRES CAN TALK ABOUT.

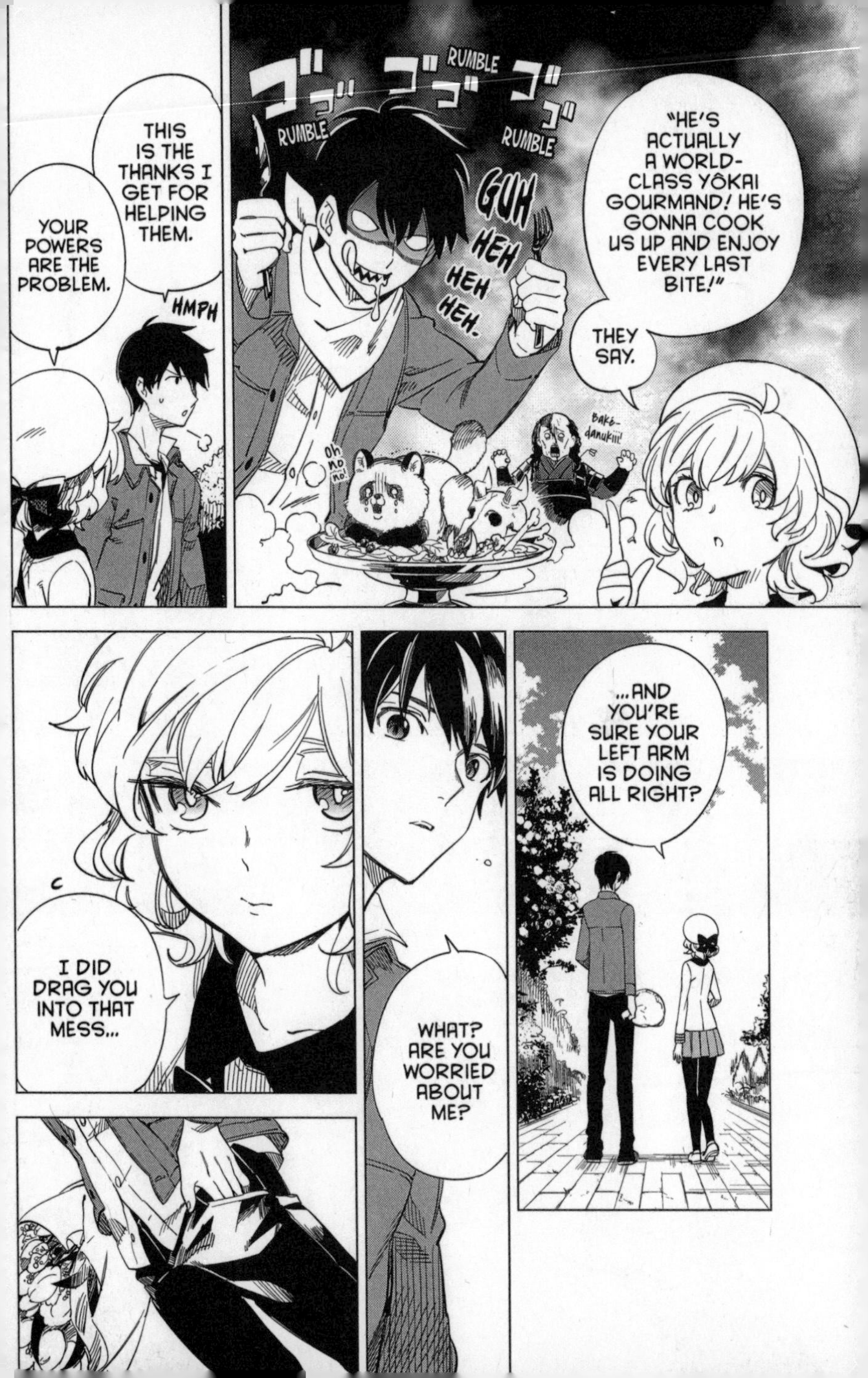
"HE'S ACTUALLY A WORLD-CLASS YÔKAI GOURMAND! HE'S GONNA COOK US UP AND ENJOY EVERY LAST BITE!"
THEY SAY.
ゴゴ RUMBLE
ゴゴ RUMBLE
ゴゴ RUMBLE
GUH HEH HEH HEH.
Baké-danukiii!
Oh no no!
THIS IS THE THANKS I GET FOR HELPING THEM.
HMPH
YOUR POWERS ARE THE PROBLEM.
...AND YOU'RE SURE YOUR LEFT ARM IS DOING ALL RIGHT?
WHAT? ARE YOU WORRIED ABOUT ME?
I DID DRAG YOU INTO THAT MESS...

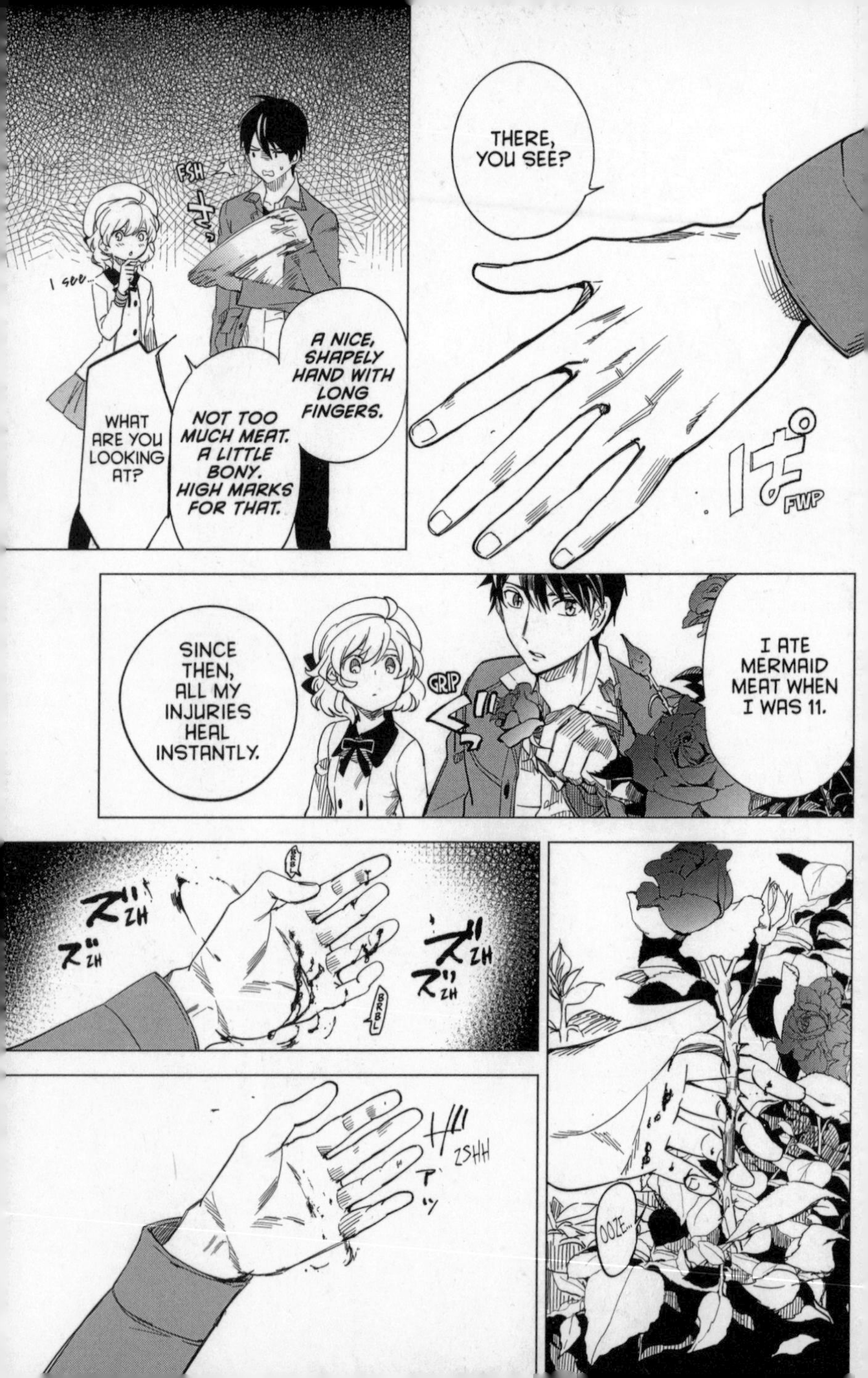

THERE, YOU SEE?
FWP
FSH
I see...
A NICE, SHAPELY HAND WITH LONG FINGERS.
NOT TOO MUCH MEAT. A LITTLE BONY. HIGH MARKS FOR THAT.
WHAT ARE YOU LOOKING AT?
I ATE MERMAID MEAT WHEN I WAS 11.
GRIP
SINCE THEN, ALL MY INJURIES HEAL INSTANTLY.
OOZE...
ZH
ZH
ZH
ZH
BRBL
ZSHH

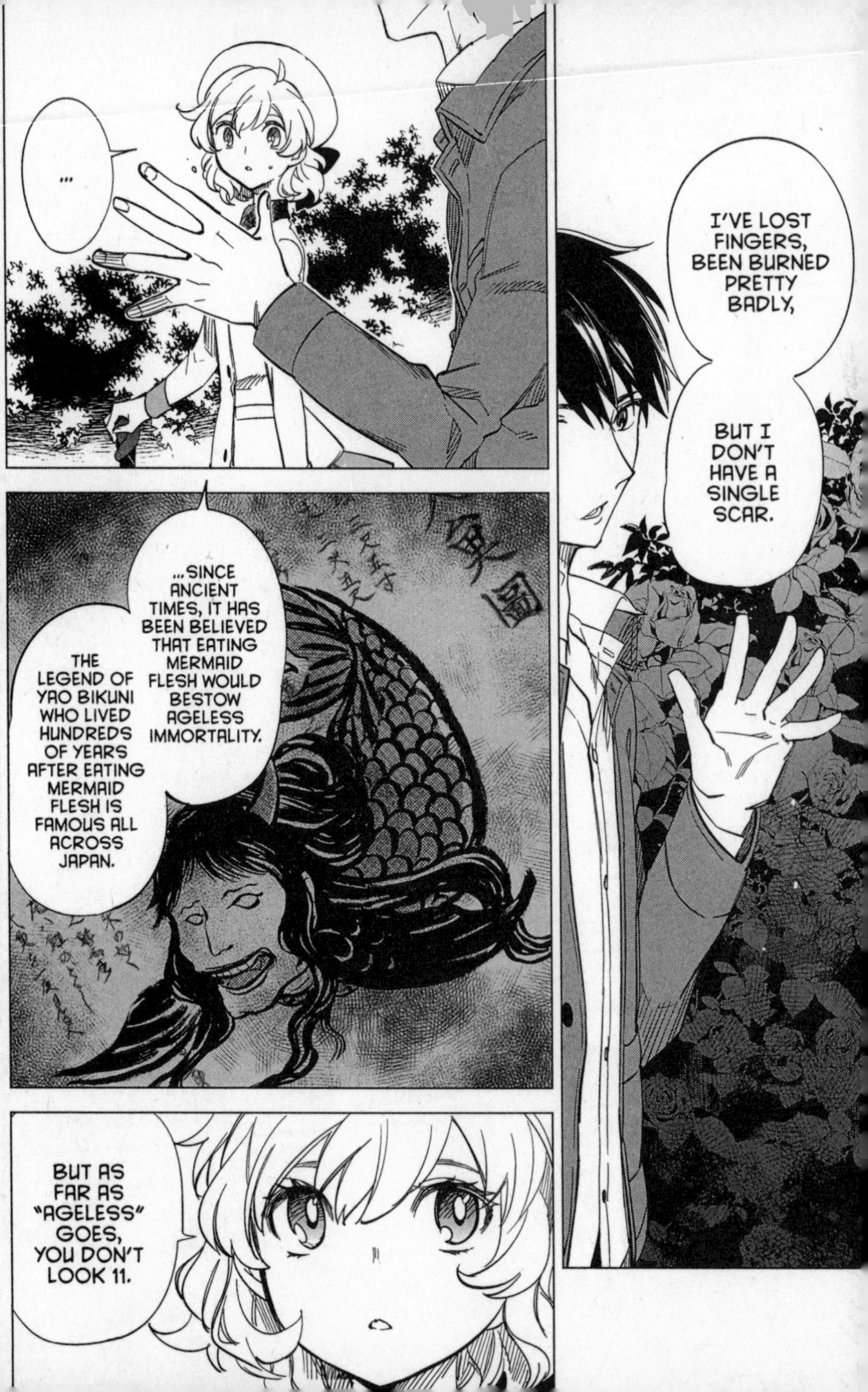
I'VE LOST FINGERS, BEEN BURNED PRETTY BADLY,
BUT I DON'T HAVE A SINGLE SCAR.
...
...SINCE ANCIENT TIMES, IT HAS BEEN BELIEVED THAT EATING MERMAID FLESH WOULD BESTOW AGELESS IMMORTALITY.
THE LEGEND OF YAO BIKUNI WHO LIVED HUNDREDS OF YEARS AFTER EATING MERMAID FLESH IS FAMOUS ALL ACROSS JAPAN.
BUT AS FAR AS "AGELESS" GOES, YOU DON'T LOOK 11.

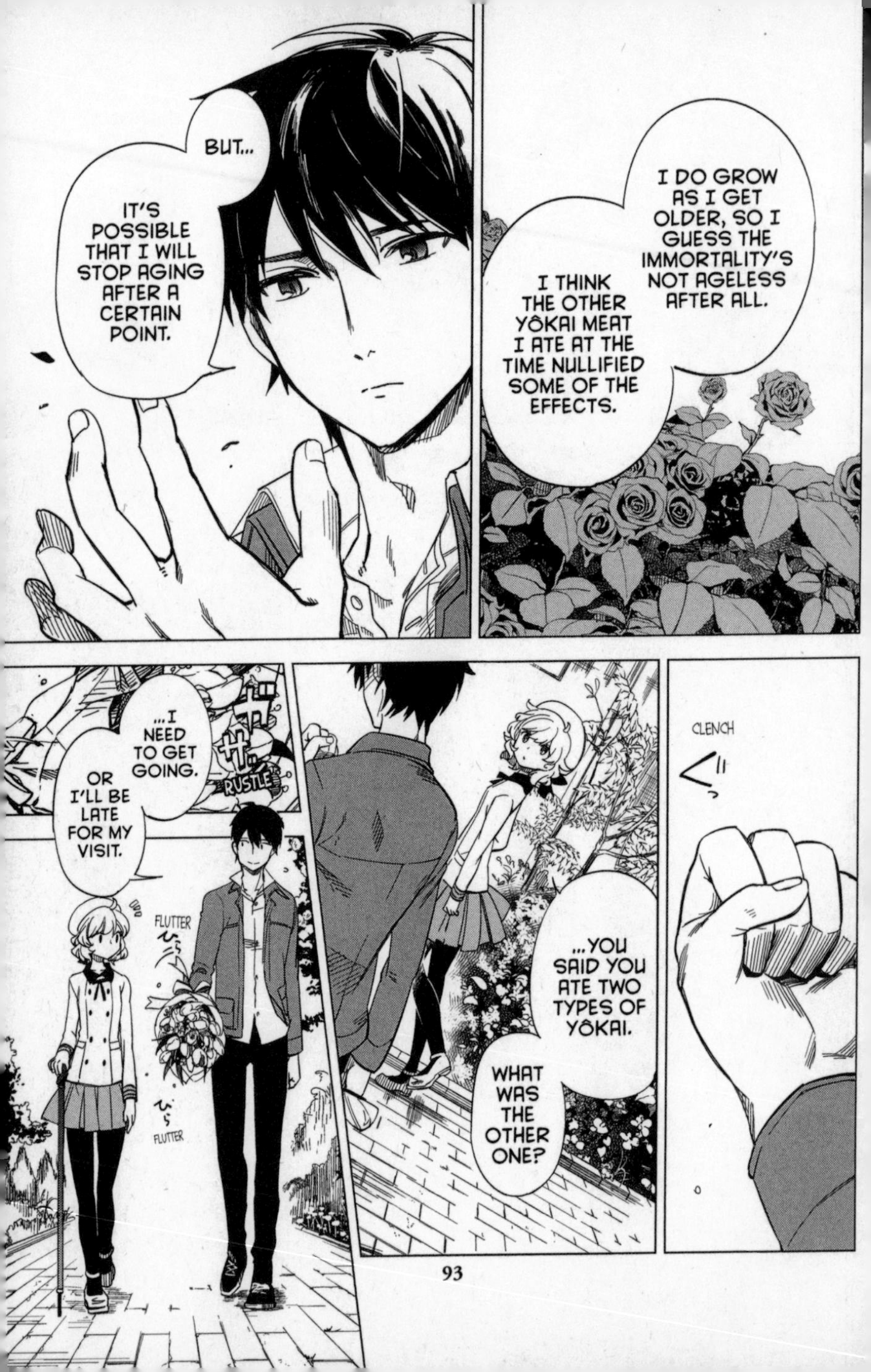
I DO GROW AS I GET OLDER, SO I GUESS THE IMMORTALITY'S NOT AGELESS AFTER ALL.
I THINK THE OTHER YÔKAI MEAT I ATE AT THE TIME NULLIFIED SOME OF THE EFFECTS.
BUT...
IT'S POSSIBLE THAT I WILL STOP AGING AFTER A CERTAIN POINT.
CLENCH
...YOU SAID YOU ATE TWO TYPES OF YÔKAI.
WHAT WAS THE OTHER ONE?
RUSTLE
...I NEED TO GET GOING.
OR I'LL BE LATE FOR MY VISIT.
FLUTTER
FLUTTER

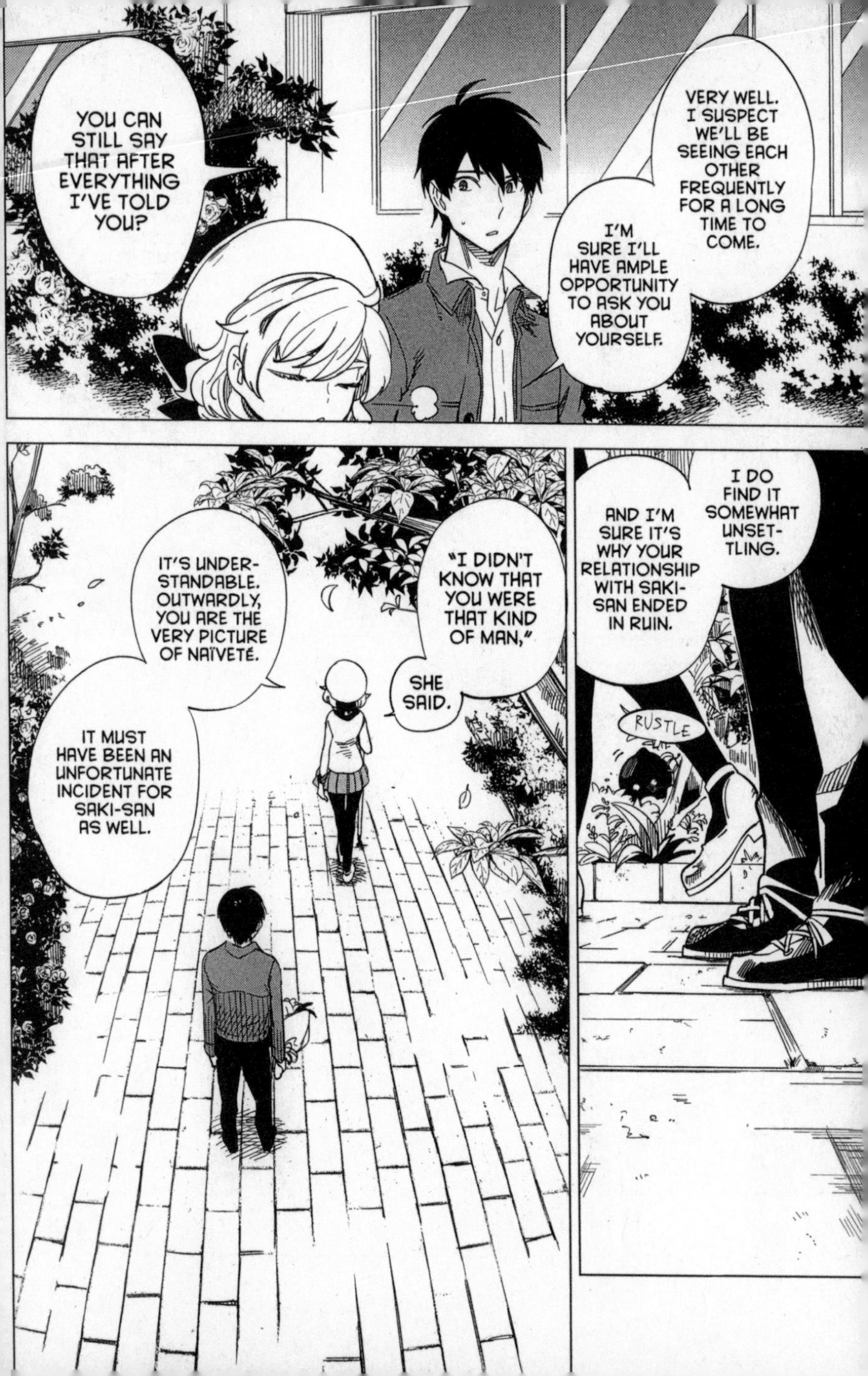
VERY WELL. I SUSPECT WE'LL BE SEEING EACH OTHER FREQUENTLY FOR A LONG TIME TO COME.
I'M SURE I'LL HAVE AMPLE OPPORTUNITY TO ASK YOU ABOUT YOURSELF.
YOU CAN STILL SAY THAT AFTER EVERYTHING I'VE TOLD YOU?
I DO FIND IT SOMEWHAT UNSET-TLING.
AND I'M SURE IT'S WHY YOUR RELATIONSHIP WITH SAKI-SAN ENDED IN RUIN.
RUSTLE
"I DIDN'T KNOW THAT YOU WERE THAT KIND OF MAN,"
SHE SAID.
IT'S UNDER-STANDABLE. OUTWARDLY, YOU ARE THE VERY PICTURE OF NAÏVETÉ.
IT MUST HAVE BEEN AN UNFORTUNATE INCIDENT FOR SAKI-SAN AS WELL.

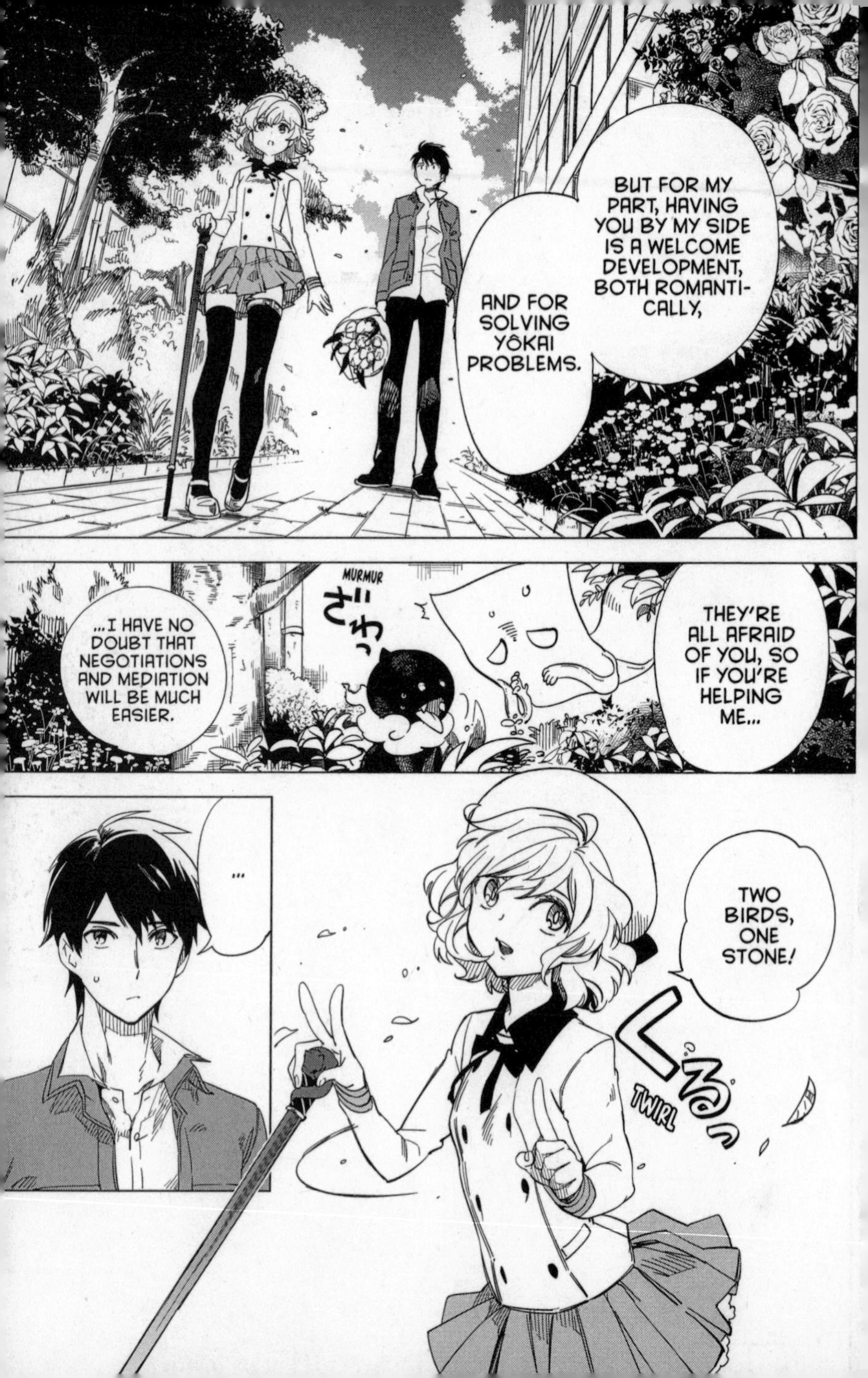
BUT FOR MY PART, HAVING YOU BY MY SIDE IS A WELCOME DEVELOPMENT, BOTH ROMANTI-CALLY,
AND FOR SOLVING YÔKAI PROBLEMS.
THEY'RE ALL AFRAID OF YOU, SO IF YOU'RE HELPING ME...
ざわっ
MURMUR
...I HAVE NO DOUBT THAT NEGOTIATIONS AND MEDIATION WILL BE MUCH EASIER.
TWO BIRDS, ONE STONE!
くるっ
TWIRL
...

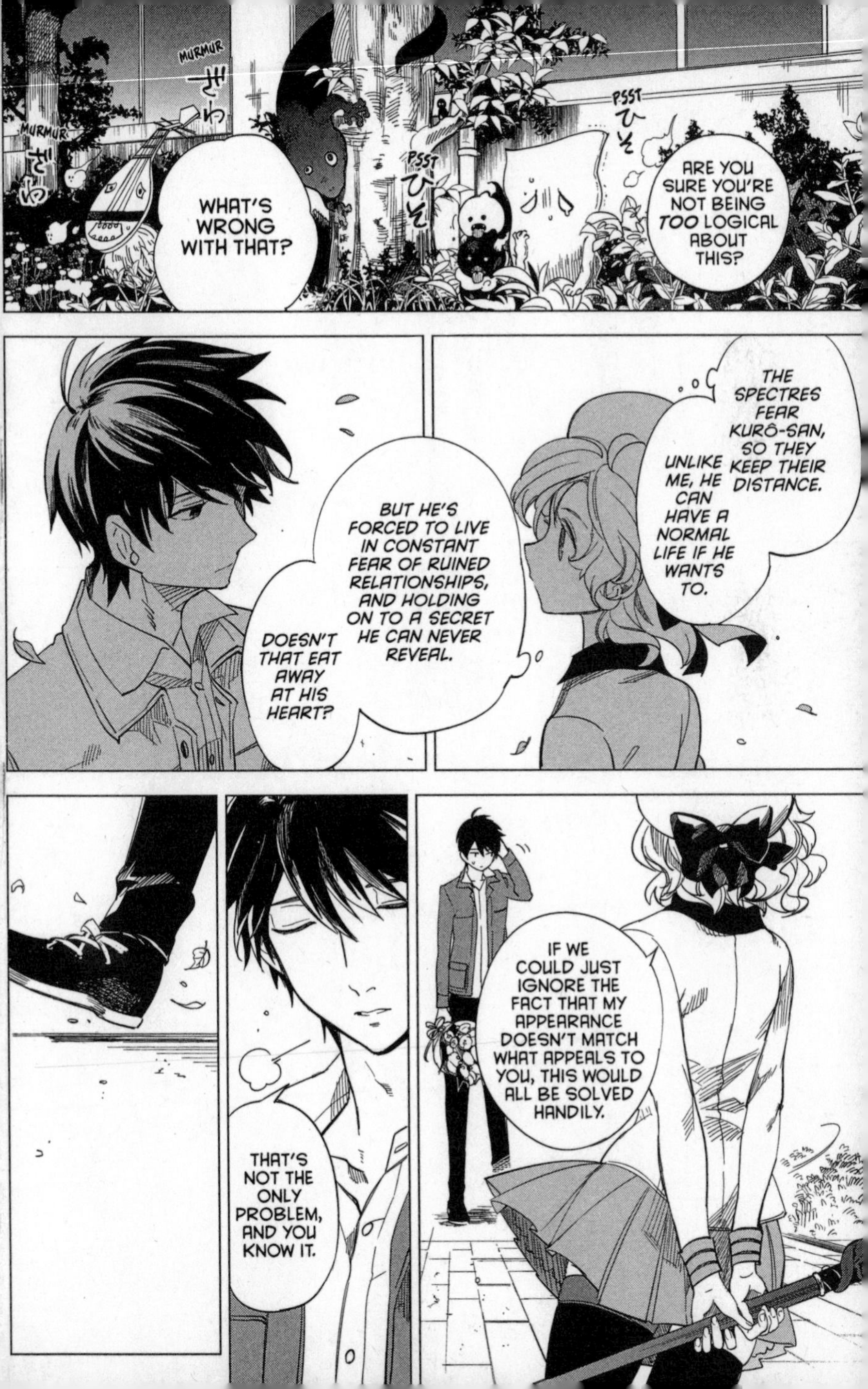
ARE YOU SURE YOU'RE NOT BEING *TOO* LOGICAL ABOUT THIS?
PSST ひそ
PSST ひそ
WHAT'S WRONG WITH THAT?
MURMUR ざわ
MURMUR ざわ
THE SPECTRES FEAR KURÔ-SAN, SO THEY KEEP THEIR DISTANCE.
UNLIKE ME, HE CAN HAVE A NORMAL LIFE IF HE WANTS TO.
BUT HE'S FORCED TO LIVE IN CONSTANT FEAR OF RUINED RELATIONSHIPS, AND HOLDING ON TO A SECRET HE CAN NEVER REVEAL.
DOESN'T THAT EAT AWAY AT HIS HEART?
IF WE COULD JUST IGNORE THE FACT THAT MY APPEARANCE DOESN'T MATCH WHAT APPEALS TO YOU, THIS WOULD ALL BE SOLVED HANDILY.
THAT'S NOT THE ONLY PROBLEM, AND YOU KNOW IT.

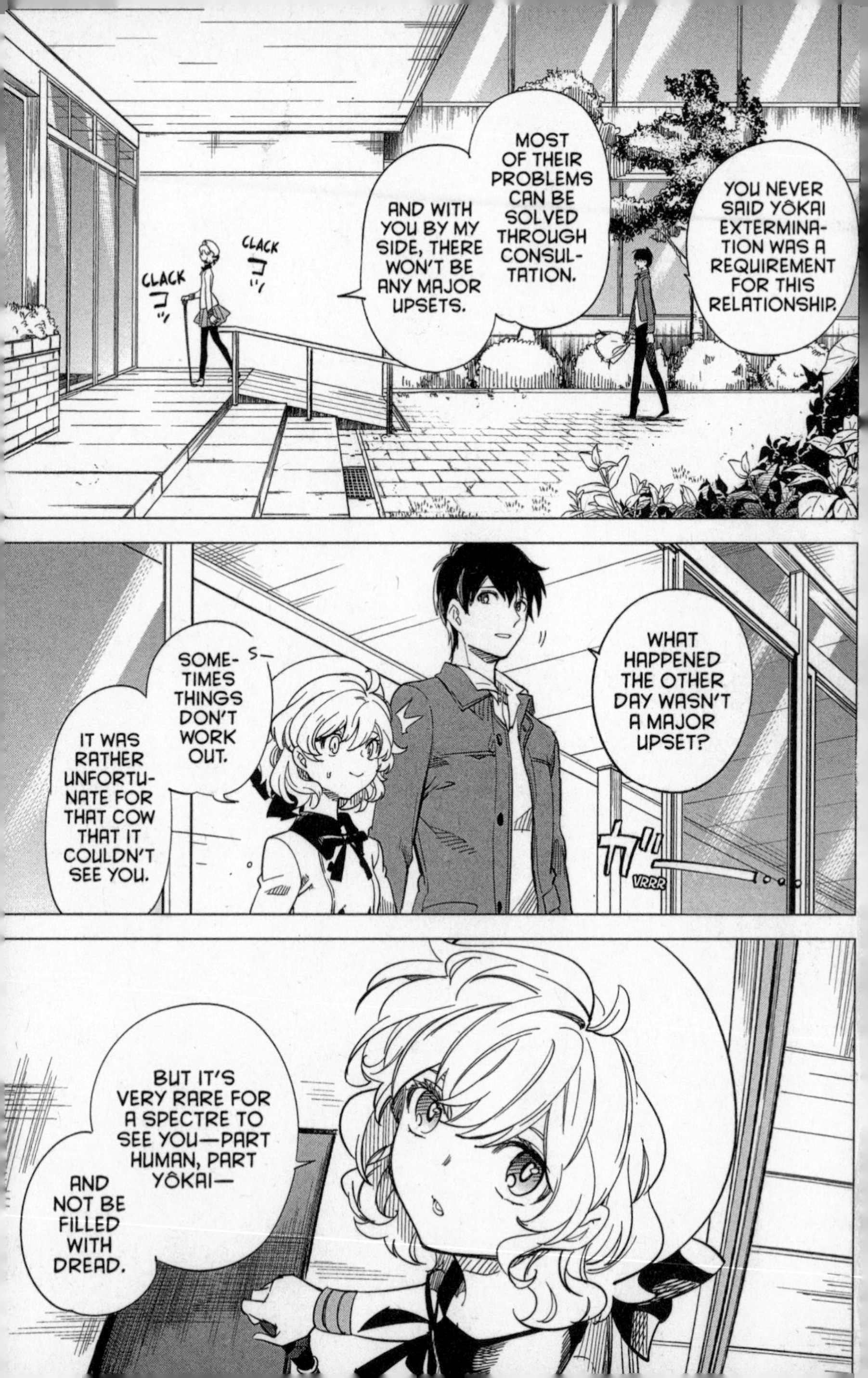
YOU NEVER SAID YÔKAI EXTERMINATION WAS A REQUIREMENT FOR THIS RELATIONSHIP.
MOST OF THEIR PROBLEMS CAN BE SOLVED THROUGH CONSULTATION.
AND WITH YOU BY MY SIDE, THERE WON'T BE ANY MAJOR UPSETS.
CLACK
CLACK
WHAT HAPPENED THE OTHER DAY WASN'T A MAJOR UPSET?
S—
SOMETIMES THINGS DON'T WORK OUT.
IT WAS RATHER UNFORTUNATE FOR THAT COW THAT IT COULDN'T SEE YOU.
VRRR
BUT IT'S VERY RARE FOR A SPECTRE TO SEE YOU—PART HUMAN, PART YÔKAI—
AND NOT BE FILLED WITH DREAD.

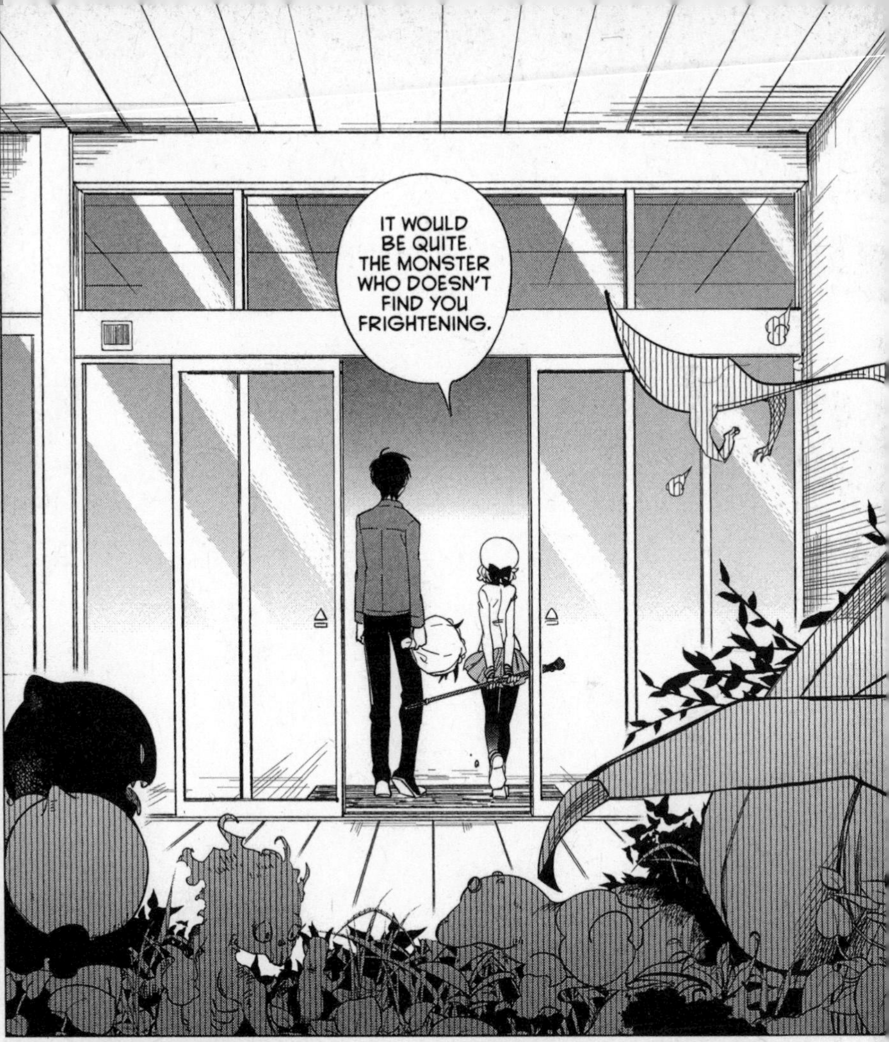
IT WOULD BE QUITE THE MONSTER WHO DOESN'T FIND YOU FRIGHTENING.

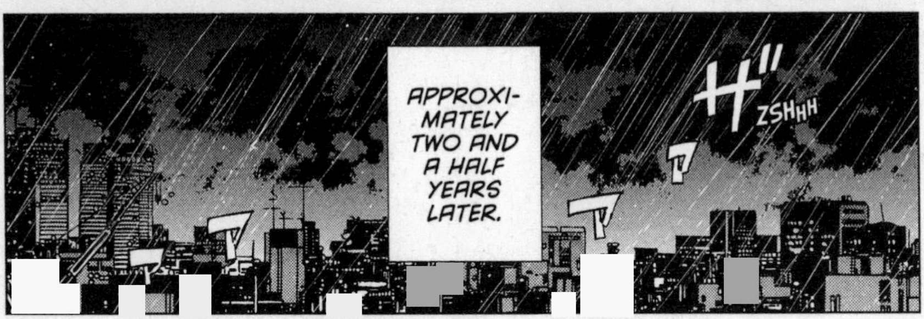
APPROXI-MATELY TWO AND A HALF YEARS LATER.
ZSHHH

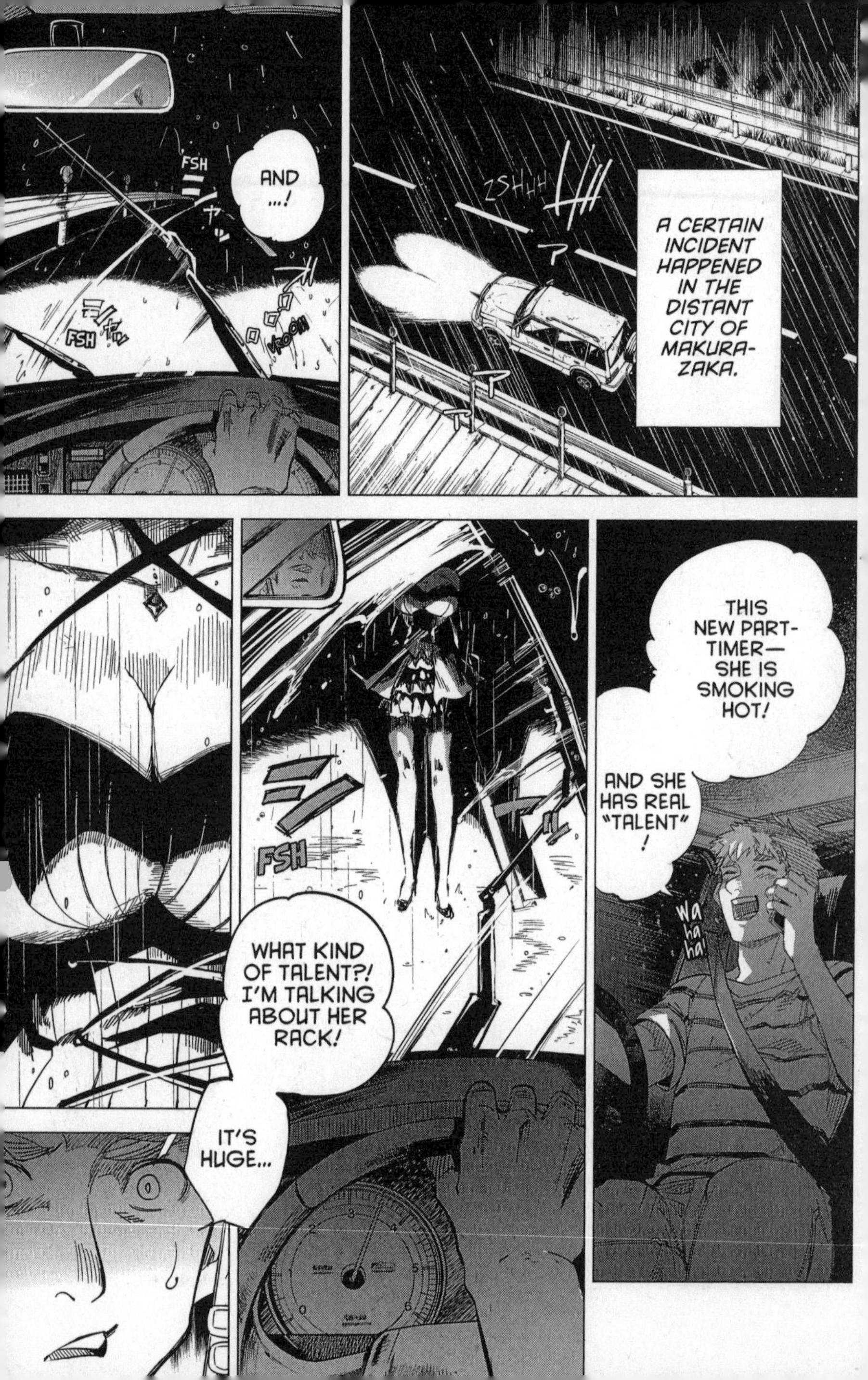
ZSHHH
A CERTAIN INCIDENT HAPPENED IN THE DISTANT CITY OF MAKURA-ZAKA.
FSH
AND ...!
VROOOM
FSH
THIS NEW PART-TIMER— SHE IS SMOKING HOT!
AND SHE HAS REAL "TALENT"!
Wa ha ha!
FSH
WHAT KIND OF TALENT?! I'M TALKING ABOUT HER RACK!
IT'S HUGE...

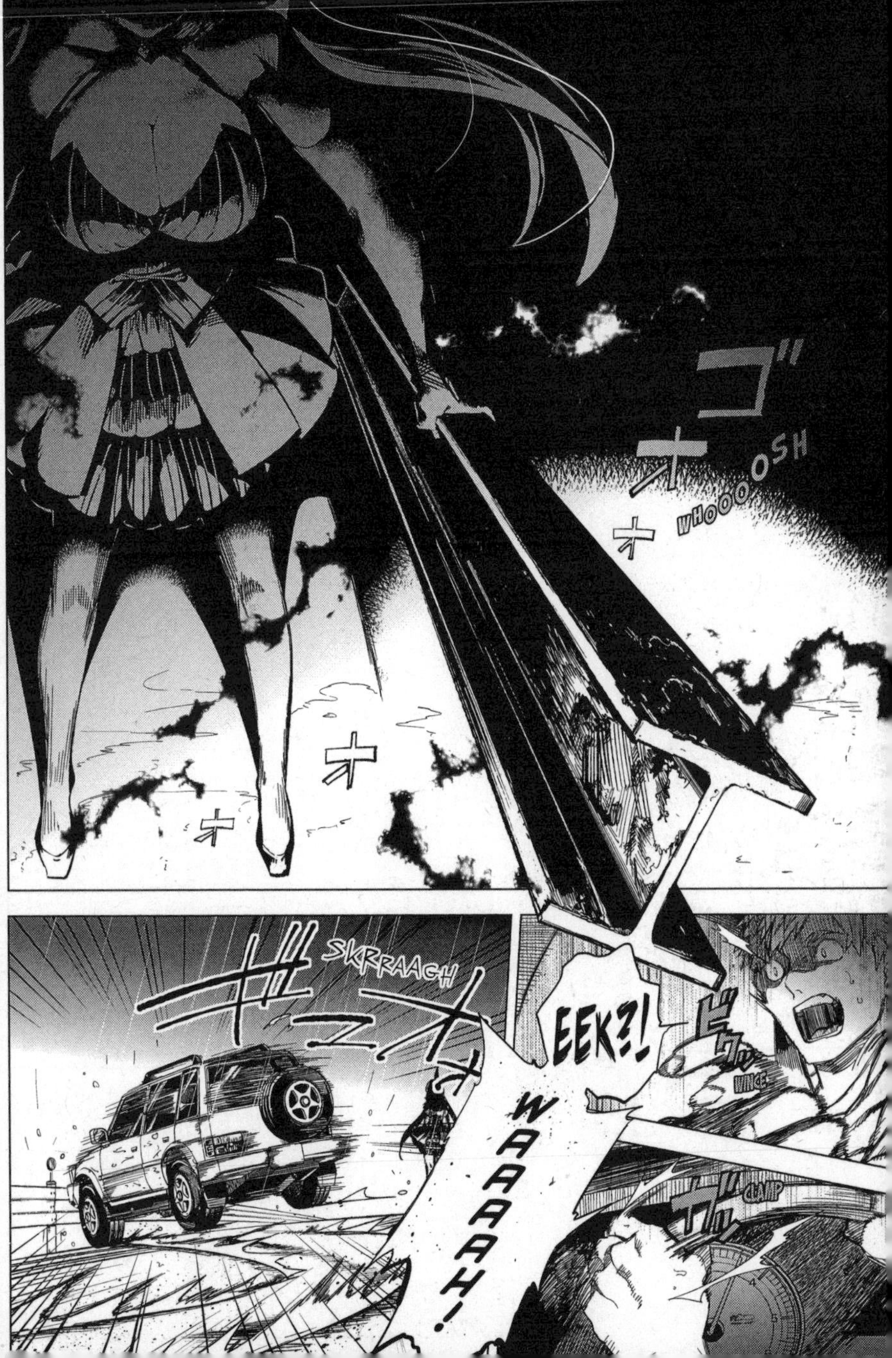
WHOOOOOSH
EEK?!
WINCE
WAAAAAH!
CLAMP
SKRRAAGH

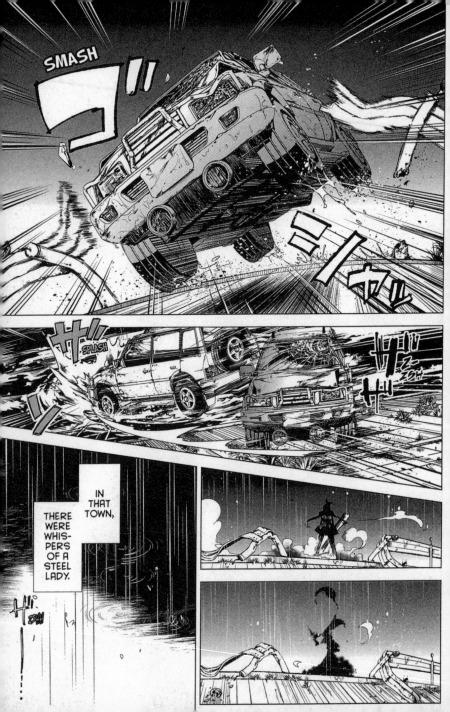

SMASH

IN THAT TOWN,

THERE WERE WHISPERS OF A STEEL LADY.

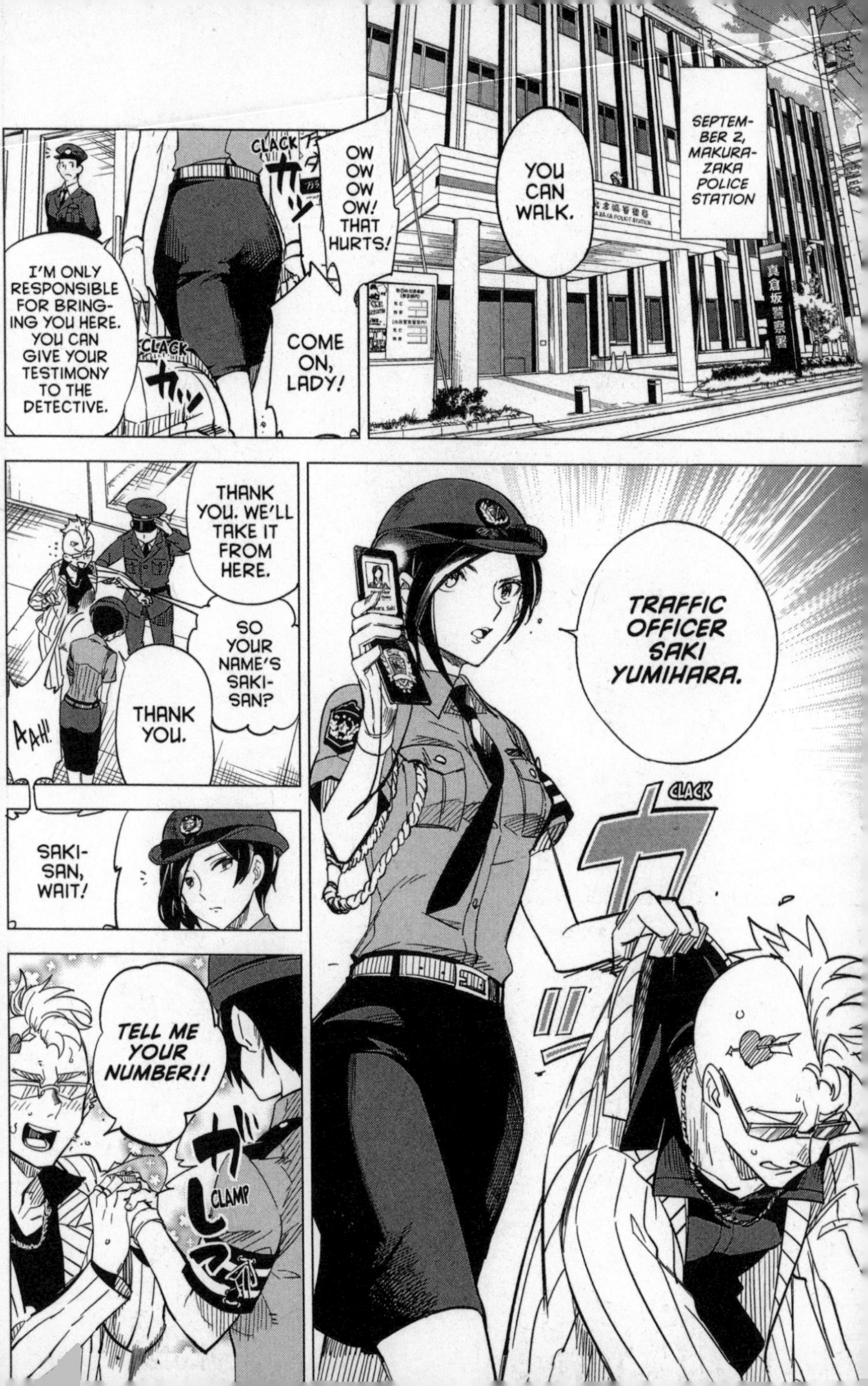
SEPTEMBER 2, MAKURA-ZAKA POLICE STATION
真倉坂警察署
YOU CAN WALK.
OW OW OW OW! THAT HURTS!
CLACK
COME ON, LADY!
I'M ONLY RESPONSIBLE FOR BRINGING YOU HERE. YOU CAN GIVE YOUR TESTIMONY TO THE DETECTIVE.
CLACK
TRAFFIC OFFICER SAKI YUMIHARA.
CLACK
THANK YOU. WE'LL TAKE IT FROM HERE.
SO YOUR NAME'S SAKI-SAN?
THANK YOU.
AAH!
SAKI-SAN, WAIT!
TELL ME YOUR NUMBER!!
CLAMP

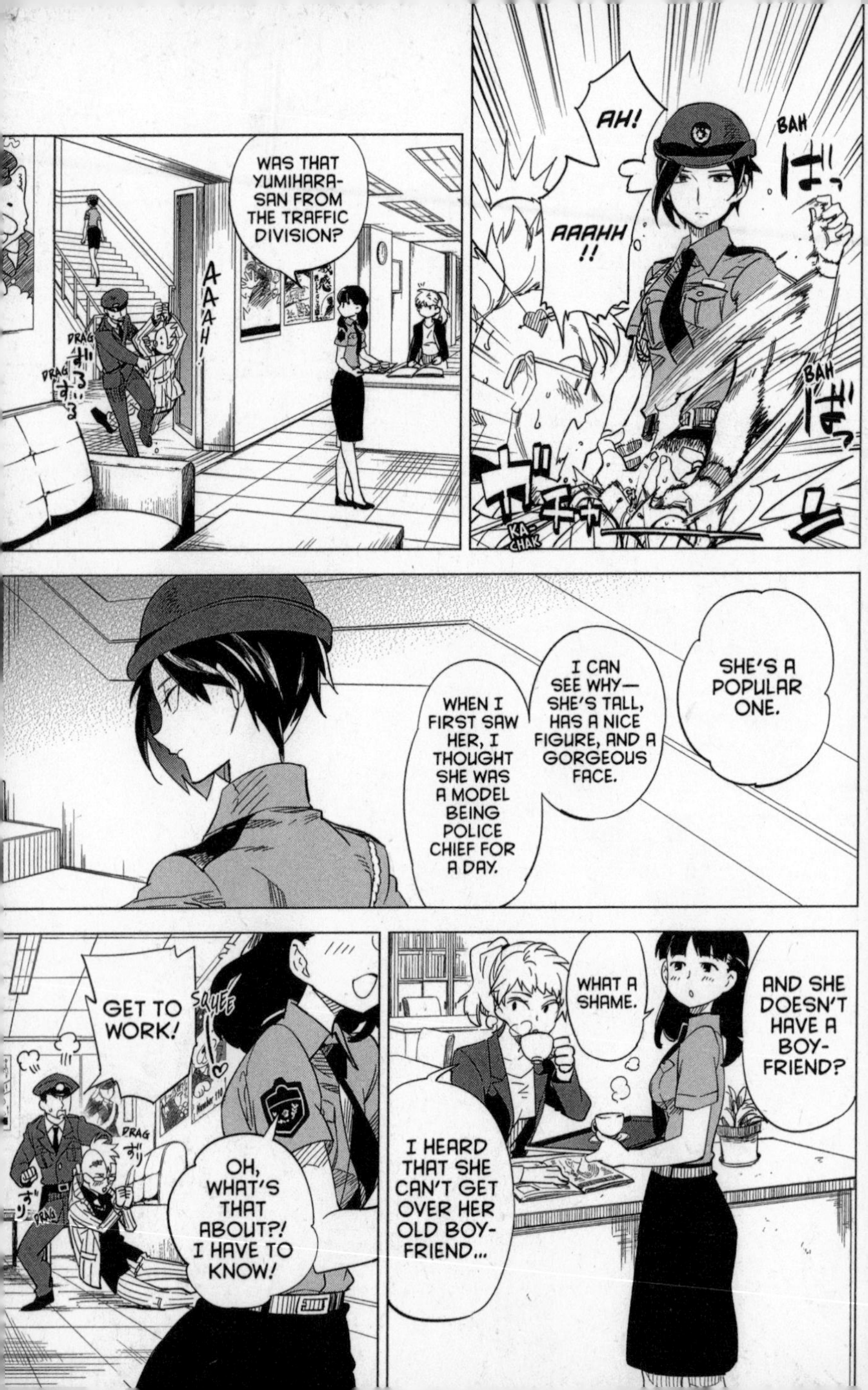
AH!
AAAHH!!
BAH
ばっ
BAH
ばっ
KA-CHAK
WAS THAT YUMIHARA-SAN FROM THE TRAFFIC DIVISION?
AAAAH!
DRAG
DRAG
SHE'S A POPULAR ONE.
I CAN SEE WHY—SHE'S TALL, HAS A NICE FIGURE, AND A GORGEOUS FACE.
WHEN I FIRST SAW HER, I THOUGHT SHE WAS A MODEL BEING POLICE CHIEF FOR A DAY.
AND SHE DOESN'T HAVE A BOY-FRIEND?
WHAT A SHAME.
I HEARD THAT SHE CAN'T GET OVER HER OLD BOY-FRIEND...
OH, WHAT'S THAT ABOUT?! I HAVE TO KNOW!
SQUEE
GET TO WORK!
DRAG
DRAG

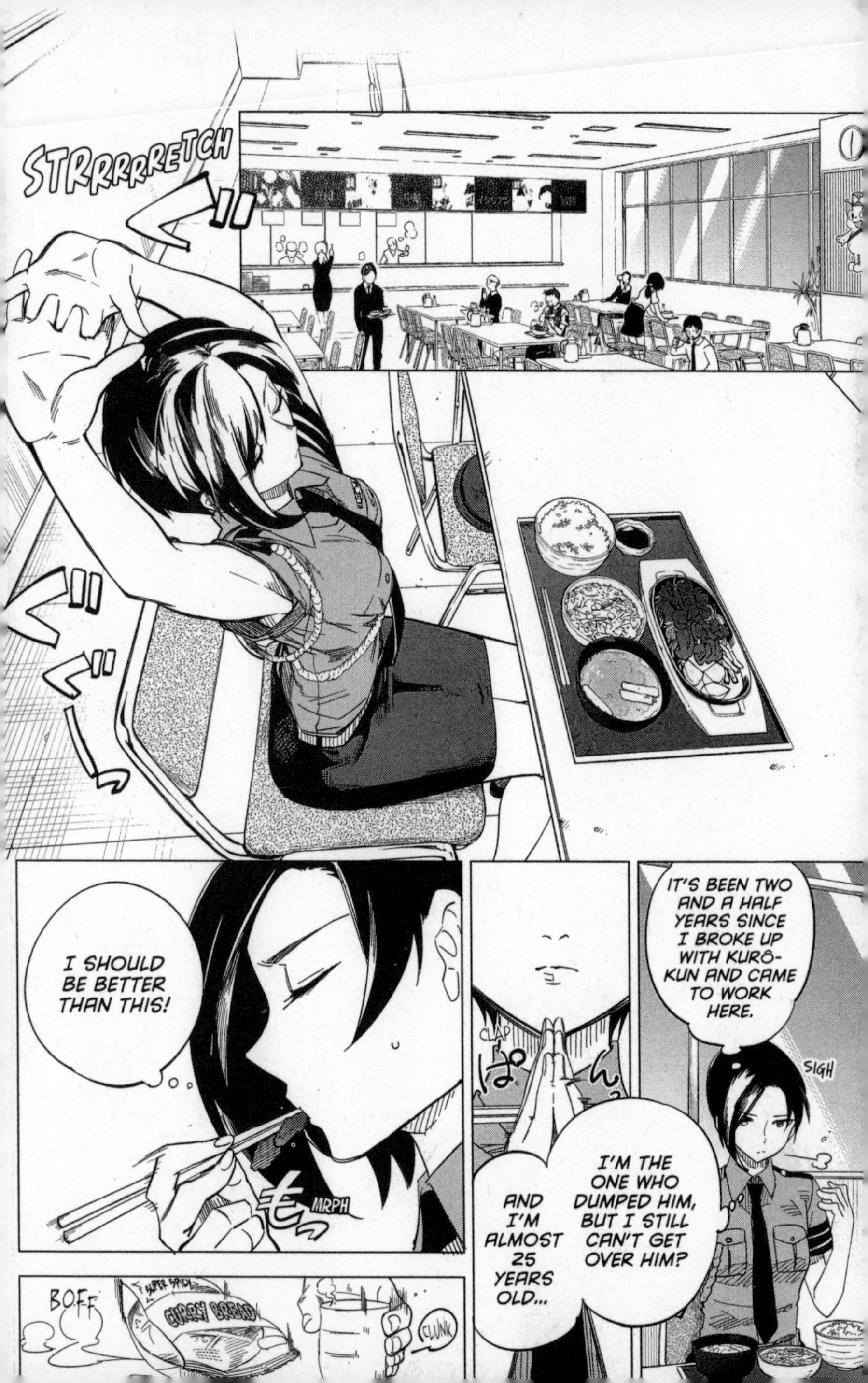

STRRRRRETCH
IT'S BEEN TWO AND A HALF YEARS SINCE I BROKE UP WITH KURÔ-KUN AND CAME TO WORK HERE.
SIGH
I'M THE ONE WHO DUMPED HIM, BUT I STILL CAN'T GET OVER HIM?
AND I'M ALMOST 25 YEARS OLD...
CLAP
I SHOULD BE BETTER THAN THIS!
MRPH
CLUNK
CURRY BREAD
BOFF

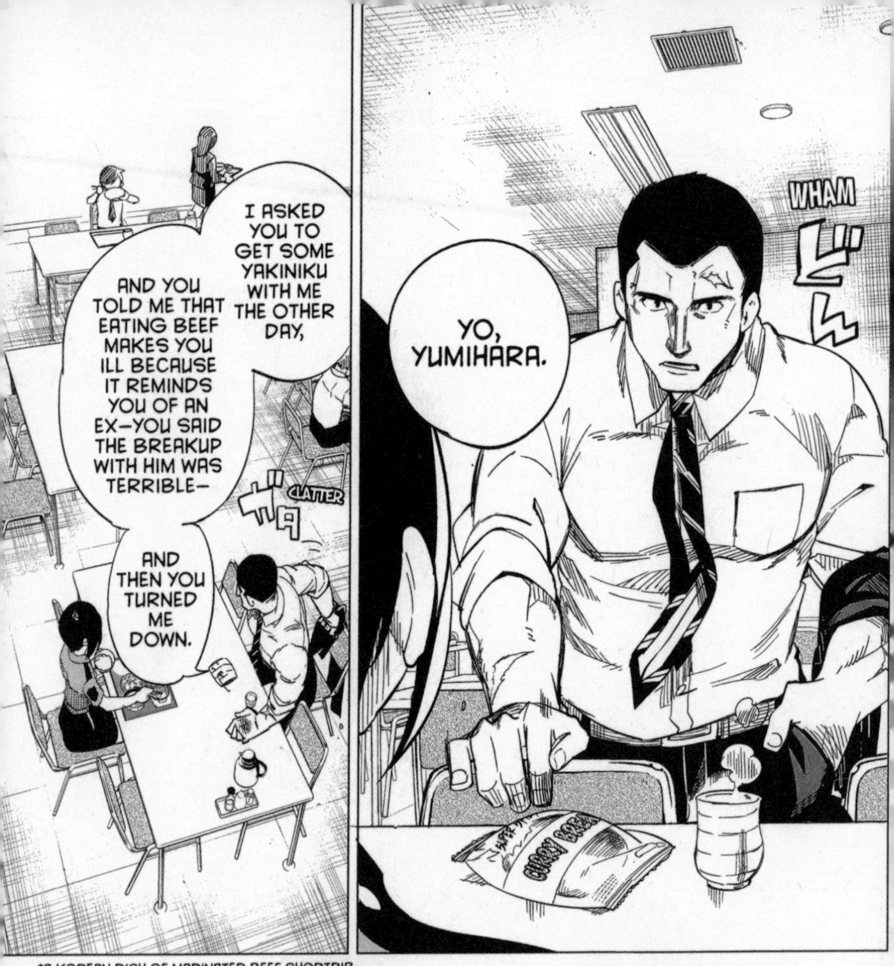
WHAM
YO, YUMIHARA.
I ASKED YOU TO GET SOME YAKINIKU WITH ME THE OTHER DAY,
AND YOU TOLD ME THAT EATING BEEF MAKES YOU ILL BECAUSE IT REMINDS YOU OF AN EX—YOU SAID THE BREAKUP WITH HIM WAS TERRIBLE—
CLATTER
AND THEN YOU TURNED ME DOWN.

*A KOREAN DISH OF MARINATED BEEF SHORTRIB

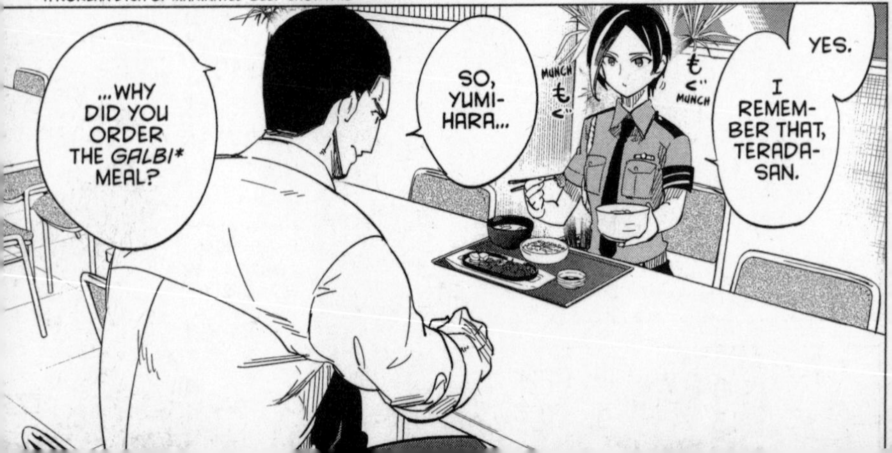
YES.
I REMEMBER THAT, TERADA-SAN.
MUNCH
MUNCH
SO, YUMIHARA...
...WHY DID YOU ORDER THE *GALBI** MEAL?

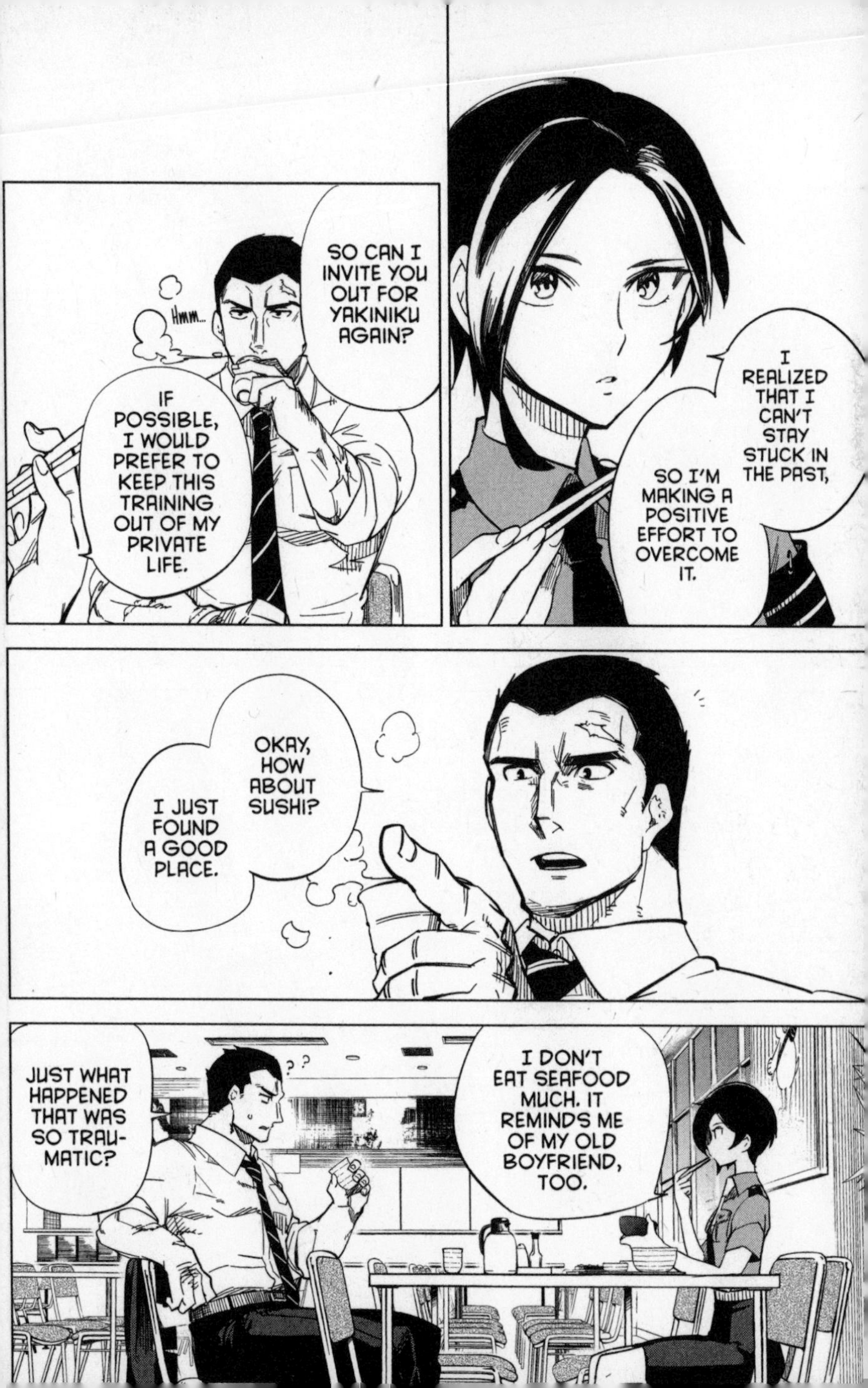
I REALIZED THAT I CAN'T STAY STUCK IN THE PAST,
SO I'M MAKING A POSITIVE EFFORT TO OVERCOME IT.
SO CAN I INVITE YOU OUT FOR YAKINIKU AGAIN?
Hmm...
IF POSSIBLE, I WOULD PREFER TO KEEP THIS TRAINING OUT OF MY PRIVATE LIFE.
OKAY, HOW ABOUT SUSHI?
I JUST FOUND A GOOD PLACE.
I DON'T EAT SEAFOOD MUCH. IT REMINDS ME OF MY OLD BOYFRIEND, TOO.
? ?
JUST WHAT HAPPENED THAT WAS SO TRAU-MATIC?

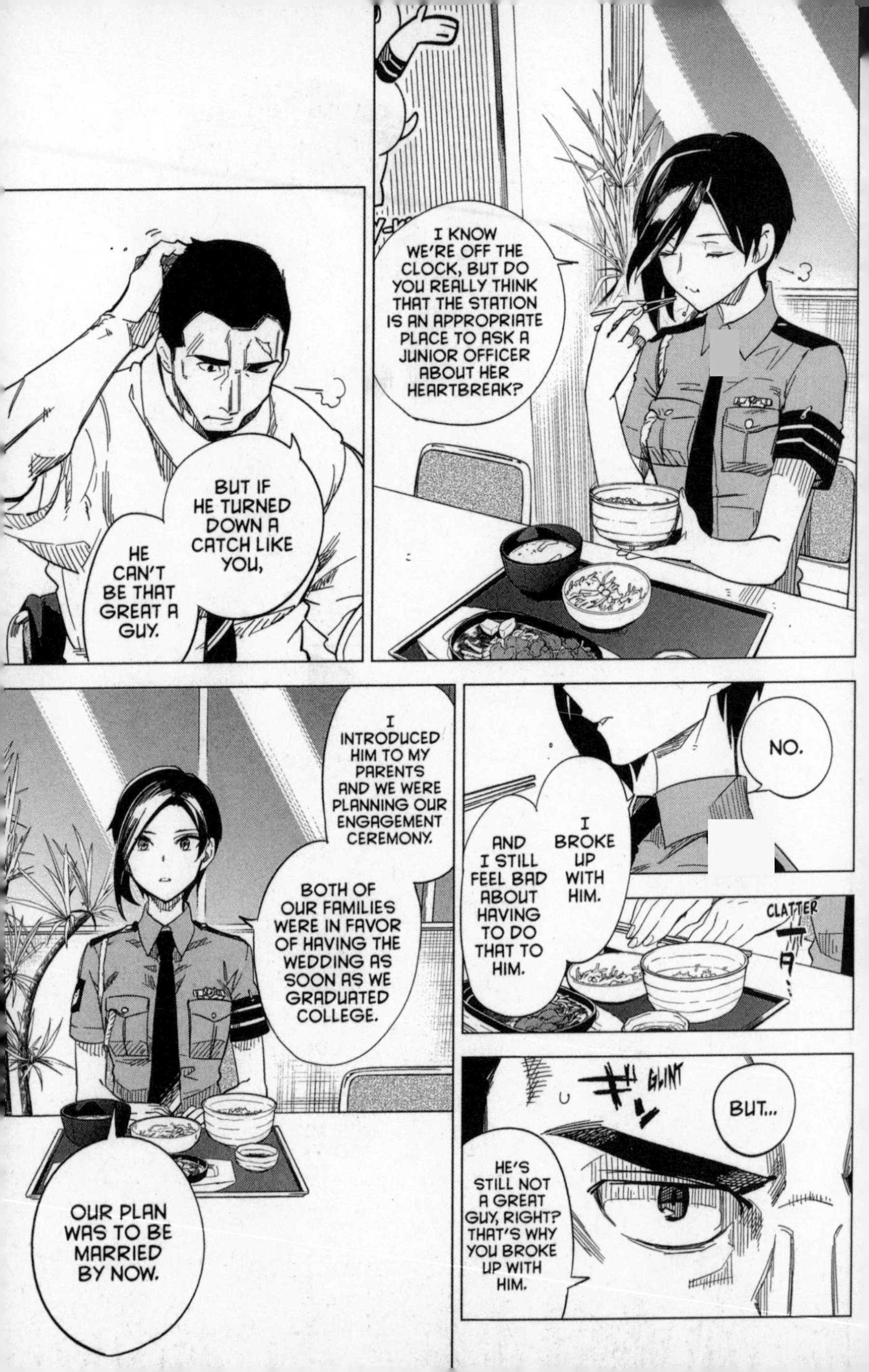
I KNOW WE'RE OFF THE CLOCK, BUT DO YOU REALLY THINK THAT THE STATION IS AN APPROPRIATE PLACE TO ASK A JUNIOR OFFICER ABOUT HER HEARTBREAK?
BUT IF HE TURNED DOWN A CATCH LIKE YOU,
HE CAN'T BE THAT GREAT A GUY.
NO.
I BROKE UP WITH HIM.
AND I STILL FEEL BAD ABOUT HAVING TO DO THAT TO HIM.
CLATTER
GLINT
BUT...
HE'S STILL NOT A GREAT GUY, RIGHT? THAT'S WHY YOU BROKE UP WITH HIM.
I INTRODUCED HIM TO MY PARENTS AND WE WERE PLANNING OUR ENGAGEMENT CEREMONY.
BOTH OF OUR FAMILIES WERE IN FAVOR OF HAVING THE WEDDING AS SOON AS WE GRADUATED COLLEGE.
OUR PLAN WAS TO BE MARRIED BY NOW.

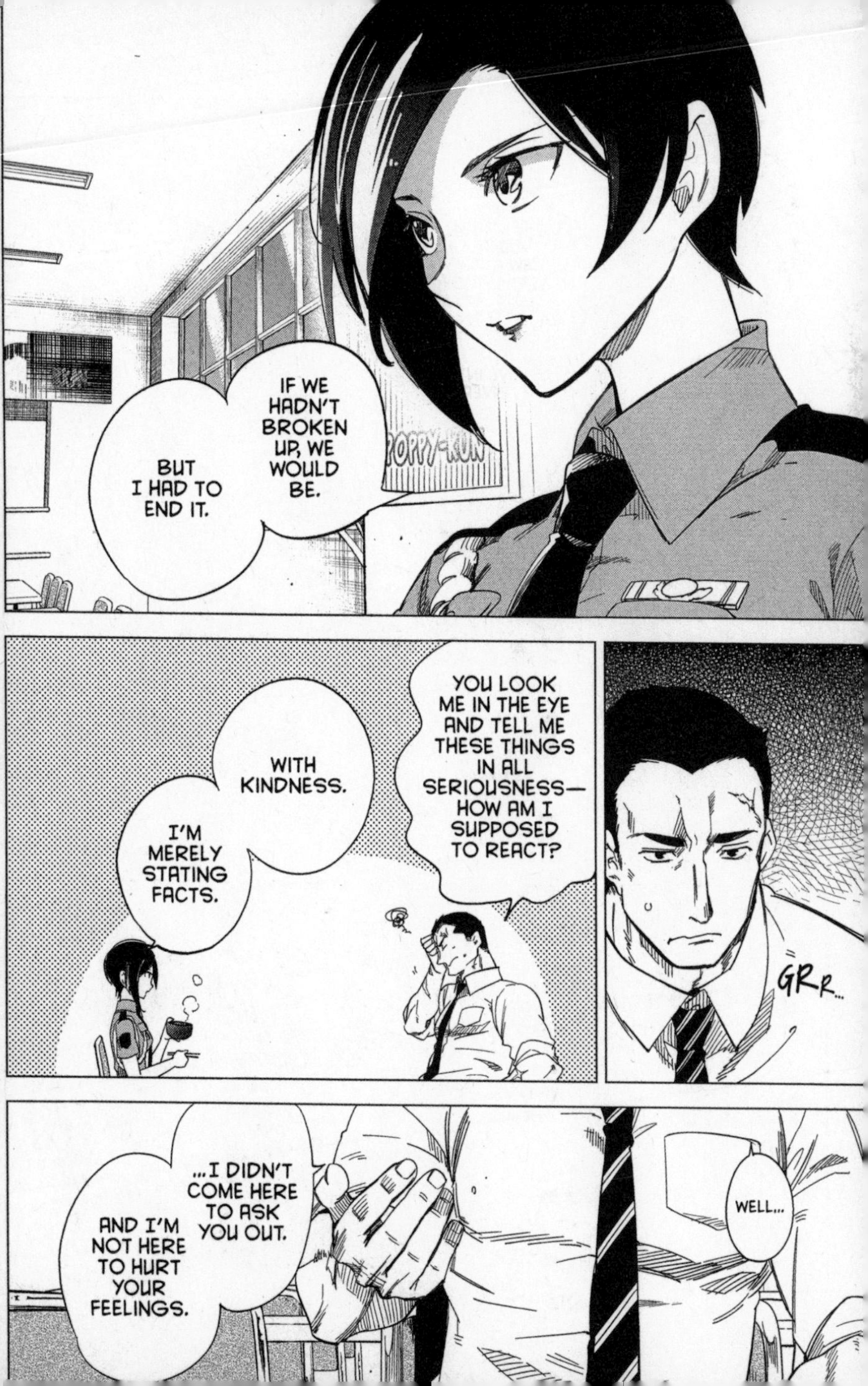
IF WE HADN'T BROKEN UP, WE WOULD BE.
BUT I HAD TO END IT.
GRr...
YOU LOOK ME IN THE EYE AND TELL ME THESE THINGS IN ALL SERIOUSNESS— HOW AM I SUPPOSED TO REACT?
WITH KINDNESS.
I'M MERELY STATING FACTS.
WELL...
...I DIDN'T COME HERE TO ASK YOU OUT.
AND I'M NOT HERE TO HURT YOUR FEELINGS.

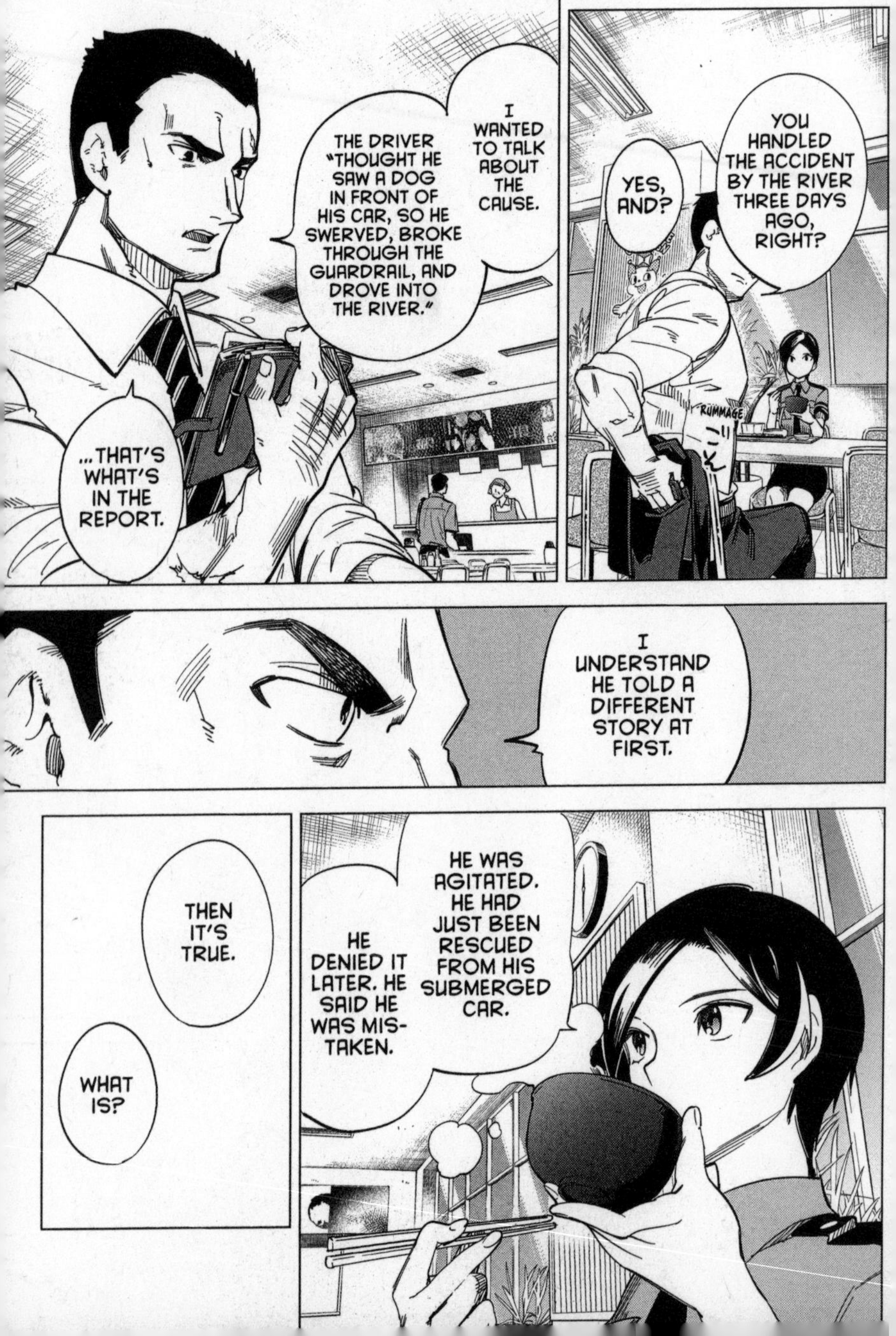

YOU HANDLED THE ACCIDENT BY THE RIVER THREE DAYS AGO, RIGHT?
YES, AND?
RUMMAGE
I WANTED TO TALK ABOUT THE CAUSE.
THE DRIVER "THOUGHT HE SAW A DOG IN FRONT OF HIS CAR, SO HE SWERVED, BROKE THROUGH THE GUARDRAIL, AND DROVE INTO THE RIVER."
...THAT'S WHAT'S IN THE REPORT.
I UNDERSTAND HE TOLD A DIFFERENT STORY AT FIRST.
HE WAS AGITATED. HE HAD JUST BEEN RESCUED FROM HIS SUBMERGED CAR.
HE DENIED IT LATER. HE SAID HE WAS MIS-TAKEN.
THEN IT'S TRUE.
WHAT IS?

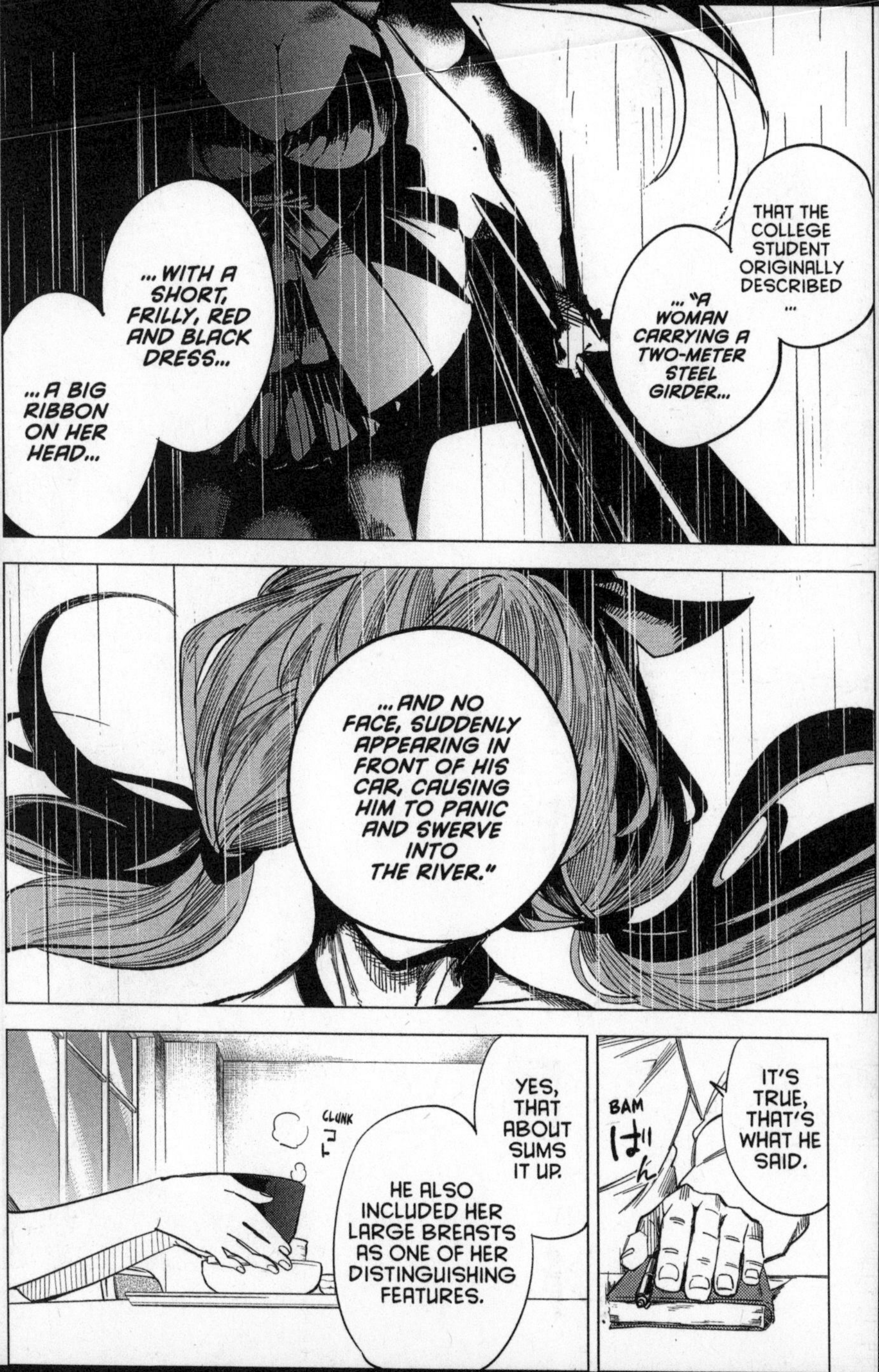
THAT THE COLLEGE STUDENT ORIGINALLY DESCRIBED ...
..."A WOMAN CARRYING A TWO-METER STEEL GIRDER...
...WITH A SHORT, FRILLY, RED AND BLACK DRESS...
...A BIG RIBBON ON HER HEAD...
...AND NO FACE, SUDDENLY APPEARING IN FRONT OF HIS CAR, CAUSING HIM TO PANIC AND SWERVE INTO THE RIVER."
IT'S TRUE, THAT'S WHAT HE SAID.
BAM
ばん
YES, THAT ABOUT SUMS IT UP.
HE ALSO INCLUDED HER LARGE BREASTS AS ONE OF HER DISTINGUISHING FEATURES.
CLUNK

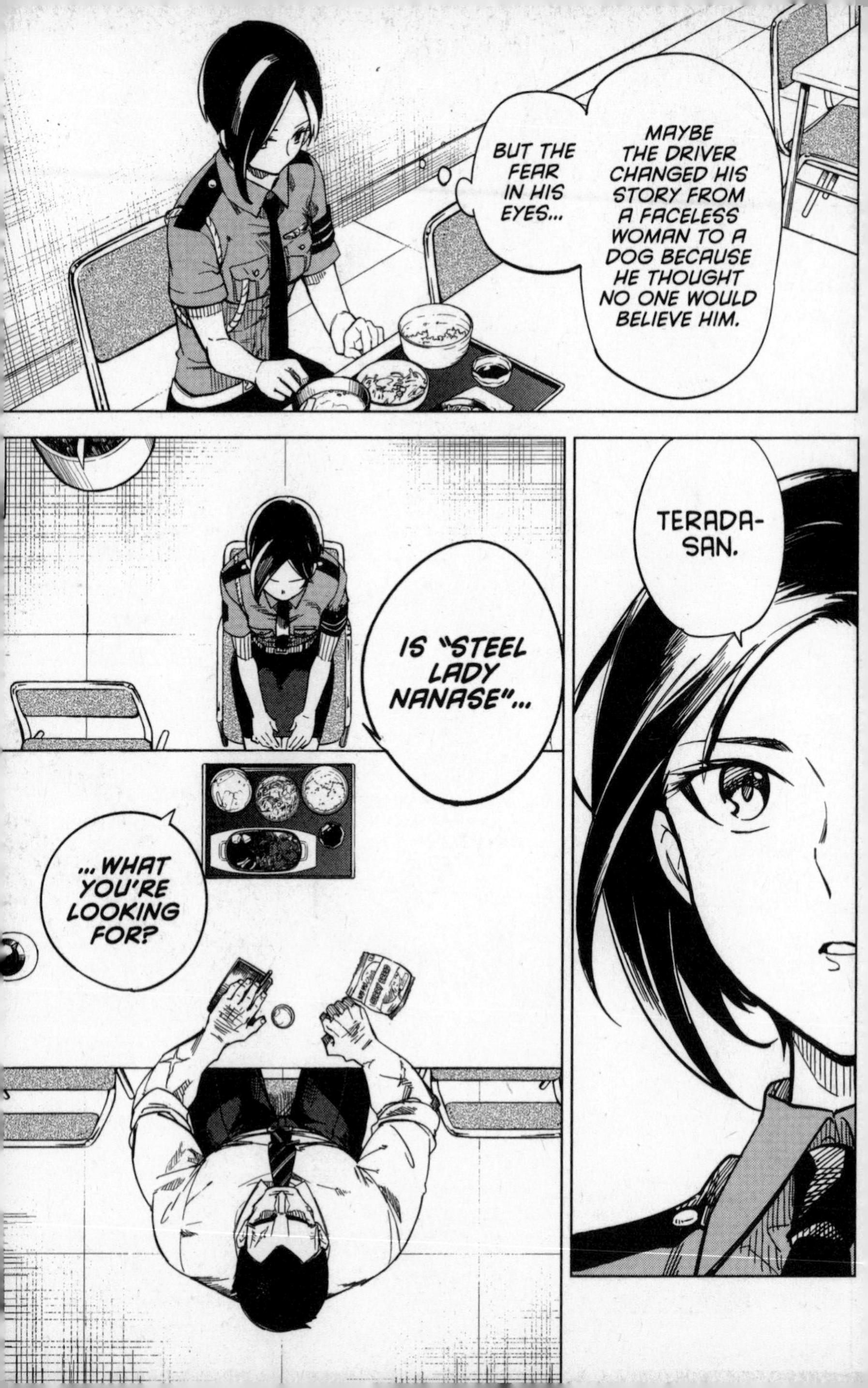
MAYBE THE DRIVER CHANGED HIS STORY FROM A FACELESS WOMAN TO A DOG BECAUSE HE THOUGHT NO ONE WOULD BELIEVE HIM.
BUT THE FEAR IN HIS EYES...
TERADA-SAN.
IS "STEEL LADY NANASE"...
...WHAT YOU'RE LOOKING FOR?

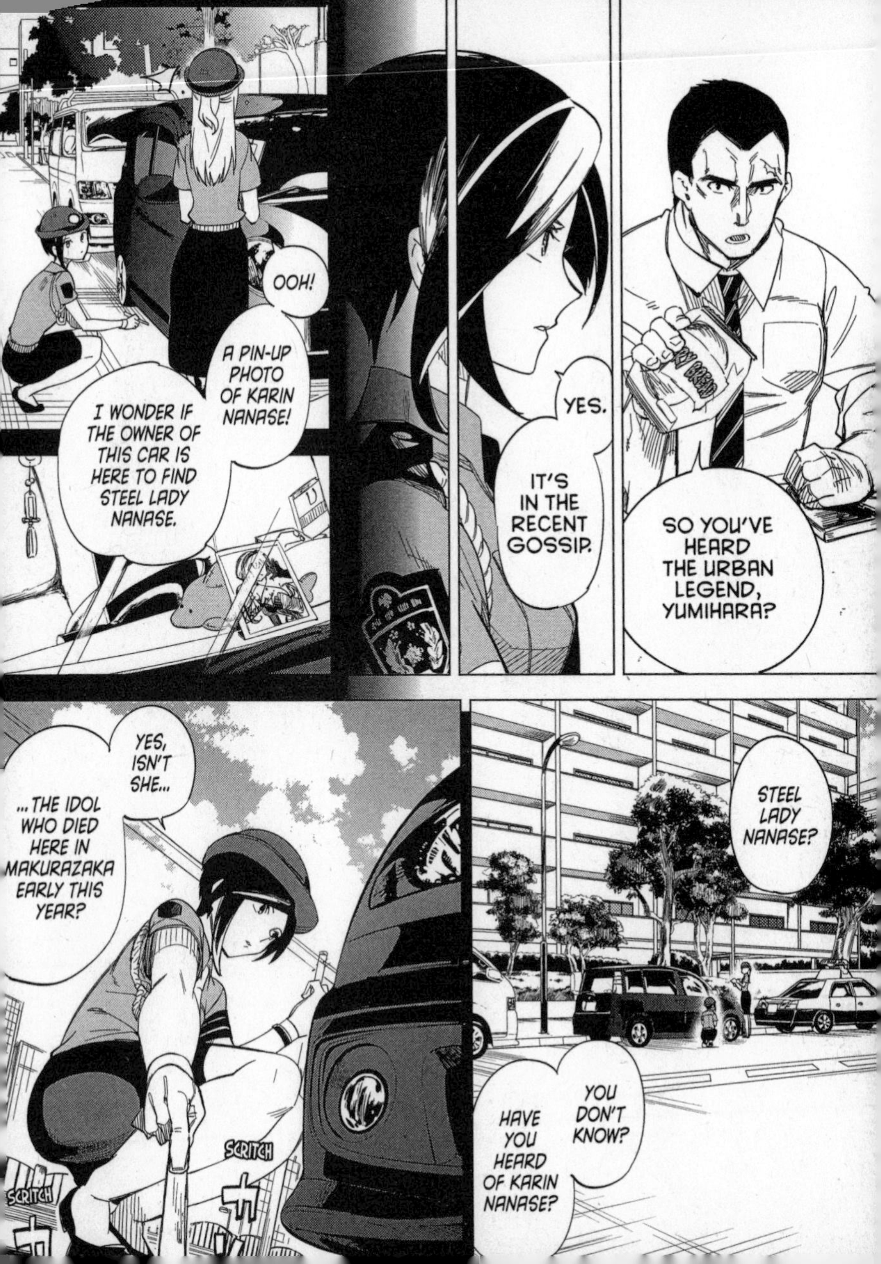
SO YOU'VE HEARD THE URBAN LEGEND, YUMIHARA?
YES.
IT'S IN THE RECENT GOSSIP.
OOH!
A PIN-UP PHOTO OF KARIN NANASE!
I WONDER IF THE OWNER OF THIS CAR IS HERE TO FIND STEEL LADY NANASE.
STEEL LADY NANASE?
YOU DON'T KNOW?
HAVE YOU HEARD OF KARIN NANASE?
YES, ISN'T SHE...
...THE IDOL WHO DIED HERE IN MAKURAZAKA EARLY THIS YEAR?
SCRITCH
SCRITCH

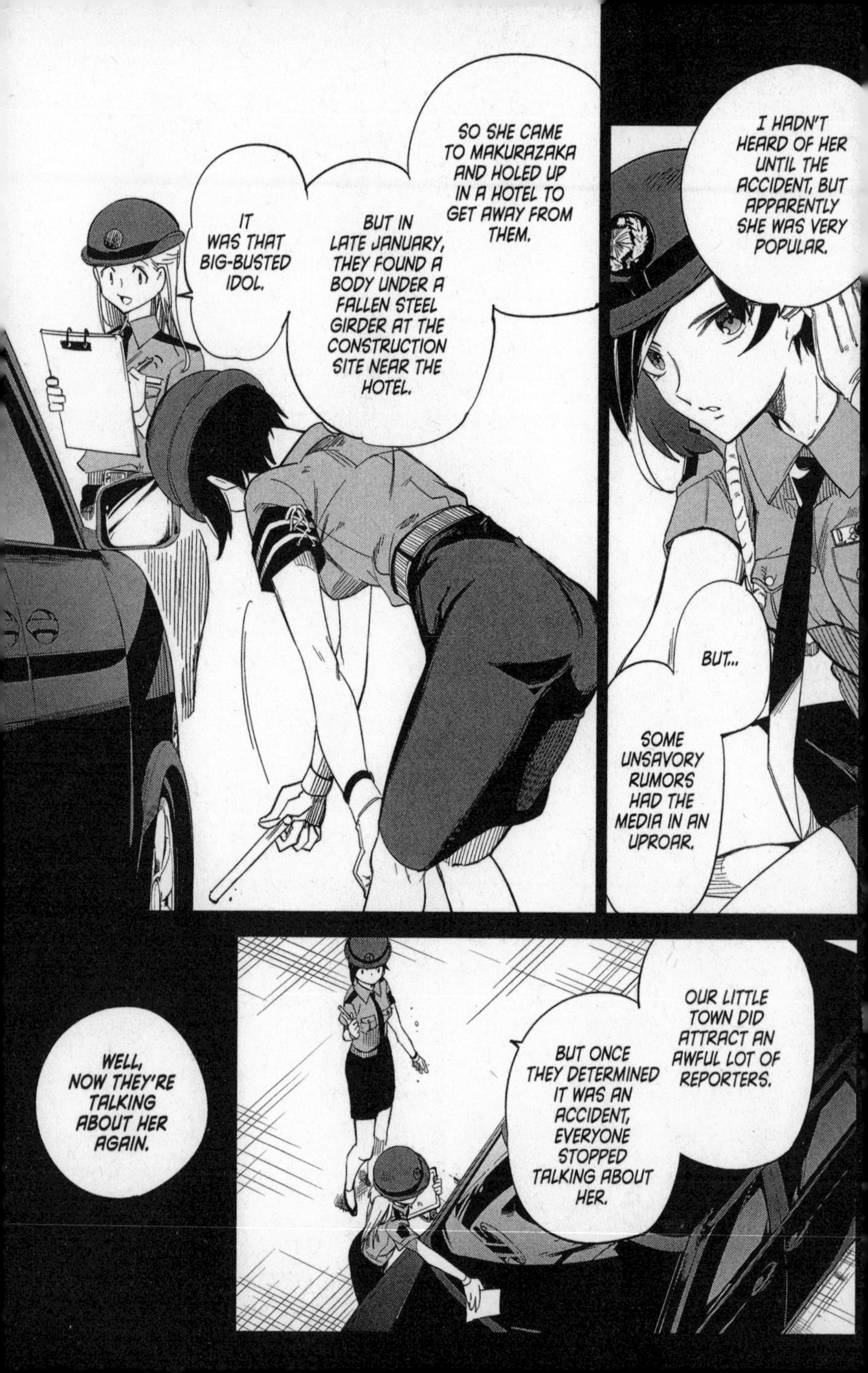
I HADN'T HEARD OF HER UNTIL THE ACCIDENT, BUT APPARENTLY SHE WAS VERY POPULAR.
BUT...
SOME UNSAVORY RUMORS HAD THE MEDIA IN AN UPROAR.
SO SHE CAME TO MAKURAZAKA AND HOLED UP IN A HOTEL TO GET AWAY FROM THEM.
BUT IN LATE JANUARY, THEY FOUND A BODY UNDER A FALLEN STEEL GIRDER AT THE CONSTRUCTION SITE NEAR THE HOTEL.
IT WAS THAT BIG-BUSTED IDOL.
OUR LITTLE TOWN DID ATTRACT AN AWFUL LOT OF REPORTERS.
BUT ONCE THEY DETERMINED IT WAS AN ACCIDENT, EVERYONE STOPPED TALKING ABOUT HER.
WELL, NOW THEY'RE TALKING ABOUT HER AGAIN.

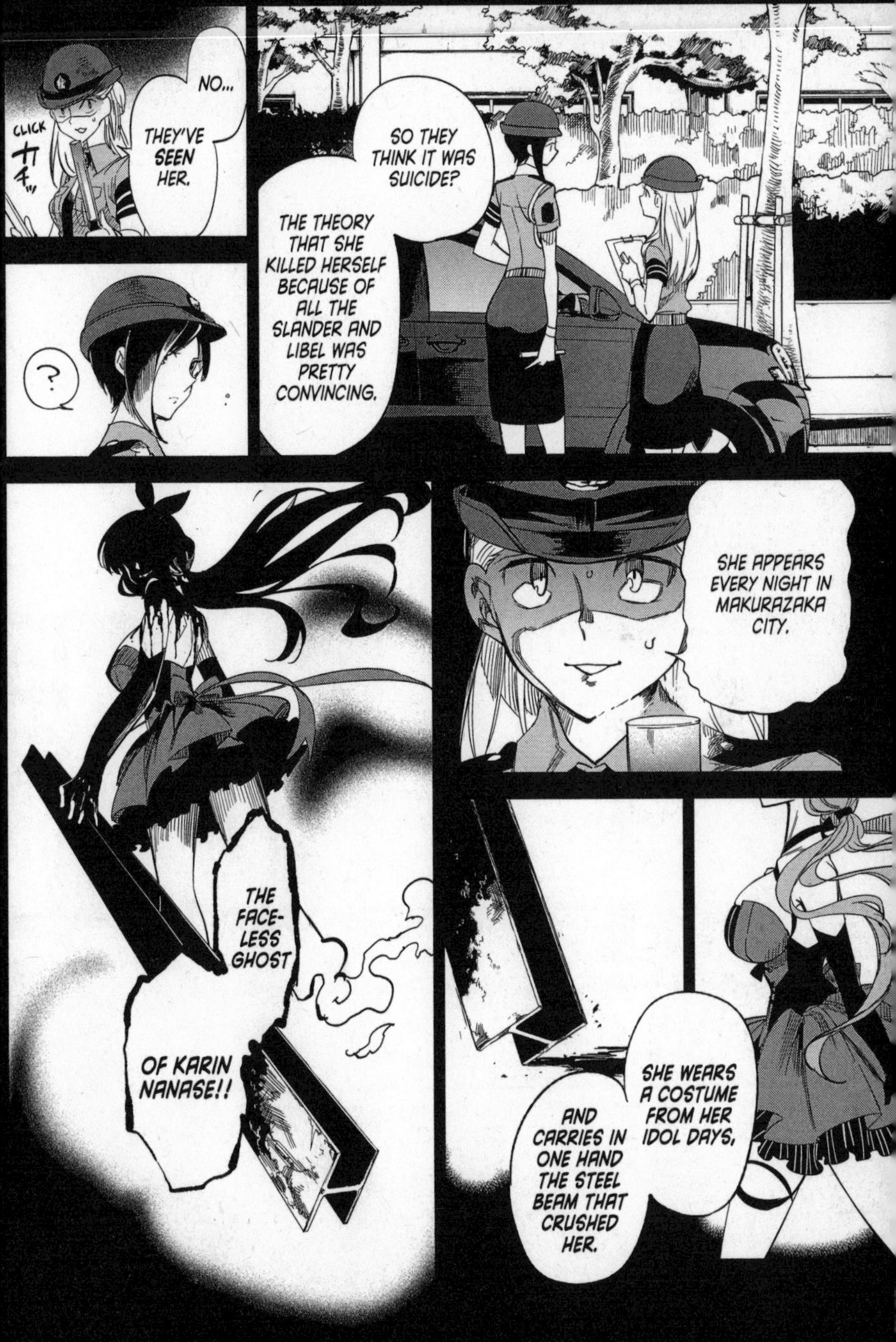
SO THEY THINK IT WAS SUICIDE?
THE THEORY THAT SHE KILLED HERSELF BECAUSE OF ALL THE SLANDER AND LIBEL WAS PRETTY CONVINCING.
NO...
THEY'VE SEEN HER.
CLICK
ガチッ
?
SHE APPEARS EVERY NIGHT IN MAKURAZAKA CITY.
SHE WEARS A COSTUME FROM HER IDOL DAYS,
AND CARRIES IN ONE HAND THE STEEL BEAM THAT CRUSHED HER.
THE FACE-LESS GHOST
OF KARIN NANASE!!

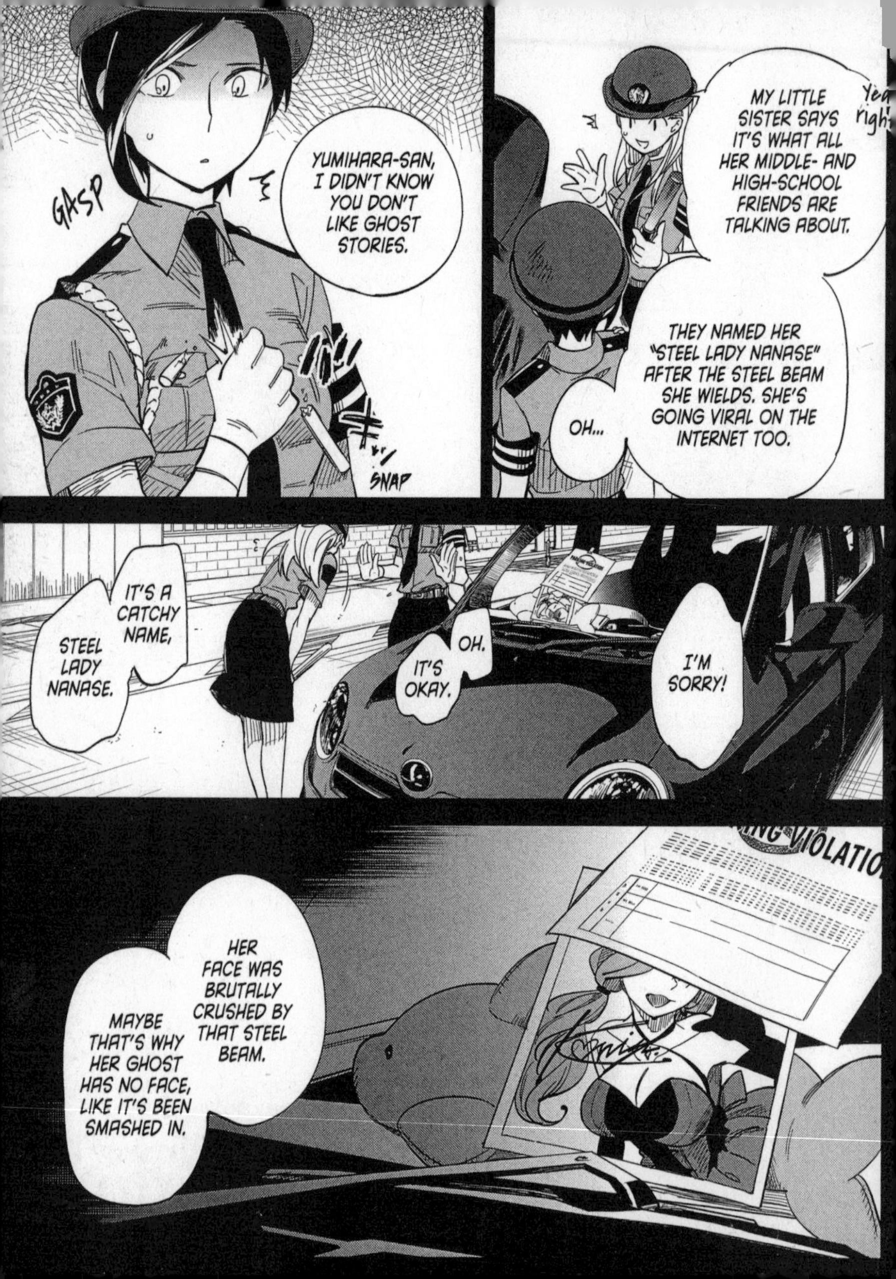
MY LITTLE SISTER SAYS IT'S WHAT ALL HER MIDDLE- AND HIGH-SCHOOL FRIENDS ARE TALKING ABOUT.
THEY NAMED HER "STEEL LADY NANASE" AFTER THE STEEL BEAM SHE WIELDS. SHE'S GOING VIRAL ON THE INTERNET TOO.
OH...
YUMIHARA-SAN, I DIDN'T KNOW YOU DON'T LIKE GHOST STORIES.
GASP
SNAP
I'M SORRY!
OH.
IT'S OKAY.
IT'S A CATCHY NAME,
STEEL LADY NANASE.
HER FACE WAS BRUTALLY CRUSHED BY THAT STEEL BEAM.
MAYBE THAT'S WHY HER GHOST HAS NO FACE, LIKE IT'S BEEN SMASHED IN.

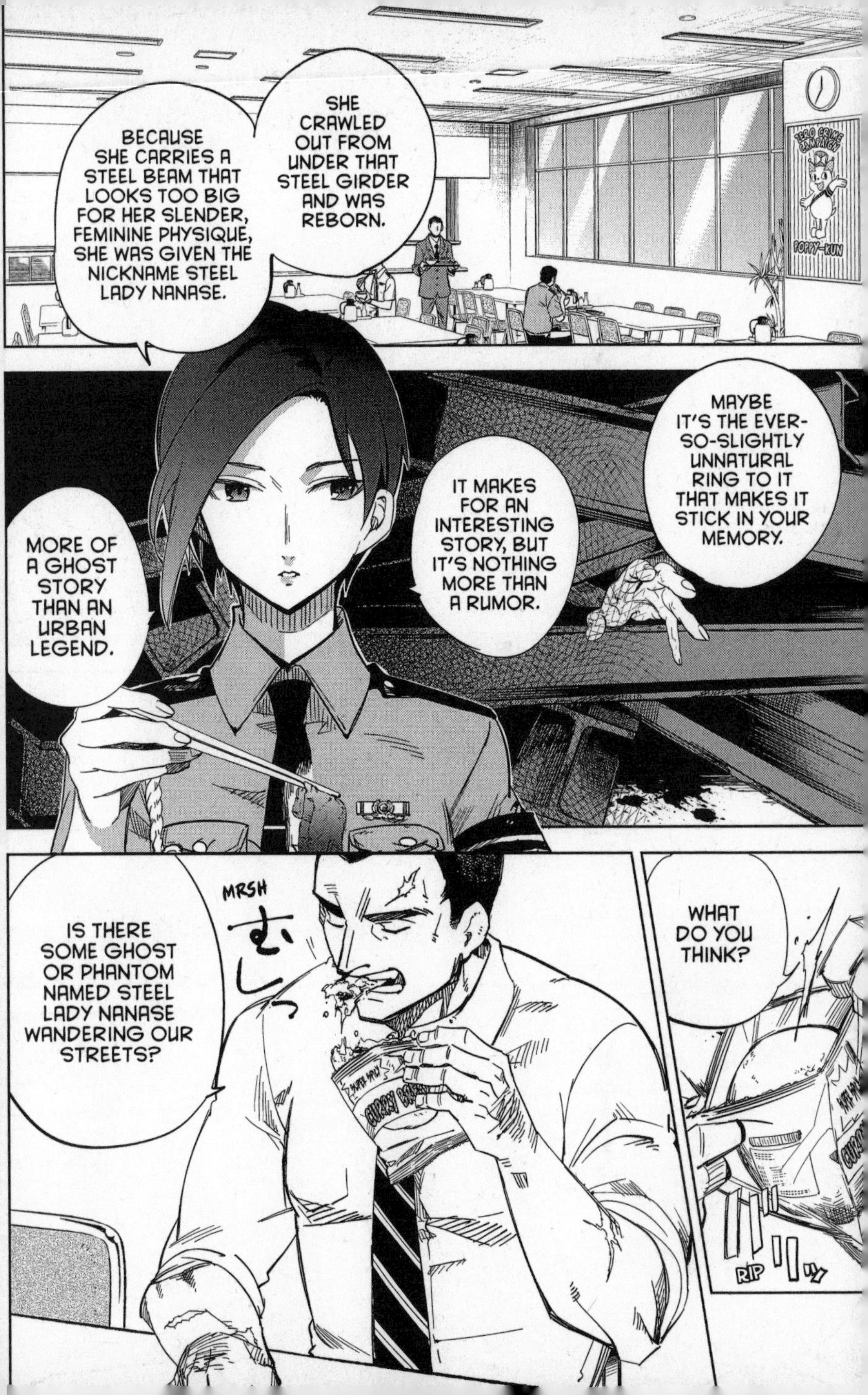
SHE CRAWLED OUT FROM UNDER THAT STEEL GIRDER AND WAS REBORN.
BECAUSE SHE CARRIES A STEEL BEAM THAT LOOKS TOO BIG FOR HER SLENDER, FEMININE PHYSIQUE, SHE WAS GIVEN THE NICKNAME STEEL LADY NANASE.
ZERO CRIME CAMPAIGN
POPPY-KUN
MAYBE IT'S THE EVER-SO-SLIGHTLY UNNATURAL RING TO IT THAT MAKES IT STICK IN YOUR MEMORY.
IT MAKES FOR AN INTERESTING STORY, BUT IT'S NOTHING MORE THAN A RUMOR.
MORE OF A GHOST STORY THAN AN URBAN LEGEND.
WHAT DO YOU THINK?
RIP
MRSH
IS THERE SOME GHOST OR PHANTOM NAMED STEEL LADY NANASE WANDERING OUR STREETS?

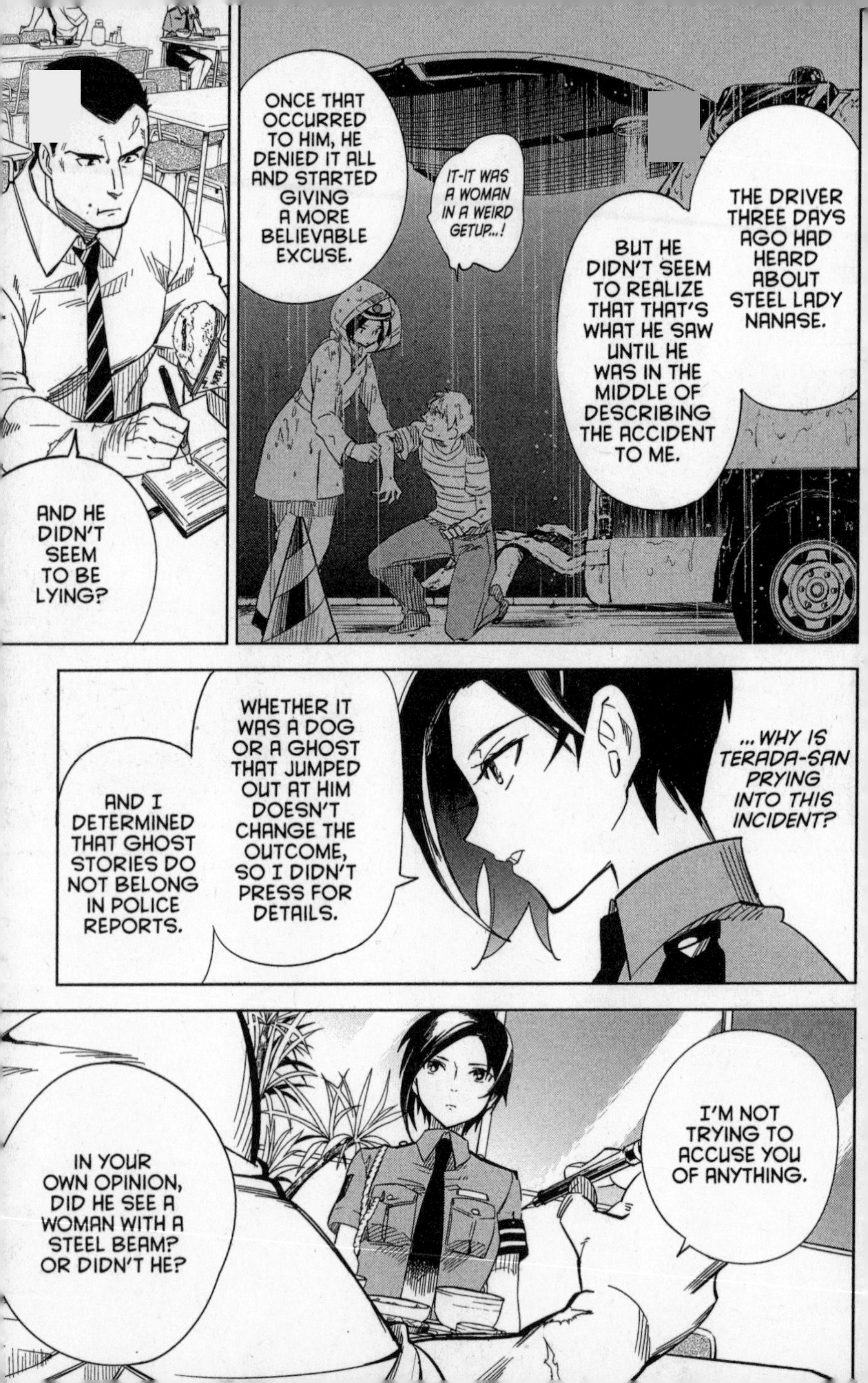
THE DRIVER THREE DAYS AGO HAD HEARD ABOUT STEEL LADY NANASE.
BUT HE DIDN'T SEEM TO REALIZE THAT THAT'S WHAT HE SAW UNTIL HE WAS IN THE MIDDLE OF DESCRIBING THE ACCIDENT TO ME.
IT-IT WAS A WOMAN IN A WEIRD GETUP...!
ONCE THAT OCCURRED TO HIM, HE DENIED IT ALL AND STARTED GIVING A MORE BELIEVABLE EXCUSE.
AND HE DIDN'T SEEM TO BE LYING?
...WHY IS TERADA-SAN PRYING INTO THIS INCIDENT?
WHETHER IT WAS A DOG OR A GHOST THAT JUMPED OUT AT HIM DOESN'T CHANGE THE OUTCOME, SO I DIDN'T PRESS FOR DETAILS.
AND I DETERMINED THAT GHOST STORIES DO NOT BELONG IN POLICE REPORTS.
I'M NOT TRYING TO ACCUSE YOU OF ANYTHING.
IN YOUR OWN OPINION, DID HE SEE A WOMAN WITH A STEEL BEAM? OR DIDN'T HE?

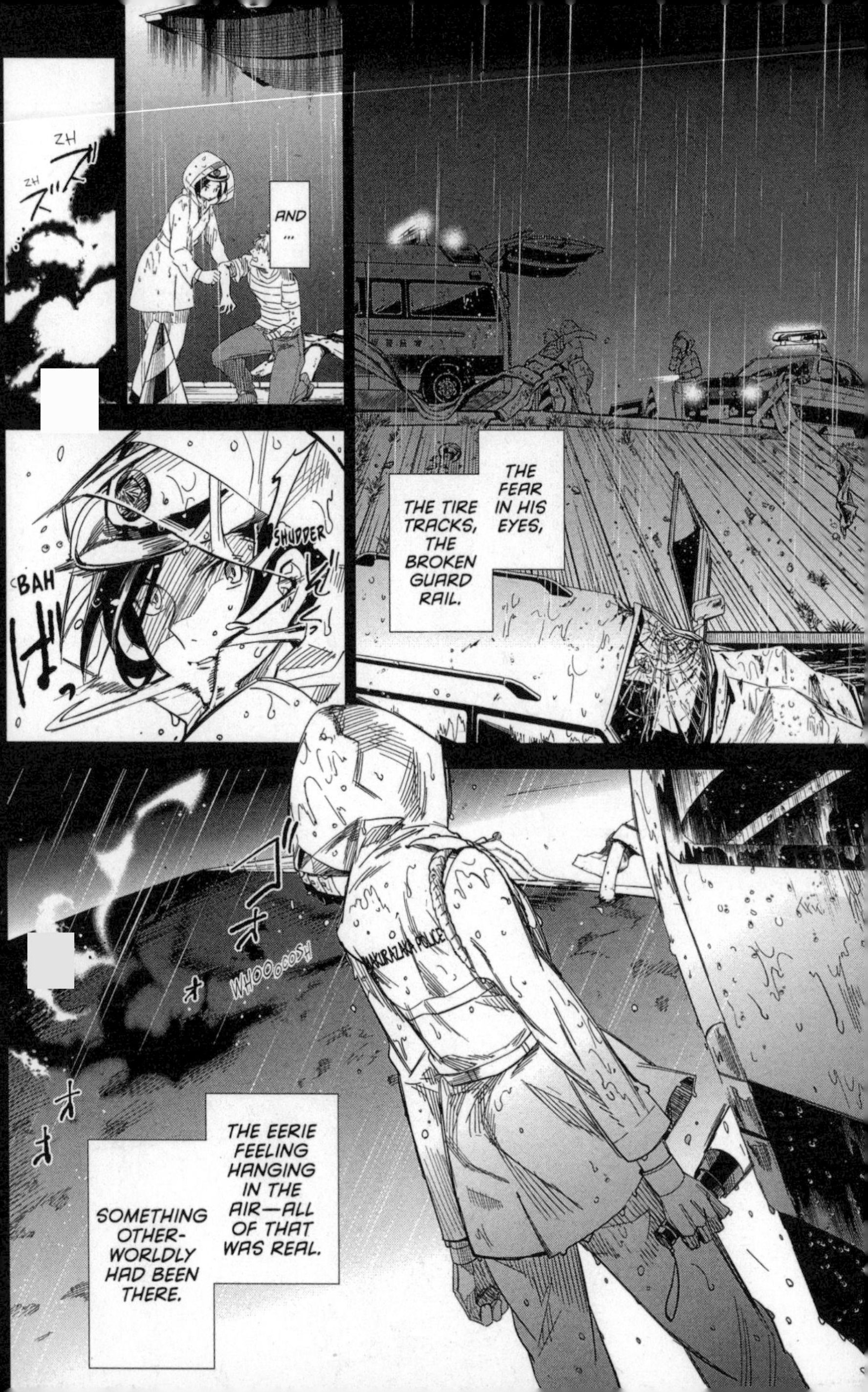
THE FEAR IN HIS EYES,
THE TIRE TRACKS, THE BROKEN GUARD RAIL.
AND ...
ZH
ZH
SHUDDER
BAH
WHOOOOOSH
MAKURAZAKA POLICE
THE EERIE FEELING HANGING IN THE AIR—ALL OF THAT WAS REAL.
SOMETHING OTHER-WORLDLY HAD BEEN THERE.

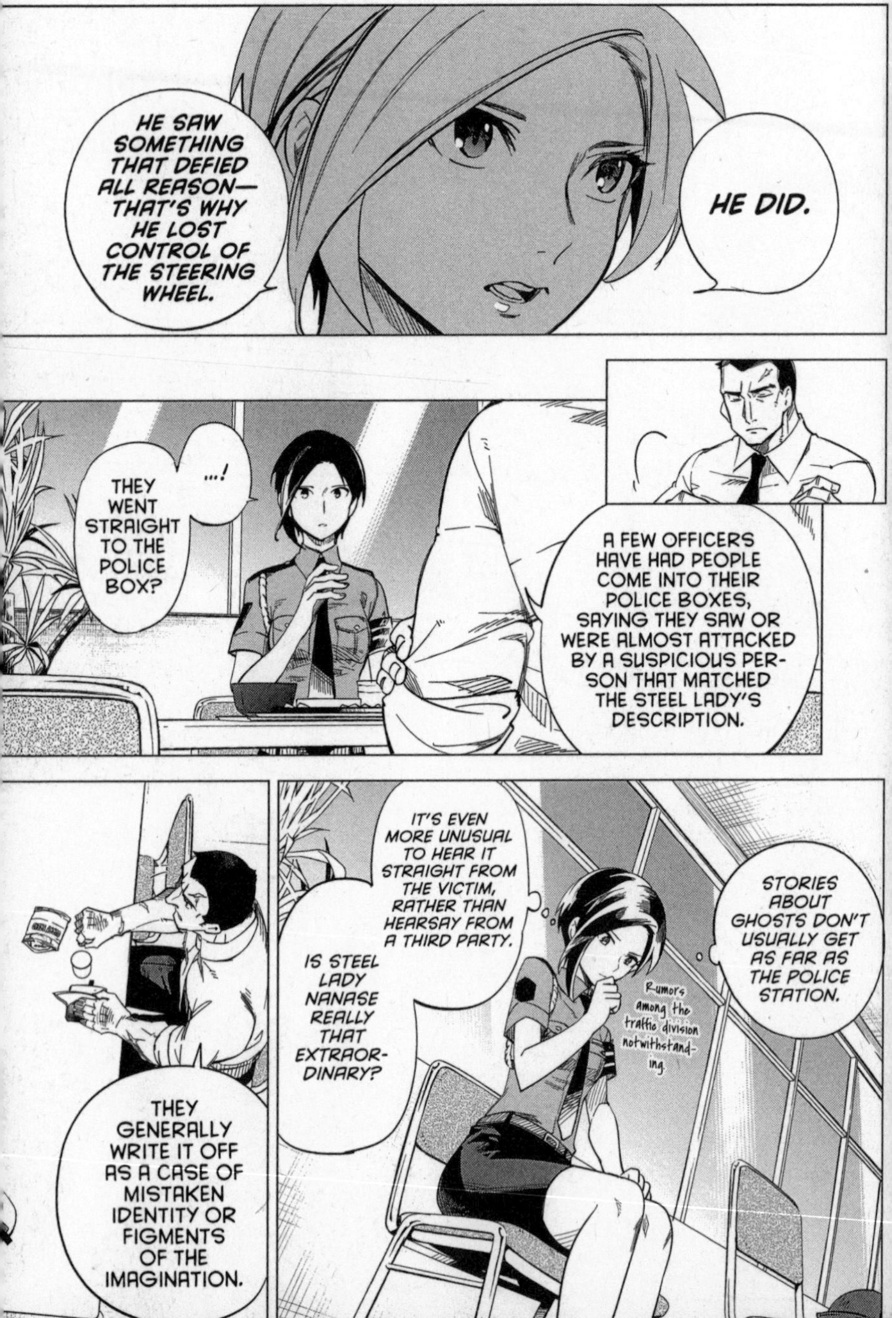
HE DID.
HE SAW SOMETHING THAT DEFIED ALL REASON—THAT'S WHY HE LOST CONTROL OF THE STEERING WHEEL.
A FEW OFFICERS HAVE HAD PEOPLE COME INTO THEIR POLICE BOXES, SAYING THEY SAW OR WERE ALMOST ATTACKED BY A SUSPICIOUS PERSON THAT MATCHED THE STEEL LADY'S DESCRIPTION.
...!
THEY WENT STRAIGHT TO THE POLICE BOX?
STORIES ABOUT GHOSTS DON'T USUALLY GET AS FAR AS THE POLICE STATION.
Rumors among the traffic division notwithstanding.
IT'S EVEN MORE UNUSUAL TO HEAR IT STRAIGHT FROM THE VICTIM, RATHER THAN HEARSAY FROM A THIRD PARTY.
IS STEEL LADY NANASE REALLY THAT EXTRAORDINARY?
THEY GENERALLY WRITE IT OFF AS A CASE OF MISTAKEN IDENTITY OR FIGMENTS OF THE IMAGINATION.

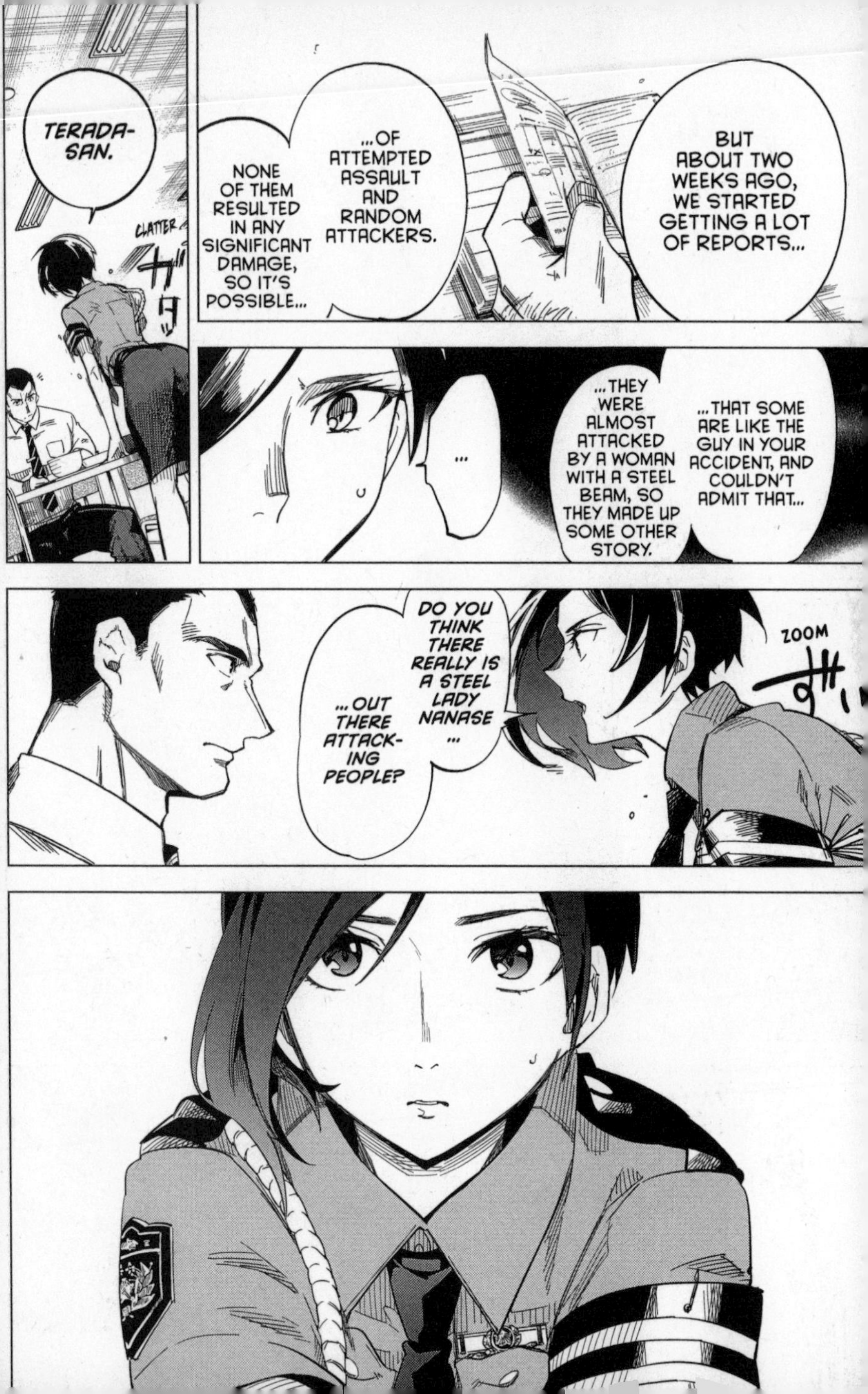
BUT ABOUT TWO WEEKS AGO, WE STARTED GETTING A LOT OF REPORTS...
...OF ATTEMPTED ASSAULT AND RANDOM ATTACKERS.
NONE OF THEM RESULTED IN ANY SIGNIFICANT DAMAGE, SO IT'S POSSIBLE...
...THAT SOME ARE LIKE THE GUY IN YOUR ACCIDENT, AND COULDN'T ADMIT THAT...
...THEY WERE ALMOST ATTACKED BY A WOMAN WITH A STEEL BEAM, SO THEY MADE UP SOME OTHER STORY.
...
TERADA-SAN.
CLATTER
ZOOM
DO YOU THINK THERE REALLY IS A STEEL LADY NANASE ...
...OUT THERE ATTACK-ING PEOPLE?

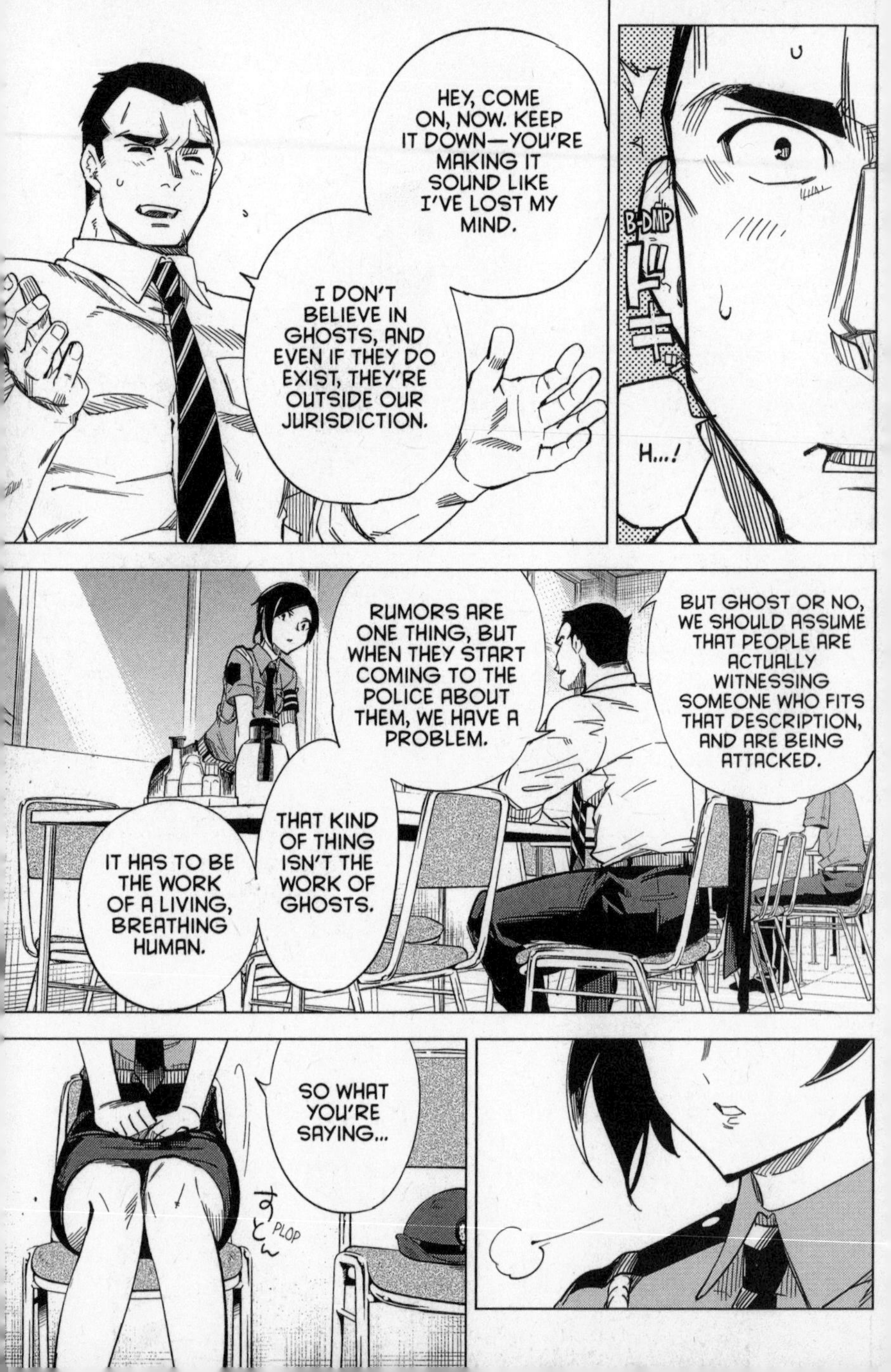
B-DMP
ドキ
H...!
HEY, COME ON, NOW. KEEP IT DOWN—YOU'RE MAKING IT SOUND LIKE I'VE LOST MY MIND.
I DON'T BELIEVE IN GHOSTS, AND EVEN IF THEY DO EXIST, THEY'RE OUTSIDE OUR JURISDICTION.
BUT GHOST OR NO, WE SHOULD ASSUME THAT PEOPLE ARE ACTUALLY WITNESSING SOMEONE WHO FITS THAT DESCRIPTION, AND ARE BEING ATTACKED.
RUMORS ARE ONE THING, BUT WHEN THEY START COMING TO THE POLICE ABOUT THEM, WE HAVE A PROBLEM.
THAT KIND OF THING ISN'T THE WORK OF GHOSTS.
IT HAS TO BE THE WORK OF A LIVING, BREATHING HUMAN.
SO WHAT YOU'RE SAYING...
すとん
PLOP

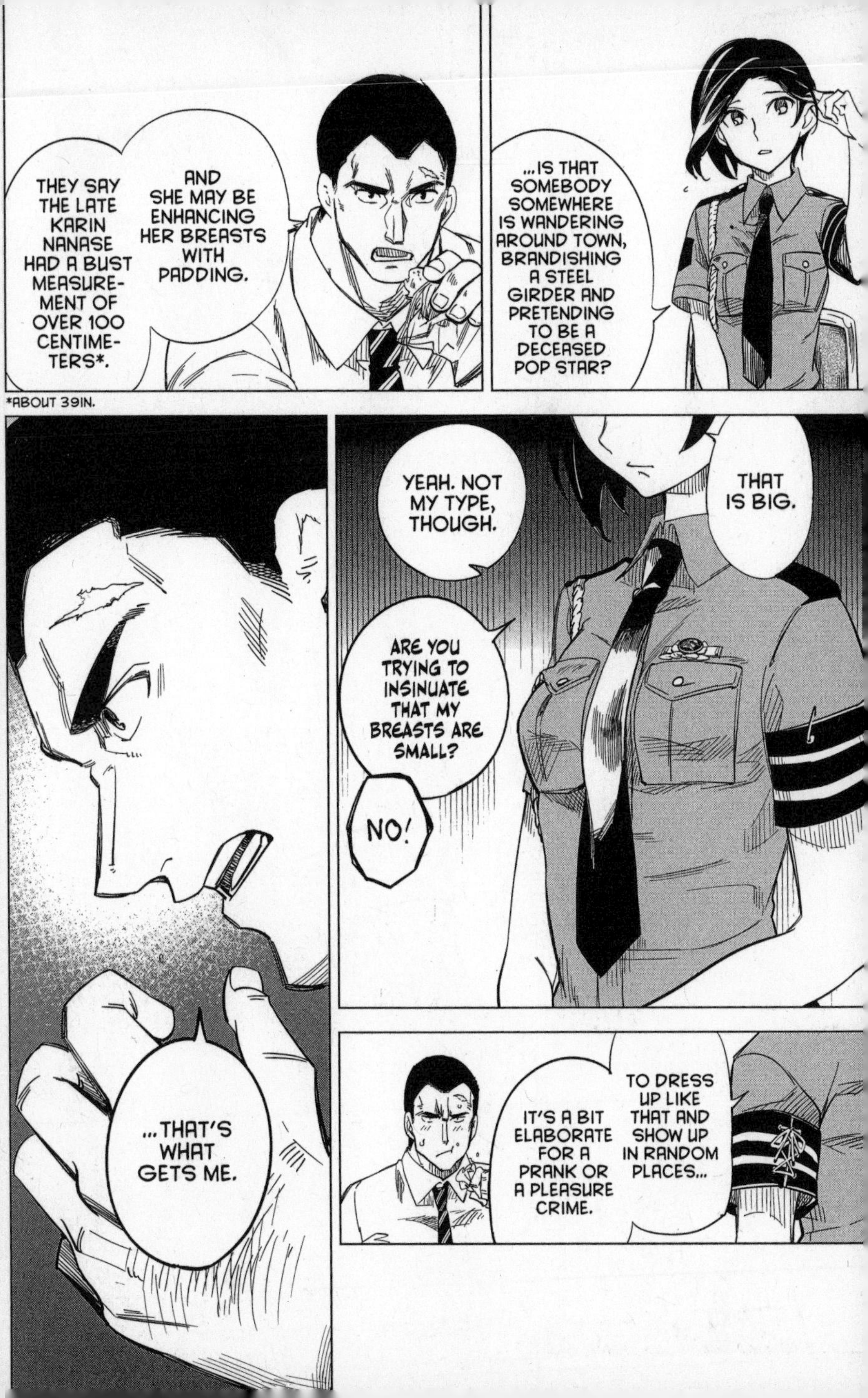
...IS THAT SOMEBODY SOMEWHERE IS WANDERING AROUND TOWN, BRANDISHING A STEEL GIRDER AND PRETENDING TO BE A DECEASED POP STAR?
THEY SAY THE LATE KARIN NANASE HAD A BUST MEASUREMENT OF OVER 100 CENTIMETERS*.
AND SHE MAY BE ENHANCING HER BREASTS WITH PADDING.
THAT IS BIG.
YEAH. NOT MY TYPE, THOUGH.
ARE YOU TRYING TO INSINUATE THAT MY BREASTS ARE SMALL?
NO!
TO DRESS UP LIKE THAT AND SHOW UP IN RANDOM PLACES...
IT'S A BIT ELABORATE FOR A PRANK OR A PLEASURE CRIME.
...THAT'S WHAT GETS ME.

*ABOUT 39IN.

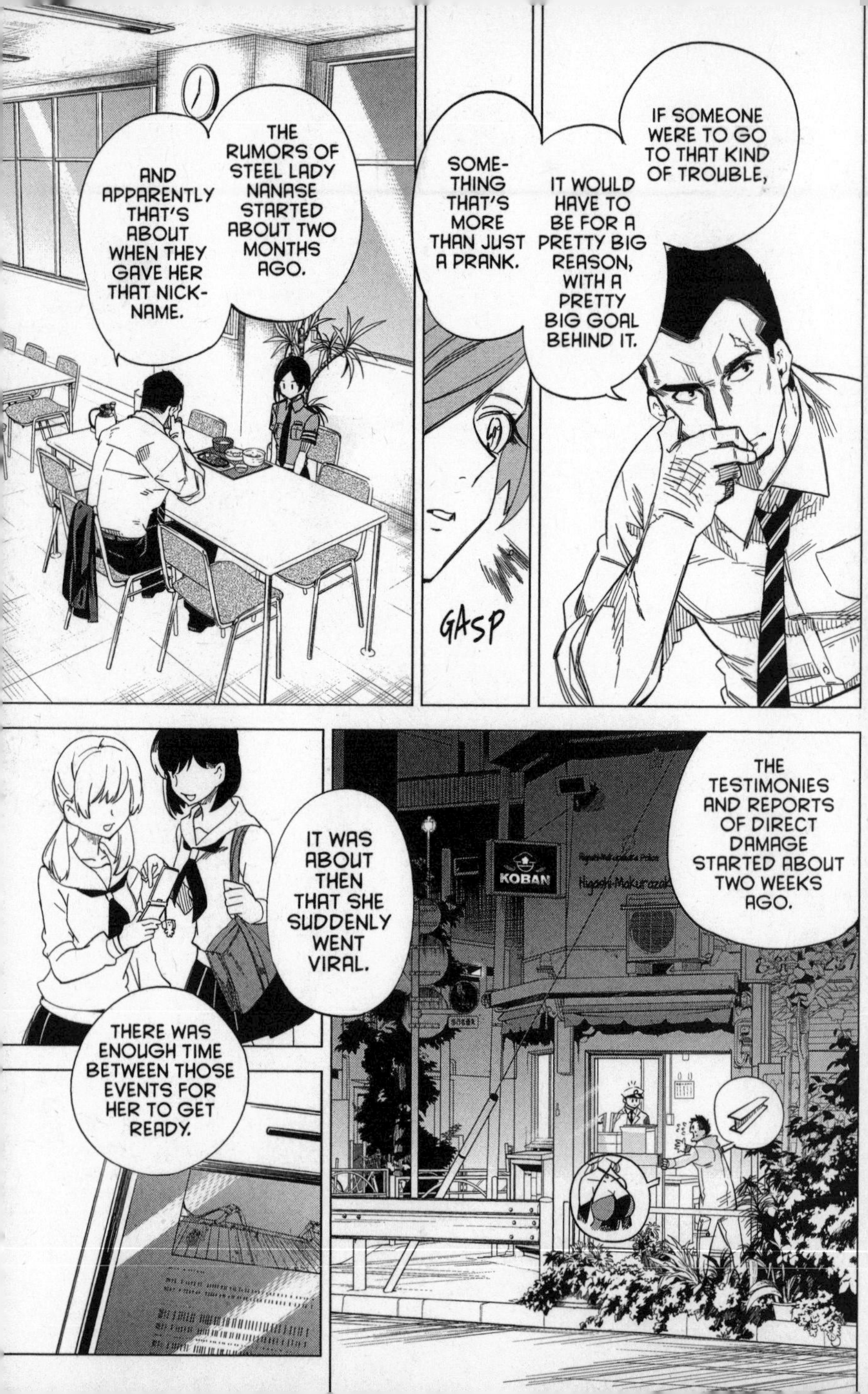
IF SOMEONE WERE TO GO TO THAT KIND OF TROUBLE,
IT WOULD HAVE TO BE FOR A PRETTY BIG REASON, WITH A PRETTY BIG GOAL BEHIND IT.
SOMETHING THAT'S MORE THAN JUST A PRANK.
GASP
THE RUMORS OF STEEL LADY NANASE STARTED ABOUT TWO MONTHS AGO.
AND APPARENTLY THAT'S ABOUT WHEN THEY GAVE HER THAT NICKNAME.
THE TESTIMONIES AND REPORTS OF DIRECT DAMAGE STARTED ABOUT TWO WEEKS AGO.
KOBAN
Higashi-Makurazaki
IT WAS ABOUT THEN THAT SHE SUDDENLY WENT VIRAL.
THERE WAS ENOUGH TIME BETWEEN THOSE EVENTS FOR HER TO GET READY.

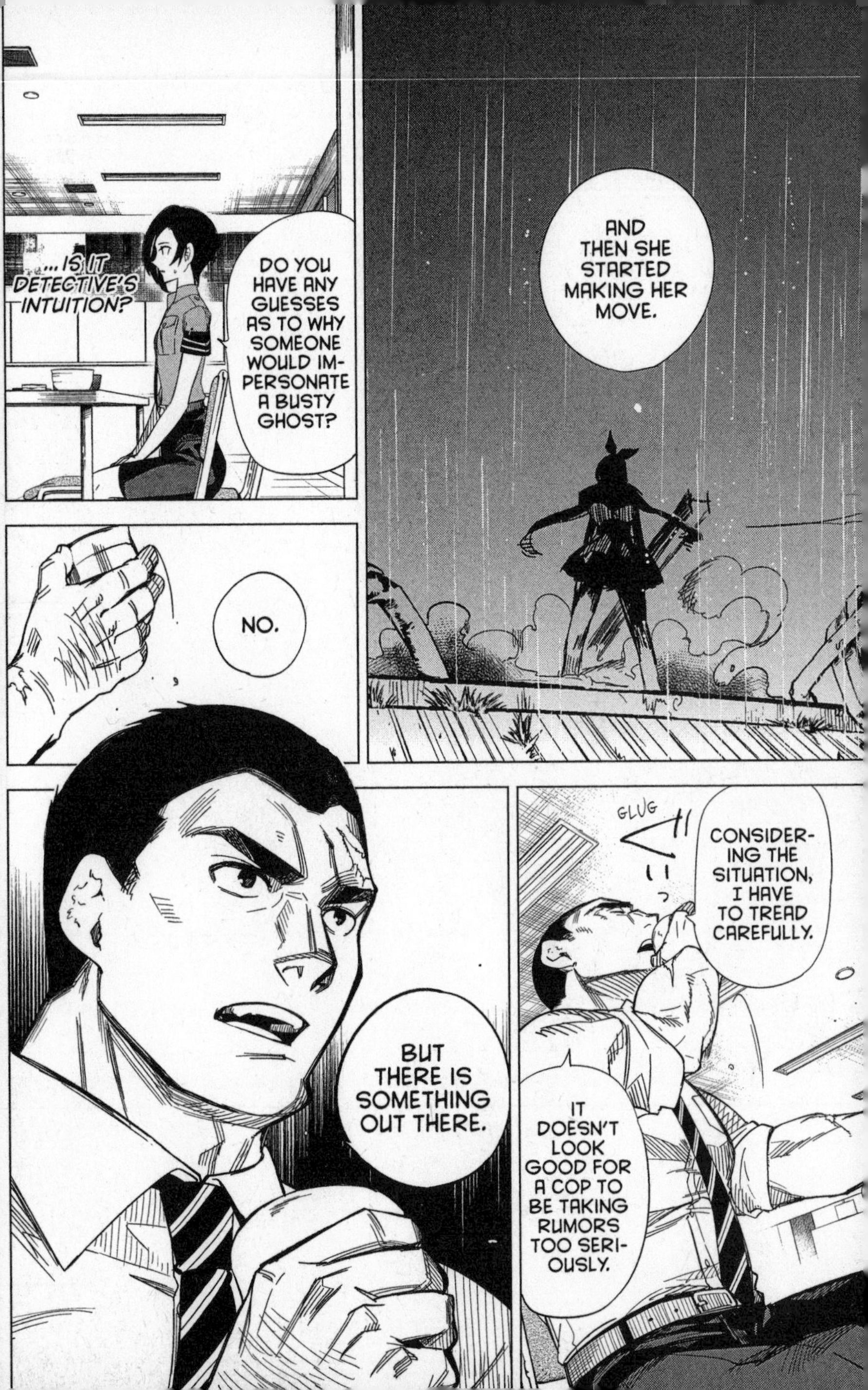
AND THEN SHE STARTED MAKING HER MOVE.
DO YOU HAVE ANY GUESSES AS TO WHY SOMEONE WOULD IMPERSONATE A BUSTY GHOST?
...IS IT DETECTIVE'S INTUITION?
NO.
CONSIDERING THE SITUATION, I HAVE TO TREAD CAREFULLY.
GLUG
IT DOESN'T LOOK GOOD FOR A COP TO BE TAKING RUMORS TOO SERIOUSLY.
BUT THERE IS SOMETHING OUT THERE.

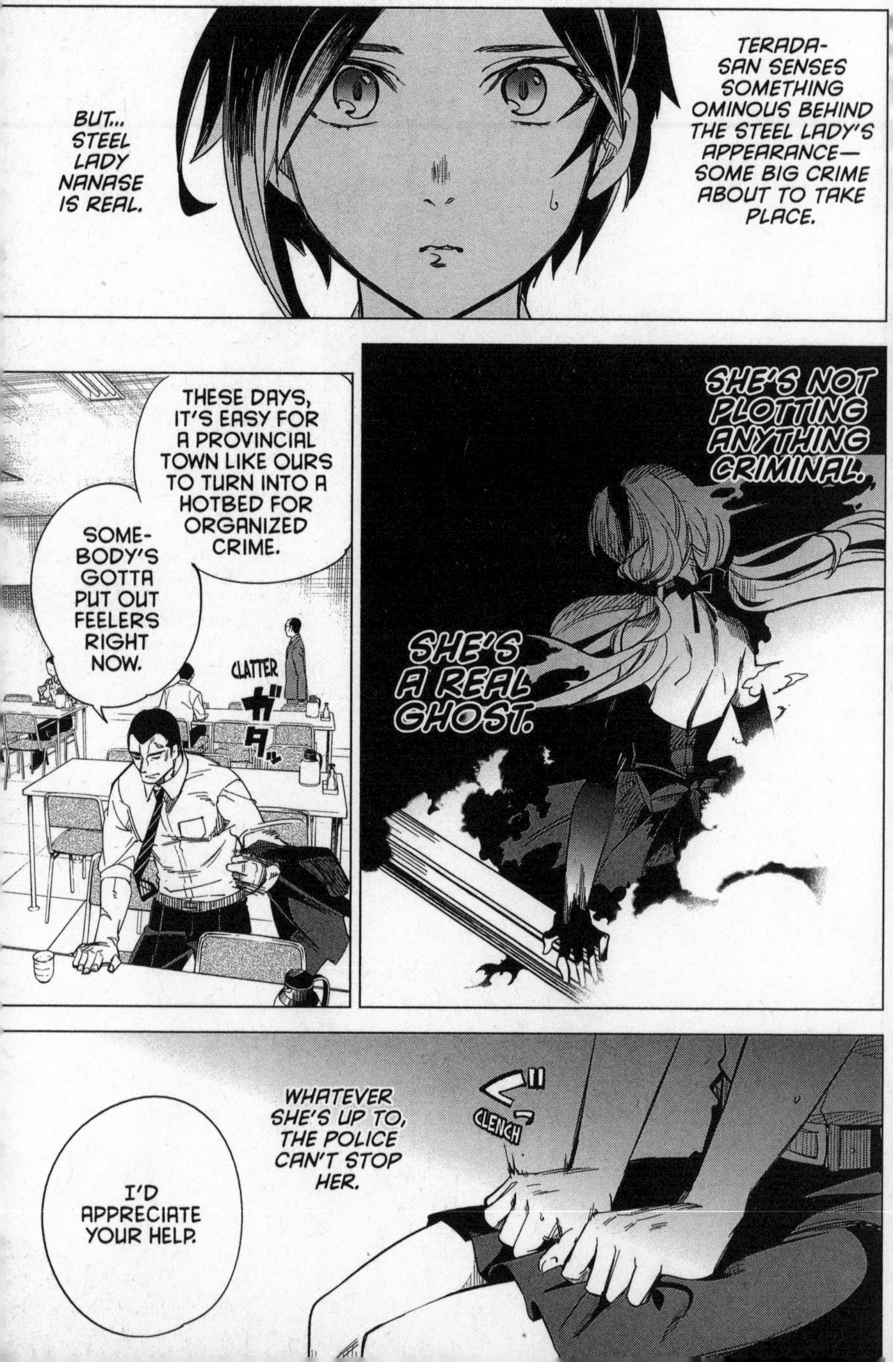
TERADA-SAN SENSES SOMETHING OMINOUS BEHIND THE STEEL LADY'S APPEARANCE—SOME BIG CRIME ABOUT TO TAKE PLACE.
BUT... STEEL LADY NANASE IS REAL.
SHE'S NOT PLOTTING ANYTHING CRIMINAL.
SHE'S A REAL GHOST.
THESE DAYS, IT'S EASY FOR A PROVINCIAL TOWN LIKE OURS TO TURN INTO A HOTBED FOR ORGANIZED CRIME.
SOME-BODY'S GOTTA PUT OUT FEELERS RIGHT NOW.
CLATTER
WHATEVER SHE'S UP TO, THE POLICE CAN'T STOP HER.
CLENCH
I'D APPRECIATE YOUR HELP.

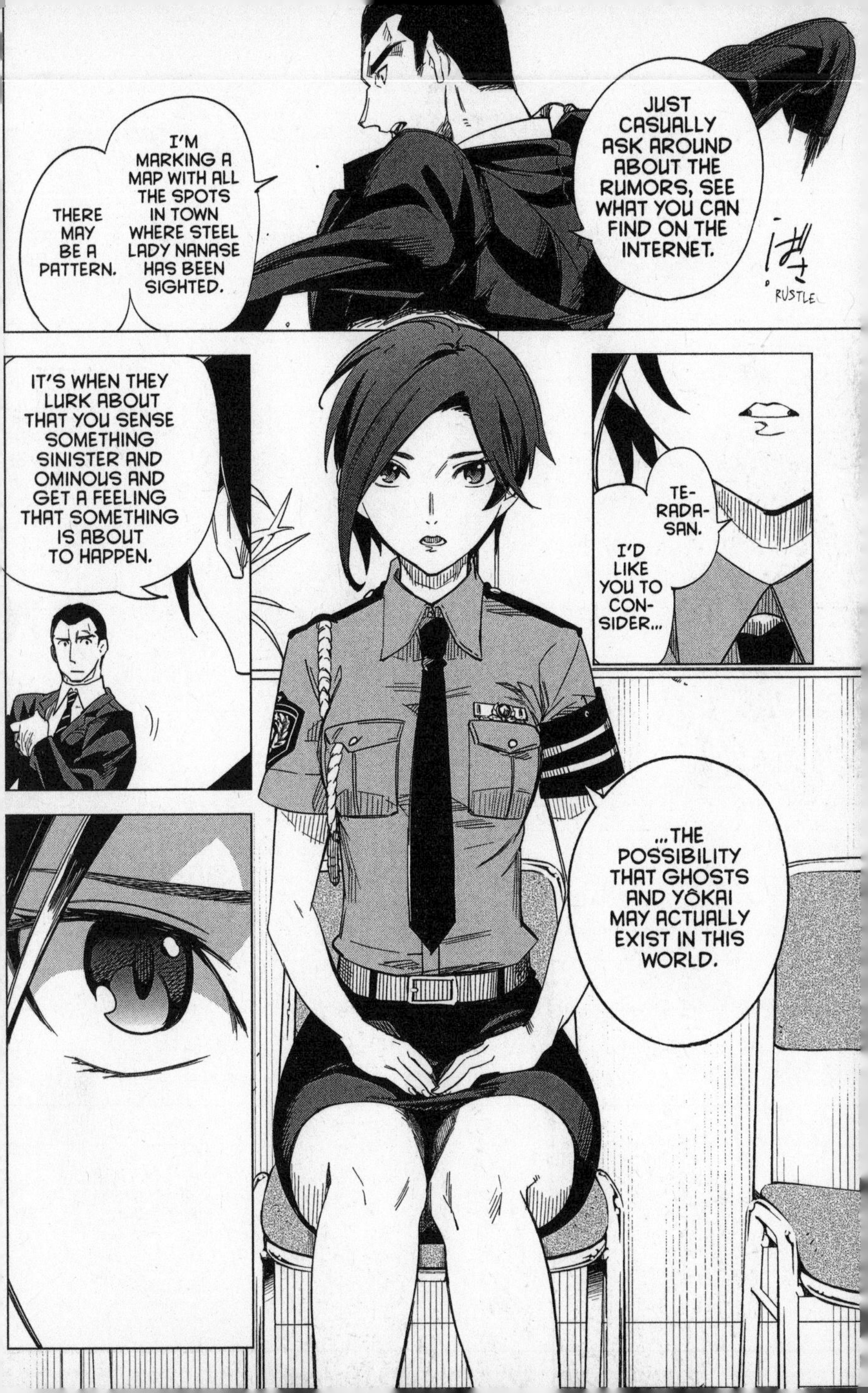
JUST CASUALLY ASK AROUND ABOUT THE RUMORS, SEE WHAT YOU CAN FIND ON THE INTERNET.
ぱさ
RUSTLE
I'M MARKING A MAP WITH ALL THE SPOTS IN TOWN WHERE STEEL LADY NANASE HAS BEEN SIGHTED.
THERE MAY BE A PATTERN.
TE-RADA-SAN.
I'D LIKE YOU TO CON-SIDER...
...THE POSSIBILITY THAT GHOSTS AND YÔKAI MAY ACTUALLY EXIST IN THIS WORLD.
IT'S WHEN THEY LURK ABOUT THAT YOU SENSE SOMETHING SINISTER AND OMINOUS AND GET A FEELING THAT SOMETHING IS ABOUT TO HAPPEN.

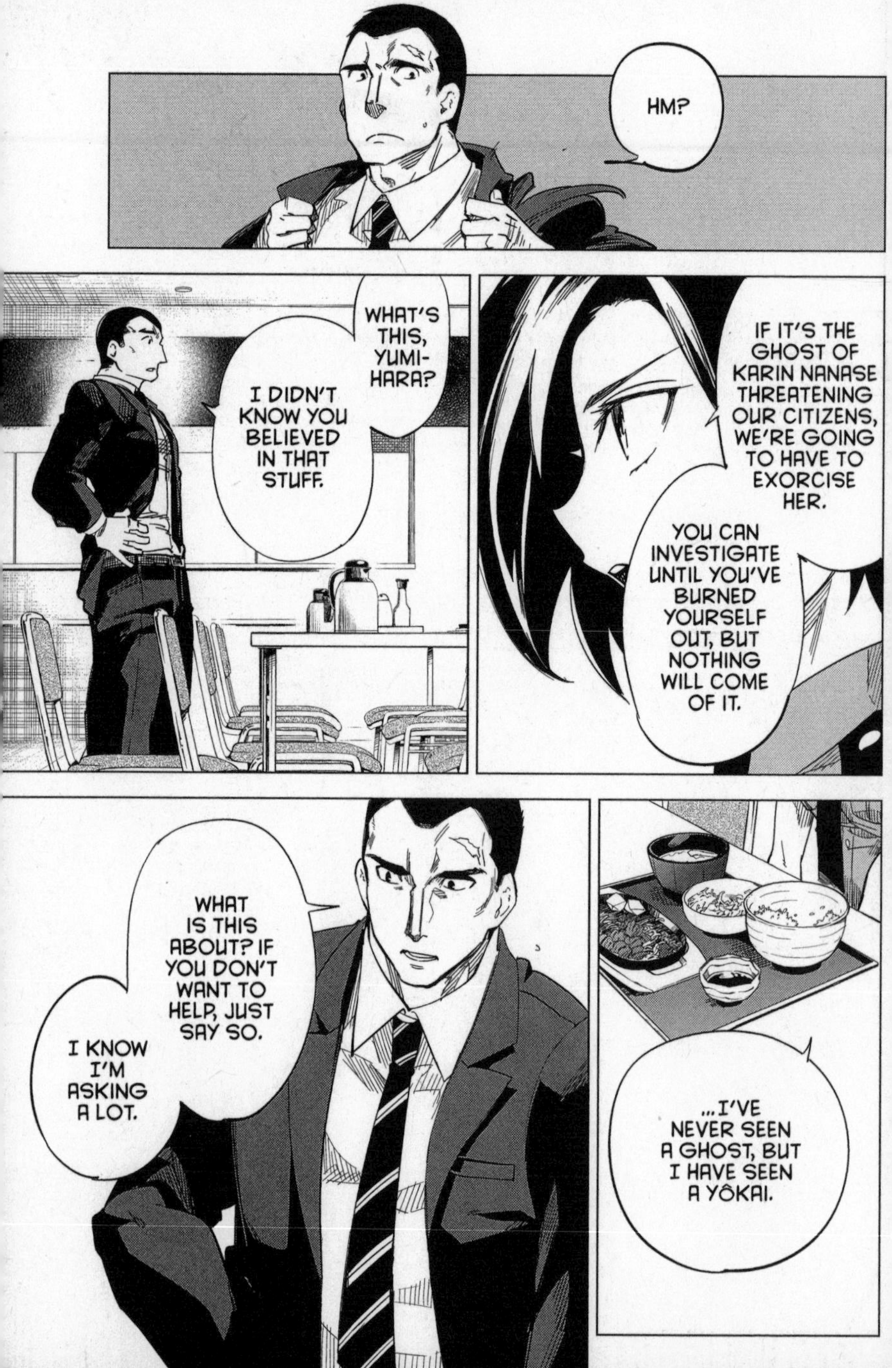
HM?
IF IT'S THE GHOST OF KARIN NANASE THREATENING OUR CITIZENS, WE'RE GOING TO HAVE TO EXORCISE HER.
YOU CAN INVESTIGATE UNTIL YOU'VE BURNED YOURSELF OUT, BUT NOTHING WILL COME OF IT.
WHAT'S THIS, YUMI-HARA?
I DIDN'T KNOW YOU BELIEVED IN THAT STUFF.
...I'VE NEVER SEEN A GHOST, BUT I HAVE SEEN A YÔKAI.
WHAT IS THIS ABOUT? IF YOU DON'T WANT TO HELP, JUST SAY SO.
I KNOW I'M ASKING A LOT.

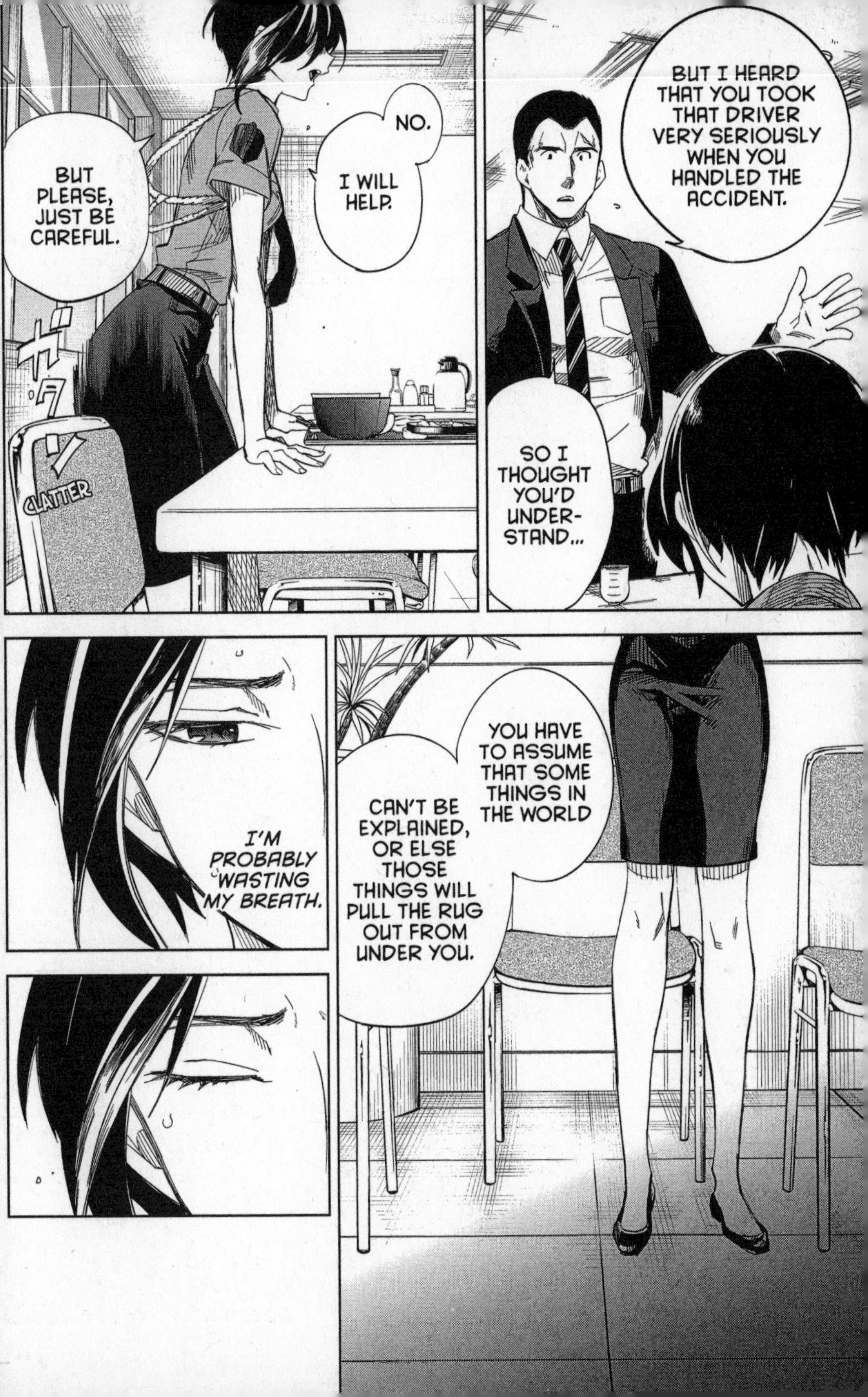
BUT I HEARD THAT YOU TOOK THAT DRIVER VERY SERIOUSLY WHEN YOU HANDLED THE ACCIDENT.
SO I THOUGHT YOU'D UNDER-STAND...
NO.
I WILL HELP.
BUT PLEASE, JUST BE CAREFUL.
CLATTER
YOU HAVE TO ASSUME THAT SOME THINGS IN THE WORLD
CAN'T BE EXPLAINED, OR ELSE THOSE THINGS WILL PULL THE RUG OUT FROM UNDER YOU.
I'M PROBABLY WASTING MY BREATH.

I DIDN'T BELIEVE IT EITHER, AND THAT'S WHY I HAD TO BREAK THINGS OFF WITH MY BOYFRIEND.

...WAS YOUR BOYFRIEND A YŌKAI OR A GHOST OR SOMETHING?

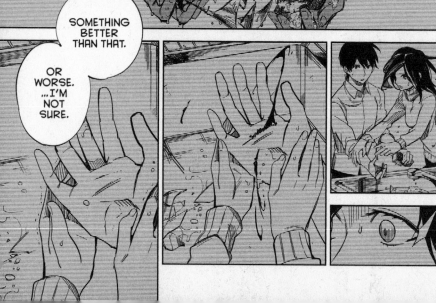

SOMETHING BETTER THAN THAT.

OR WORSE. ...I'M NOT SURE.

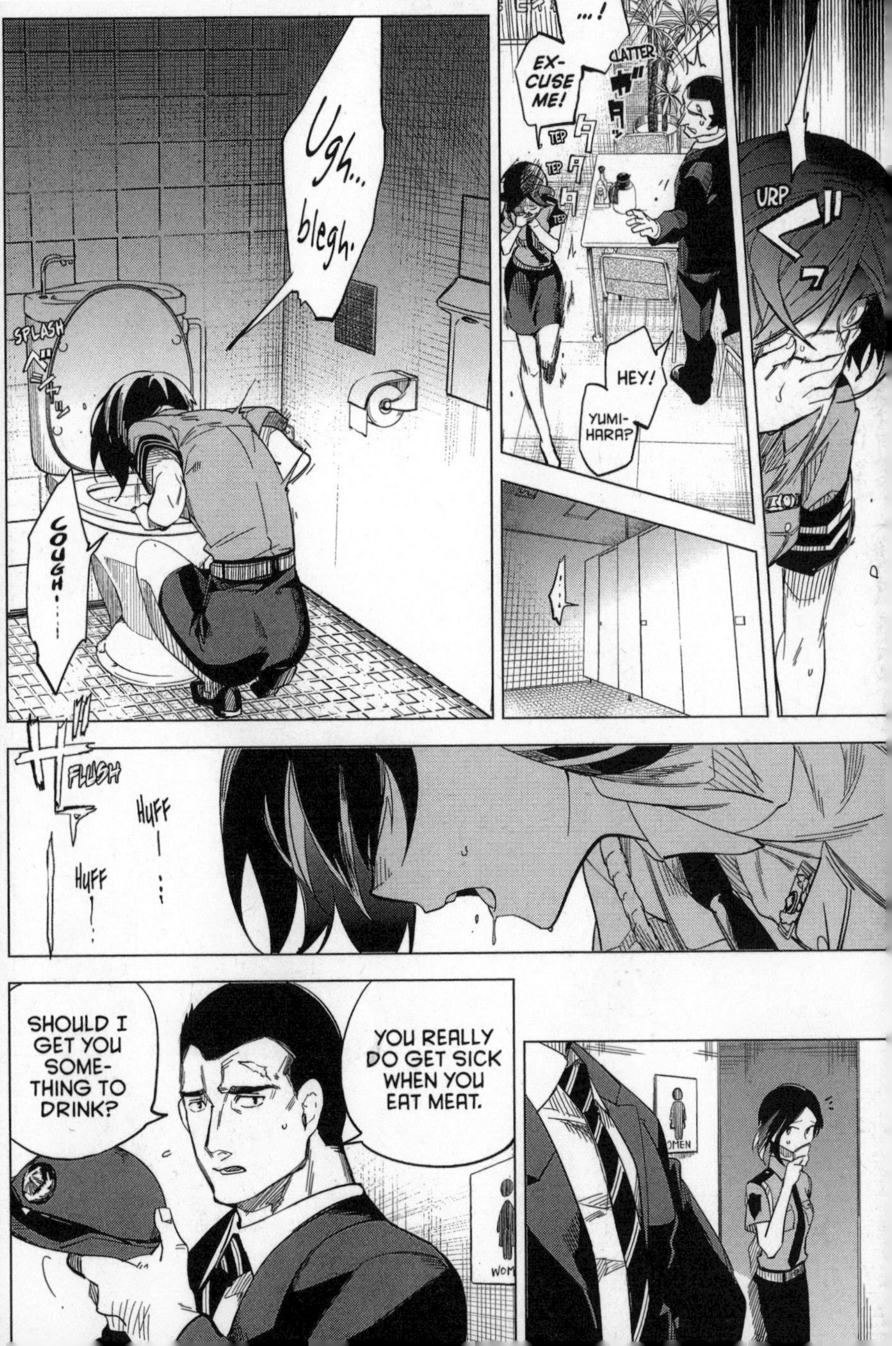
URP
...!
EX-CUSE ME!
CLATTER
TEP
TEP
HEY!
YUMI-HARA?
Ugh... blegh.
SPLASH
COUGH.....
FLUSH
HUFF
HUFF
WOMEN
YOU REALLY DO GET SICK WHEN YOU EAT MEAT.
SHOULD I GET YOU SOME-THING TO DRINK?

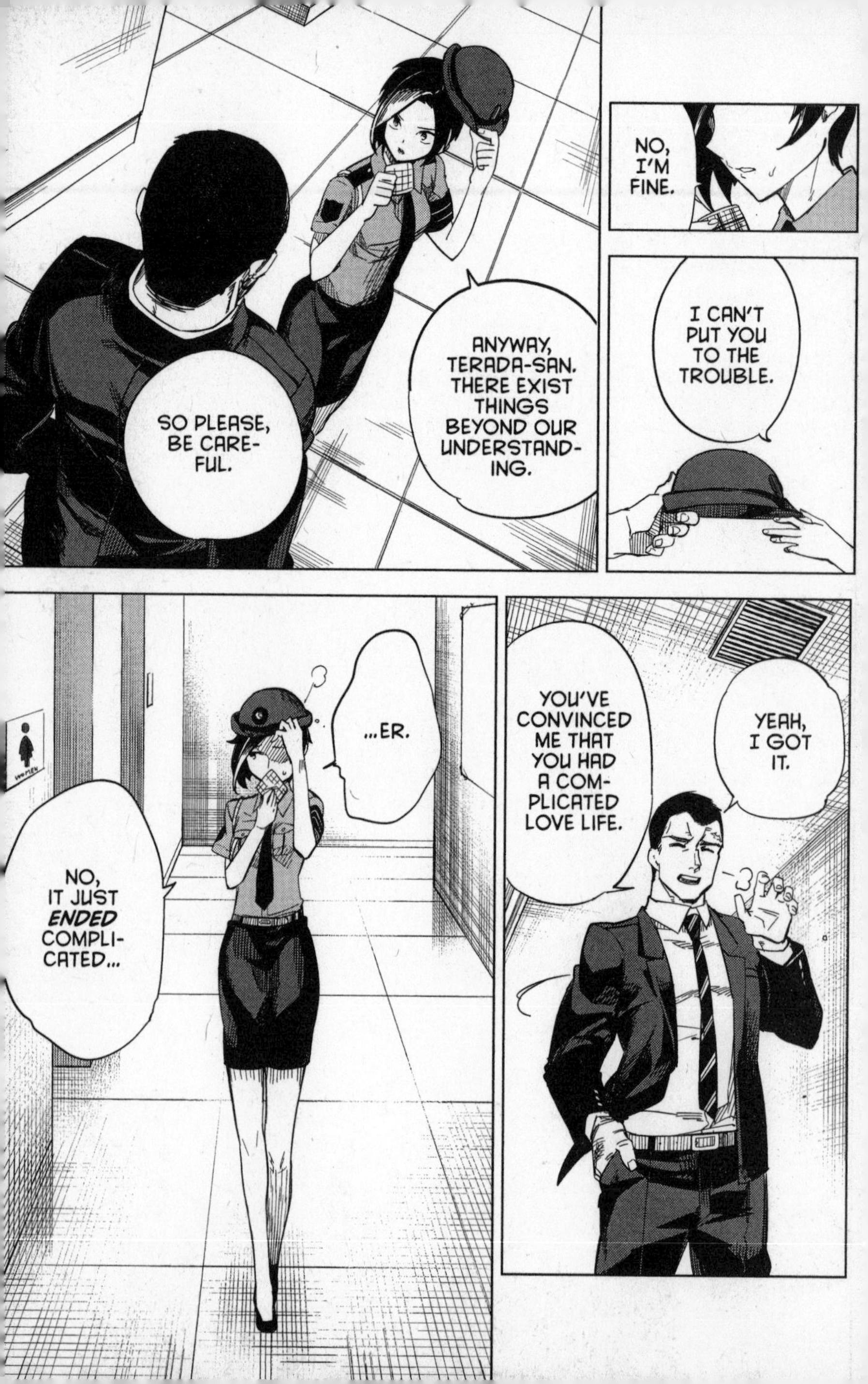
NO, I'M FINE.
I CAN'T PUT YOU TO THE TROUBLE.
ANYWAY, TERADA-SAN. THERE EXIST THINGS BEYOND OUR UNDERSTAND-ING.
SO PLEASE, BE CARE-FUL.
YEAH, I GOT IT.
YOU'VE CONVINCED ME THAT YOU HAD A COM-PLICATED LOVE LIFE.
...ER.
NO, IT JUST *ENDED* COMPLI-CATED...

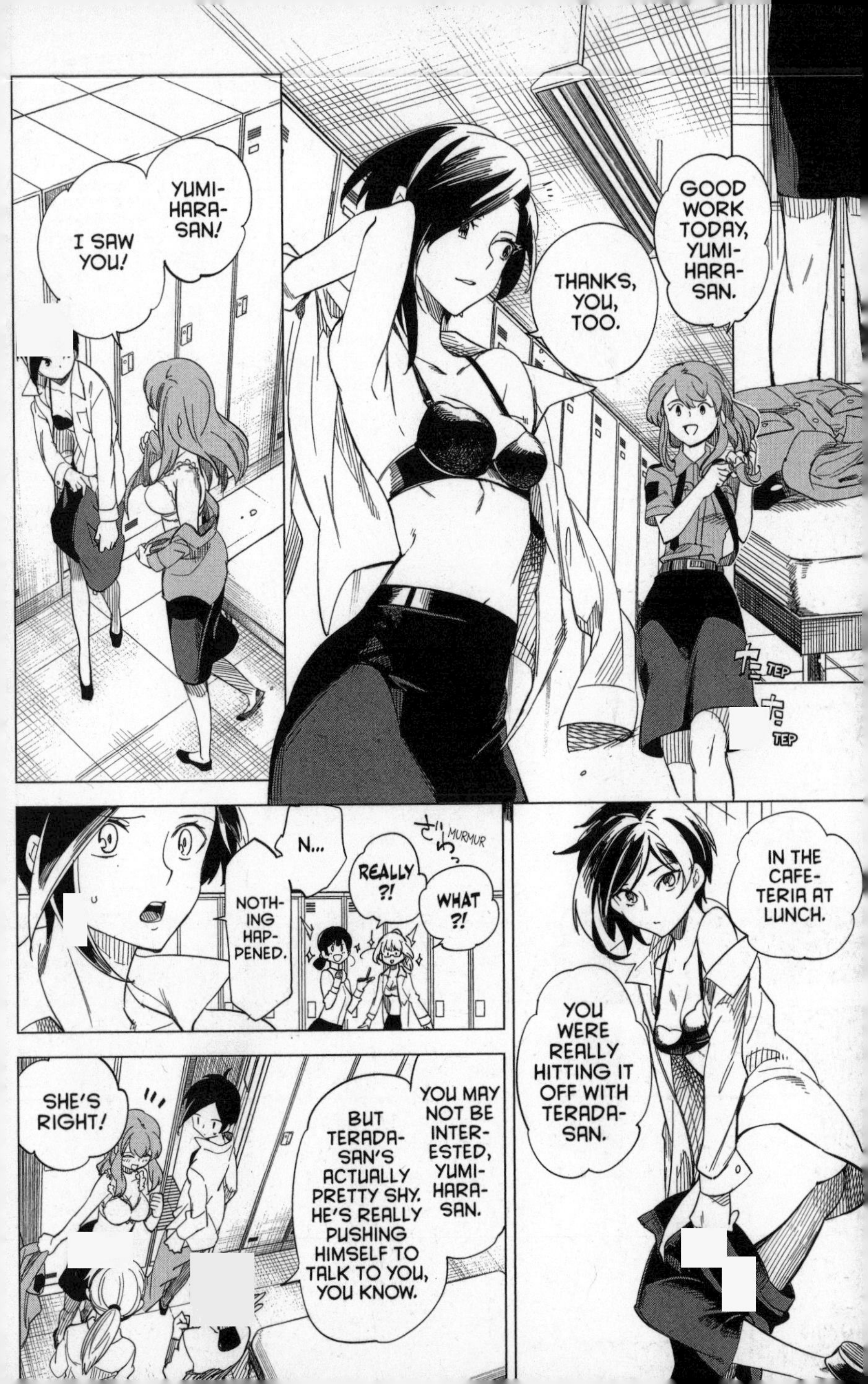
GOOD WORK TODAY, YUMIHARA-SAN.
THANKS, YOU, TOO.
TEP
TEP
YUMIHARA-SAN!
I SAW YOU!
IN THE CAFETERIA AT LUNCH.
YOU WERE REALLY HITTING IT OFF WITH TERADA-SAN.
N...
NOTHING HAPPENED.
MURMUR
WHAT?!
REALLY?!
YOU MAY NOT BE INTERESTED, YUMIHARA-SAN.
BUT TERADA-SAN'S ACTUALLY PRETTY SHY. HE'S REALLY PUSHING HIMSELF TO TALK TO YOU, YOU KNOW.
SHE'S RIGHT!

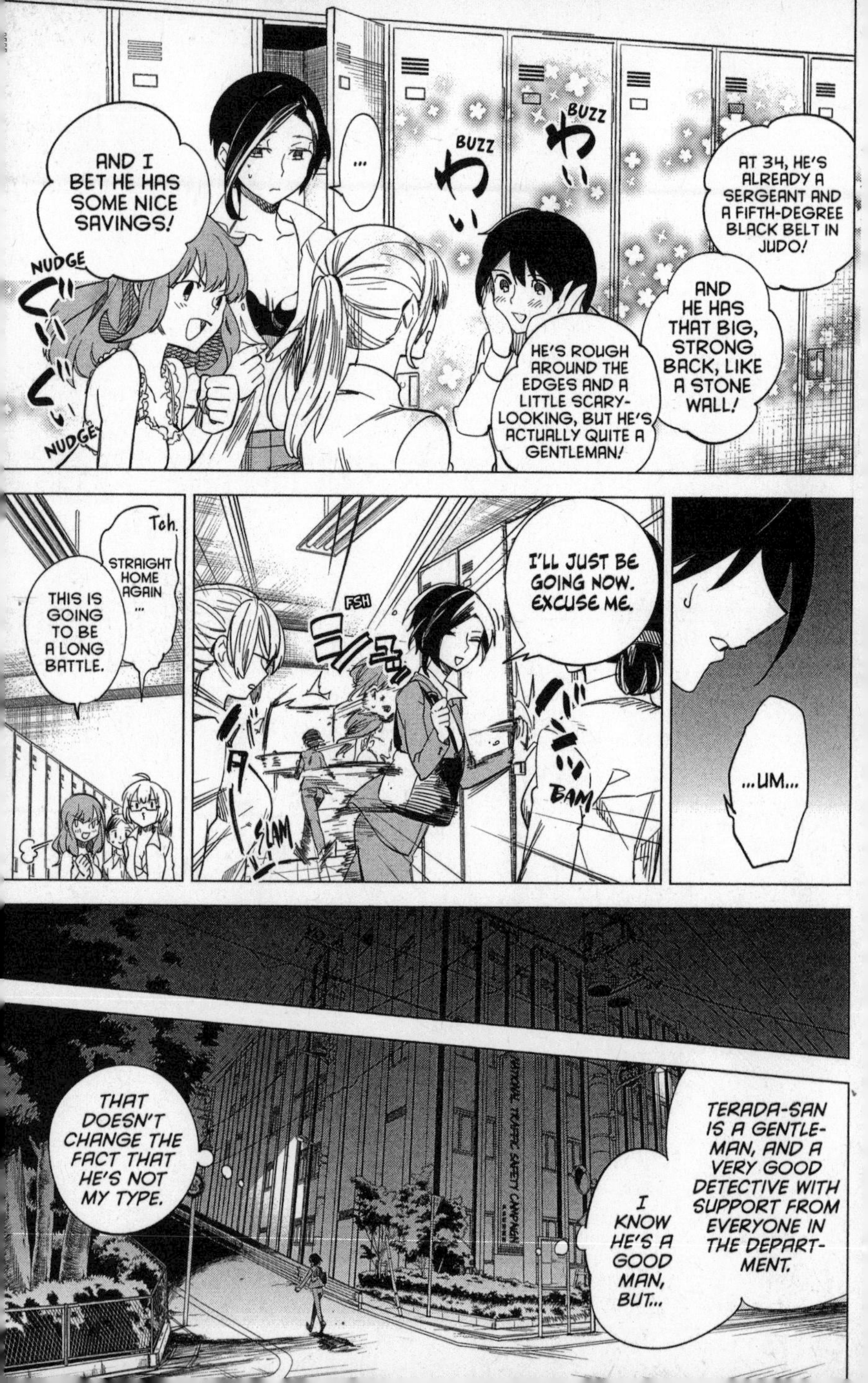
AT 34, HE'S ALREADY A SERGEANT AND A FIFTH-DEGREE BLACK BELT IN JUDO!
AND HE HAS THAT BIG, STRONG BACK, LIKE A STONE WALL!
HE'S ROUGH AROUND THE EDGES AND A LITTLE SCARY-LOOKING, BUT HE'S ACTUALLY QUITE A GENTLEMAN!
BUZZ
BUZZ
...
AND I BET HE HAS SOME NICE SAVINGS!
NUDGE
NUDGE
...UM...
I'LL JUST BE GOING NOW. EXCUSE ME.
FSH
BAM
SLAM
Tch.
STRAIGHT HOME AGAIN ...
THIS IS GOING TO BE A LONG BATTLE.
TERADA-SAN IS A GENTLE-MAN, AND A VERY GOOD DETECTIVE WITH SUPPORT FROM EVERYONE IN THE DEPART-MENT.
I KNOW HE'S A GOOD MAN, BUT...
THAT DOESN'T CHANGE THE FACT THAT HE'S NOT MY TYPE.

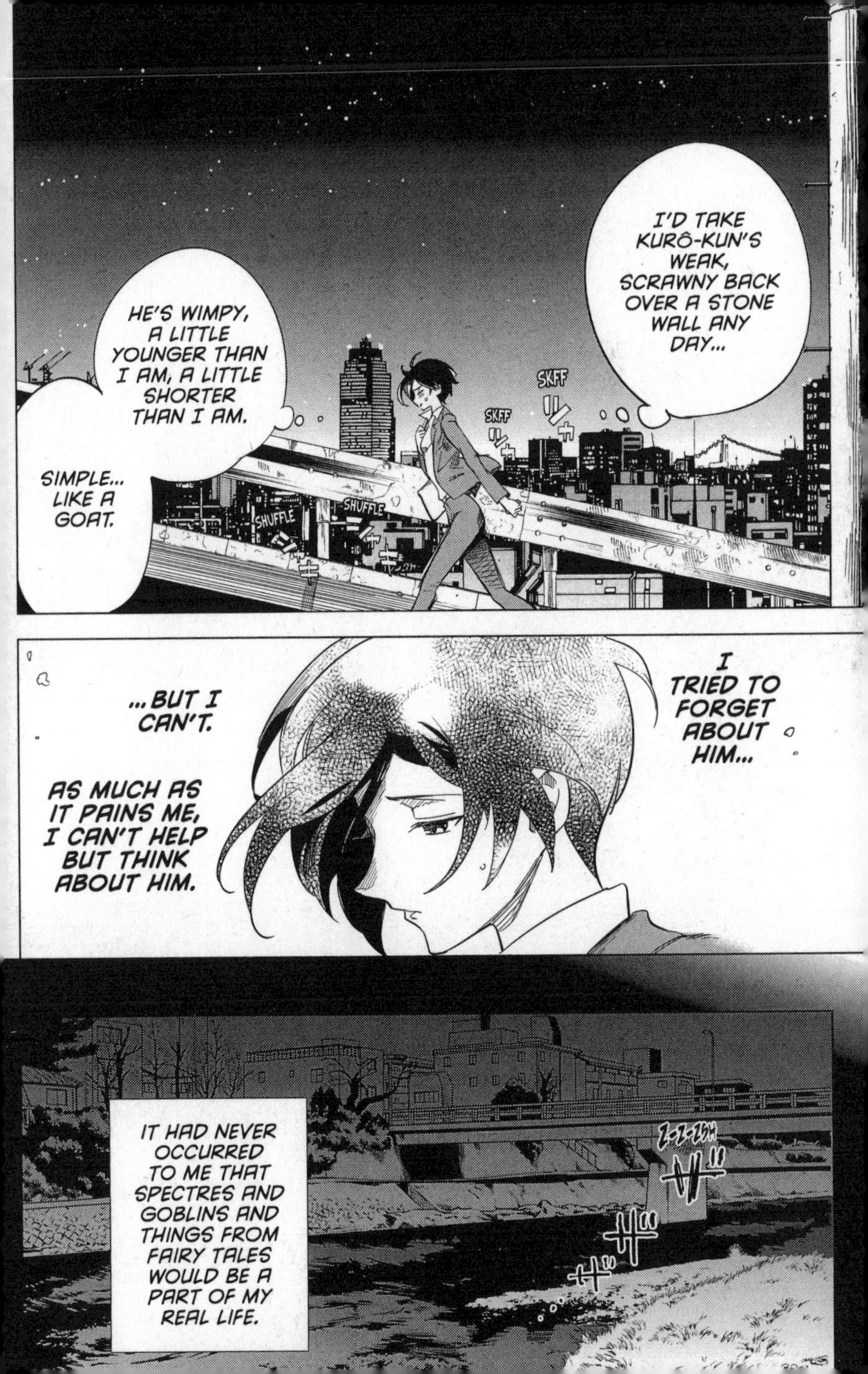
I'D TAKE KURÔ-KUN'S WEAK, SCRAWNY BACK OVER A STONE WALL ANY DAY...
SKFF
SKFF
HE'S WIMPY, A LITTLE YOUNGER THAN I AM, A LITTLE SHORTER THAN I AM.
SIMPLE... LIKE A GOAT.
SHUFFLE
SHUFFLE
I TRIED TO FORGET ABOUT HIM...
...BUT I CAN'T.
AS MUCH AS IT PAINS ME, I CAN'T HELP BUT THINK ABOUT HIM.
Z-Z-ZSH
IT HAD NEVER OCCURRED TO ME THAT SPECTRES AND GOBLINS AND THINGS FROM FAIRY TALES WOULD BE A PART OF MY REAL LIFE.

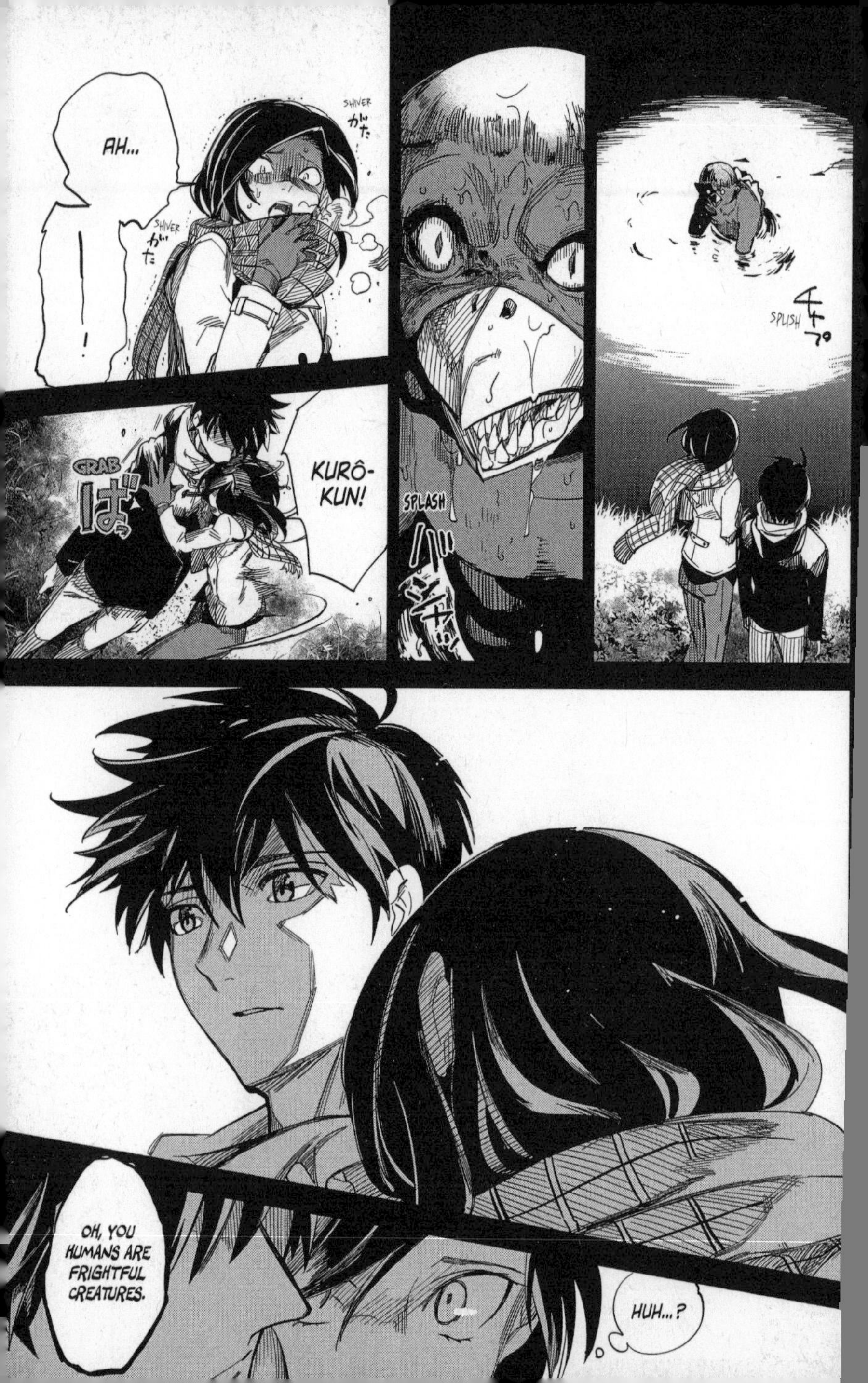
SPLISH
チャプ
SPLASH
SHIVER
がた
SHIVER
がた
AH...
—!
GRAB
ばっ
KURÔ-KUN!
HUH...?
OH, YOU HUMANS ARE FRIGHTFUL CREATURES.

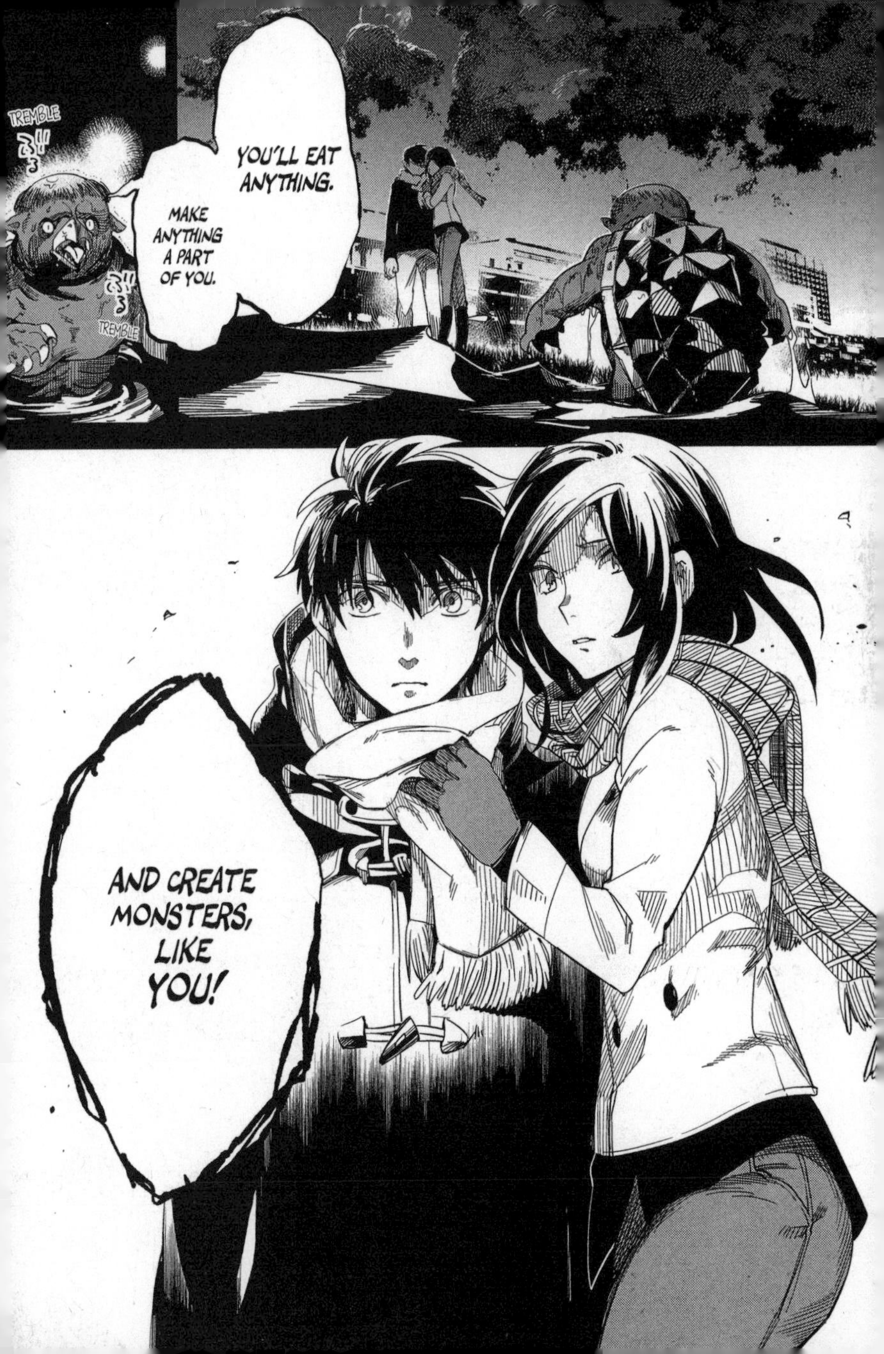
YOU'LL EAT ANYTHING.
MAKE ANYTHING A PART OF YOU.
TREMBLE
TREMBLE
AND CREATE MONSTERS, LIKE YOU!

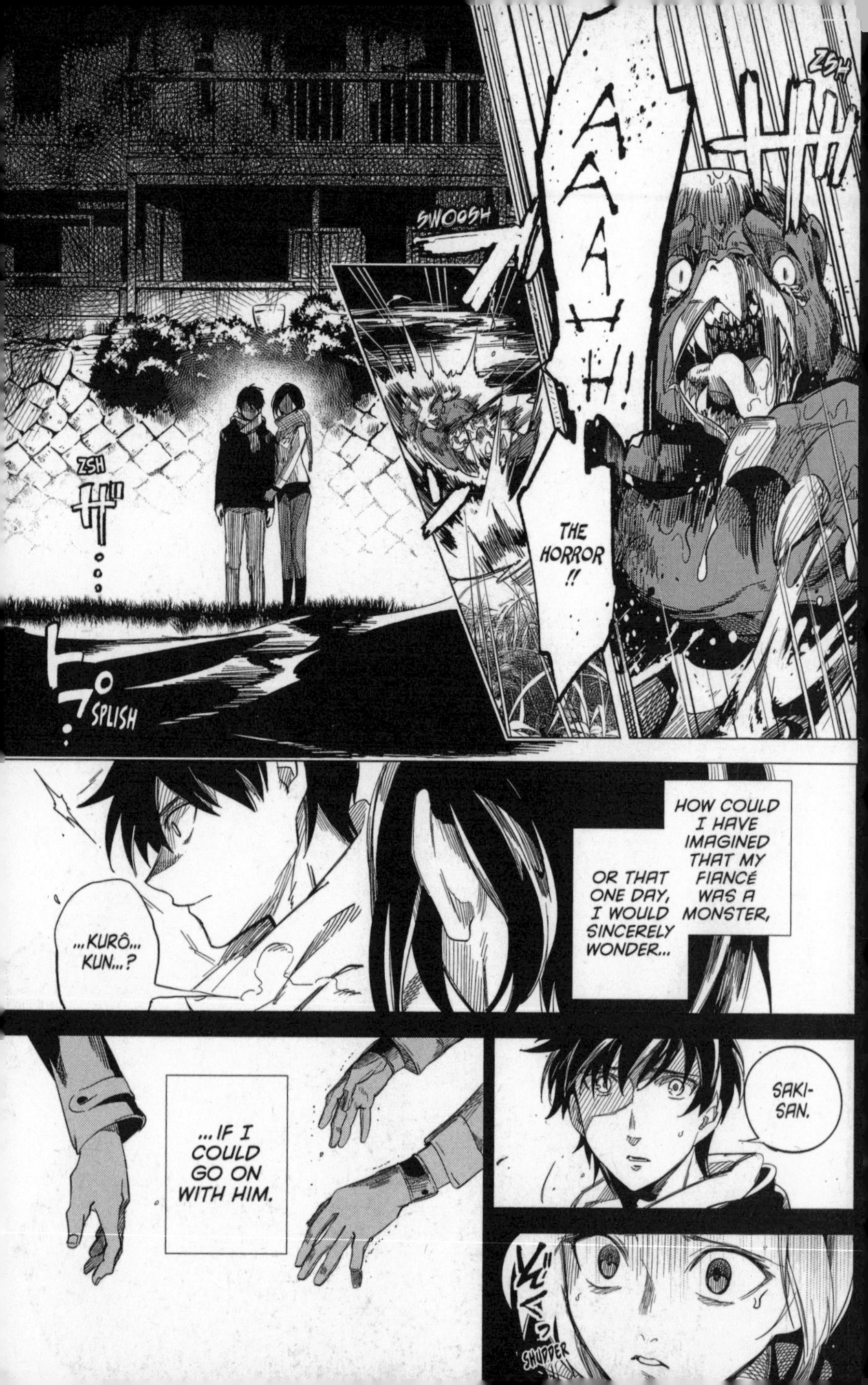
ZSH
AAAHH!
THE HORROR!!
SWOOSH
ZSH
...
SPLISH
HOW COULD I HAVE IMAGINED THAT MY FIANCÉ WAS A MONSTER,
OR THAT ONE DAY, I WOULD SINCERELY WONDER...
...KURÔ... KUN...?
SAKI-SAN.
SHUDDER
...IF I COULD GO ON WITH HIM.

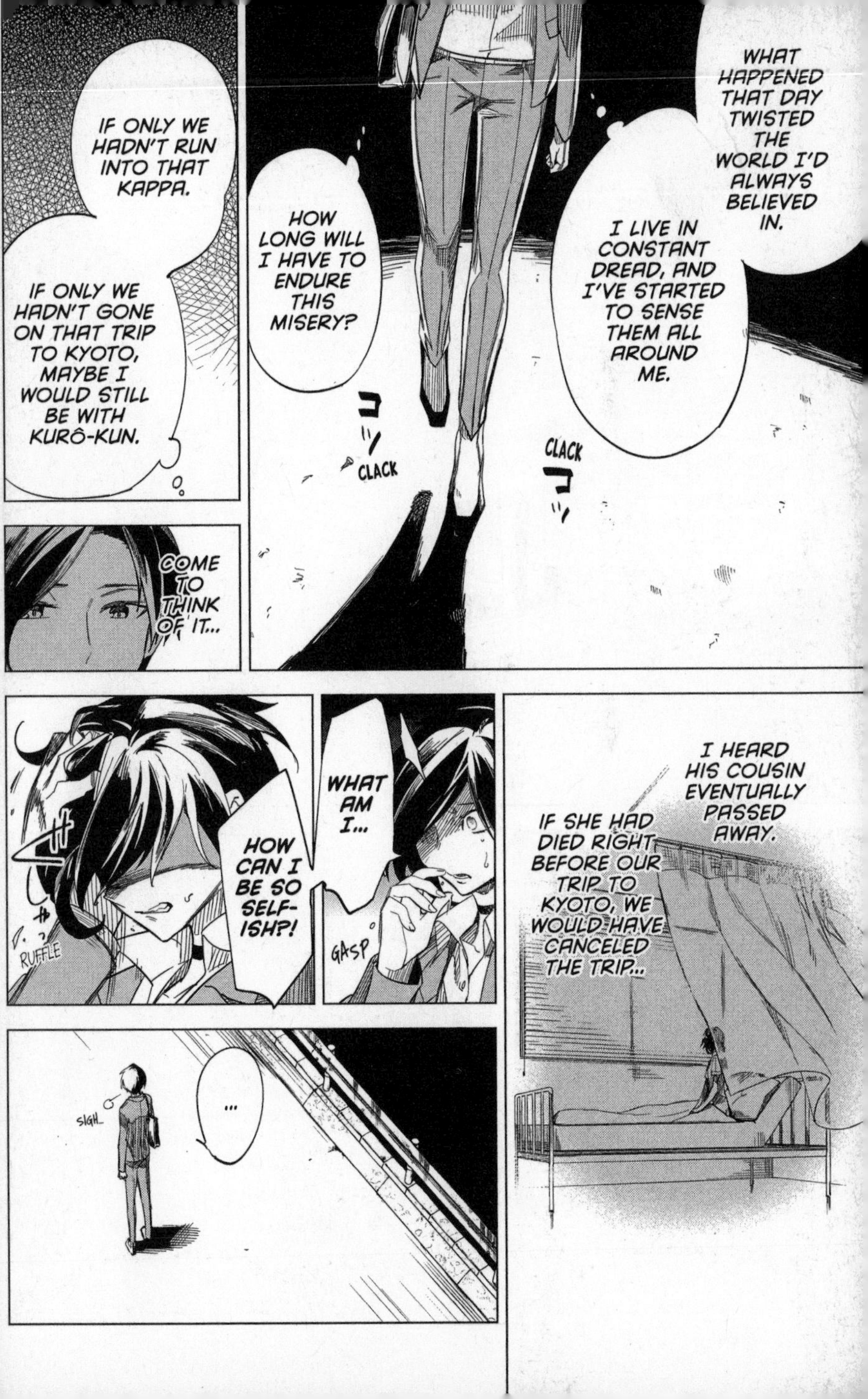
WHAT HAPPENED THAT DAY TWISTED THE WORLD I'D ALWAYS BELIEVED IN.
I LIVE IN CONSTANT DREAD, AND I'VE STARTED TO SENSE THEM ALL AROUND ME.
HOW LONG WILL I HAVE TO ENDURE THIS MISERY?
CLACK
CLACK
IF ONLY WE HADN'T RUN INTO THAT KAPPA.
IF ONLY WE HADN'T GONE ON THAT TRIP TO KYOTO, MAYBE I WOULD STILL BE WITH KURÔ-KUN.
COME TO THINK OF IT...
I HEARD HIS COUSIN EVENTUALLY PASSED AWAY.
IF SHE HAD DIED RIGHT BEFORE OUR TRIP TO KYOTO, WE WOULD HAVE CANCELED THE TRIP...
WHAT AM I...
GASP
HOW CAN I BE SO SELF-ISH?!
RUFFLE
...
SIGH

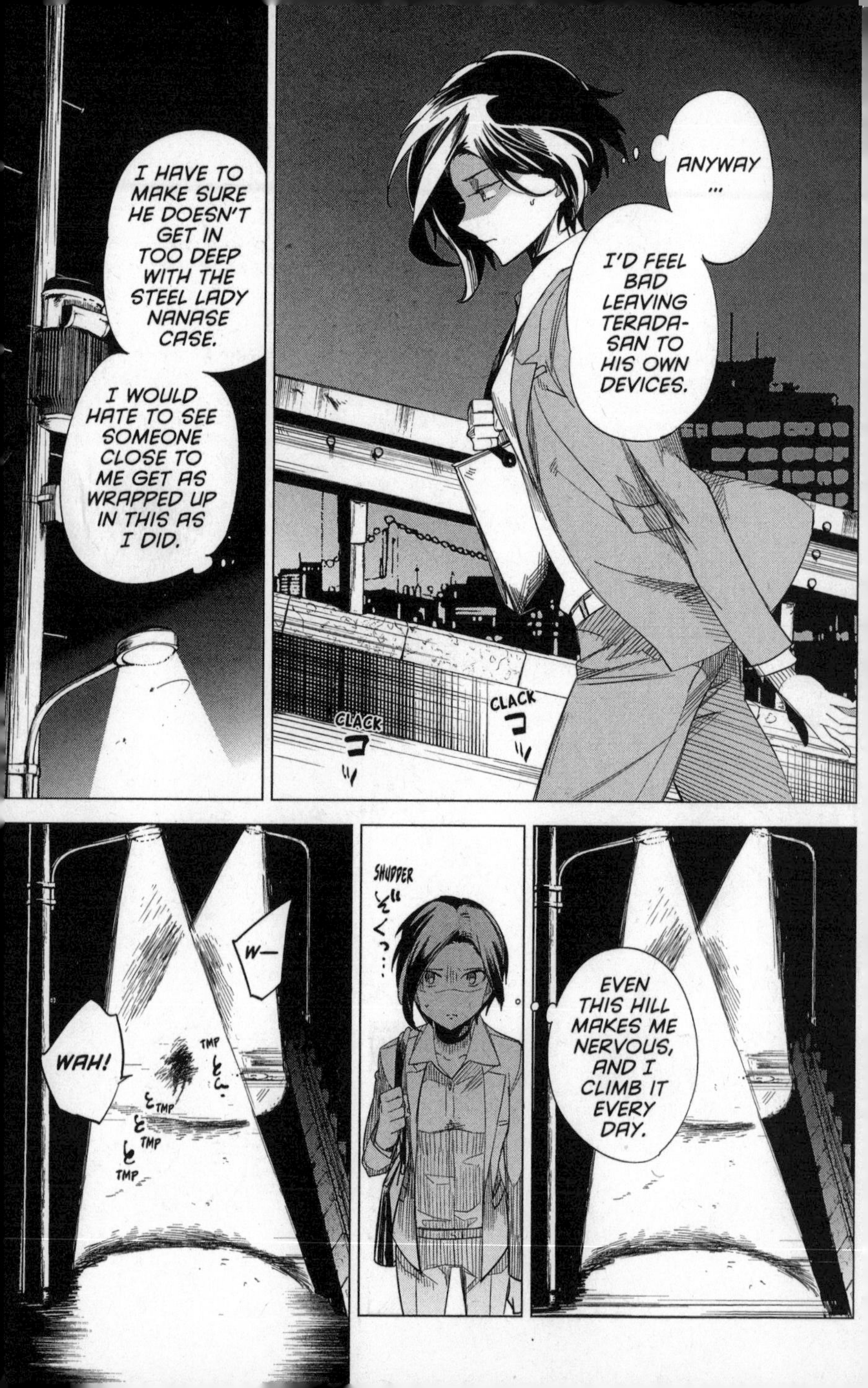
ANYWAY ...
I'D FEEL BAD LEAVING TERADA-SAN TO HIS OWN DEVICES.
CLACK コツ
CLACK コツ
I HAVE TO MAKE SURE HE DOESN'T GET IN TOO DEEP WITH THE STEEL LADY NANASE CASE.
I WOULD HATE TO SEE SOMEONE CLOSE TO ME GET AS WRAPPED UP IN THIS AS I DID.
EVEN THIS HILL MAKES ME NERVOUS, AND I CLIMB IT EVERY DAY.
SHUDDER ぞくっ…
W—
WAH!
TMP と
TMP と
TMP と
TMP と

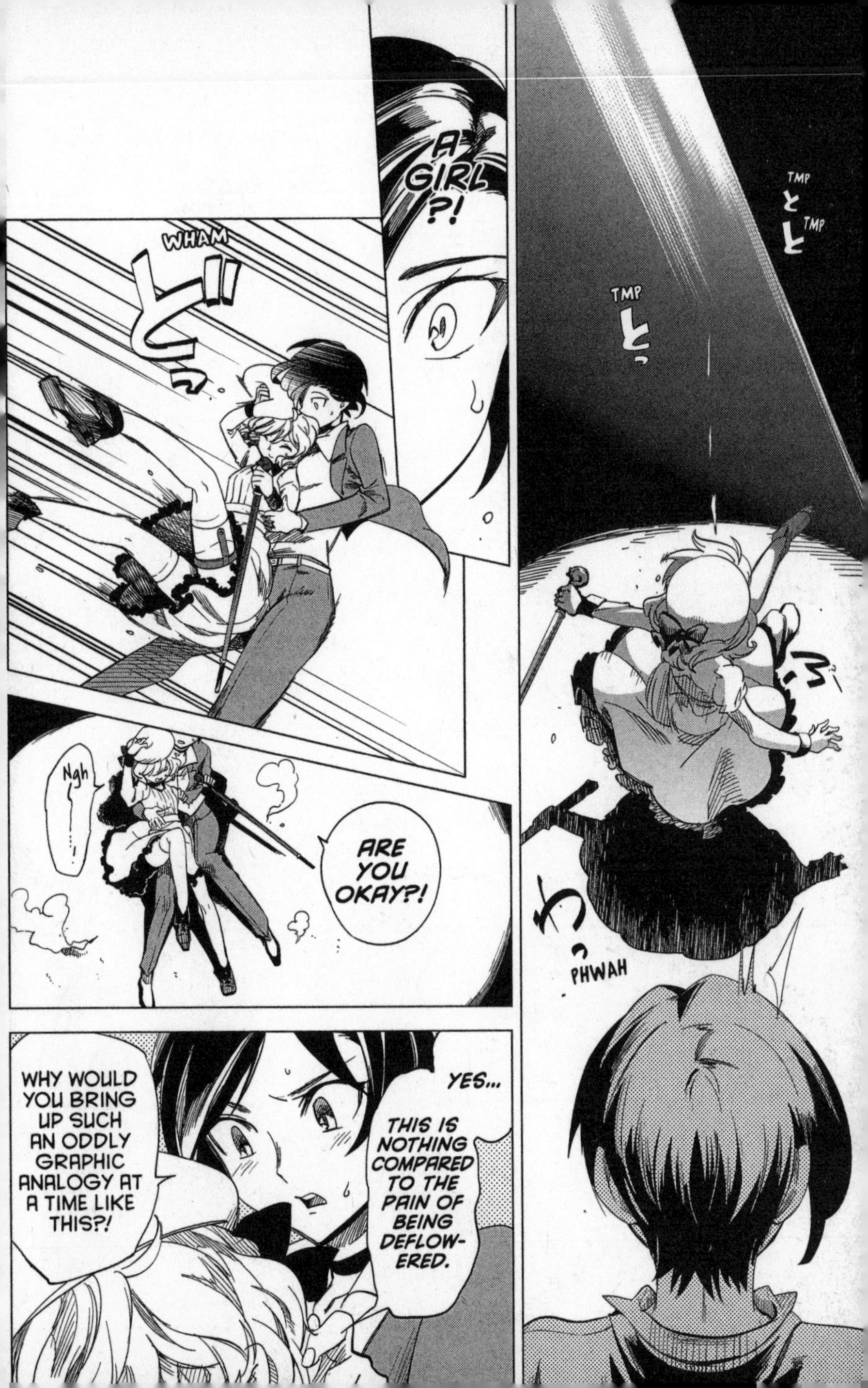

TMP と
TMP と
TMP とっ
PHWAH わっ
A GIRL?!
WHAM どしゃ
Ngh
ARE YOU OKAY?!
YES...
THIS IS NOTHING COMPARED TO THE PAIN OF BEING DEFLOW-ERED.
WHY WOULD YOU BRING UP SUCH AN ODDLY GRAPHIC ANALOGY AT A TIME LIKE THIS?!

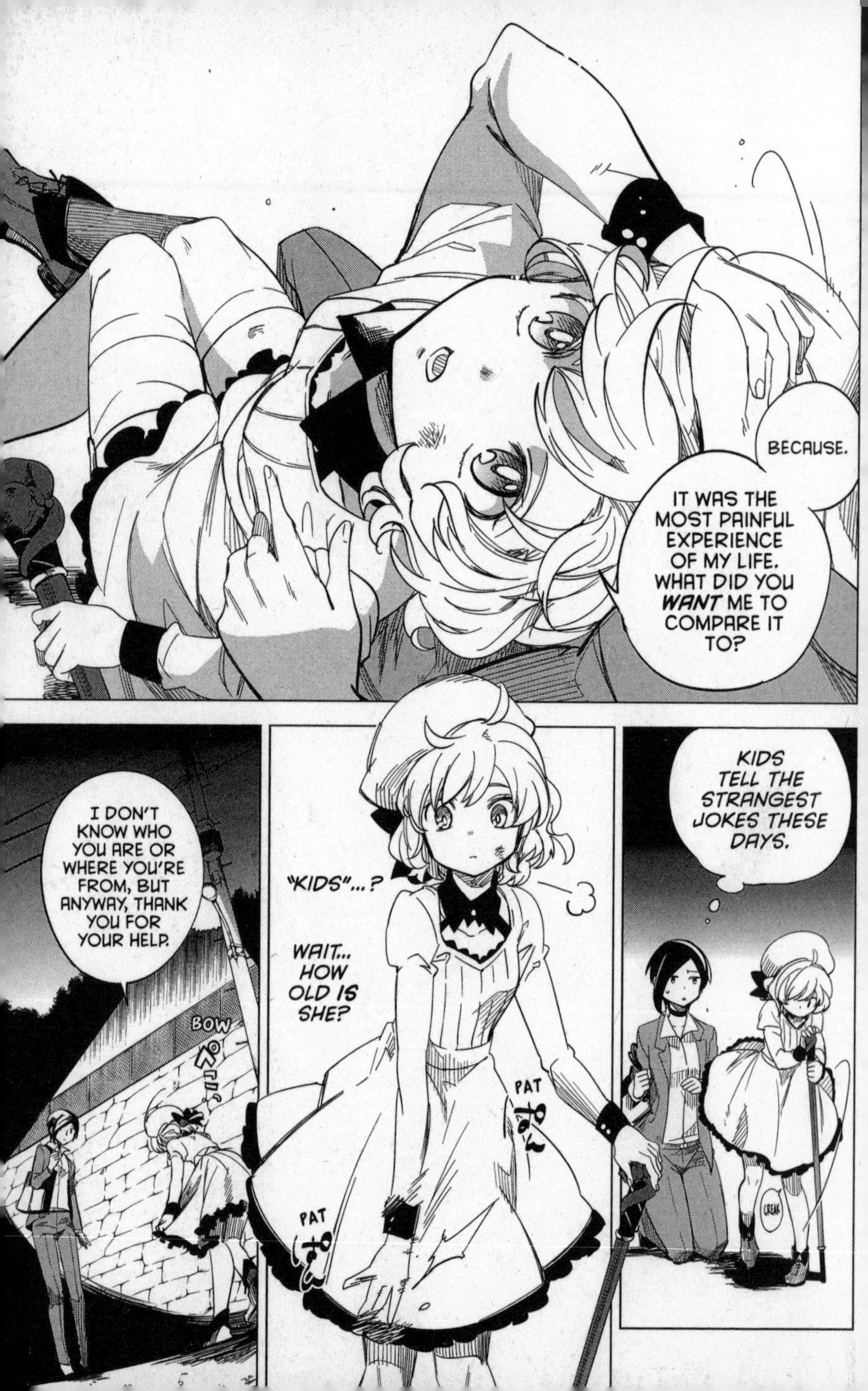
BECAUSE.
IT WAS THE MOST PAINFUL EXPERIENCE OF MY LIFE. WHAT DID YOU *WANT* ME TO COMPARE IT TO?
KIDS TELL THE STRANGEST JOKES THESE DAYS.
CREAK
"KIDS"...?
WAIT... HOW OLD IS SHE?
PAT
PAT
I DON'T KNOW WHO YOU ARE OR WHERE YOU'RE FROM, BUT ANYWAY, THANK YOU FOR YOUR HELP.
BOW

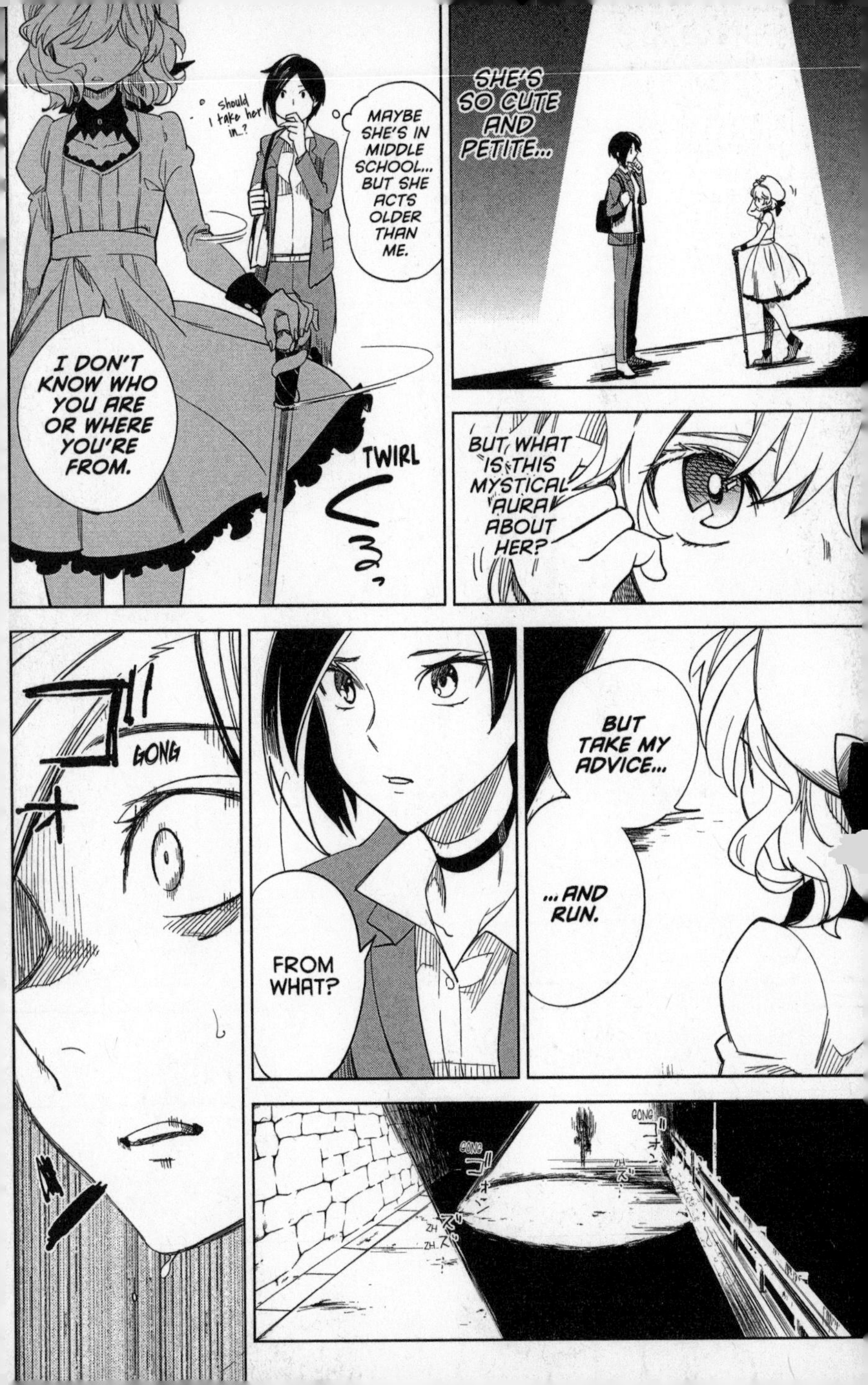
SHE'S SO CUTE AND PETITE...
BUT WHAT IS THIS MYSTICAL AURA ABOUT HER?
MAYBE SHE'S IN MIDDLE SCHOOL... BUT SHE ACTS OLDER THAN ME.
should I take her in..?
I DON'T KNOW WHO YOU ARE OR WHERE YOU'RE FROM.
TWIRL
BUT TAKE MY ADVICE...
...AND RUN.
FROM WHAT?
GONG
GONG
ZH
ZH
ZH
GONG

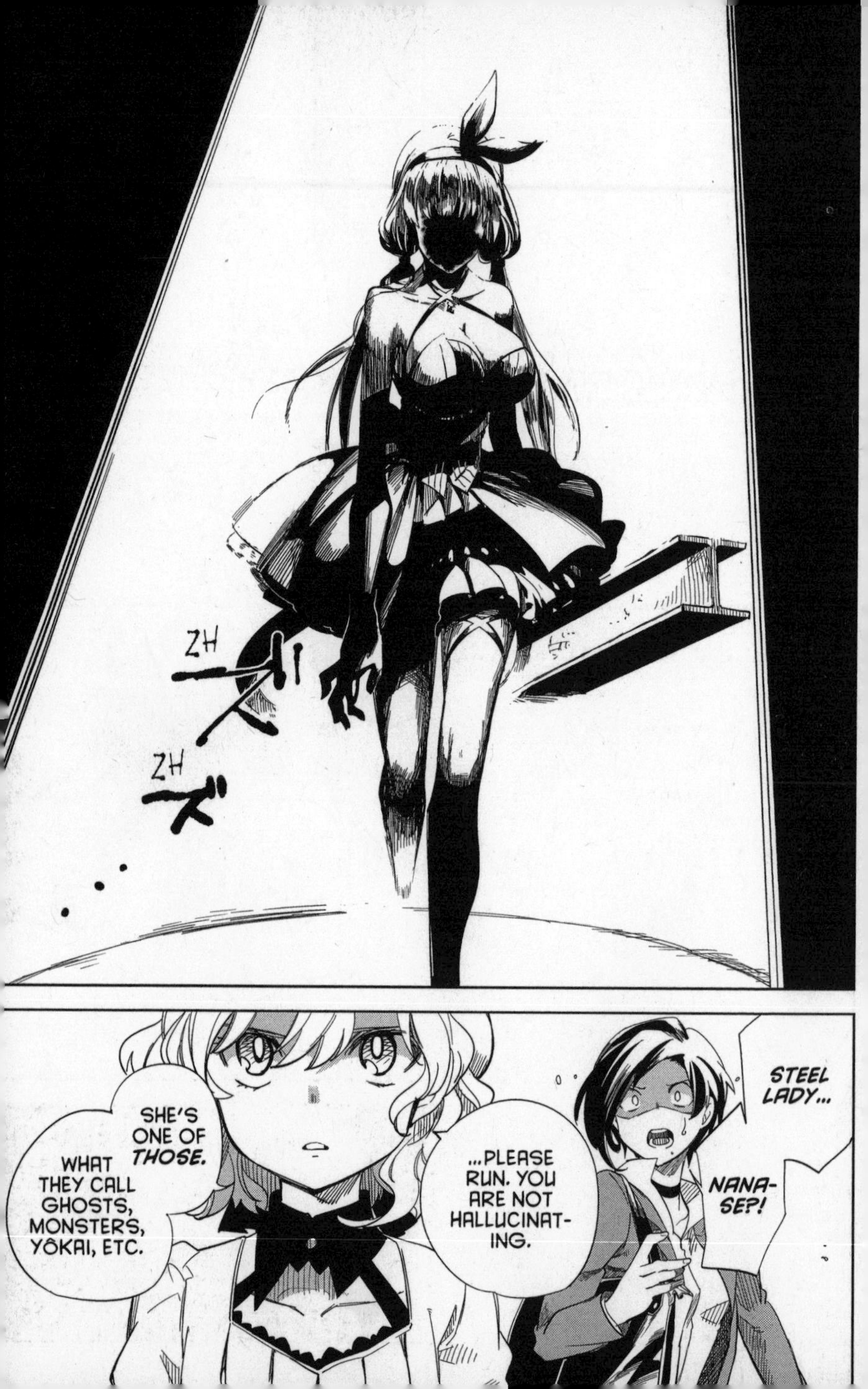
ZH
ZH
STEEL LADY...
NANA-SE?!
...PLEASE RUN. YOU ARE NOT HALLUCINAT-ING.
SHE'S ONE OF *THOSE.*
WHAT THEY CALL GHOSTS, MONSTERS, YÔKAI, ETC.

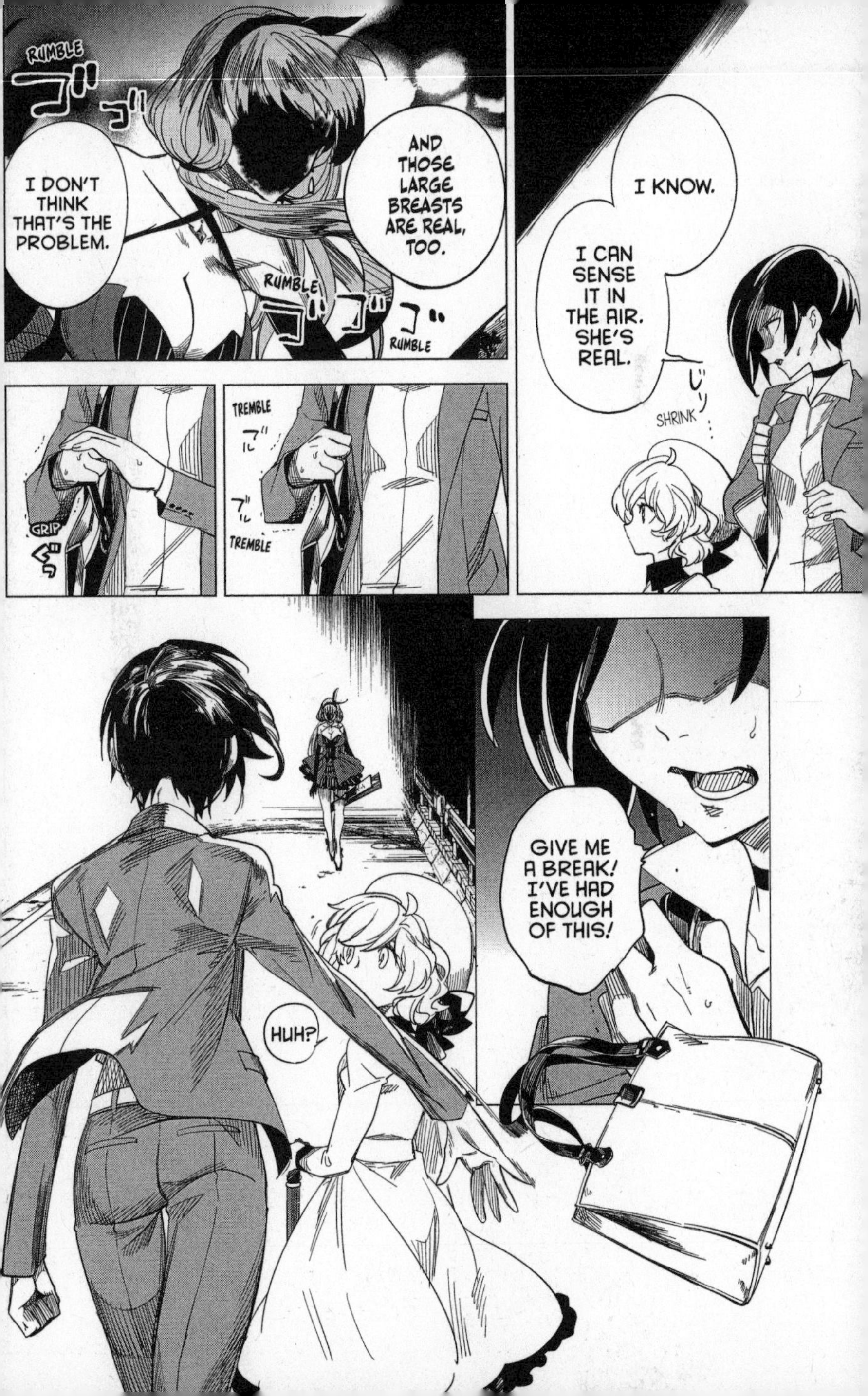
I KNOW.
I CAN SENSE IT IN THE AIR. SHE'S REAL.
SHRINK
RUMBLE
AND THOSE LARGE BREASTS ARE REAL, TOO.
I DON'T THINK THAT'S THE PROBLEM.
RUMBLE
RUMBLE
TREMBLE
TREMBLE
GRIP
GIVE ME A BREAK! I'VE HAD ENOUGH OF THIS!
HUH?

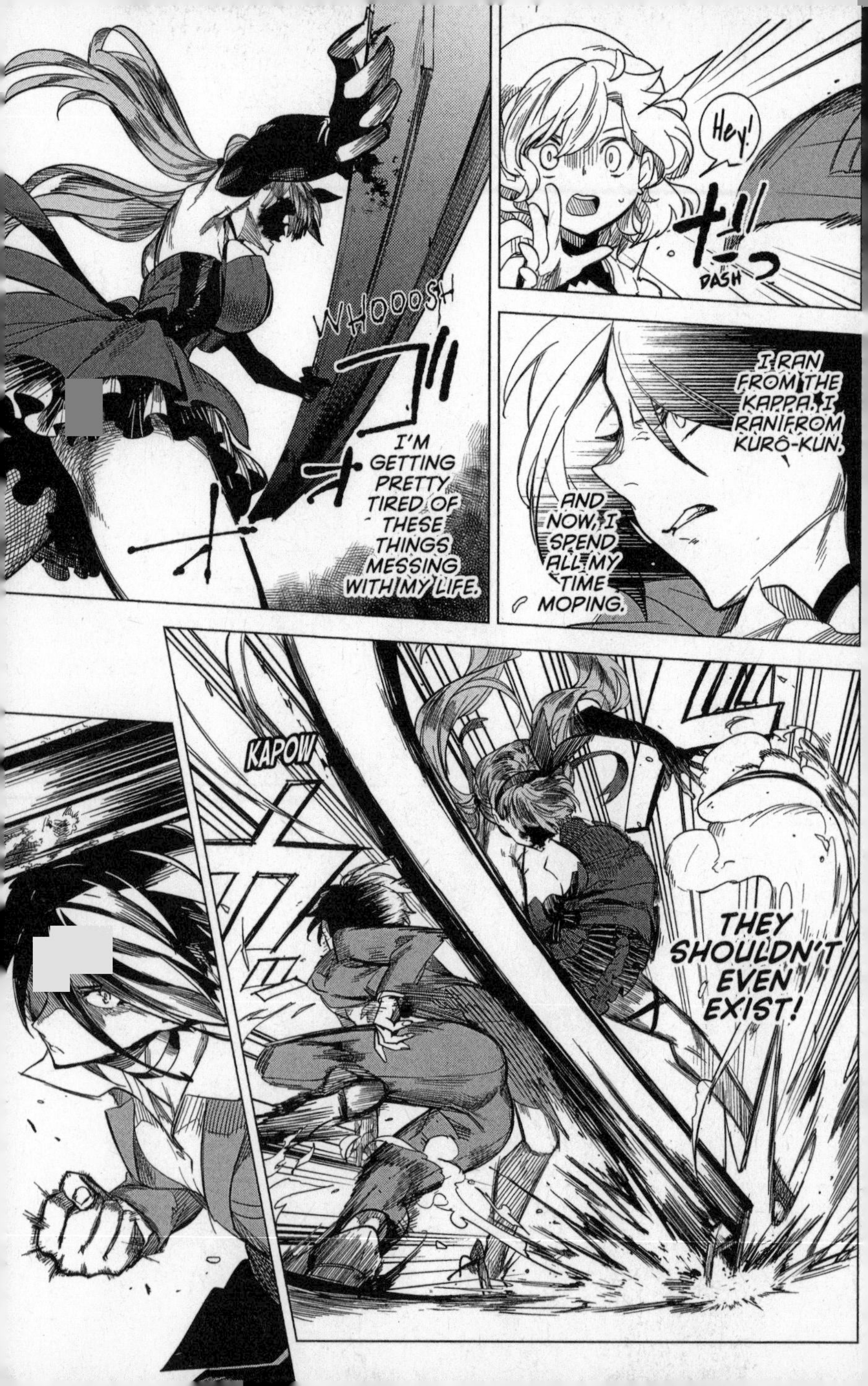
Hey!
DASH
I RAN FROM THE KAPPA. I RAN FROM KURÔ-KUN.
AND NOW, I SPEND ALL MY TIME MOPING.
WHOOOSH
I'M GETTING PRETTY TIRED OF THESE THINGS MESSING WITH MY LIFE.
THEY SHOULDN'T EVEN EXIST!
KAPOW

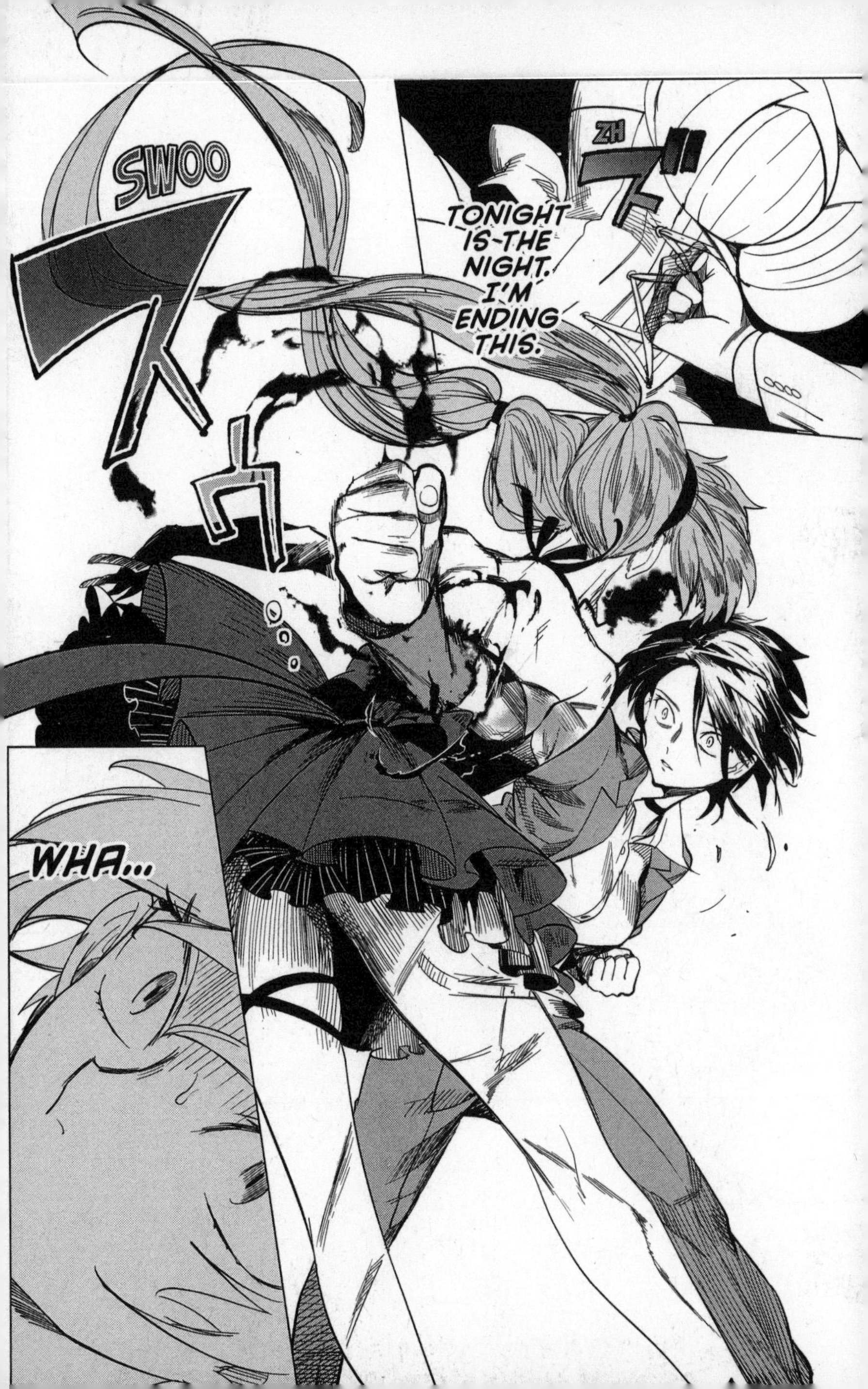
ZH
TONIGHT IS THE NIGHT. I'M ENDING THIS.
SWOO
WHA...

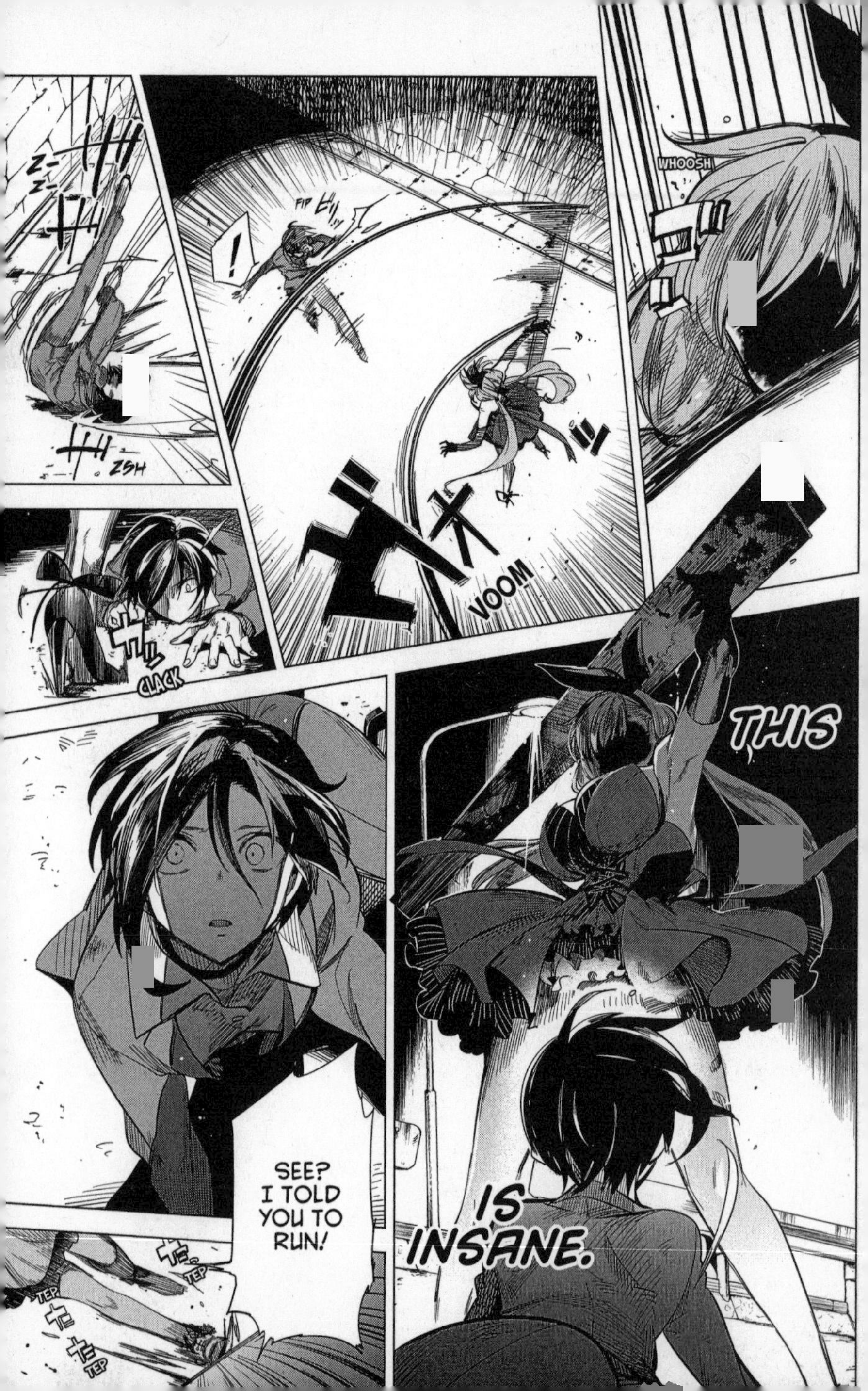
WHOOSH
FIP
!
VOOM
ZSH
CLACK
THIS
IS INSANE.
SEE? I TOLD YOU TO RUN!
TEP
TEP
TEP

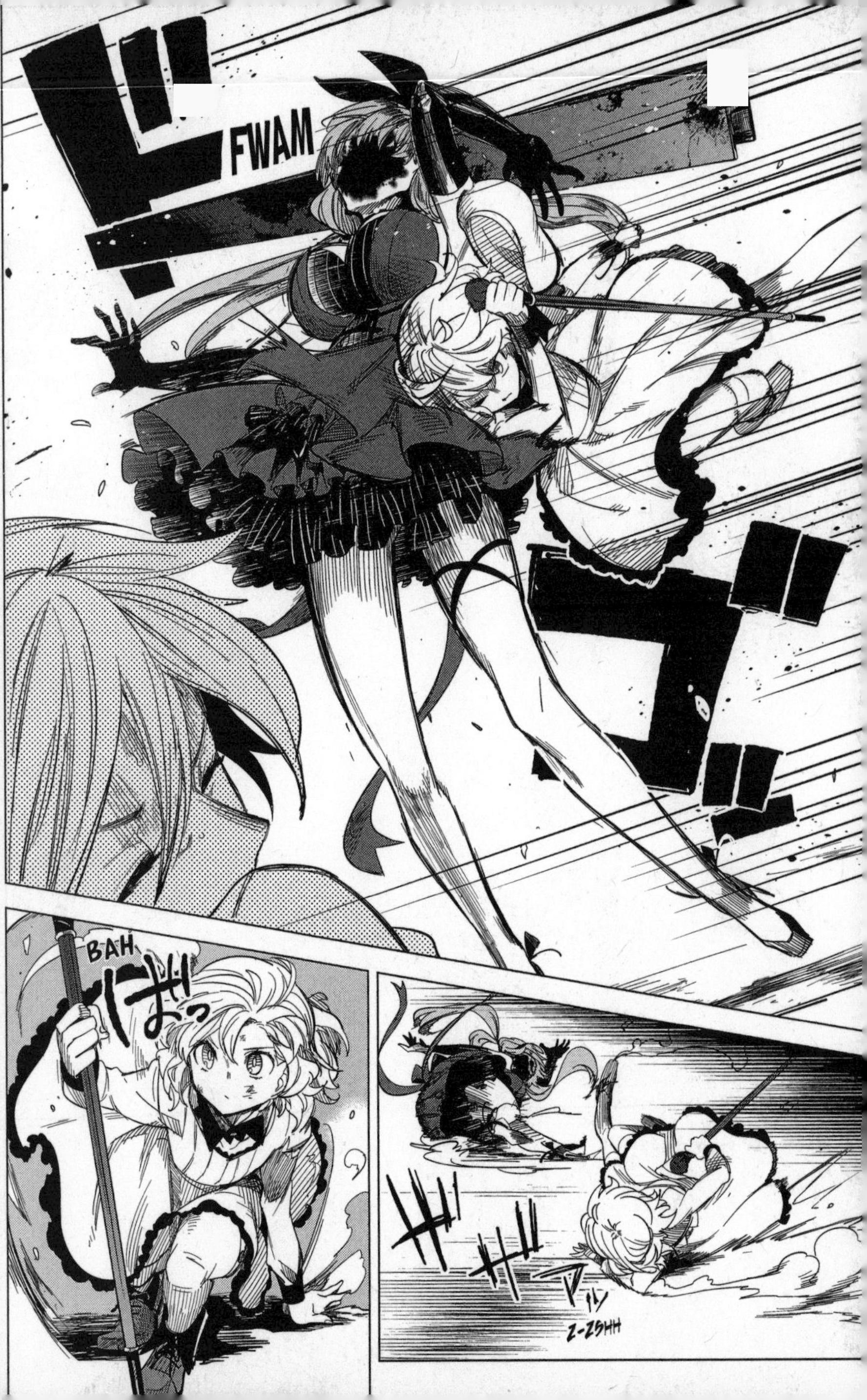
FWAM
ぱっ
BAH
Z-ZSHH

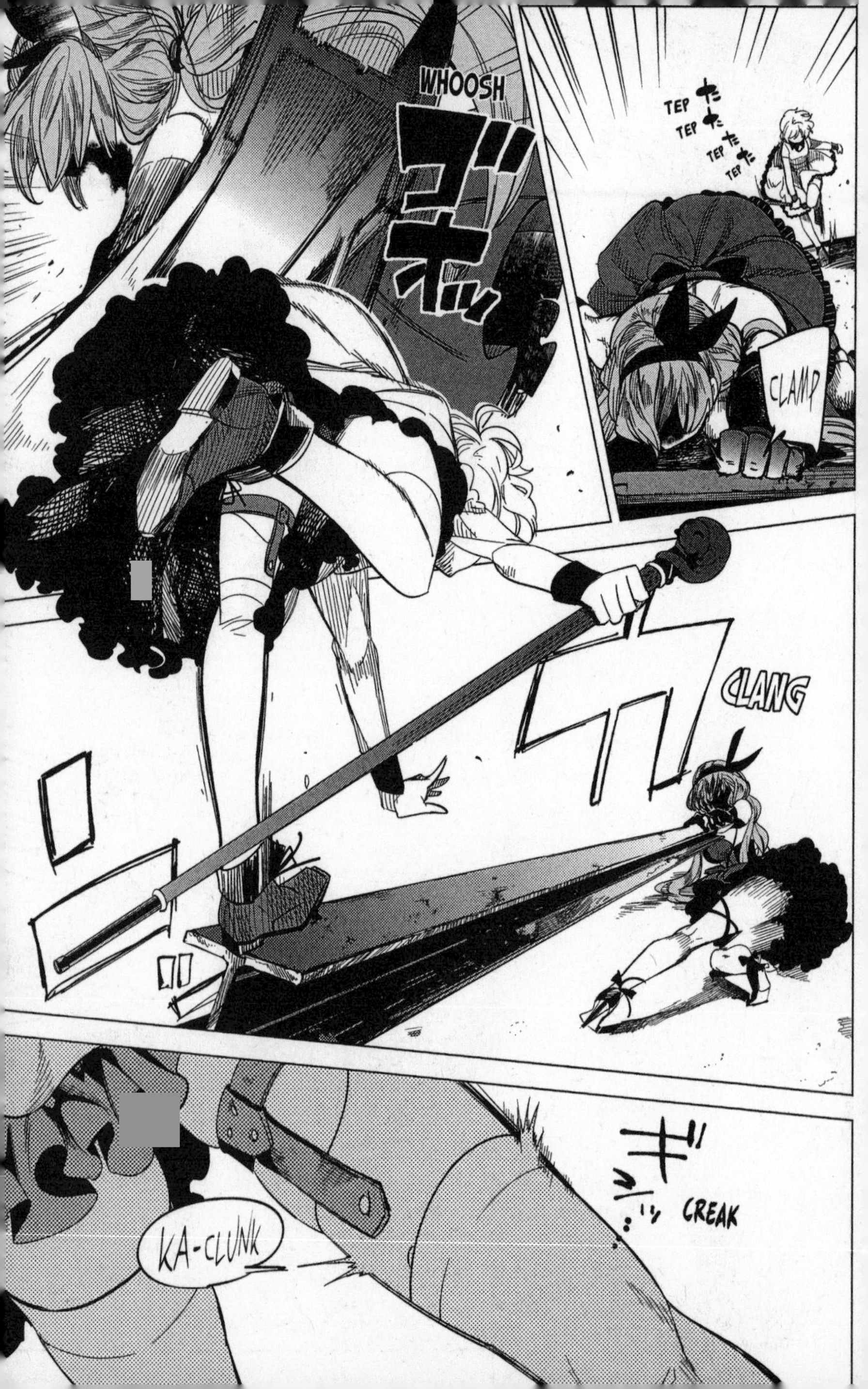
TEP
TEP
TEP
TEP
CLAMP
WHOOSH
CLANG
CREAK
KA-CLUNK

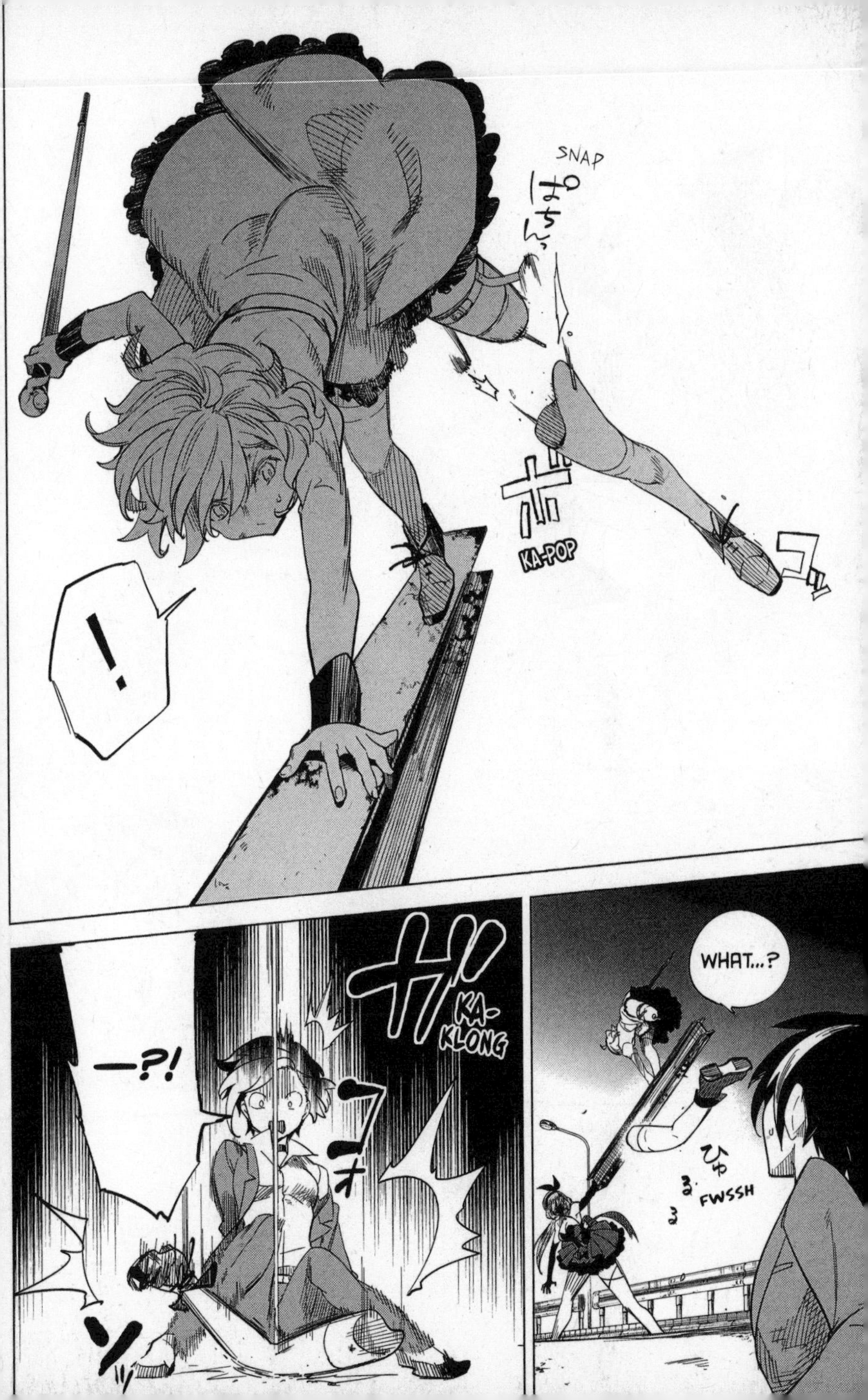
SNAP
ぱちんっ
KA-POP
!
WHAT...?
ひゅるる
FWSSH
KA-KLONG
—?!

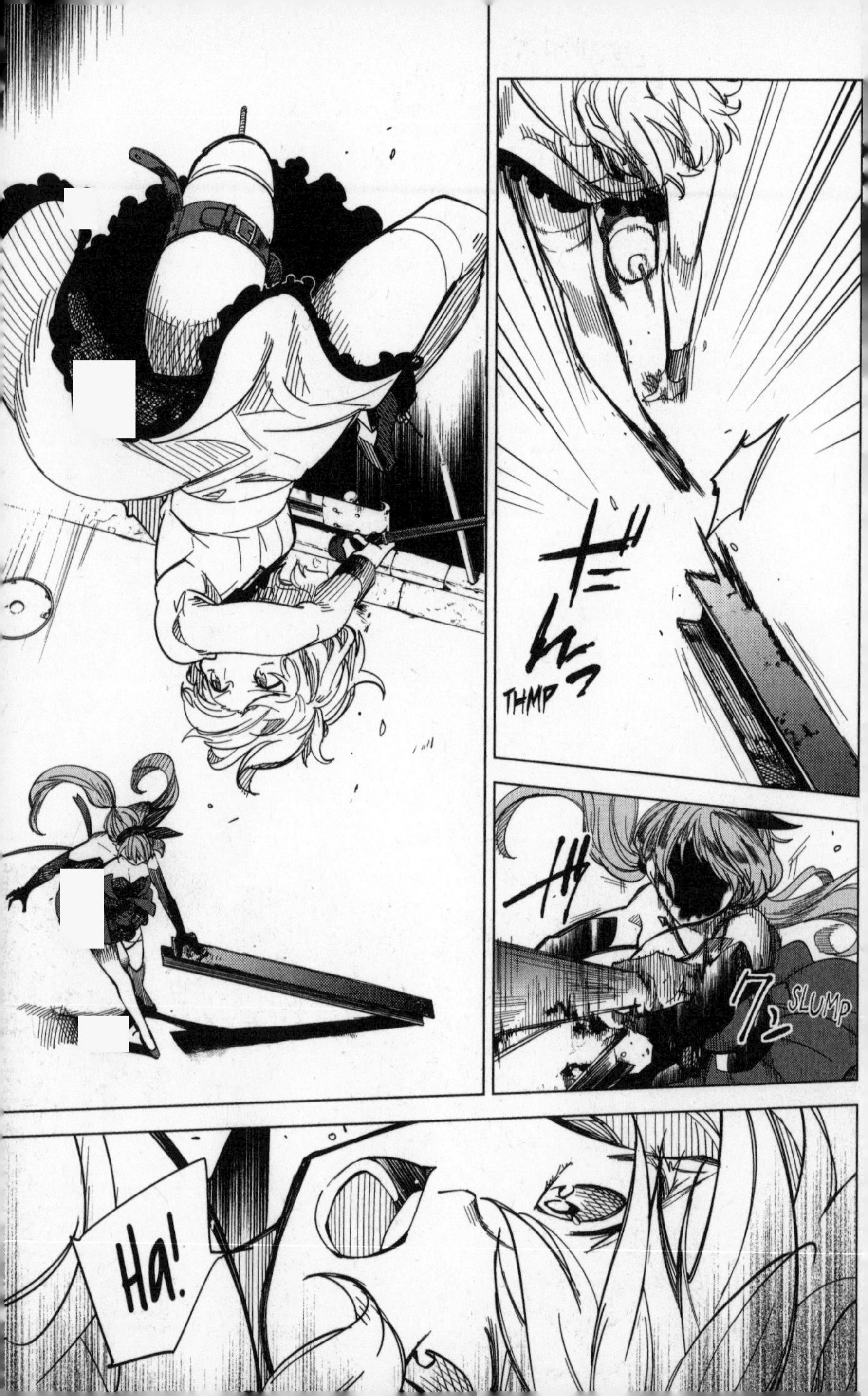
THMP
SLUMP
Ha!

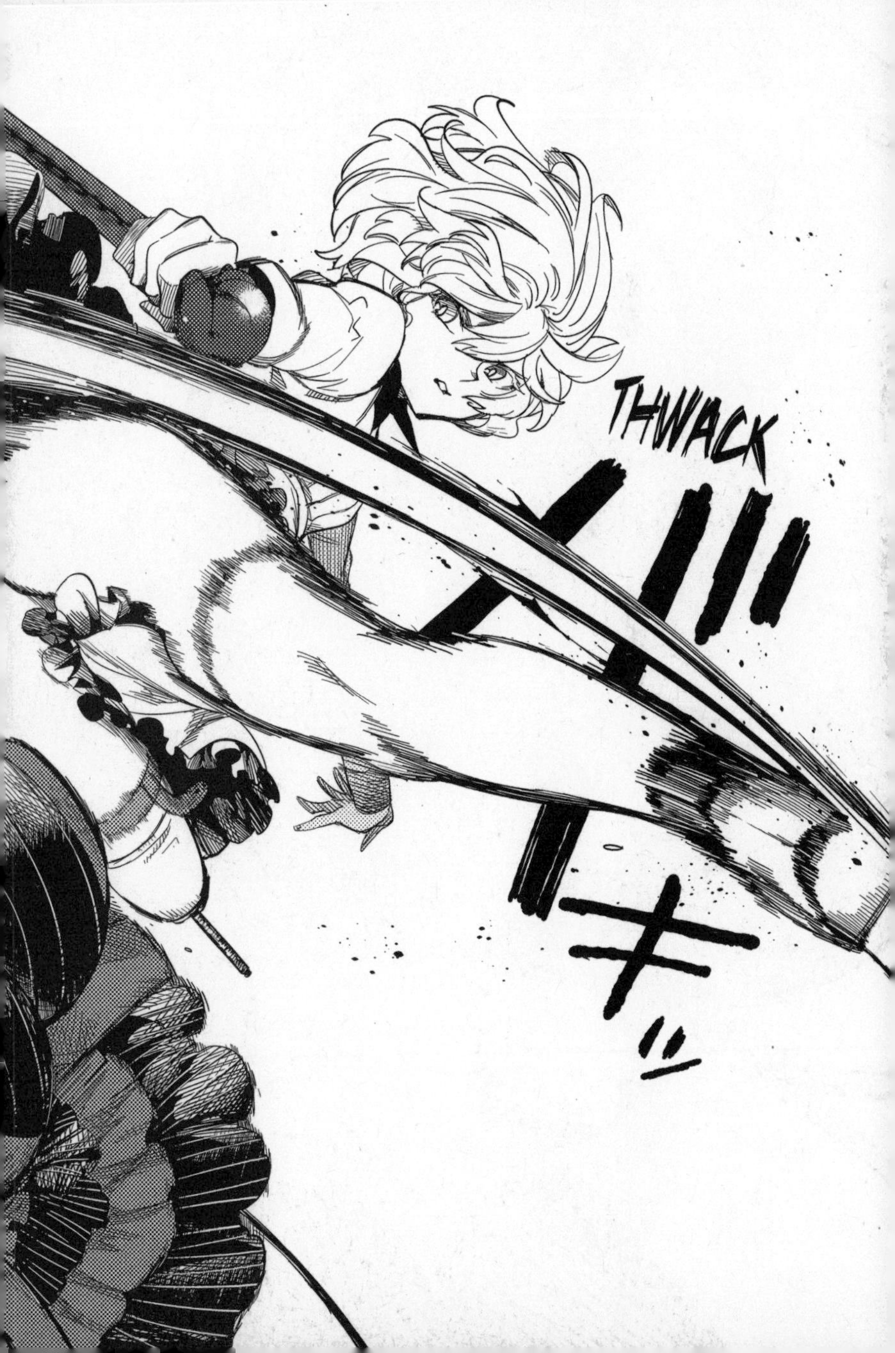
THWACK

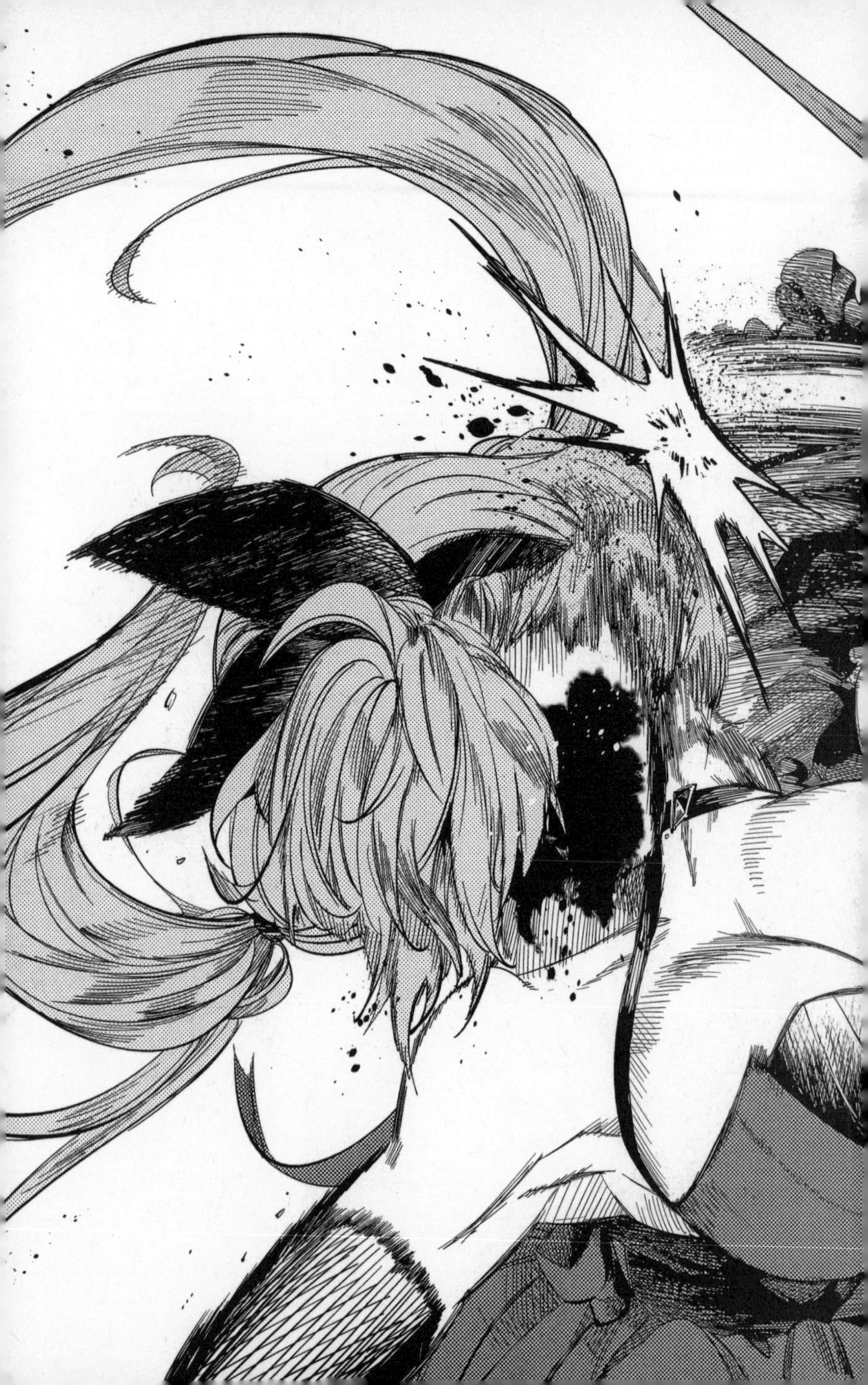

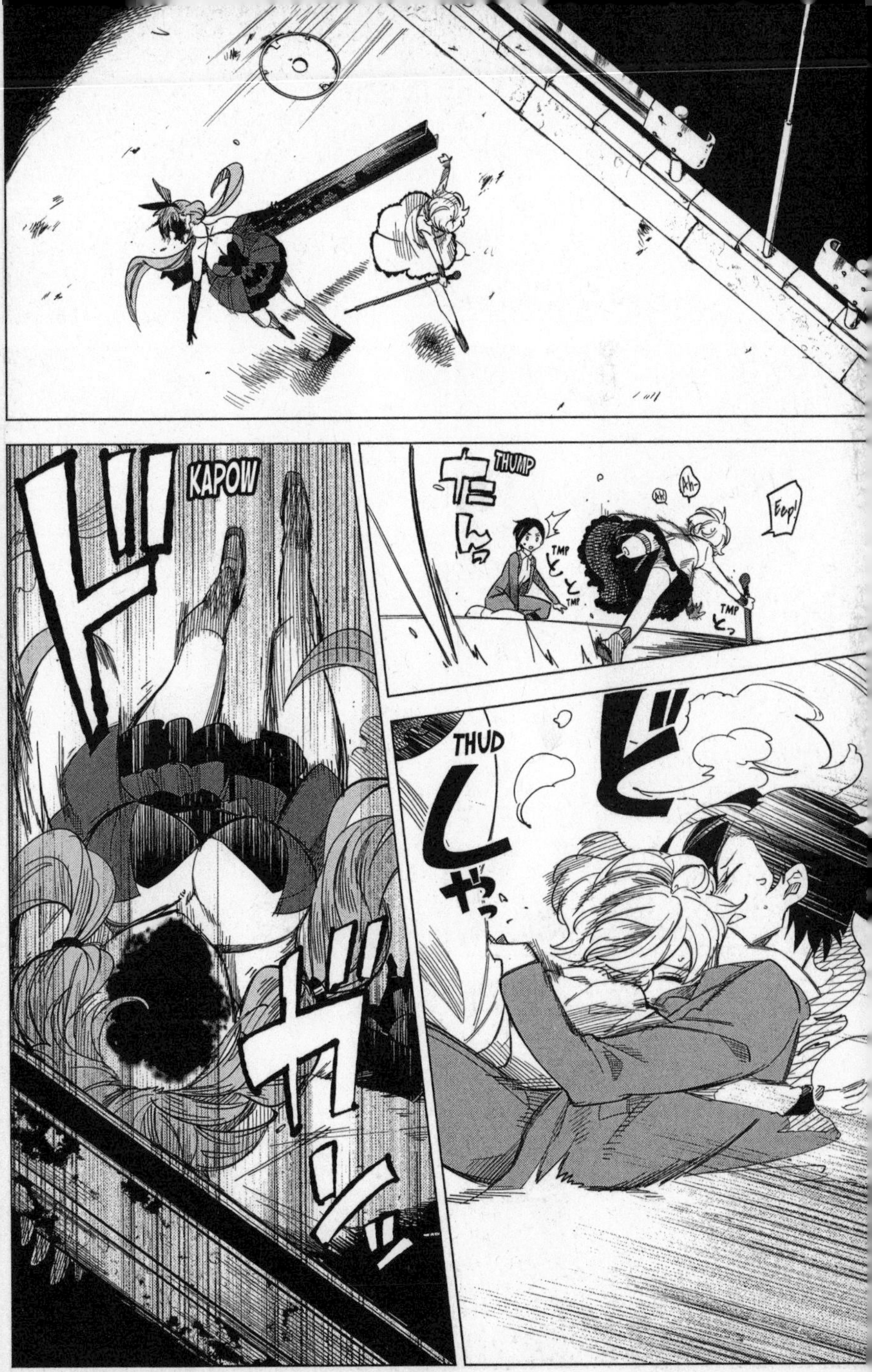
Eep!
Ah-
Ah!
THUMP
たん
TMP
TMP
TMP
THUD
どしゃっ
KAPOW
ドッ
ガッ

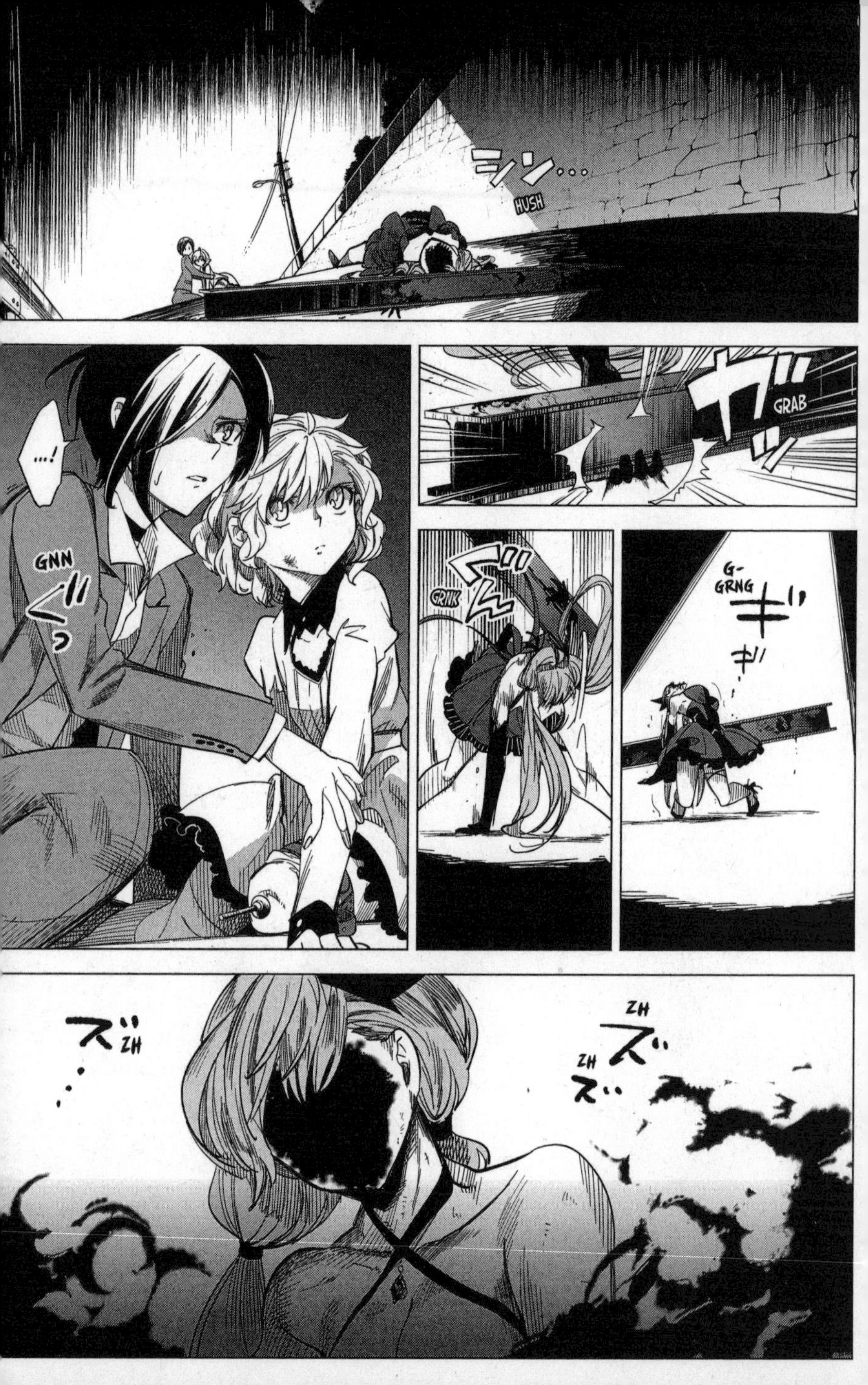

シン…
HUSH
GRAB
G-GRNG
GRNK
...!
GNN
ZH
ZH
ZH

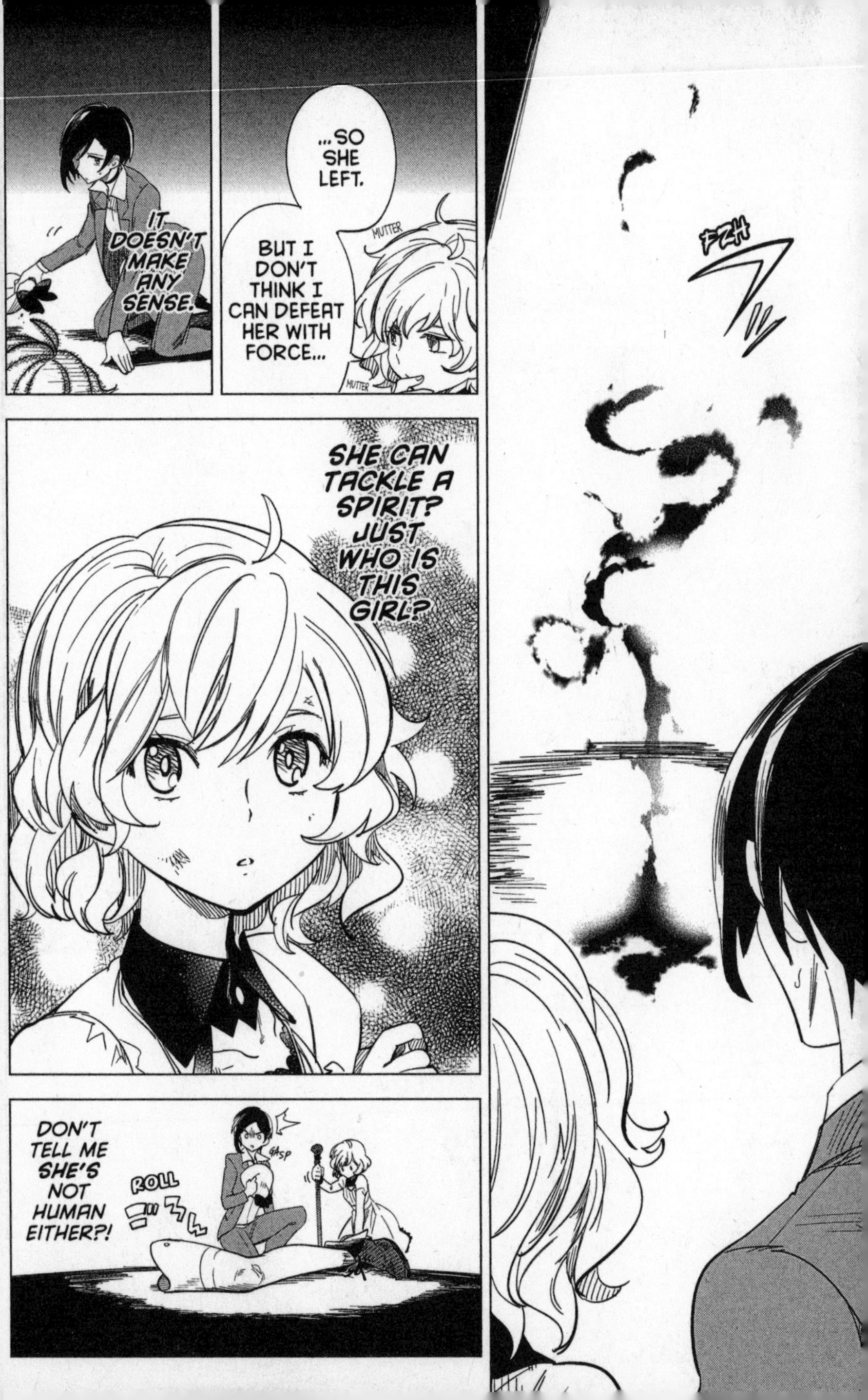
FZH
...SO SHE LEFT.
MUTTER
BUT I DON'T THINK I CAN DEFEAT HER WITH FORCE...
MUTTER
IT DOESN'T MAKE ANY SENSE.
SHE CAN TACKLE A SPIRIT? JUST WHO IS THIS GIRL?
GASP
ROLL
DON'T TELL ME SHE'S NOT HUMAN EITHER?!

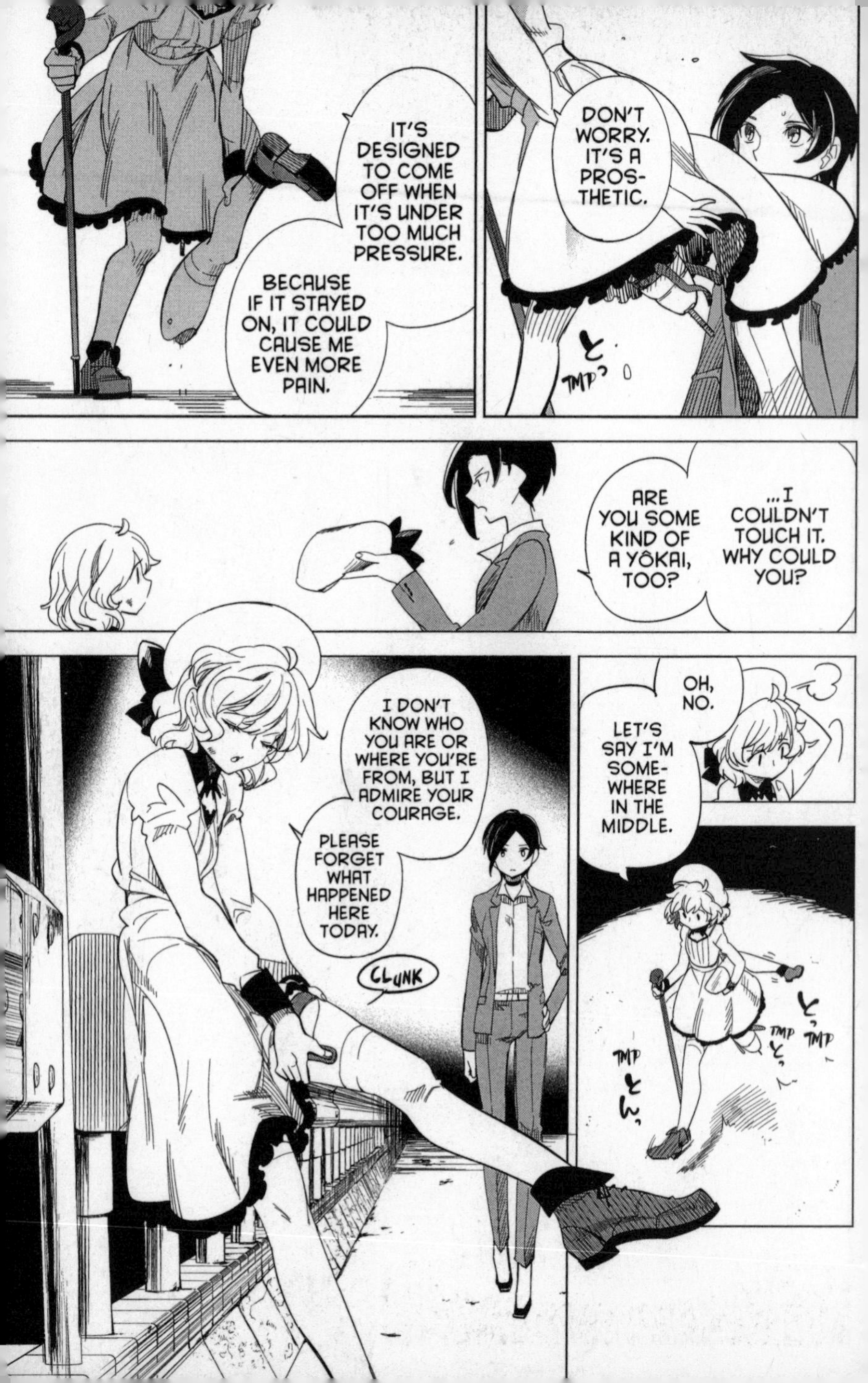
DON'T WORRY. IT'S A PROSTHETIC.
と
TMP
IT'S DESIGNED TO COME OFF WHEN IT'S UNDER TOO MUCH PRESSURE.
BECAUSE IF IT STAYED ON, IT COULD CAUSE ME EVEN MORE PAIN.
...I COULDN'T TOUCH IT. WHY COULD YOU?
ARE YOU SOME KIND OF A YÔKAI, TOO?
OH, NO.
LET'S SAY I'M SOME-WHERE IN THE MIDDLE.
と、TMP
と、TMP
とん、TMP
I DON'T KNOW WHO YOU ARE OR WHERE YOU'RE FROM, BUT I ADMIRE YOUR COURAGE.
PLEASE FORGET WHAT HAPPENED HERE TODAY.
CLUNK

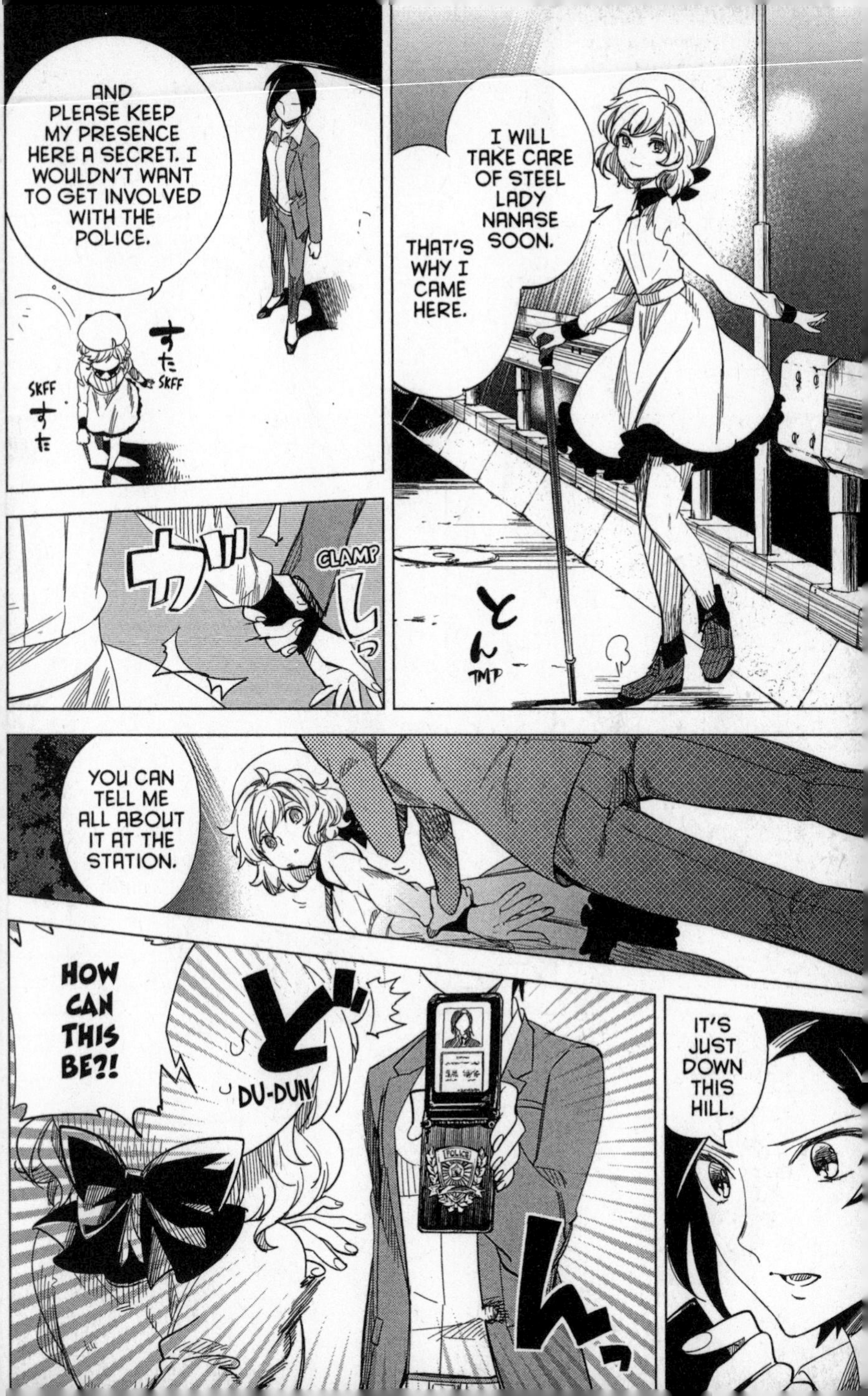
I WILL TAKE CARE OF STEEL LADY NANASE SOON.
THAT'S WHY I CAME HERE.
とん
TMP
AND PLEASE KEEP MY PRESENCE HERE A SECRET. I WOULDN'T WANT TO GET INVOLVED WITH THE POLICE.
すた
SKFF
SKFF
すた
ガッ
しっ
CLAMP
YOU CAN TELL ME ALL ABOUT IT AT THE STATION.
IT'S JUST DOWN THIS HILL.
POLICE
ん
HOW CAN THIS BE?!
ど
DU-DUN

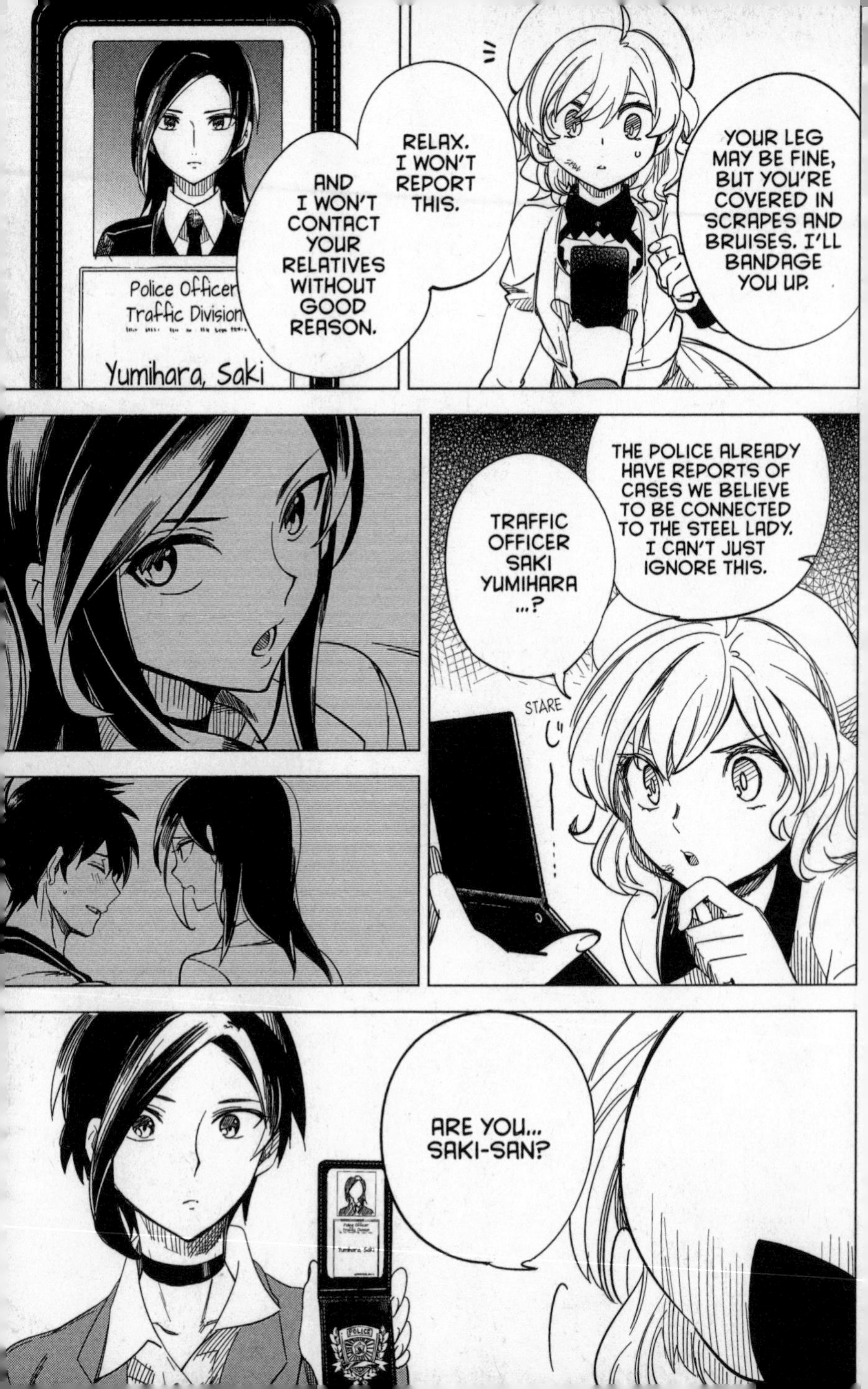
YOUR LEG MAY BE FINE, BUT YOU'RE COVERED IN SCRAPES AND BRUISES. I'LL BANDAGE YOU UP.
RELAX. I WON'T REPORT THIS.
AND I WON'T CONTACT YOUR RELATIVES WITHOUT GOOD REASON.
Police Officer
Traffic Division
Yumihara, Saki
THE POLICE ALREADY HAVE REPORTS OF CASES WE BELIEVE TO BE CONNECTED TO THE STEEL LADY. I CAN'T JUST IGNORE THIS.
TRAFFIC OFFICER SAKI YUMIHARA ...?
STARE
ARE YOU... SAKI-SAN?

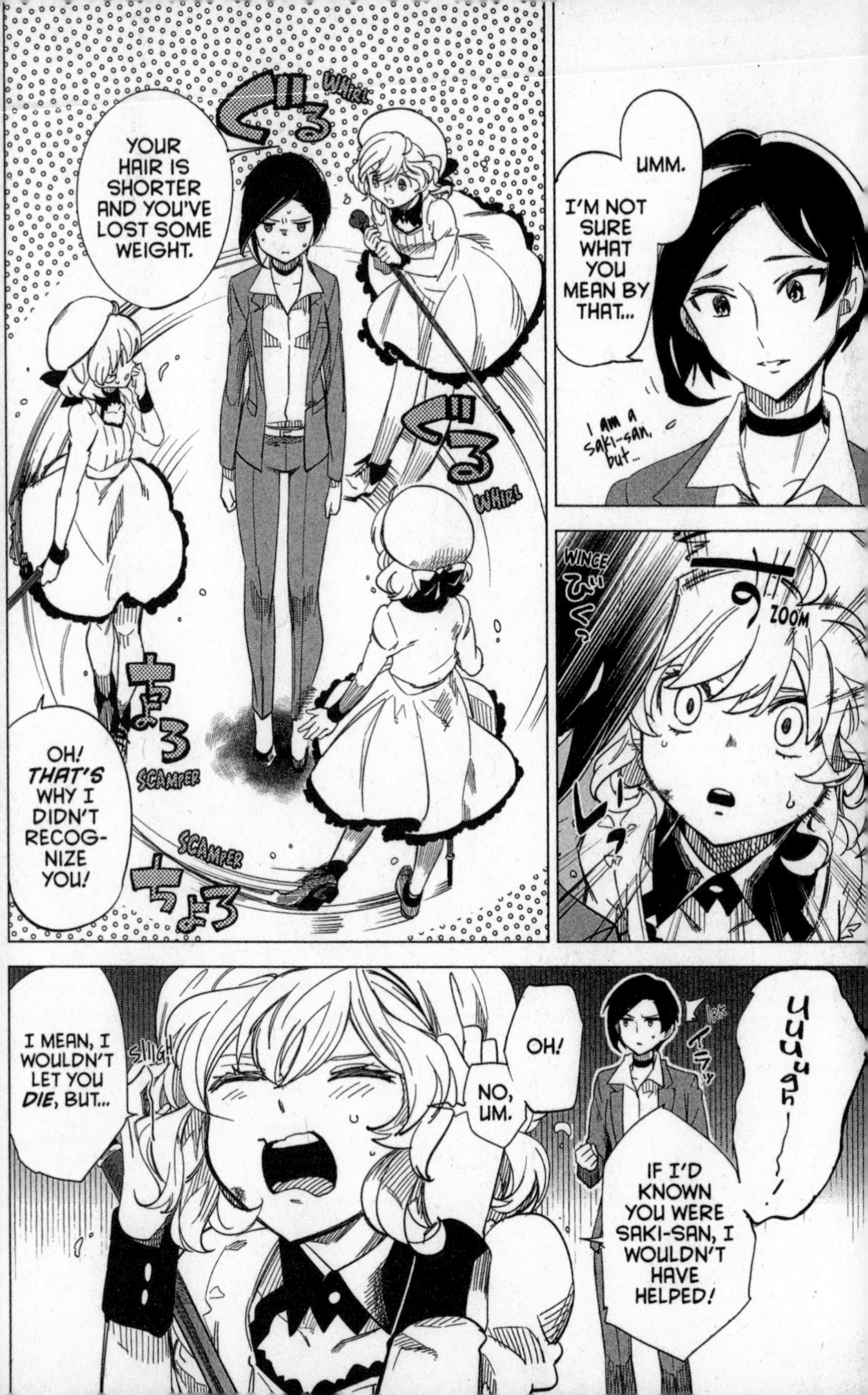
UMM.
I'M NOT SURE WHAT YOU MEAN BY THAT...
I am a Saki-san, but...
WINCE
びくっ
ZOOM
WHIRL
ぐる
YOUR HAIR IS SHORTER AND YOU'VE LOST SOME WEIGHT.
ぐる
WHIRL
ちょろ
SCAMPER
OH! *THAT'S* WHY I DIDN'T RECOG-NIZE YOU!
SCAMPER
ちょろ
Uuuugh---
IRK
イラッ
IF I'D KNOWN YOU WERE SAKI-SAN, I WOULDN'T HAVE HELPED!
OH!
NO, UM.
SLIIGH
I MEAN, I WOULDN'T LET YOU *DIE*, BUT...

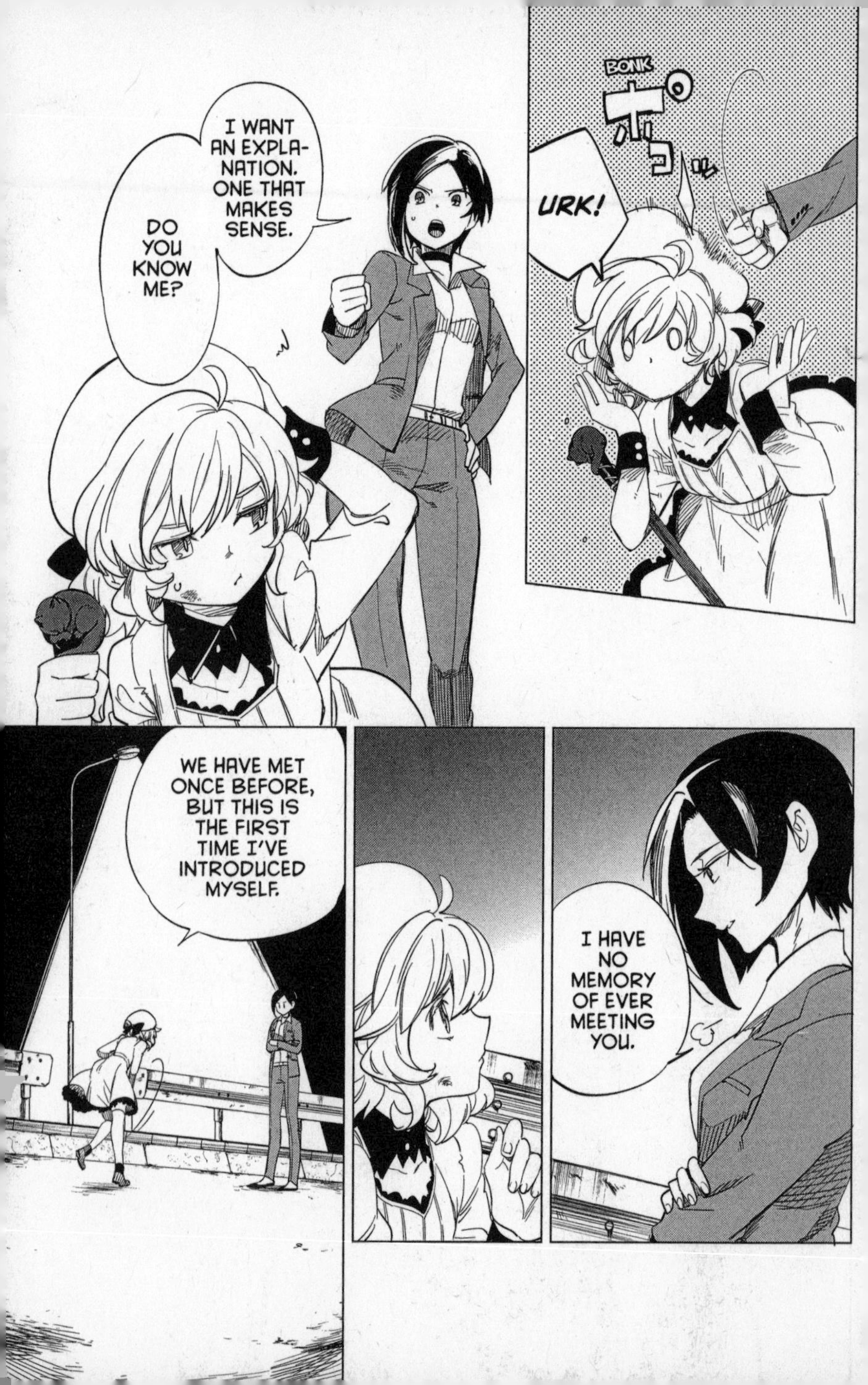
BONK
URK!
I WANT AN EXPLANATION. ONE THAT MAKES SENSE.
DO YOU KNOW ME?
I HAVE NO MEMORY OF EVER MEETING YOU.
WE HAVE MET ONCE BEFORE, BUT THIS IS THE FIRST TIME I'VE INTRODUCED MYSELF.

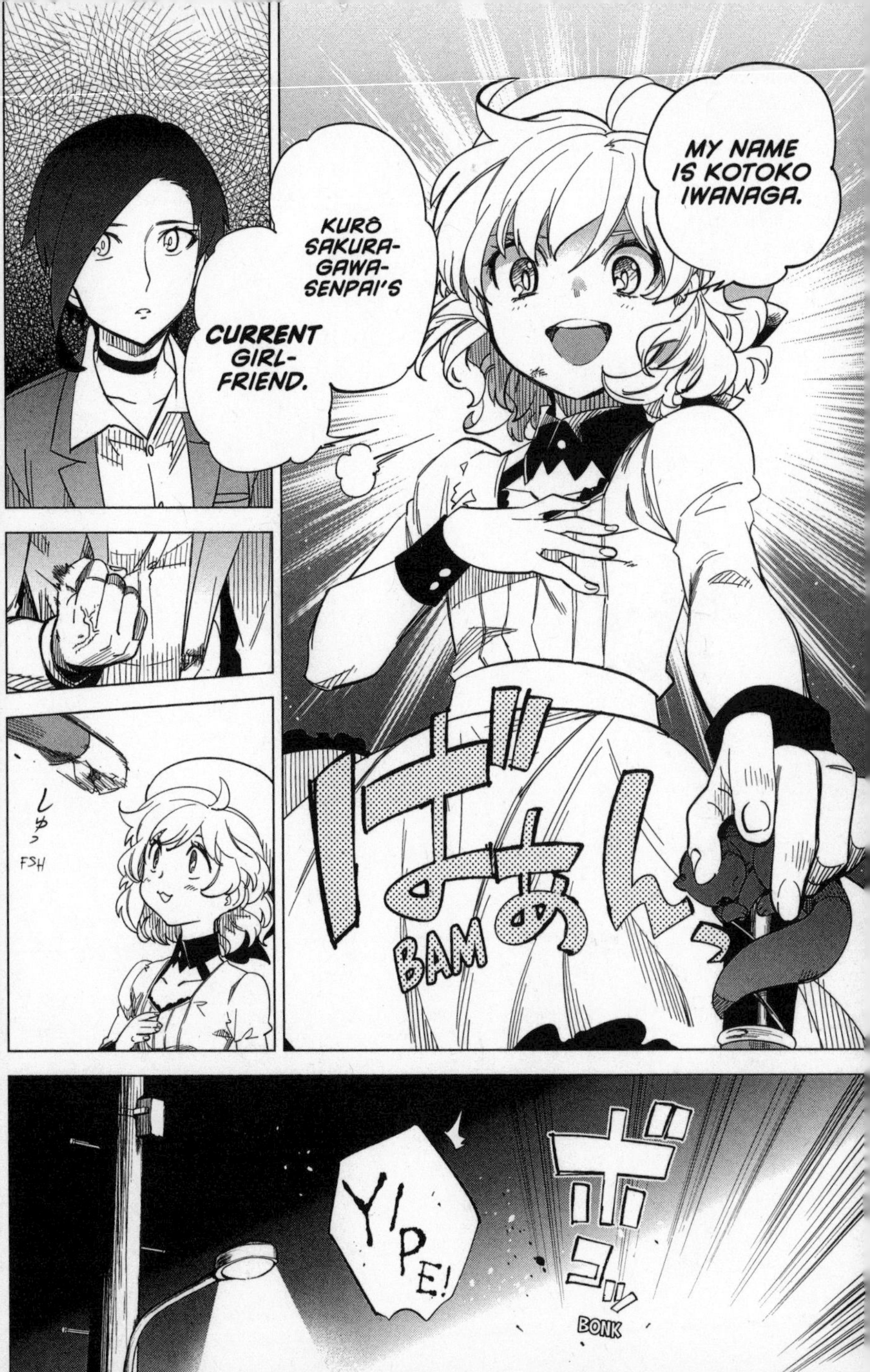
MY NAME IS KOTOKO IWANAGA.
KURÔ SAKURA-GAWA-SENPAI'S CURRENT GIRL-FRIEND.
BAM
FSH
YIPE!
BONK

◆ TO BE CONTINUED IN VOLUME 2

Something Like a Greeting from the Author

I am Kyo Shirodaira, the one credited on the cover and frontispiece as writing the "story." This is volume one. To those of you who know my name and those who don't, thank you for picking up this book.

Now, this manga, known as *In/Spectre*, is the graphic novel version of the story I wrote as a novel in 2011, and published as *Invented Inference: Steel Lady Nanase*. At the time that I was writing the novel, I had no idea that it would become a manga.

And this time, I didn't write any new scenarios or tweak the continuity like I often do with manga of my work; I just gave Chashiba Katase-sensei the book and said, "Don't worry about my feelings at all, just draw whatever you think is interesting in whatever way you think it's interesting. If possible, I'd prefer you don't make it too serious." It's a pretty different relationship than what I usually have with a manga artist.

Because Chapter 1 was the first one, and we were just starting out, I did make some comments before it was drawn about some lines of dialogue and the story details, but other than that, I had no idea what was going on with it until it was published in the magazine. I just sat back and thought to myself, "Wow, I'm not doing anything, but this is really turning into a good manga. There are more good scenes than there were before." Part of my lack of involvement comes from a fear that, since the story already exists as a published novel, if I were to get too involved, the manga would be constrained by the novel. I felt it would be a better manga if I left it to someone else's interpretation and story sense.

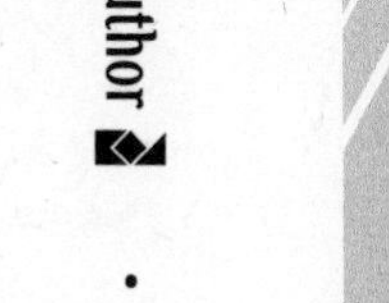

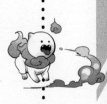

As for the content of this particular volume, while the plot and dialogue are pretty much straight from the novel, there are scenes, expressions, and ideas everywhere that are unique to the manga, and it's turning into something that will have different highlights from the novel, giving readers a different impression. In fact, an acquaintance of mine read Chapter 1 and said, "It's so faithful to the novel, but so much more refreshing."

Even the same scene with the same lines will have differences; maybe it's because the humanity of the writer shows through. It's scary.

Incidentally, the title makes reference to detective work, but there is nothing resembling a mystery story in this book; instead, we have yôkai and ghosts, and on top of that, it focuses on people with powers that aren't really explained. So if anyone picked it up hoping for a mystery manga, and you're getting mad and thinking, "Are you going to have any mystery in this at all?!", then direct all your complaints to me, because it's faithful to the original.

The story should become a little more of a "mystery" as it goes on (there are police officers in it, after all). When the novel was published, I got reviews from both camps, claiming that it was a mystery novel and that it wasn't one. In regards to that, I hide behind my excuse of, "It's made of the same substance as mystery."

That's really not very refreshing, is it?

Well, I hope you'll read the next volume.

Kyo Shirodaira

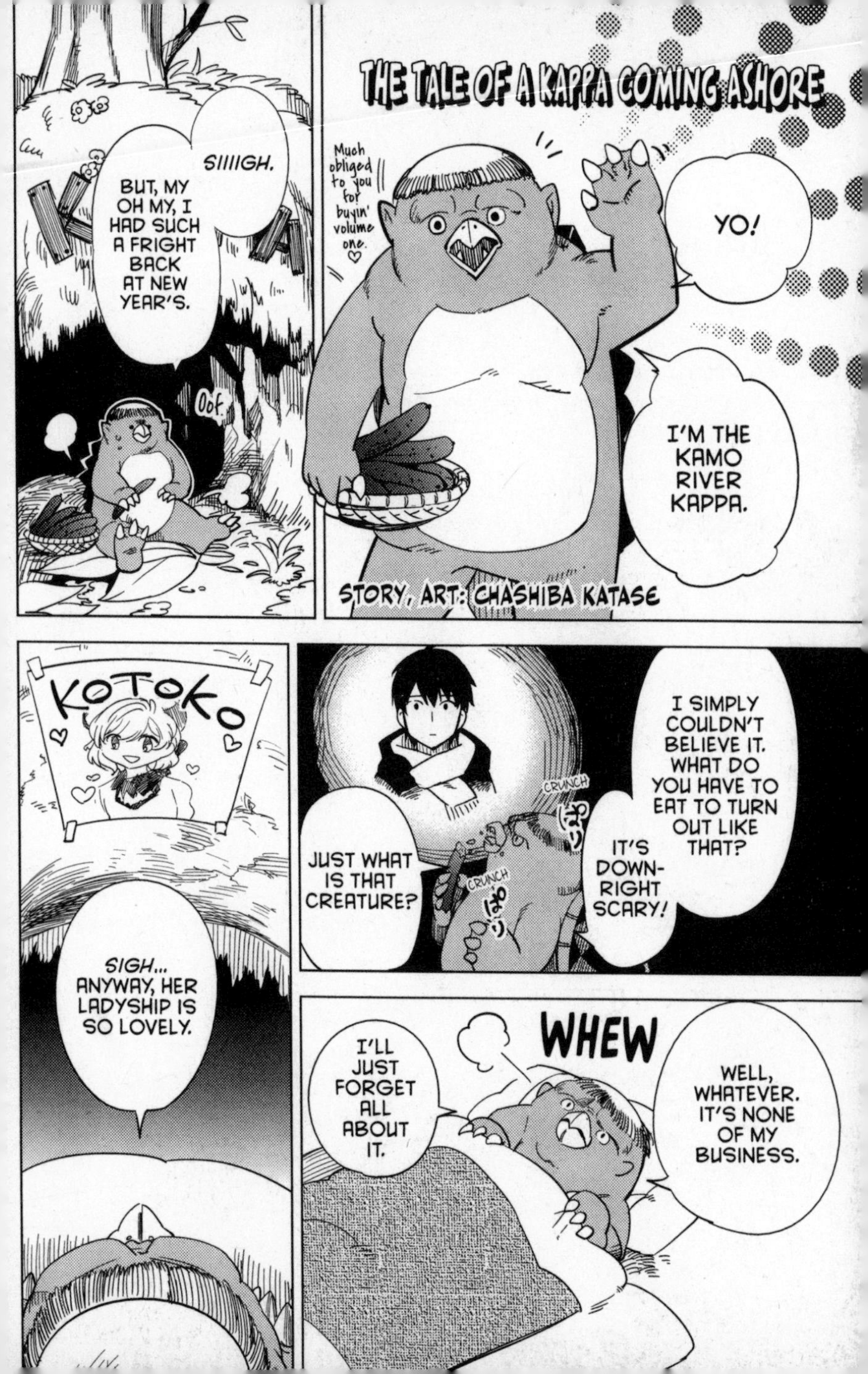
THE TALE OF A KAPPA COMING ASHORE
YO!
I'M THE KAMO RIVER KAPPA.
Much obliged to you for buyin' volume one.
STORY, ART: CHASHIBA KATASE
SIIIGH.
BUT, MY OH MY, I HAD SUCH A FRIGHT BACK AT NEW YEAR'S.
Oof.
I SIMPLY COULDN'T BELIEVE IT. WHAT DO YOU HAVE TO EAT TO TURN OUT LIKE THAT?
IT'S DOWN-RIGHT SCARY!
CRUNCH
ぱり
CRUNCH
ぱり
JUST WHAT IS THAT CREATURE?
WELL, WHATEVER. IT'S NONE OF MY BUSINESS.
WHEW
I'LL JUST FORGET ALL ABOUT IT.
KOTOKO
SIGH... ANYWAY, HER LADYSHIP IS SO LOVELY.

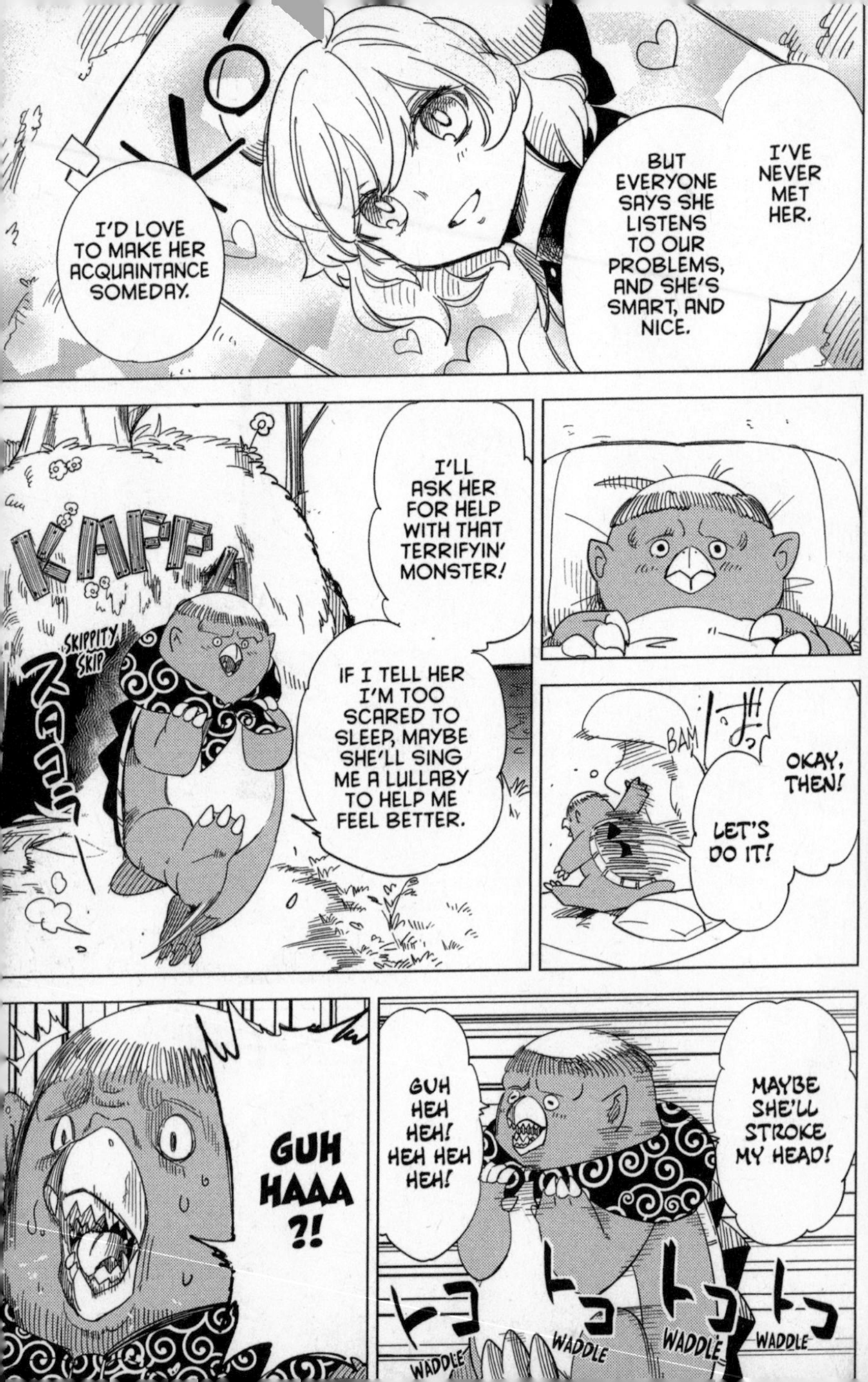
I'VE NEVER MET HER.
BUT EVERYONE SAYS SHE LISTENS TO OUR PROBLEMS, AND SHE'S SMART, AND NICE.
I'D LOVE TO MAKE HER ACQUAINTANCE SOMEDAY.
BAM
OKAY, THEN!
LET'S DO IT!
I'LL ASK HER FOR HELP WITH THAT TERRIFYIN' MONSTER!
IF I TELL HER I'M TOO SCARED TO SLEEP, MAYBE SHE'LL SING ME A LULLABY TO HELP ME FEEL BETTER.
KAPPA
SKIPPITY SKIP
MAYBE SHE'LL STROKE MY HEAD!
GUH HEH HEH! HEH HEH HEH!
WADDLE
WADDLE
WADDLE
WADDLE
GUH HAAA ?!

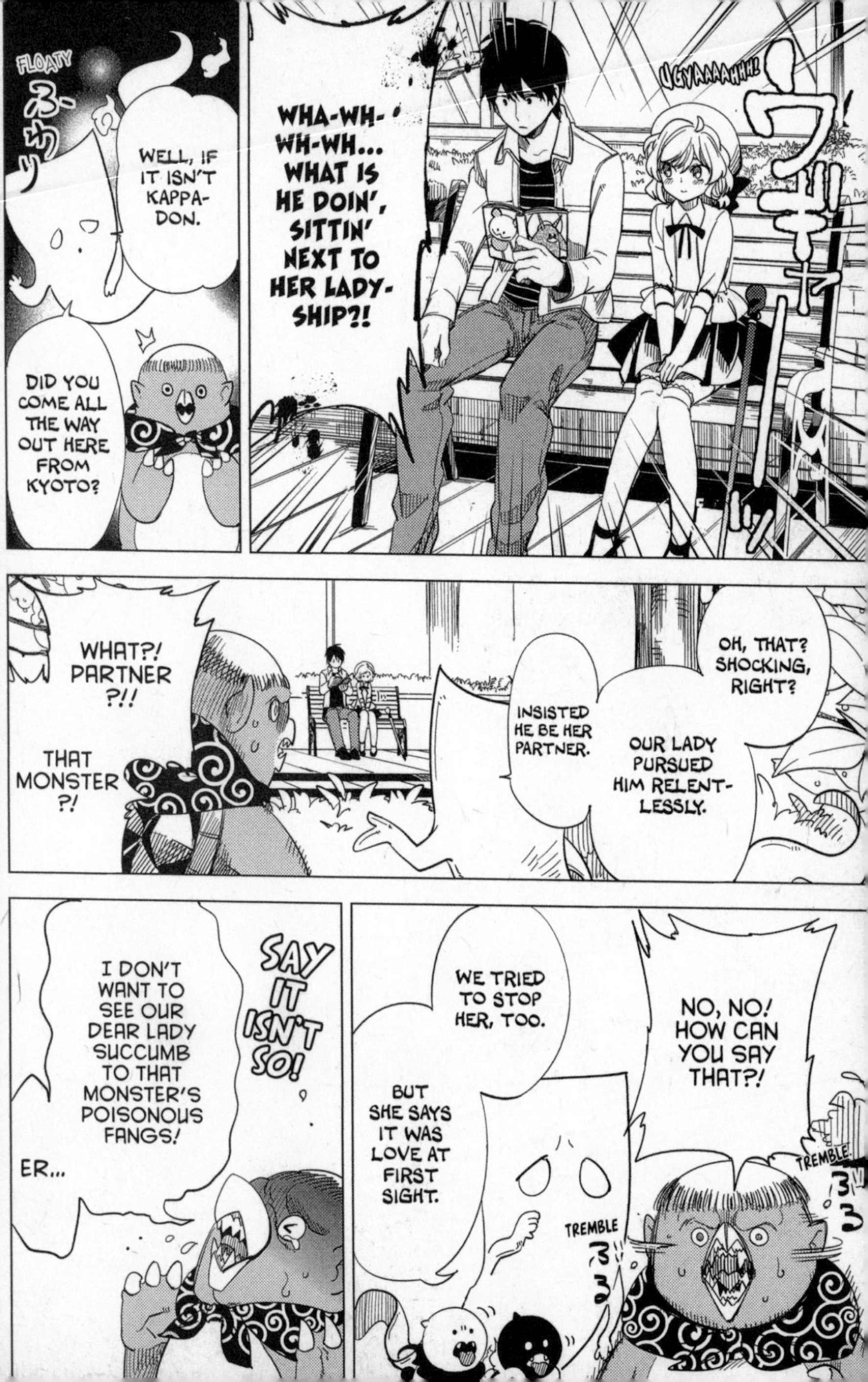
UGYAAAAHH!
WHA-WH-WH-WH... WHAT IS HE DOIN', SITTIN' NEXT TO HER LADY-SHIP?!
FLOATY
ふわり
WELL, IF IT ISN'T KAPPA-DON.
DID YOU COME ALL THE WAY OUT HERE FROM KYOTO?
OH, THAT? SHOCKING, RIGHT?
OUR LADY PURSUED HIM RELENT-LESSLY.
INSISTED HE BE HER PARTNER.
WHAT?! PARTNER ?!!
THAT MONSTER ?!
TREMBLE
NO, NO! HOW CAN YOU SAY THAT?!
TREMBLE
WE TRIED TO STOP HER, TOO.
BUT SHE SAYS IT WAS LOVE AT FIRST SIGHT.
SAY IT ISN'T SO!
I DON'T WANT TO SEE OUR DEAR LADY SUCCUMB TO THAT MONSTER'S POISONOUS FANGS!
ER...

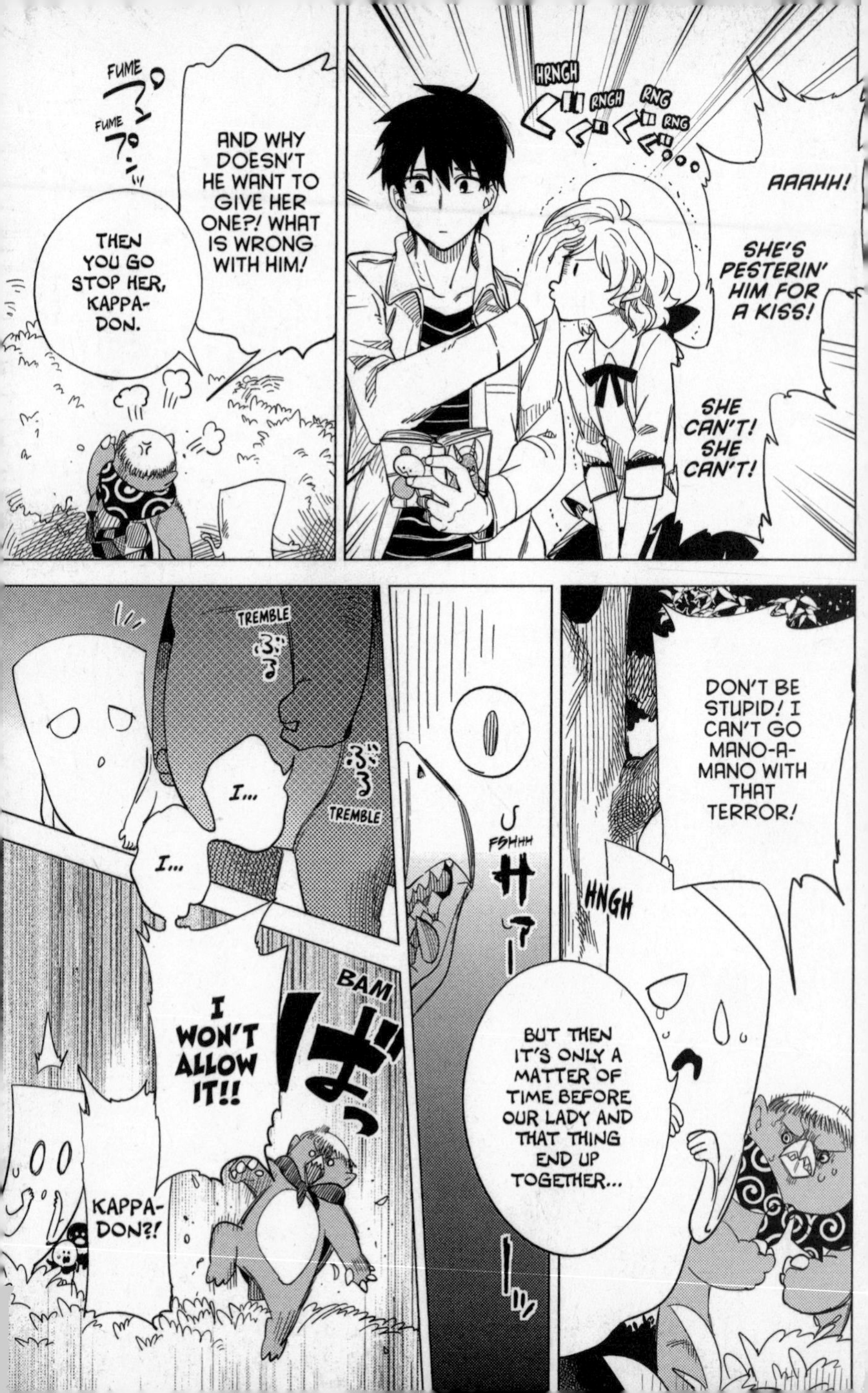
HRNGH
RNGH
RNG
RNG
AAAHH!
SHE'S PESTERIN' HIM FOR A KISS!
SHE CAN'T! SHE CAN'T!
AND WHY DOESN'T HE WANT TO GIVE HER ONE?! WHAT IS WRONG WITH HIM!
FUME
FUME
THEN YOU GO STOP HER, KAPPA-DON.
DON'T BE STUPID! I CAN'T GO MANO-A-MANO WITH THAT TERROR!
HNGH
BUT THEN IT'S ONLY A MATTER OF TIME BEFORE OUR LADY AND THAT THING END UP TOGETHER...
FSHHH
TREMBLE
TREMBLE
I...
I...
BAM
I WON'T ALLOW IT!!
KAPPA-DON?!

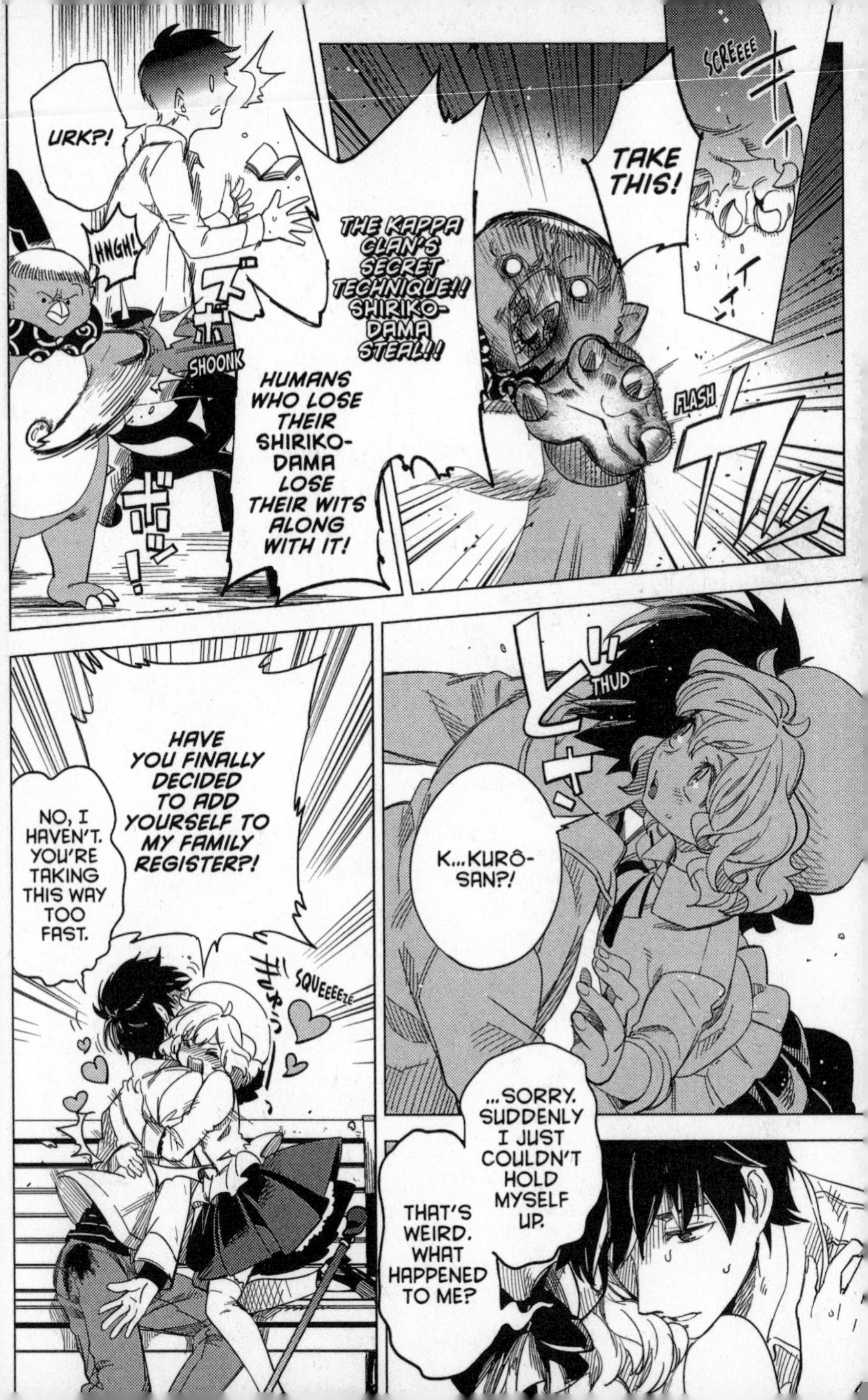
SCREEEE
TAKE THIS!
THE KAPPA CLAN'S SECRET TECHNIQUE!! SHIRIKO-DAMA STEAL!!
FLASH
URK?!
HUMANS WHO LOSE THEIR SHIRIKO-DAMA LOSE THEIR WITS ALONG WITH IT!
HNGH!
SHOONK
THUD
K...KURÔ-SAN?!
...SORRY. SUDDENLY I JUST COULDN'T HOLD MYSELF UP.
THAT'S WEIRD. WHAT HAPPENED TO ME?
HAVE YOU FINALLY DECIDED TO ADD YOURSELF TO MY FAMILY REGISTER?!
NO, I HAVEN'T. YOU'RE TAKING THIS WAY TOO FAST.
SQUEEEEZE

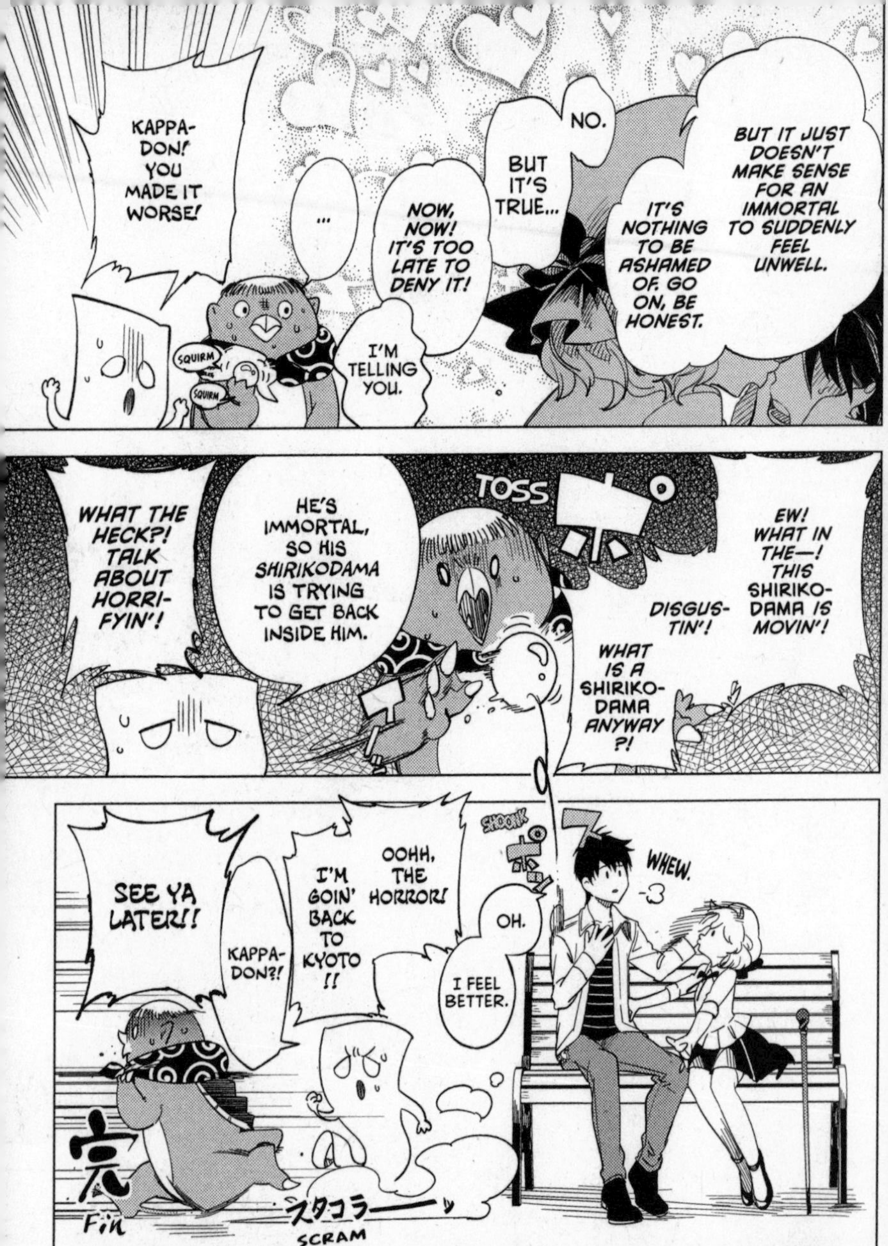
BUT IT JUST DOESN'T MAKE SENSE FOR AN IMMORTAL TO SUDDENLY FEEL UNWELL.
IT'S NOTHING TO BE ASHAMED OF. GO ON, BE HONEST.
NO.
BUT IT'S TRUE...
NOW, NOW! IT'S TOO LATE TO DENY IT!
I'M TELLING YOU.
...
KAPPA-DON! YOU MADE IT WORSE!
SQUIRM
SQUIRM
EW! WHAT IN THE—! THIS SHIRIKODAMA IS MOVIN'!
DISGUSTIN'!
WHAT IS A SHIRIKODAMA ANYWAY?!
TOSS
HE'S IMMORTAL, SO HIS SHIRIKODAMA IS TRYING TO GET BACK INSIDE HIM.
WHAT THE HECK?! TALK ABOUT HORRIFYIN'!
WHEW.
SHOONK
OH.
I FEEL BETTER.
OOHH, THE HORROR!
I'M GOIN' BACK TO KYOTO!!
KAPPA-DON?!
SEE YA LATER!!
完
Fin
スタコラー
SCRAM

Thank you very much!
I hope you'll read volume two. KATASE

Staff: Kuro Shima, Tonpu, Yutsu Editors: O-kawa, T-da (honorifics excluded)

TRANSLATION NOTES

Japanese is a tricky language for most Westerners, and translation is often more art than science. For your edification and reading pleasure, here are notes on some of the places where we could have gone in a different direction in our translation of the work, or where a Japanese cultural reference is used.

Eating grass, page 12

There may be some significance to this observation that Kurô is like an herbivorous goat. In recent years, the Japanese word for "herbivore" has been applied to men who are low on carnal ("carnivorous") desires. In other words, Kurô doesn't actively seek out romantic relationships.

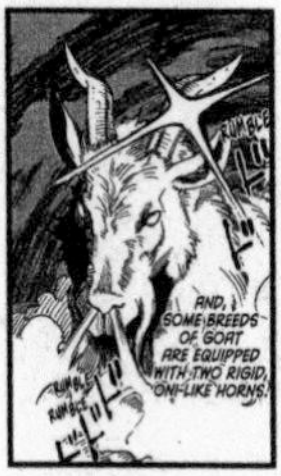
AND, SOME BREEDS OF GOAT ARE EQUIPPED WITH TWO RIGID, ONI-LIKE HORNS.

Oni, page 13

An *oni* is a creature from Japanese folklore. The word is often translated to "ogre", as *oni* do tend to be ugly man-eaters. *Oni* come in many shapes and sizes, but one thing they have in common is horns. Some have only one horn, but the most common depictions of oni have two, much like a goat. The word *oni* is also used to describe people who are tough, unsparing, and/or heartless.

Engagement ceremony, page 19

When a couple gets engaged in Japan, it is tradition to have a formal dinner during which the parents of the soon-to-be married couple exchange symbolic gifts. These gifts all represent things such as a long-lasting marriage, happiness, good fortune, etc. If Kurô and Saki are planning such a ceremony, it means both of their parents have agreed to the match, and there's little chance that either of them will back out.

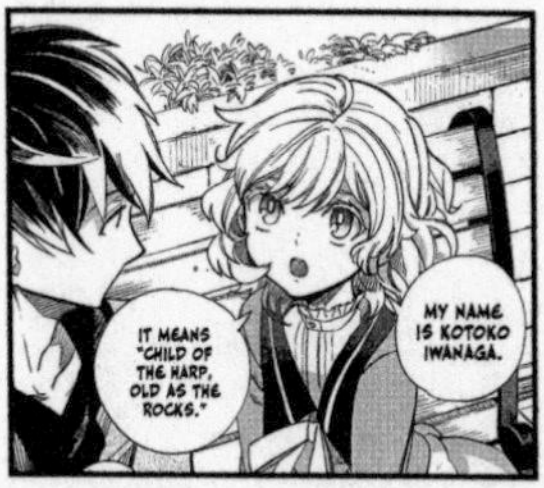
MY NAME IS KOTOKO IWANAGA.
IT MEANS "CHILD OF THE HARP, OLD AS THE ROCKS."

Kotoko Iwanaga means..., page 24

Kotoko isn't necessarily assuming that Kurô would have any interest in what her name means, or that the meaning of her name will impress him in any way. Because the Japanese writing system uses ideographs (one symbol that represents a word or idea), the meaning of her name would tell him which characters to use to write it. She's basically telling him how to write or "spell" her name, in case he ever decides to look her up.

First temple visit, and the New Year's Bell, page 32

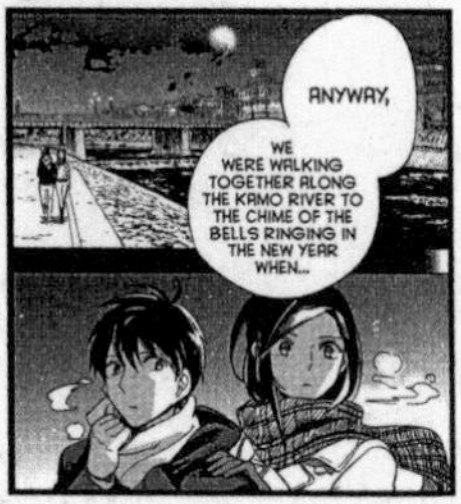
ANYWAY,
WE WERE WALKING TOGETHER ALONG THE KAMO RIVER TO THE CHIME OF THE BELLS RINGING IN THE NEW YEAR WHEN...

In Japan, it's a New Year's tradition to visit a shrine or temple within the first three days of the new year, to express gratitude for the previous year and pray for a good new year. The New Year's Bell is rung 108 times, around midnight on New Year's Eve. One theory as to why this is, is that the number 108 represents the types of worldly desires that exist in the world, and hearing the bell ring can purify your heart of those worldly desires that had built up over the last year. However, the number of rings can vary from temple to temple, sometimes ringing more than 200 times.

***Gatarô*, *suiko*, and *hyôsube*, page 33**

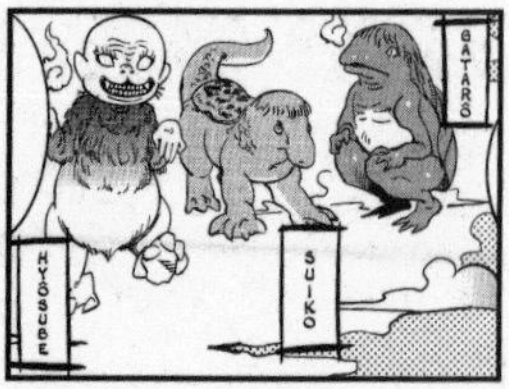
GATARÔ
SUIKO
HYÔSUBE

As the reader may have guessed from the context, these are all supernatural water creatures, like the more well-known kappa. All of them live by rivers and interact with humans with varying degrees of hostility. As an expert in regard to all Japanese supernatural creatures, Kotoko wants to make sure she has all the details right.

Sushi and shrimp crackers, page 34

Kotoko is referring to the fact that there is a popular chain of sushi restaurants called Kappa-Zushi, and a brand of shrimp flavored crackers which also bears the name of the aquatic creatures.

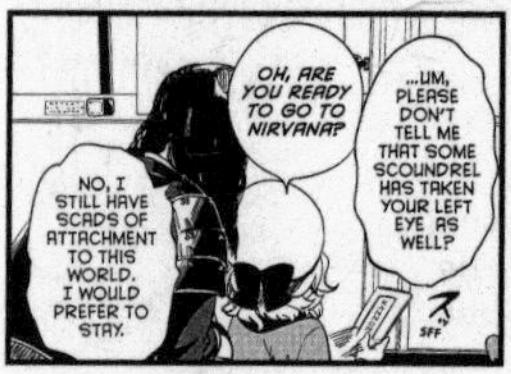
...UM, PLEASE DON'T TELL ME THAT SOME SCOUNDREL HAS TAKEN YOUR LEFT EYE AS WELL?
OH, ARE YOU READY TO GO TO NIRVANA?
NO, I STILL HAVE SCADS OF ATTACHMENT TO THIS WORLD. I WOULD PREFER TO STAY.
SFF

Kannon, page 53

Kannon, or Guanyin, is a bodhisattva—one who has attained Nirvana but has come back to earth to help show others the way. She is also considered a goddess of mercy, including leading souls of the deceased toward the pure land. In other words, Kotoko is going to enlist her help to send this ghost to nirvana.

***The Warrior's Way to My Heart*, page 53**

The translators confess that this is not a direct translation of this particular novel title, but such is the way of translating book and movie titles. The Japanese title of the book is *Mushaburui LOVE*, where *mushaburui* means "trembling with excitement or anticipation," but this particular ghost would be attracted to the *musha* part, which means "warrior." The translators chose to focus on that as the main point of the English title.

Good things come to those who sleep, page 59

Here, Kotoko is accurately reciting the Japanese version of "good things come to those who wait", which translates more literally to, "If you want good fortune, go to sleep and wait for it." Unfortunately, the English version doesn't include the part about sleep, so the translators had to tweak it a little.

Tea lunch, page 64

More accurately, Kotoko states that she has eaten a *kaiseki* meal. *Kaiseki* is a very high-class Japanese cuisine, and usually consists of miso soup and three side dishes. When written with the Chinese characters that Kotoko used, it refers to a meal served in conjunction with a formal tea ceremony. In keeping with the high level of the meal, Kyoto heirloom vegetables, or *kyô yasai*, are expensive vegetables served mainly in upscale restaurants, and they are very nutritious.

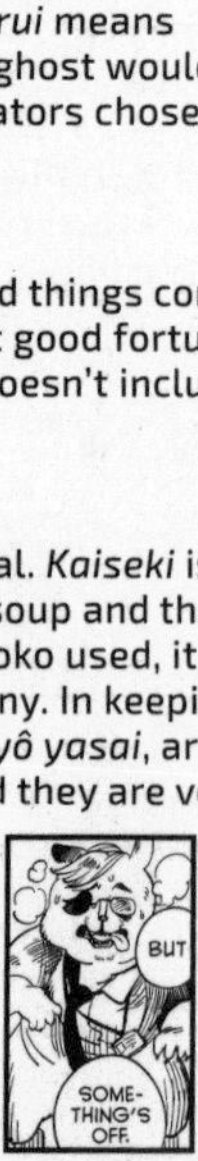
BUT
SOME-THING'S OFF.

***Baké-Danuki*, page 66**

A tanuki is a Japanese raccoon dog. While tanuki are normal, everyday animals, a *baké-danuki* (or "transforming tanuki") is supernatural one capable of shapeshifting.

Protective barrier, page 66

The word our tanuki friend uses here for "protective barrier" is *kekkai*, literally "bound world." Often translated to "barrier," a *kekkai* is a boundary marking off the border between the sacred and the profane. The area inside the barrier is supposed to be protected from harm.

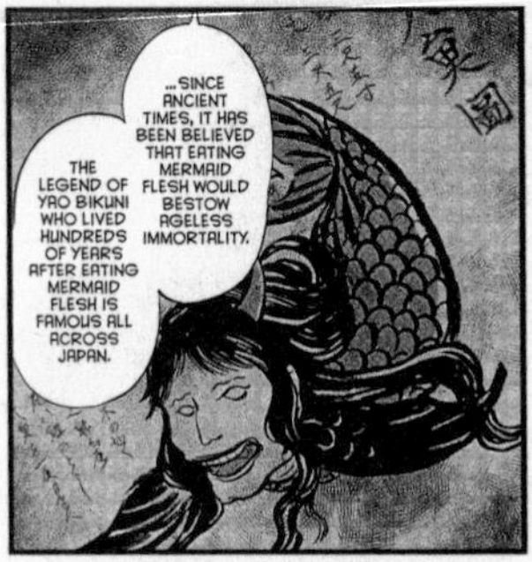
...SINCE ANCIENT TIMES, IT HAS BEEN BELIEVED THAT EATING MERMAID FLESH WOULD BESTOW AGELESS IMMORTALITY.
THE LEGEND OF YAO BIKUNI WHO LIVED HUNDREDS OF YEARS AFTER EATING MERMAID FLESH IS FAMOUS ALL ACROSS JAPAN.

Yao Bikuni, page 92

Although Kotoko relates the significant parts of the tale, the reader may be interested in a slightly more detailed account of Yao Bikuni. There are regional differences to the story, but the gist of it is that a man was invited to dinner at a fisherman's house and discovered by chance that the fisherman was serving mermaid meat. Repulsed at the idea, he didn't eat the meat but wrapped it up and took it home to discard later. Either his daughter or his wife then ate the meat before he could warn her not to, and lived for centuries thereafter. After being widowed several times and losing all her friends, she became a nun and traveled the country, helping the poor.

Police boxes, page 119

Police boxes, loosely translated from *kôban*, are like miniature police stations, spread throughout the community, bringing the police close to the community so they can respond more readily to the citizens' needs.

Pleasure crime, page 122

A "pleasure crime," or *yukaihan*, is committed by someone who does it just to get a rise out of people, or for the fun of it.

Should I take her in, page 142

Specifically, Saki wonders if she should *hodô* Kotoko. The purpose of *hodô*, which means "guidance," is to identify minors who are committing—or look like they might commit—a crime, and to provide guidance to prevent them from resorting to such behavior. Kotoko is suspicious because she is out late at night, when most good children would be at home.

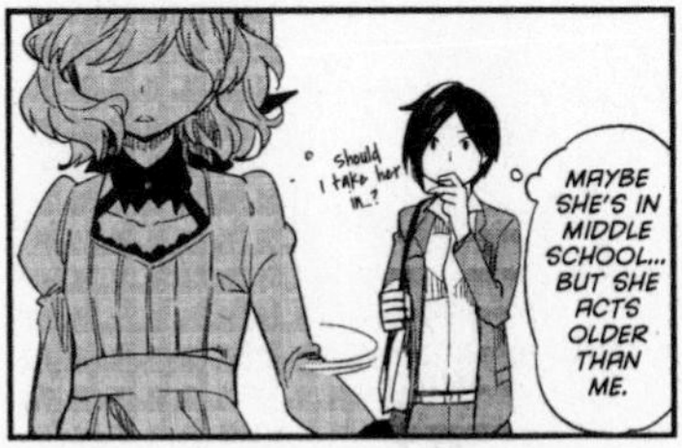
MAYBE SHE'S IN MIDDLE SCHOOL... BUT SHE ACTS OLDER THAN ME.
should I take her in..?

The Kamo River Kappa, page 166

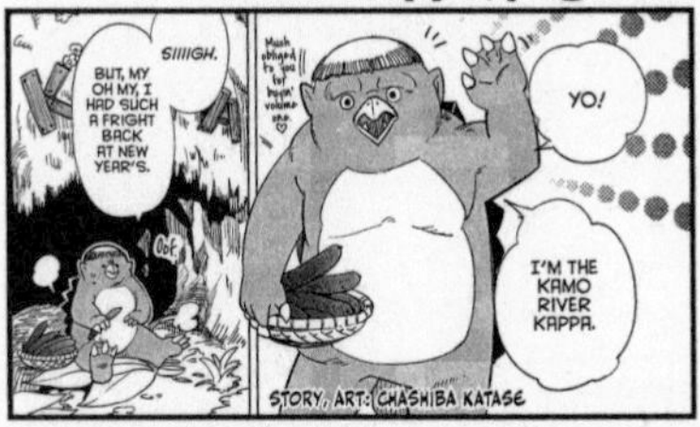
YO!
I'M THE KAMO RIVER KAPPA.
SIIIIGH.
BUT, MY OH MY, I HAD SUCH A FRIGHT BACK AT NEW YEAR'S.
STORY, ART: CHASHIBA KATASE

This kappa is a native of Kyoto, and although he used the standard Japanese dialect in the main story, here in the bonus manga, he speaks with a Kyoto dialect. The dialects from this region of Japan are often translated into an American Southern dialect. This is because people from this region are seen by the Japanese in a similar way as people from the American South are seen by residents of the Unites States—some are simple and humorous, while others are refined and proud.

Shirikodama, page 170

Translated roughly as "rear-end jewel," a *shirikodama* is a mythical crystal believed to exist in humans' anuses. According to legend, the reason kappa attack people is to obtain this jewel.